# Our Robertsons

## Descendants of the Brothers
## Thomas and John Robertson
## of the Shetland Islands

Reuben Buck Robertson III
and
Blanche and James Boyd Robertson

Our Robertsons
Descendants of the Brothers Thomas and John Robertson
of the Shetland Islands



ISBN    979-8-218-21649-8 (Hardcover)
ISBN    979-8-218-21650-4 (Softcover)
LCCN  2023910093

Shetland map courtesy of Finlay McWalter CC BY-SA 3.0, https://commons.
wikimedia.org



Portions of the text previously appeared in Coontin Kin, the journal of the Shetland Family History Society, Lerwick.

Cover photo of Seafield reprinted with permission of the Shetland Museum and Archives.

Book design by Nan Barnes, StoriesToTellBooks.com

# Our Robertsons

Descendants of the Brothers
Thomas and John Robertson
of the Shetland Islands

# CONTENTS

## Part III  The Ever-Spreading Family Tree

# Greetings

This project started almost three decades ago, when Jim and Blanche Robertson left their home in North Carolina to visit the Shetland Islands in 1970. Having met several Robertson relatives there and on later trips to New Zealand and Australia in 1976, they undertook to record what is known of "Our Robertsons" in the past and today. Jim and Blanche later returned to Shetland, New Zealand and Australia, meeting more cousins and compiling more information for the family tree. I signed on to help complete the project in 1994, after a wonderful family visit to Shetland.

We have had great help in this effort from many family members who have helped gather and freely shared information about Our Robertsons. They include Dr. Eddie Robertson, our distinguished cousin from New Zealand; Margaret Fowlds from New Zealand; the late George Robertson of Waterloo in Walls, Shetland, and his sons George and Angus; the late Charlotte Gibson of Levin, New Zealand; Alice Drury of Devon, England; the Mitchell family of Nelson, New Zealand, who shared their family research and mapmaking skills; Delphine Slattery of Queensland, Australia; Margaret Ridland of Shetland; Eileen Kelley of British Columbia, Canada; Elizabeth Shamblin in Raleigh, North Carolina, who is helping us set up a website on the internet for *Our Robertsons;* and many, many others.

Some outside of our family have also contributed greatly, including Stuart Robertson, a Shetlander now living in Scotland, Allan Beatty and other officials of the Shetland Family History Society. Our thanks to all who have helped.

Inevitably, a project such as this one will have numerous mistakes and omissions, for which we would humbly apologize in advance. Names may have been misspelled or left out entirely. Other vital information shown here may be incorrect. Please understand that any errors that appear in this book are unintentional, and please send us the correct information to include the next time around.

We hope you will enjoy reading about our extended family—and getting to know more about our interesting ancestors and cousins around the world—as much as we have enjoyed working on it.

~Reuben Robertson, October, 1999

## *Reuben Buck Robertson III*
## *1939–2000*

It is hard to describe the joy that Reuben found in researching his family history. He especially loved making connections with distant relatives from around the globe. He found that most of those Robertson descendants were also eager to participate in this evolving history project. He received countless letters and packages of family information from relatives who were generous with their time and memories. His research unfortunately came to an abrupt end in late 1999 shortly after his unexpected diagnosis of metastasized colon cancer. He hoped at that time to share with this far-flung family what he had collected, researched, and written. Finally, we are able to attempt to do that for him with this book. This history starts in the early 1700s and ends in December, 1999… just as Reuben wrote it.

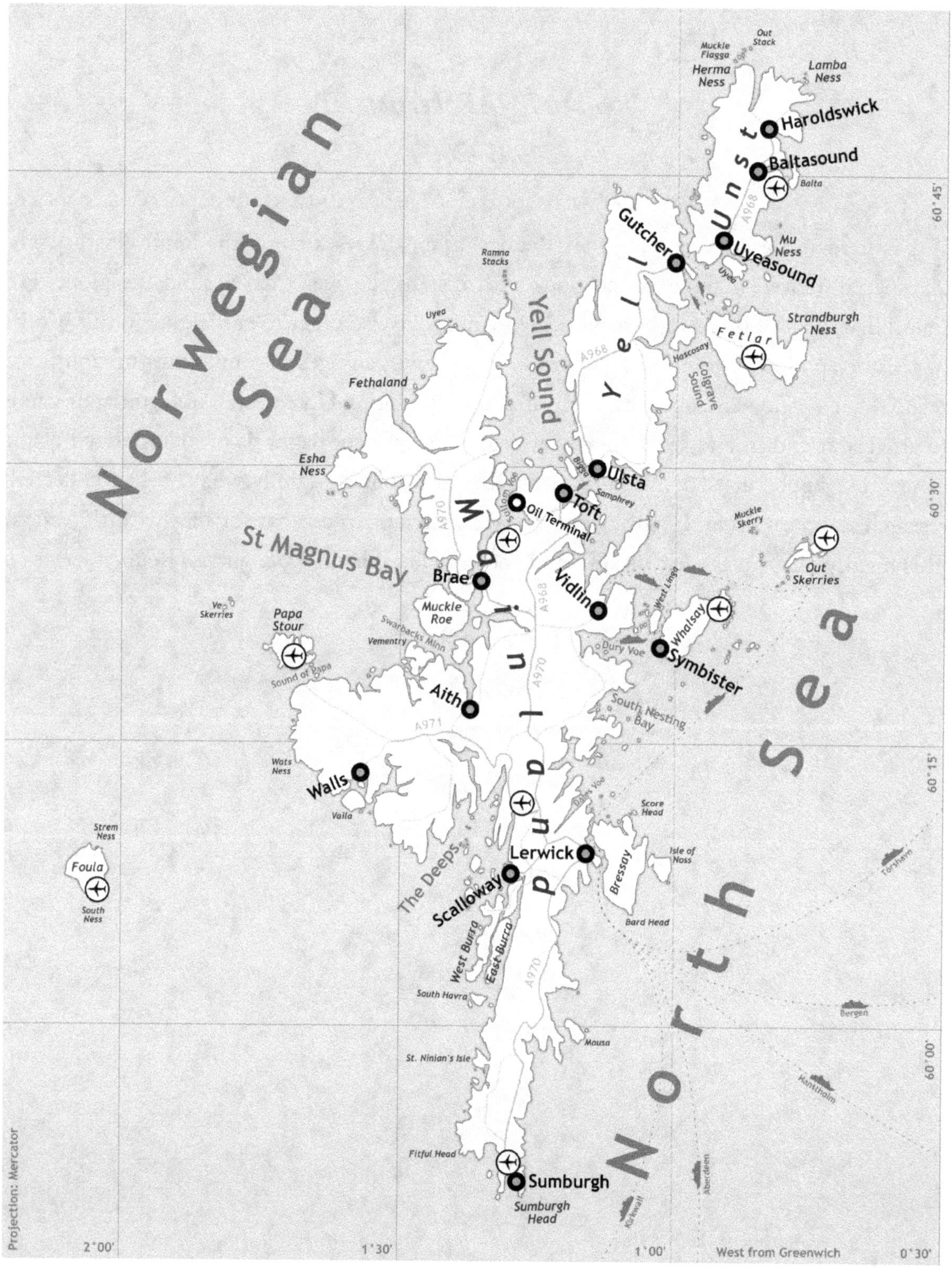
Norwegian Sea
North Sea
Out Stack
Muckle Flagga
Herma Ness
Lamba Ness
Haroldswick
Baltasound
Balta
Unst
Gutcher
Mu Ness
Uyeasound
Uyea
Strandburgh Ness
Ramna Stacks
Fetlar
Uyea
Yell Sound
A968
Yell
Hascosay
Colgrave Sound
Fethaland
Esha Ness
Ulsta
Samphrey
Muckle Skerry
Toft
Oil Terminal
Out Skerries
St Magnus Bay
A970
Mainland
Brae
Vidlin
West Lingø
A968
Muckle Roe
Whalsay
Ve Skerries
Swarbacks Minn
Papa Stour
Vementry
Dury Voe
Symbister
A970
Sound of Papa
South Nesting Bay
Aith
A971
Wats Ness
Walls
Vaila
Score Head
Dales Voe
The Deeps
Lerwick
Bressay
Isle of Noss
Strem Ness
Foula
Scalloway
Bard Head
Tornhavn
South Ness
West Burra
East Burra
A970
South Havra
Bergen
St. Ninian's Isle
Mousa
Rusthholm
Fitful Head
Sumburgh
Sumburgh Head
Kirkwall
Aberdeen
Projection: Mercator
2°00'
1°30'
1°00'
West from Greenwich
0°30'
60°45'
60°30'
60°15'
60°00'

# Part I

## Our Shetland Heritage

Hundreds of us around the world have a unique and very special ancestral distinction. We are the descendants of one or both of two brothers who appeared in the Shetland Islands, to the north of mainland Scotland, in the second half of the eighteenth century. Those two brothers, who lived and raised families in Shetland some two and a half centuries ago, were called Thomas and John Robertson. This book is the culmination of efforts by many family members in Shetland, elsewhere in the United Kingdom, in New Zealand, Australia, and America, to find and tell the stories, as best we can, of the two Robertson brothers in Shetland and their progeny, "Our Robertsons," around the globe.

### The Shetland Setting

The Shetland Islands are located between the Atlantic Ocean and the North Sea, about 200 miles north of Aberdeen, Scotland, and 220 miles west of Bergen, Norway. Shetland—called Hjaltland by the Norse, later written as Hetland or Zetland—is an archipelago consisting of about 100 islands; only twenty or so are inhabited today. Most Shetlanders live on the largest of the islands, sometimes locally called the "Mainland."

These hilly, windswept islands are the most northern part of the British Isles. They are situated on latitude 61° north, the same as Hudson Bay in Canada, the southern end of Greenland, and Anchorage, Alaska. On the shortest day in the Shetland winter, the sun is up only six hours and there are eighteen hours of dusk and darkness. But the "Simmer Dim"—a Shetland phrase for the longest days of summer—brings almost twenty-four hours of daylight.

The Shetland coastline is jagged, punctuated by long "voes" or inlets from the sea. No part of Shetland is more than three miles from the sea. Parts of the coastline feature precipitous cliffs with vertical drops plunging hundreds of feet into the sea. The islands have almost no trees, making the round, bare hills seem like the backs of enormous whales rising out of the sea.

The Gulf Stream swings in on the Atlantic Ocean close to the Shetland Islands. This makes for a reasonably mild climate with few extremes of temperature, little snow, and no oppressive summer heat. But balanced against those pleasant features are frequent high winds and gales, dense fogs, and gray and drizzly days of a maritime climate. Charles D. Robertson vividly recalled the fearsome magic of winter storms of Shetland:

> *On those weather beaten islands, their heather covered hills are bleak and dreary enough in summer, but in winter storms they possess an incommunicable charm. When the heavens are charged with impending tempest, when the sun is obscured, the mighty swell of the Atlantic Ocean rolls in on the ragged and jagged coast line, leaping from peak to peak with its irresistible force, until it dashes its mass with thundering roar against the vertical rocks. . . .*
>
> *But when the hurricane has passed, and the stars come out to look down on the desolate scene, the glorious Aurora breaks forth over the blue vault with its blushing light purpling the sky in soft tranquility, the voice of its rushing currents being audible like the roll of a mystic sea on mystic shores, a phenomenon recognized by the ancient Norse as the lights of the Valkyries riding forth to carry to Valhalla the brave from the battlefields."*

## Shetland Life and Culture

The earliest recorded settlements on the Shetland Islands were those of Viking raiders who came over the sea from Norway and apparently drove out the earlier Picts who had come from the Scottish mainland thousands of years before. The Picts left behind fortress-like stone structures called *brochs,* whose remnants are still found in the islands. Brochs in Shetland consist of circular stone towers about forty feet high and forty feet in diameter, built of flat stones put together without mortar. Pictish brochs were placed at regular intervals throughout the islands and, apparently, served both as signal towers and defense fortresses, with spaces for storing food and supplies and for sleeping. Nearly all the ancient brochs are in ruin, in part because later Shetlanders have carried away many of the original stones to make buildings and walls for their own use.

The Shetland Islands were controlled by Norway until the fifteenth century, when they came under Scottish rule. Christian I, King of Norway and Denmark, wanted his daughter, Princess Margaret, to marry King James III of Scotland and had to produce a suitable dowry to accompany the bride. Because he was short of funds, a portion of the dowry was a "pledge" of the Shetland Islands, securing his promise to pay more later. But the pledge was never redeemed, and the islands came under the permanent control of Scottish kings.

Over five centuries later, Shetland is still influenced by Norwegian culture and tradition. Many of the names of towns and places come from ancient Norse words. Each January, in the dark of winter, Shetlanders celebrate *Up-Helly-Aa*, a traditional festival said to be of Norse origin. In 1916, our ancestor James D. Robertson of Walls, Shetland, wrote to a niece in America, telling of the events: "It consisted of a boat made like an old Viking ship, dragged about and finally set on fire. The company who dragged it was about 50 men, all in disguise and in fantastic wigs, singing the old war song of Odin and Thor. After the ceremony a dance was held till morning." Up-Helly-Aa is much the same today.

The official language of Shetland is English. But the traditional dialect of the islands is a distinctive blending of three languages: Norn, the ancient Norse language, Middle Scots, and English. Few Shetlanders today speak the dialect, and those who do live mainly on the outlying islands; its use is now mainly in folk culture and literature.

One of "Our Robertsons" was an acclaimed poet in the Shetland dialect as well as English. Recognized as "Shetland's finest lyric poet," he was Thomas Alexander Robertson (1909–1973), who wrote under the pen name "Vagaland." (See 5-A.3 below). T.A. Robertson was also a renowned teacher and a leading expert on the grammar, vocabulary, and linguistic characteristics of the Shetland dialect. His widow, Martha Robertson, described how the dialect came into being: "Incomers from Scotland, and later from England, who settled in the islands from the sixteenth century onwards, could not understand the Norn language and its use was more and more discouraged. But the native Norn speech must have persisted for a long time, for the original Norn ballads were still being recited in the remote island of Foula in 1774, more than 300 years after the transfer of the islands."

A sample of Vagaland's work is the poem "Burgawater," describing an ancient broch built by Picts on a small island in a lake near Sandness, on the western peninsula of Shetland.

### BURGAWATER

*The birds of storm are seaward flying*
*From burgawater, lonely lying,*
*And summer's glories fade.*
*Above the ruins the gulls are crying,*
*Where once the pict-folk stayed.*
*Nothing remains of their toil and trouble,*
*Their broch a heap of stones and rubble,*
*And a green-growing mound;*
*For foes came like the plough through stubble*
*And razed it to the ground.*
*Here in the hush of western billow*
*Low they lie with the earth for pillow —*
*Kind to the dispossessed —*
*With wild white roses and fronds of willow*
*To mark their place of rest.*

T.A. Robertson's poetry was compiled in *The Collected Poems of Vagaland*, published by Shetland Times, Ltd. in Lerwick, now out of print. He also co-authored *Grammar and Usage of the Shetland Dialect* (1952), reprinted by Shetland Times in 1991.

The sea has always had an enormous influence on the lives and fortunes of the Shetland people. Catching, curing, and exporting fish was the major industry of Shetland for centuries. In the past, and to a lesser extent today, young Shetland men almost automatically went to sea, either as fisherman or as seamen on merchant ships. The most common Shetland fishing vessel was a six-man wooden rowing boat with no deck or cabin, called a "sixareen." These boats were taken far out to sea for days or even weeks at a time to find and harvest the fishing grounds, which might be fifty miles or farther from land. The life of the fisherman at sea was extremely perilous, as sudden storms could easily capsize their boats with the loss of all aboard. For this reason, and because many of the men who went off as seamen never returned, Shetland was a place where women far outnumbered the men.

The old fisherman's expression "Rowin Foula doon" tells much. Foula, the westernmost island of the Shetlands, features cliffs rising over 1,200 feet above sea level, some of the highest in the British Isles. "Rowin Foula doon" was going so far out that the top of Foula went below the horizon. Vagaland wrote of this in *Da Sang o Da Papa Men*, a sea chantey in dialect:

> *OOT BEWAST DA HORN O PAPA*
>
> *ROWIN FOULA DOON!*
>
> *OWER A HIDDEN PIECE O WATER,*
>
> *ROWIN FOULA DOON!*
>
> *ROOND DA BOAT DA TIDE-LUMPS MAKKIN*
>
> *SUNLICHT TROWE DA CLOUDS IS BRAKKIN;*
>
> *WE MAAN GENG WHAAR FISH IS TAKKIN,*
>
> *ROWIN FOULA DOON!*[1]

Both men and women had to spend much of their time working to raise food crops to sustain their families and livestock. Peat had to be cut, stacked, and dried for fuel to warm the Shetlanders' homes. Generally, the people did not own their farms or "crofts" but were tenants to "lairds" or landowners. Under the oppressive croft-tenancy system of the past, landlords not only required tenants to turn over a large part of their annual harvest of crops but also required the crofters to fish for them, turning over a substantial portion of the catch. This almost feudal system, which remained in effect for centuries, kept most of the population of Shetland at the lairds' mercy and prevented most families from accumulating any significant wealth.[2]

"The Shetlander," wrote Reuben Robertson Sr., "is something of an amphibian, a combination of farmer and fisherman, living part of his time in his boats and part in his fields, equally at home in both places." Most of our Robertsons who lived in Shetland before this century were farmers, fishermen, and seamen, but others were merchants, teachers, doctors, and builders.

The seat of local government, Shetland's major port and commercial center, is Lerwick—its name came from the Norse word *Leirvik,* meaning "muddy bay"—on the eastern side of the mainland. Norah Kendall, in her book, *Naught But Kin Behind Them,* has written, "Perhaps there is not another place in the whole world quite like Lerwick. A dozen or more lanes navigate their steep descent around the dull grey look-alike buildings that grew up on the banks of creeks on the hill which rises from the shore. These quiet lanes seem to burst open into busy Commercial Street which winds its way around the shops housed in the original old merchant buildings and taverns that once lined the shore."

Getting around Shetland was always difficult and sometimes treacherous, often requiring transportation by boat and walking over hills and bogs. There were virtually no roads in the islands until the middle of the nineteenth century when a road-construction program was set up to provide work for impoverished Shetlanders.

Most of our Robertsons lived in the outlying areas of Walls and Sandsting & Aithsting parishes on the western peninsula of the main island of Shetland. Many lived in and around the village of Walls. (Walls is a mistranslation of the original name *Waas,* a Norn word meaning "voes" or inlets of the sea). Walls is located on Vaila Sound, a natural harbor protected by Vaila Island, abutting the Atlantic Ocean about twenty-five miles west of Lerwick.

The first school in Shetland was built in Walls in 1768—a century before education became compulsory in the United Kingdom—on land donated by the parish minister and called "Happy Hansel." For many years Happy Hansel was the principal school in the Shetland Islands and the only one where Latin was taught. The schoolhouse at Walls had great significance for Vagaland and, through the years, many others of our family who received a wonderful education there, some who taught children there, and others who—as explained in 3-C below—found shelter there as a home when times were hard. The name "Happy Hansel" is of ancient vintage and roughly means "a fortuitous gift or blessing." Charles D. Robertson wrote about it in a letter to his son in 1918:

> *It is doubtful if there is any place of the same name in the world, excepting the one in the Shetland Islands, situate on the top of a hill over-looking Vaila Sound. The site was the original school house and school grounds, and was occupied by mother when I was last there. . . .*

*The word "hansel" or "handsel" is probably Danish in its origin. I think it is used sometimes as a noun, and sometimes as a verb, but generally it means a gift handed to a person for good luck; at weddings, for instance, a young man who was known to be generous in "hanselling" the bride was a favorite wedding guest. Those hansellings were generally money, put in the bride's hand after she had been put to bed!*

*If a tradesman opens a new shop, his friends will hansel him, or hansel the shop, by buying there; and the first money taken in is kissed, then spat upon, and put away by itself—all for luck! The custom of fishermen, I think, is from the same root. The first fish caught is supposed to be a gift from the Sea God; so the mouth of the fish is opened, and the fisherman spits in its mouth for good luck. Very few fishermen overlook that ceremony.*

## Research Challenges and Sources

The purpose of this book is to trace and document, as best we can, the lives of the earliest Robertsons we know of and their descendants. Unfortunately, records of peoples' lives two or more centuries ago are very limited and often confusing—far from the kind of information we have in today's detail-oriented, computer-assisted world.

Before 1855, there was no national system in Scotland to register births, marriages, or deaths. That data was maintained primarily by parish officials in the Church of Scotland in what are now referred to as Old Parish Records or "OPRs." For various reasons, the parish registers were incomplete (for example, deaths were infrequently listed), handwriting was often poor or difficult to decipher, and spelling was erratic. It is hard to imagine that all knowledge and memory of many individuals who lived fruitful and loving lives have been totally lost over time, including many of the ancestors of our Robertsons.

Starting in 1855, a national system for recording births, marriages, and deaths was implemented throughout Scotland by law, with civil registrars being designated in the various parishes with the duty of recording vital data. These records are maintained in Edinburgh at the General Register Office (GRO) for Scotland.

Other useful information for family-history research can be found in Kirk Session Minutes of the Church of Scotland. In the Presbyterian structure of the Church of Scotland, created under the leadership of John Knox, the Kirk Session was a somewhat democratic local church body consisting of elders of the various congregations and moderated by the local minister. The Kirk Session was responsible for organization and administration of the local church's affairs, including discipline of members and providing support for the poor. Records of Kirk Session meetings reveal interesting and vital information about the local parish and its members.

The development and use of family names like Robertson has helped genealogical research greatly but is also a potential source of confusion. Robertson is a very common name in Scotland, used not only by families connected with the Robertsons of Clan Donnachaidh but also by unrelated families who obtained the surname through the ancient *patronymic* system of naming children based upon their fathers' first, or Christian, names. Under that tradition, if a son William was born to John Thomson, he would be known as William Johnson; William's son John would be John Williamson; and so on. A man named Robertson in those days might be called that because he was, literally, *Robert's son*. There were numerous families using patronymic naming in the same areas of Shetland that our ancestors occupied, and this continued well into the nineteenth century. Thus, when we find a record referring to someone named Robertson, we need to check that it was not about an unrelated person who happened to have had a father named Robert.

Another naming convention can be quite helpful in research—the traditional pattern which called for the first son to be given the first, or Christian, name of the paternal grand-father, the second son being named after the maternal grandfather, and the third son after the father. For girls, the traditional pattern was to name the first daughter after the maternal grandmother, the second daughter after the paternal grandmother, and the third daughter after the mother. A later child would be named for an uncle or aunt and, sometimes, for the local doctor, minister, teacher, or dominant landowner. This traditional naming pattern, where followed, provides valuable cross-checks and clues for research.

We are most fortunate that the Shetland Family History Society (SFHS), based in Lerwick, is active and has been helpful and supportive of our research into the Robertsons and related families of Sandsting & Aithsting, Walls, and neighboring areas.[3] Another most helpful source is the Shetland Archives in Lerwick, which maintains copies of old court records, land deeds, newspapers, photographs, and other historical information about Shetland. Other information about our Robertsons has been compiled through the years by family members from official records, family Bibles, notes and letters, old newspapers, grave markers and cemetery inscriptions, and other sources. It has been a group effort, continuing to this day, as our Robertsons around the globe continue working together to unlock the secrets of our ancestors.

In trying to identify our ancestors and reconstruct their lives, we have been aided greatly by work of the Mormons, more formally known as the Church of Jesus Christ of Latter Day Saints (LDS), who are dedicated to genealogical research. The Mormons maintain a system called the International Genealogical Index (IGI), which is a listing of vital statistics compiled from original records that are available in particular countries and areas, such as baptismal and marriage records kept by church officials, and birth and death records, sometimes made by local government and parish clerks. Much of what we know about our Robertsons is based upon or confirmed by data in the IGI.[4]

Roman numerals are used throughout the manuscript to designate generations. Thus, the original Robertson brothers are identified as generation I, their great-grandchildren are designated generation IV, the great-grandchildren of those individuals are generation VII, and so on. We have divided the book into chapters roughly representing the successive generations, with sections within each chapter covering various branches of the family tree.

Most if not all of the members of the fifth generation were born in the nineteenth century, over one hundred years ago, and we believe all of them have probably died by now. The sixth generation, the great-great-great-grandchildren of the original Robertson brothers Thomas and John, have now become the senior members of our Robertsons. As we now enter the twenty-first century, there are many energetic young Robertsons comprising the ninth generation of descendants of the brothers—and the beginnings of the tenth generation.

## Where Did the Robertson Brothers Come From?

We have not been able to trace our Robertson ancestry further back than Thomas and John Robertson, both believed to have been born in the 1740s. But where did they originally come from? How and when, and why, did they—or their ancestors—first come to Shetland? What follows is the myth of our family's origin, handed down for generations.

Our Robertsons by tradition came from the Robertsons of Struan, a leading sept or branch of the Clan Donnachaidh of the central Highlands of Scotland. The Robertson families of Clan Donnachaidh once occupied vast hereditary lands stretching "from the Moor of Rannoch to the gates of Perth," the ancient capital of Scotland. Eminent Scots historian W.F. Skene described the Robertsons of Struan as "the oldest family in Scotland, being the sole remaining branch of the Royal House which occupied the throne of Scotland during the 11th and 12th Centuries."[5]

However, all of our known Robertson ancestors were born in the remote Shetland Islands, far from traditional Robertson homelands in the Scottish Highlands. Why and when would they have made such a move? A possible answer lies in the story of Culloden, one of the unhappiest and cruelest chapters of Scottish history.

The Robertsons of Struan traditionally supported the royal House of Stuart, which ruled Scotland and England until King James II was exiled to France in 1688. Many of the clansmen were Jacobites who sought to regain the crown for the Stuarts. This movement coupled the nationalistic sentiments of many Highland Scots with the Catholicism of the Stuarts and the French leaders, with whom they had been aligned since the time of Mary, Queen of Scots. Open rebellion by Jacobite forces in Scotland arose on several occasions. The last of these Jacobite uprisings started in 1745, as Charles Edward Stuart—"Bonnie Prince Charlie"—came out of exile in France and renewed the struggle to return the English throne to Stuart control.

The final battle of that uprising, the disastrous Battle of Culloden, was fought on a soggy, windswept moor in northern Scotland on April 16, 1746. There, the Jacobite troops were routed and many Highlanders were slaughtered. After hiding for weeks in remote coastal islands and hills, Bonnie Prince Charlie fled Scotland and returned to France to live out the rest of his life. The English army occupied Scotland, and for months waged a brutal campaign of terror against the Highland people. Anyone suspected of having supported or sympathized with the young pretender was in great peril. The Highland clans and their distinctive tartans and dress were formally outlawed, the Gaelic language was suppressed, and heads of the leading families lost their properties and estates by forfeiture. Many were thrown into prison or simply murdered.[6]

The Robertsons of Struan began to scatter. According to family legend, our Robertson ancestors and other Scottish families, with support or aid from a sister of either the Duke of Atholl or the Duke of Argyll, fled Scotland by sailing vessel. Somehow, two of our ancestors, by this account, landed on Shetland near the hamlet of Brindister. Possibly, they were headed for America or some other haven but were shipwrecked on the Shetland coast; on the other hand, they could have been going to Shetland by plan.

This is the traditional, romantic vision of our family origins, casting our ancestors as brave young refugees from political and military repression. Some of our Robertsons are skeptical of this story. For one thing, Angus Robertson says, "the legend of the two brothers arriving by boat is common to several families on the West Side of Shetland and does tend to strain credulity a bit." In addition, the Presbyterian communities of Shetland were not generally friendly to the Jacobite cause and its Catholic religious orientation. In 1745, the Kirk Session of Walls "held a day of humiliation and fasting and prayer when they heard of 'the Dangerous Insurrection in Scotland in favor of the Popish Pretender to the Throne of these Nations'; and they held a Thanksgiving when they heard—six months after it was fought—of the battle of Culloden." Thus, Angus notes, "it seems unlikely that a colony of Jacobite sympathizers would have existed here at that time."

The legend is vague in important details but still may hold a grain of truth. It is not certain that the Robertson brothers named Thomas and John were the same ones who supposedly came to Shetland from Scotland. In fact, there was a previous Jacobite uprising in 1715, a generation earlier, in which Alexander Robertson of Struan, chief of Clan Donnachaidh and a devoted Jacobite, played an important role, as a result of which he went into exile and lost his estates by forfeiture. Could the first of our Robertsons in Shetland actually have had some connection with the rebellion of 1715 and come to Shetland at that time?

It may also be incorrect to assume that the immigrant brothers (or their families) were on the *pro*-Jacobite side. The Duke of Atholl and the Duke of Argyle were both loyal to Anne, Queen of England, and hostile to the Jacobites. Certainly, not all Robertsons were Jacobites. Indeed, Clan Donnachaidh's chief, Alexander Robertson of Struan, had a sister, Margaret Robertson (whom he nicknamed "Black Margaret"), who was loyal to the Crown and with whom he was embroiled in years of financial, legal, and personal disputes. Struan even accused his sister of spying and plotting against the Jacobite cause, including the transporting of secret intelligence between the Duke of Atholl and the Duke of Argyle. Although Queen Anne and the Duke of Atholl tried to protect Margaret from her brother, Struan caused her to be kidnapped, beaten, and held prisoner for months in 1714 and 1715. By the time she was freed, the Jacobite uprising of 1715 was over and Struan was in exile. This historical episode suggests that the Robertson brothers who first landed on Shetland *could* have had some direct or indirect connection to Margaret Robertson. Perhaps they were sent to Shetland to escape the harassment and threats of her ardent Jacobite brother. But this too remains unproven speculation.

Another theory is that our Robertsons did not emerge from the Highland clans at all but came from an old Shetland family. Charles Gifford of Lerwick has a theory that our Robertsons descend from Magnus Norsk, a native of Norway who came to Shetland as a preacher and was ordained as a minister in the parish of Unst in 1593. By this hypothesis, Magnus Norsk had a grandson named Robert, whose sons were called Robertson in the patronymic custom and, thereafter, the surname was retained. Whether this theory can be proved remains to be seen. In any event, there is a real possibility that our Robertsons came from old Shetland-Viking stock, not from mainland Scotland at all, and got their surname by patronymic usage.

The short answer to the mystery of our origins is that we still have no knowledge of where our ancestors Thomas and John Robertson came from.

Chapter 1

# THE TWO BROTHERS

According to family lore passed down by the late George Robertson of Waterloo, Walls Parish, the brothers who were the first of our Robertsons to appear in Shetland were tall, fair-haired, and blue-eyed. The dates and circumstances of their arrival, like the names and origins of their parents, remain shrouded in mystery. All we know about these brothers is included in this chapter.

## 1-A: THOMAS ROBERTSON, THE ELDER BROTHER

I. **Thomas Robertson** was reportedly born in 1740. According to the OPRs for Sandsting & Aithsting Parish, Thomas was married there on February 25, 1766, to _Katharin Brown_.[7] His wife, a daughter of Thomas Brown, was born on January 25, 1741, in Uyeasound, Sandsting & Aithsting Parish.[8] Our Robertsons had several links through marriage with the Brown family of Clousta, Aithsting.

Katharin and Thomas Robertson had several children. We were long aware of their sons Thomas, James, and Jerom, and a daughter named Agnes. Help from the Shetland Family History Society enabled us to identify another daughter, Helen Robertson. And, as there is a three-year gap between Thomas and Katharin's marriage and the birth of their first known child, who was given the name of his maternal grandfather, Thomas, it seems quite possible that an earlier son was born and named after the paternal grandfather.

It appears that Thomas and Katharin at one time lived in Uyeasound (now called Vementry) in Sandsting & Aithsting Parish. But by the early 1780s, the family was in Unifirth, near Brindister Voe, about four miles from Uyeasound. In the summer of 1781, a Thomas Robertson of Unifirth was one of numerous individuals named as defenders in a court summons filed on behalf of Robert Ross, a merchant in Weisdale Parish. Thomas was still living in Unifirth on December 10, 1795, when his son Jerom was married in Walls, about five miles south of Brindister in the adjacent parish.

Thomas Robertson died after 1795, probably in Unifirth, Sandsting & Aithsting Parish.

## Children of Thomas Robertson

II. **<u>Thomas Robertson</u>** was born in Uyeasound, the first known child of Katharin Brown and Thomas Robertson. He was baptized on February 26, 1769, in Sandsting & Aithsting Parish, Shetland, indicating that his birth was probably not long before.[9] He married his cousin *<u>Beatrice Jamieson</u>* (called "Bessie"), and they had three children. (*SEE SECTION 2-A.*)

II. **<u>Jerom Robertson</u>**, son of Katharin Brown and Thomas Robertson, was born in Uyeasound, Sandsting & Aithsting Parish, Shetland. There is confusion about when he was born—possibly 1771 or 1772, as parish records indicate (which may conflict with his brother James's birthdate), or 1775, as his son recorded (which may conflict with his sister Helen's birthdate). He married his first cousin *<u>Umphray Robertson</u>*, and they had five children. Jerom died on May 12, 1840, in Stove, Walls Parish. He was reported to be sixty-nine years of age. (*SEE SECTION 2-B.*)

II. **<u>James Robertson</u>**, another son of Katharin Brown and Thomas Robertson, was born in Uyeasound and baptized in 1772 in Sandsting & Aithsting Parish, Shetland.[10] On October 24, 1803, in that parish, James married *<u>Christian Yell</u>*,[11] whose parents' names are unknown. James and his wife lived in Aith, a few miles southeast of Uyeasound by water. They had at least three children, and possibly, there were others who have not yet been discovered in our research.

### Children of James Robertson

III. **<u>Mary Robertson</u>**, daughter of Christian Yell and James Robertson, was born March 15, 1806, in Aith and baptized on May 18, 1806, in Sandsting & Aithsting Parish, Shetland.[12] Mary had a cousin six years younger with the same name, the daughter of her uncle Thomas, also in Sandsting & Aithsting Parish.

The Mary Robertson who was the daughter of James Robertson appears to have married *<u>Thomas Henry</u>* on December 3, 1828, when she was twenty-two.[13]

Another possibility is that she or her younger cousin Mary married *Robert Christie* on November 21, 1833.[14]

To confuse matters further, there was still another Mary Robertson born in Clousta in Sandsting & Aithsting Parish about May 17, 1805, some ten months before James's daughter. This older Mary was the daughter of a Malcolm Robertson, whose connection to our Robertsons, if any, remains unknown.[15]

III. **James Robertson**, son of Christian Yell and James Robertson, was born in Aith, Sandsting & Aithsting Parish, Shetland, and was baptized May 14, 1809.[16]

III. **Clementina Robertson**, daughter of Christian Yell and James Robertson, was born in Aith, Sandsting & Aithsting Parish, Shetland. She was baptized there on November 18, 1813.[17]

II. **Helen Robertson (Thomson)**, daughter of Katharin Brown and Thomas Robertson, died on March 16, 1858, in Brindister, Sandsting & Aithsting Parish, Shetland. The death record states that she was eighty-three years old when she died, indicating that she was born in 1774 or early 1775; however, no birth or baptismal records have been found for her. Also, the death register listed her under the surname Thomson, which would mean that she had been married to a Mr. Thomson or that she was given that name at birth under the patronymic system. Tony Gott of the SFHS informs us that it was not uncommon for some daughters to be given patronymic names while sons in the same family were given the father's surname.

II. **Agnes Robertson**, daughter of Katharin Brown and Thomas Robertson, was born in Unifirth and baptized on June 2, 1782, in Sandsting & Aithsting Parish, Shetland.[18] No other information has surfaced about her in our research.

## 1-B: John, the Younger Brother

I. **John Robertson**, the younger brother of Thomas, is believed to have been born in 1745. He had at least one son, Robert, and two daughters, Agnes and Umphray (who married her first cousin, a son of John Robertson's brother, Thomas).

John Robertson lived in Bardister in Walls Parish, near the village of Walls, and he may also have lived for a while in nearby Elvister. His wife's name and origins are unknown. However, an Agnes Robertson died in May 1840 in Bardister, Walls Parish, and was buried in Walls Churchyard; she was reported to be ninety-three years of age, which would put her birth in approximately 1747. Possibly, she was the widow of our John Robertson of Bardister.

John Robertson probably died in Bardister in Walls Parish, but the date of his death has not been ascertained. We know it was before November 21, 1786, because the marriage records of Walls Parish concerning his daughter Umphray's contract for marriage on that date described her father as "the deceased John Robertson, sometime residenter in Bardister."

**Children of John Robertson**

II. **Robert Robertson**, son of John Robertson, was born about 1765. He married *Margaret Doul* in 1786, and they had three children. This Robert Robertson died in 1827. (*SEE SECTION 2-C.*)

II. **Agnes Robertson**, daughter of John Robertson, was born about 1768. She was identified in the Walls Parish birth register as "Agness Robertsdaughter"— possibly a variant of the old patronymic naming custom, as she was actually John's daughter, not Robert's. Agnes (again listed in the Walls Parish marriage register as Agnes "Robertsdaughter") married *James Laing* of Stennestwatt, Walls Parish, son of Gilbert Laing; they had two sons. Later, she married *James Twatt*, with whom she had two daughters and two more sons, and on that record was listed as Agnes "Johnsdaughter." (*SEE SECTION 2-D.*)

The two children of Agnes and James Laing were named Gilbert and John. Assuming that they were following the traditional pattern for giving first names— first son named after the father's father and the second son after the mother's father—their names tend to confirm that this Agnes Robertson was in fact the daughter of John Robertson and that her husband was the son of Gilbert Laing.

II. **Umphray Robertson**, daughter of John Robertson, was born in 1770 in Bardister, Walls Parish, Shetland, and died on April 21, 1842. Umphray married her cousin *Jerom Robertson* in 1795. (*SEE SECTION 2-B.*)

## 1-C: Who Were the Other Robertsons in Shetland?

Wherever Thomas and John Robertson may have originally come from, it is clear that other Robertsons were already living in the same parts of Shetland they settled in: Sandsting & Aithsting Parish and Walls Parish. Although the villages and hamlets in these areas are relatively remote and sparsely settled, available records make clear that there were at least one or two other Robertson families in each parish having marriages and births during the same time periods as our Robertsons.

To complicate things further, the parents and children in these families often had the same first names. For example, Thomas Robertson of our Robertson's first generation had a son Jerom, born in Sandsting & Aithsting Parish in around 1771 or 1772, but there was also another person named Jerome or Jarome Robertson in Sandsting (the adjacent parish) or Sandsting & Aithsting who was the father of at least eight children born from 1752 to 1769 who had such names as Agnes (baptized August 18, 1752), Robert, Andrew, James, Katherin, and Magnus that have been used repeatedly by our Robertsons. Later, there were at least five other Robertson fathers in Sandsting & Aithsting who had sons named Jerom: James, whose son Jerom was born in 1794; Thomas, son born February 11, 1796; Malcolm, son born June 7, 1801; Gideon, son born October 18, 1801; and Laurence, whose Jerom was born June 19, 1814.

In addition to the Agnes mentioned above, another Agnes Robertson was born to a James Robertson in Sandsting & Aithsting and baptized on August 15, 1748.[19] Both brothers, Thomas and John Robertson, gave their daughters the name Agnes.

Another example is the unusual name Umphray. That is what John Robertson named his second daughter, born in 1770 in Walls Parish, and the name was later used for several generations of our Robertsons, both male and female. Another child named Umphray was born to a James Robertson in Sandsting & Aithsting Parish and was baptized on July 31, 1749[20]—but this one was a male according to the IGI records.[21] Another interesting fact is that a James Robertson in Sandsting & Aithsting had a son named John baptized on June 4, 1745—the same year our ancestor John Robertson was born.[22]

These and numerous other overlaps lead us to believe that at least some of the Robertson families in Walls and Sandsting & Aithsting were linked to ours, although others were not.[23]

If that is so, Thomas and John may have been born on Shetland; possibly, their parents or grandparents, whose names are unknown to us, initially came from the Scottish mainland. If they *were* the immigrants, Thomas and his brother John quite possibly came to Shetland to live with Robertson relatives already there. Thus, it seems likely that at least some of the other Robertsons living in the western peninsula—and possibly other parts of Shetland— were parents, siblings, or cousins of the two brothers.

# Chapter 2

# THE SECOND GENERATION

## 2-A: THOMAS ROBERTSON (1769-18??)
### Son of Thomas Robertson

**II. T**homas Robertson**, born in Uyeasound in Sandsting & Aithsting Parish, Shetland, was baptized on February 26, 1769. He was the first known son of Thomas Robertson, the eldest of the two earliest Robertson brothers, and his wife, Katharin Brown, from a family whose Aithsting roots go back at least several generations.

At the age of thirty-three, Thomas married *Beatrice Jamieson* (or *Jamesdaughter*) on January 6, 1803, in Sandsting & Aithsting Parish.[24] Bessie was born in 1775 to Marian Brown and James Jamieson, a blacksmith. As her mother was a sister of Thomas's mother, Katharin Brown, Thomas and Bessie were first cousins.

Thomas Robertson was a fisherman and crofter. He and Bessie lived in Unifirth in Sandsting & Aithsting Parish. They had at least six children: James, Catherine, Thomas, Mary, Jerom, and Magnus Robertson.

Bessie died on August 2, 1866, in West Houlland, in Sandsting & Aithsting Parish, at age ninety-one. The death was registered by her son Jerom.

**Children of Thomas Robertson**

III. **James Robertson** was born on June 3, 1804, in Unifirth, Sandsting & Aithsting Parish, Shetland; James's and his father's surnames are entered in the abbreviated form "Robson" in the IGI.[25] James married *Barbara Tait* in Sandsting & Aithsting Parish, Shetland, on New Year's Eve, 1835.[26] They had at least eight children, all of whom may have been born in Unifirth.

**Children of James Robertson**

IV. <u>**Thomas Robertson**</u>, born on December 23, 1836, in Sandsting & Aithsting Parish, Shetland.[27]

IV. <u>**James Robertson**</u>, born on October 25, 1838, in Sandsting & Aithsting Parish, Shetland.[28]

IV. <u>**Laurence Robertson**</u>, born on August 10, 1840, in Unifirth, Sandsting & Aithsting Parish, Shetland.[29] He married *Agnes Walterson* on December 20, 1885, in Lerwick. They had five children of whom we are aware. The family suffered a horrible tragedy when the first three children were all drowned on a winter day in 1895 when the ice broke while they were playing on a pond. The family moved out of the parish not long afterward.

**Children of Laurence Robertson**

V. <u>**Laurence Robertson**</u>, born on September 17, 1887. He was one of the three children who died on January 9, 1895, when the ice broke on a frozen pond they were playing on. He was seven years old.

V. <u>**James Robertson**</u>, born on November 28, 1888. Died at age six, also in the pond accident on January 9, 1895.

V. <u>**Walter Robertson**</u>, born on November 25, 1891, in Brindister, Sandsting & Aithsting Parish, Shetland. The youngest of the three brothers who fell through the ice on January 9, 1895, he was only three years old.

V. <u>**Thomas Robertson**</u>, born on December 7, 1892.

V. <u>**Robina Margaret Robertson**</u>, born on October 6, 1895.

IV. <u>**John Robertson**</u>, born on August 4, 1841.

IV. <u>**Peter Robertson**</u>, born on August 18, 1845, in Sandsting & Aithsting Parish, Shetland.[30]

IV. <u>**Jeremiah Robertson**</u>, born on December 27, 1847, in Sandsting & Aithsting Parish, Shetland.[31]

IV. <u>**Magnus Robertson**</u>, born on February 19, 1850, in Sandsting & Aithsting Parish, Shetland.[32]

IV. **Margaret Robertson**, born on November 28, 1851, in Sandsting & Aithsting Parish, Shetland.[33]

III. **Catherine Robertson**, daughter of Bessie Jameson and Thomas Robertson, was born in Unifirth and baptized on September 28, 1806, in Sandsting & Aithsting Parish, Shetland.[34] She married her first cousin *John Robertson* in 1826, and they had seven children. Katie died on December 2, 1886, in Westerskeld. (*SEE SECTION 3-A.*)

III. **Thomas Robertson**, son of Bessie Jameson and Thomas Robertson, was born about 1809 and baptized on May 7, 1809, in Unifirth, Sandsting & Aithsting Parish, Shetland.[35]

III. **Mary Robertson**, daughter of Bessie Jameson and Thomas Robertson, was born in 1812 in Unifirth, Sandsting & Aithsting, Shetland. She was baptized on October 13, 1812.[36] The IGI lists several marriages of "Mary Robertson" in Sandsting & Aithsting Parish that could have involved this Mary or her cousin Mary, daughter of Christian Yell and James Robertson. (See 1-A above.) Possibly, this younger Mary Robertson married *Robert Christie* on November 21, 1833,[37] when she was twenty-one years old. Another possible (but less likely) marriage would have been at the age of sixteen to *Thomas Henry* on December 3, 1828.[38]

III. **Jerom Robertson**, son of Bessie Jameson and Thomas Robertson, was born about 1819 in Sandsting & Aithsting Parish, Shetland (according to old parish records). He married *Elizabeth Irvine* on January 2, 1849, in Sandsting & Aithsting Parish.[39] Elizabeth was born about 1816 and baptized on February 16 of that year. Her parents were Agnes Peterson and Peter Irvine, who had married in Walls Parish on November 14, 1811, but moved to Unifirth in Sandsting & Aithsting Parish soon afterward.

Elizabeth and Jerom Robertson had at least two children (listed below). Based on the gap between the date of their marriage and these children's birthdates, and on the daughter's name, they may have had one or more earlier children who have not been discovered in our research (possibly girls, as the name Thomas would have been appropriate for a first son).

Elizabeth died on May 27, 1889, in Houlland in Sandsting & Aithsting Parish, Shetland. Jerom Robertson died on October 13, 1890—approximately seventy-one years of age—at Murrister in Sandsting & Aithsting Parish.

### Children of Jerom Robertson

IV. **Thomas Robertson**, born on July 24, 1853.

IV. **Barbara Robertson**, born on November 16, 1856, in Sandsting & Aithsting Parish, Shetland.[40]

III. **Magnus Robertson**, son of Bessie Jameson and the second Thomas Robertson, is an ancestor we discovered by working backwards to find the way in which his granddaughter Margaret Robertson Williamson was related to our Robertsons. Reuben Robertson Sr. met Margaret on a visit to Shetland in 1935, when she was living in the home of his late uncle James David Robertson in Riskaness, Walls, and they maintained correspondence for some time. From those letters we know that Margaret's maiden name was Robertson, that her grandfather had the name Magnus, and that he was a first cousin of Reuben's grandfather Thomas Robertson. But we were unable to find the actual connection between these branches of the family. The mystery was solved by fellow Shetland researcher Stuart Robertson in August 1997 when he located records in the Scottish government archives in Edinburgh that identified Magnus Robertson and his parents.

Magnus was born on January 6, 1822, in Unifirth, Sandsting & Aithsting Parish, Shetland. He married *Marion Hunter* in Tingwall Parish, and they had six children. Their progeny include many of our Robertsons who are living in Shetland, England, and Canada. Magnus Robertson died on September 16, 1901, in Houlland, Sandsting & Aithsting Parish. (*SEE SECTION 3-B.*)

## 2-B: UMPHRAY (1770-1842) AND JEROM ROBERTSON (C.1770-1840)

II. **Umphray Robertson** was born in 1770 in Bardister, Walls Parish, in the western part of Mainland Shetland. She was the third child of John Robertson, the younger of the original Robertson brothers (1-B above). She married *Jerom Robertson* (below).

II. **Jerom Robertson**, Umphray's first cousin, was the second son of Katharin Brown and Thomas Robertson (1-A above). He was born in Uyeasound in Sandsting & Aithsting Parish, Shetland, but the date and year of his birth are uncertain. According to the IGI, Jerom (there spelled Gerom) was baptized on September 25, 1772, meaning that his birth was obviously on or before that date.[41] However, the "Day Book" in which his son Thomas Robertson wrote down birthdays and other information about family members listed the year of Jerom's birth as 1775. When Jerom died in May of 1840, the Index of Deaths for Walls Parish listed his age as sixty-nine, which is consistent with a birth in 1770 or 1771. He was a fisherman and probably also a crofter.

Jerom and Umphray Robertson were married in Walls Parish on December 10, 1795.[42] The marriage register for Walls contains the following entry dated November 21, 1795: "Jerom Robertson lawful son to Thomas Robertson in Unifirth and Umphray Robertson, lawful daughter to the deceased John Robertson, sometime residenter in Bardister were contracted in order for marriage." The register further shows they were married on December 10, 1795, by Rev. David Thomson, minister of the Church of Scotland.[43] Jerom and Umphray had five sons, all of whom were baptized by Rev. Thomson in Walls.

In March 1789, one Jerom Robertson entered into an agreement to lease Vementry, a small, irregularly-shaped island close to the Shetland Mainland and northwest of Aithsting, from Gideon Gifford of Busta. The Giffords of Busta, Northmaven Parish, were long among Shetland's most prominent lairds or landowners, according to author Norah Kendall.[44]

The complex lease between Jerom and Gideon Gifford contemplated a lifetime arrangement for tenant farming in which the tenant and his family would live in the homestead on the island. Rent for the island involved not only a yearly monetary payment of twelve pounds Scots, but also a variety of goods and services to be provided by the tenant—including tending the landlord's stock of almost 500 sheep on the island,[45] delivering 300 pounds

Dutch weight of wool by June 20 every year, and operating "a six manned six oared boat" (a kind of rowed fishing boat known as a "sixareen") for deep sea fishing out of Stenness "or where you shall appoint," from which the landlord was to receive one third of the catch. The tenant also was required to turn over all "white fish, gill and herring caught by me or any residing in my family" at prices set by Gifford, plus all the butter he produced, at a stipulated price; and in addition, Gifford required that "any fishermen, sons, servants or others residing with you from Lammas [August 1] to the fishing season shall fish to me." Such arrangements, which often proved to be very onerous for tenants, had been originated by the Giffords, as Norah Kendall explains:

*The survival of the proprietors [landowners] necessitated their undertaking the fish-curing and marketing of the produce. In the early part of the eighteenth century, until the markets were established, these were lean times for all. Thomas Gifford of Busta was the pioneer of this venture which became known as "fishing tenures" or "Zetland method." This was, perhaps, at the time a necessity but as it developed the tenants became bound to deal only with their landlord. They were no longer able to negotiate their own prices for their fish or for the provisions which they purchased. In many cases they lived under the threat of eviction, bound to buy their provisions at inflated prices and to sell their fish at their proprietor's stipulated prices. . . .*

*With their markets established by the 1740s, the proprietors bought larger boats and the men went further out to sea, being away days at a time. Some landowners increased their numbers of fishermen by absorbing the people evicted by those who chose sheep and cattle farming to tenants. . . . The measure of wealth was determined by the numbers of tenant-fishermen rather than the size of the estate. . . .*

*There were about twenty large proprietors and a considerable number of small ones. The land rent amounted to about £5000, but the proprietors make as much more, from the profits of the fishery, carried on by the fishermen settled on the estates, who are obliged to purchase from their landlords the articles that they want, and to dispose of the fish they catch to them, at a rate sufficient to admit of a considerable profit when resold. . . . This system has the unhappy effect of making the people pay very little attention to agriculture, or at least to consider it as an object of secondary importance; but at the same time, has been the means of raising an incredible number of seafaring people, in proportion to the number of inhabitants.[46]*

Like many other tenants under this rigid system, Jerom Robertson was unable to survive financially. In March of 1797, he was sued by Gideon Gifford with a so-called "Summons of Removing," alleging failure to provide fish to the landlord as required. When Jerom failed to answer in court in Lerwick on the appointed day, an order of eviction was entered.[47]

We do not know whether the tenant in this case was our Jerom Robertson. As noted above, there was an another, considerably older Jerom Robertson in Sandsting & Aithsting. But there are some reasons to believe that the Jerom of Vementry may have been one of our Robertsons, although our Jerom would have been very young at the commencement of the lease in 1789—only eighteen or nineteen, if he was born in 1770 or 1771—and still unmarried. The correspondence with Mr. Gifford indicates that he was already in possession of the property. It is possible that Jerom succeeded his father, Thomas Robertson, or an uncle or grandfather as the tenant on Vementry. IGI records reflect that Jerom's mother, Katherin Brown, and two of her brothers, as well as Jerom himself and two of his brothers, were all born in Uyeasound, a hamlet almost immediately next to the island and now itself known as Vementry. It is entirely possible that they were actually born on Vementry Island in the tenant home there. The birth records of Sandsting & Aithsting Parish indicate that a John Robertson in Vementry had a daughter named Katharine about December 1740. Could he also have been one of our Robertsons?

Jerom Robertson was married in 1795, and his first son, Thomas, was born in September 1796. While parish records seem to indicate that Thomas was born in Walls Parish,[48] Thomas reportedly told his son, years later, that he had been born on an island in the north—perhaps meaning he was born on Vementry, consistent with Thomas's father still having tenancy of that island until March 1797.

At some point after their marriage, Jerom and Umphray settled in Walls Parish, where most of their children were born and all, apparently, were raised. He seems to have been residing in Bardister, Walls Parish (where Umphray's late father had lived), when the second son was born in November 1798. Perhaps the young family had moved into the father's home after losing the leasehold in Vementry, or perhaps they decided to move first and then let the lease go. Within a few years, Jerome and Umphray were in the hamlet of Stove, barely a half mile from Bardister. The old parish records listed Jerome's residence as Stove when more children were born in 1801, in 1803, and in 1806.

Jerom Robertson died on May 12, 1840, in Stove, Walls Parish, and was buried in the Walls Churchyard. His age was recorded as sixty-nine. In June 1841, Umphray Robertson and her thirteen-year-old grandson were listed in the official census as residing in Stove in the cottage next to her son Thomas. She died there on April 21, 1842, about seventy-two years of age.

### Children of Umphray and Jerom Robertson

III. **Thomas Robertson**, oldest son of Umphray and Jerom Robertson, was born on September 6, 1796, in Bardister, Walls Parish, Shetland,[49]and died on January 9, 1873, age seventy-six. He married three times and had nine children. (*SEE SECTION 3-C.*) This Thomas is the direct ancestor of most members of our Robertsons now known to be living in the United States and of many in New Zealand.

III. **John Robertson**, second son of Umphray and Jerom Robertson, was born on November 14, 1798, in Bardister, Walls Parish, Shetland,[50] and died on December 20, 1887, in Westerskeld in Sandsting Parish. He married a first cousin, *Catherine Robertson*, and they had seven children. (*SEE SECTION 3-A.*)

III. **Oliver Robertson**, third son of Umphray and Jerom Robertson, was born on November 30, 1801, in Stove in Walls Parish, Shetland.[51] (According to Dr. Eddie Robertson, Oliver's birth was in November 1801, not April.) No further information is available about him.

III. **Robert Robertson**, fourth son of Umphray and Jerom Robertson, was born on May 15, 1803, in Stove in Walls Parish, Shetland.[52] He died on March 22, 1827, in the age of twenty-three, and was buried in Walls Churchyard, according to the Register of Deaths for Walls.

III. **James Greig Robertson**, fifth son of Umphray and Jerom Robertson, was born on May 8, 1806, in Stove in Walls Parish, Shetland.[53] His second name may have been given in respect to the longtime master of Happy Hansel school in Walls, Archibald Greig. James married a first cousin, *Helen Twatt*, and they had eight children. They settled in Scalloway, Tingwall Parish, where James died in 1876. (*SEE SECTION 3-D.*)

## 2-C: ROBERT ROBERTSON (C. 1765-1827)
### Son of John Robertson

II. **Robert Robertson**, born in Shetland about 1765,[54] was the son of John Robertson, the younger of the brothers from whom Our Robertsons are descended, and a mother whose name remains unknown (1-B above).

On November 20, 1786, Robert was married in Sandsting & Aithsting Parish to *Margaret Doul.* The marriage was also recorded in Walls Parish with the date November 28, 1786.[55] Born on June 10, 1767, in West Burrafirth in Sandsting & Aithsting Parish,[56] Margaret was the daughter of Elizabeth Johnsdaughter and Andrew Doul. The Doul or Doull family (also sometimes spelled "Dowl" or "Dowel") is found in West Burrafirth for several generations before Margaret. The first in Shetland appears to have been a man named MacDougal, who reportedly came there with Cromwell's army and was the great-grandfather of Andrew Doul.

Margaret and Robert Robertson had nine sons, of whom seven apparently survived to maturity: twin brothers John and Andrew, Robert, Anthony, Oliver, Archibald Henry, and Erasmus. This family demonstrates the use of the naming pattern—first son named after paternal grandfather (John), second son after maternal grandfather (Andrew Doul), third son after the father (Robert), and others named for uncles and family friends. The two first-born children, named John and Andrew, must have died in infancy, as the next children were given the same names.

**Children of Robert Robertson**

III. **John Robertson**, born about 1787 or 1789, must have died as a small child before November 1792, when the same name was given to another baby.

III. **Andrew Umphray Robertson**, born on September 8, 1790, probably died in infancy before November 1792, when the parents named another baby Andrew.

III. **John Robertson**, a twin son of Margaret Doul and Robert Robertson, born on November 10, 1792, in Walls Parish, Shetland,[57] and baptized by Rev. David Thomson, Minister of the Gospel of the Church of Scotland.

III. **Andrew Robertson**, son of Margaret Doul and Robert Robertson and twin brother of John, born on November 10, 1792, in Walls Parish, Shetland,[58] and also baptized by Rev. Thomson. Andrew died on January 9, 1872, in Walls, at the age of seventy-nine.

III. **Robert Robertson**, son of Margaret Doul and Robert Robertson, was born on July 6, 1794, in Elvister in Walls Parish, Shetland.[59] Robert married *Margaret Fraser*. His wife was born on August 29, 1795. She was the daughter of Barbara Williamsdaughter and Laurence Fraser of Seater, Walls Parish. The Walls Parish records show that Robert and Margaret "contracted in order for marriage" on January 29, 1820, and were married five days later, on February 3, 1820, by Rev. David Thomson.[60] Margaret and Robert had one daughter, Robina, who ultimately settled in Australia and who is the ancestor of many of Our Robertsons in that nation.

**Child of Robert Robertson**

IV. **Robina Robertson** was born in Elvister, Walls Parish, Shetland, on December 8, 1821, (according to the IGI.)[61]—or on that date in 1822, according to her husband's record in a family Bible.

In her mid-twenties, Robina married *Thomas Gifford Jamieson* in Lerwick. Thomas, a schoolteacher, was born in Brae, Delting Parish, on March 28, 1821. His mother's name was Janet Robertson. The names of her parents, and whether they had any relationship to our Robertsons, are unknown. Thomas's father was Peter Jamieson or Jameson, a fisherman and a crofter in Brae.[62]

Robina and Thomas immigrated to Victoria, Australia, in the mid-1850s. They had twelve children, of whom no more than six lived to maturity. Robina died in March 1876 in Victoria. (*SEE SECTION 4-G.*)

III. **Anthony Robertson**, son of Margaret Doul and Robert Robertson, was born on May 16, 1796, in Elvister, Walls Parish, Shetland,[63] and was baptized by Rev. David Thomson. He died at the age of twelve in December 1807 and was buried in Walls Churchyard.

III. **<u>Oliver Robertson</u>**, son of Margaret Doul and Robert Robertson, was born on August 20, 1801, in Walls Parish, Shetland.[64]

III. **<u>Archibald Henry Robertson</u>**, son of Margaret Doul and Robert Robertson, was born on May 15, 1803, in Walls Parish, Shetland.[65]

Archibald and *<u>Elizabeth Robertson</u>* (called "Bessy") were married in Lerwick, Shetland, on October 21, 1832,[66] (recorded November 1, 1832) in the parish of Sandsting & Aithsting.[67] Although Bessy's family name was Robertson, we do not yet know who her parents were or whether she was a cousin of Archibald. We know of six children in this family.

**Children of Archibald Henry Robertson**

IV. **<u>Margaret Robertson</u>**, baptized on November 21, 1833, in Lerwick, Shetland, and given the name of her father's mother.[68]

IV. **<u>Robert Robertson</u>**, baptized on July 16, 1837, in Sandsting & Aithsting Parish, Shetland, apparently named after his paternal grandfather.[69]

IV. **<u>Helen Robertson</u>**, baptized on March 15, 1839, in Sandsting & Aithsting Parish, Shetland.[70] Based upon conventional naming patterns, her given name is probably a good clue to the first name of Bessy's mother.

IV. **<u>Archibald Robertson</u>**, baptized on December 26, 1840, in Sandsting & Aithsting Parish, Shetland.[71]

IV. **<u>Elizabeth Robertson</u>**, baptized on May 25, 1843, in Sandsting & Aithsting Parish, Shetland.[72]

IV. **<u>Olla Robertson</u>**, baptized on April 29, 1845, in Sandsting & Aithsting Parish, Shetland.[73]

III. **<u>Erasmus Robertson</u>**, son of Margaret Doul and Robert Robertson, born on November 1, 1805, in Elvister, Walls Parish, Shetland.[74]

## 2-D: AGNES ROBERTSON (C. 1768-1841?)
### Daughter of John Robertson
### Matriarch of the Laing and Twatt Branches

II. **Agnes Robertson**, daughter of John Robertson, was born about 1768, probably in Bardister in Walls Parish, Shetland. The name of her mother is unknown.

Agnes first married *James Laing* in Bardister on November 22, 1787. The marriage register for Walls Parish records the union between "James Laing lawful son to Gilbert Laing residenter in Stenistwat and Agness Robertsdr lawful daughter to the deceased John Robertson sometime residenter in Bardister" and reflects that the ceremony was performed by Rev. David Thomson.[75] James Laing was born about 1762, the son of Katherine Anderson and Gilbert Laing of Stennestwatt, Walls Parish.[76] They had two sons. Apparently, James Laing died young, because Agnes remarried as a widow in 1795.

The second husband of Agnes Robertson was *James Twatt*, who was born about 1770. They were married by Rev. Thomson of the Church of Scotland in Walls Parish on October 29, 1795,[77] but this time the bride was listed in the parish register as "Agnes Johnsdr, widow in Bardister." The husband was identified as "James Twat lawful son to the deceased Thomas Twat in Sandness." Agnes and James Twatt had four children. The Twatt family had long been in Shetland. Then known by the surname Thveit, they removed from western Norway, around Bergen, in the tenth century and settled in the Faroe Islands. Later, they left the Faroes for Shetland, where they had settled by the seventeenth century using the name Twatt.[78]

James Twatt died on September 1, 1841, about seventy-one years old. The death register for Walls Parish shows that a widow, Agnes Robertson, died in Voe on February 8, 1850, and was buried in the Walls Churchyard. If that was "our" Agnes (which we believe it was, as her son Robert lived in Voe with his family), she would have been about eighty-one.

**Children of Agnes Robertson**

III. **Gilbert Laing**, first son of Agnes Robertson and James Laing, was born on August 28, 1788, in Walls Parish, Shetland.[79] The birth register identifies him as "lawful son to James Laing and Agnes Johnsdr." Gilbert married *Elizabeth Peterson* on December 26, 1811, (contracted in order for marriage on November 16) in Walls Parish, Shetland. The ceremony was performed by Rev. David Thomson. The marriage register indicates that Gilbert was then living in Burraland and Agnes was in Elvister. She was born about 1785. They had four children. Gilbert Laing died on November 14, 1848.

**Children of Gilbert Laing**

IV. **Mary Laing**, born on January 25, 1813, in Elvister, Walls Parish, Shetland;[80] baptized there by Rev. Thomson; died in Norby, Sandness, on May 15, 1888. Her death certificate describes her as unmarried and a pauper. Mary apparently had two children.

**Children of Mary Laing**

V. **Anderina Laing**, born 1831. She died in Bousta, Sandness, Shetland, on February 4, 1915, at age eighty-three. The death certificate lists her name as Anderina Slater and describes her as a farm servant, unmarried; it also lists her reputed father as William Slater, a seaman.

V. **Henry Laing**, born 1836. He died on August 28, 1869, in Norby, Sandness, Shetland, and is described in the death certificate as single, with no father identified.

IV. **James Laing**, born in Walls Parish, Shetland, on December 18, 1814, and baptized by Rev. David Thomson.[81] He married *Susan McKenzie* of Tumlin on May 23, 1837, as reflected in the Walls Parish records.[82] (Also recorded in Tingwall on May 27, 1837.[83]) She was born on August 7, 1814. They resided in Scalloway and had eight children.

Apparently, Susan died on January 21, 1855, at age forty, not long after the birth of her youngest child. The parish records show a marriage of James Laing to *Helen Ellen Hay* in Tingwall on December 18, 1855[84] (his forty-first birthday). She was born on July 26, 1820.

**Children of James Laing**

V. **<u>Elizabeth Laing</u>**, born on August 30, 1837, Walls Parish, Shetland,[85] and named for her paternal grandmother.

V. **<u>Barbara Laing</u>**, born on April 24, 1839, per Walls Parish records.[86]

V. **<u>John Laing</u>**, born on December 16, 1840, Tingwall[87]; apparently died in childhood before 1848, as another child was given the same name then.

V. **<u>James Laing</u>**, born on September 26, 1842, in Tingwall, Shetland.[88]

V. **<u>Mary Laing</u>**, born on September 27, 1844, in Tingwall, Shetland.[89]

V. **<u>John Laing</u>**, born on December 4, 1848, in Tingwall, Shetland.[90]

V. **<u>William Laing</u>**, born on May 3, 1851, in Tingwall, Shetland.[91]

V. **<u>Robert Laing</u>**, born on June 2, 1854, in Tingwall, Shetland.[92]

V. **<u>Ann Tait Laing</u>**, born on December 28, 1861, was the child of James Laing and Helen Ellen Hay, according to SFHS information.

IV. **<u>John Laing</u>**, born on November 25, 1817, in Walls Parish, Shetland,[93] and baptized by Rev. David Thomson.

IV. **<u>Agness Laing</u>**, born on December 9, 1822, in Curcagirth, Walls Parish, Shetland,[94] and baptized by Rev. Thomson.

III. **<u>John Laing</u>**, the second son of Agnes Robertson (or Johnsdaughter) and James Laing, was born on February 7, 1791, in Bardister, Walls Parish, Shetland. On November 23, 1820, in Walls Parish, he married *Margaret Smith*,[95] who was born in 1799. They had one child.

**Child of John Laing**

IV. **<u>James Scott Laing</u>**, born in Walls Parish, Shetland, on August 26, 1822.[96]

III. **<u>Margaret Twatt</u>**, daughter of Agnes Robertson (or Johnsdaughter) and James Twatt, was born on September 25, 1796, in Bardister, Walls Parish, Shetland.[97] She married *James Jeromson*, the son of Elizabeth Wishart and Jerom Manson (1769 – 1836), and they had five children.[98] (*SEE SECTION 3-E.*) Margaret died in 1876, about eighty years of age.

III. **James Twatt**, son of Agnes Robertson (or Johnsdaughter) and James Twatt, was born on August 12, 1798. He married *Andrina Robertson*, and they had four children. Andrina was the daughter of Olla Robertson of Northmavine, whose relationship to our Robertsons, if any, is unknown. After his first wife died, James married *Margaret Williamson*; they had no children. (*SEE SECTION 3-F.*) James Twatt died in 1876, about seventy-eight years of age.

III. **Helen (or Hellan) Twatt**, younger daughter of Agnes Robertson and James Twatt, was born on October 25, 1802, in Burraland, Walls Parish, Shetland. She married her first cousin *James Greig Robertson* in 1834. They lived in Scalloway and had eight children. Helen died in 1876. (*SEE SECTION 3-D.*)

III. **Robert Twatt**, younger son of Agnes Robertson and James Twatt, was born in 1805. He married *Jean Anderson*. They lived in Walls Parish and had twelve children. He died in 1869, about sixty-four years of age. (*SEE SECTION 3-G.*)

# Chapter 3

# THE THIRD GENERATION

**3-A: CATHERINE (1806-86) AND
JOHN ROBERTSON (1798-1887)**

III. <u>**Catherine Robertson**</u> (called "Katie"), daughter of Bessie Jamieson and Thomas Robertson (2-A above), granddaughter of the first Thomas Robertson and his wife, Katharin Brown, was born on September 28, 1806, in Unifirth in Sandsting & Aithsting Parish, Shetland. She married her first cousin *John Robertson* (below):

III. **John Robertson**, son of Jerom and Umphray Robertson (2-B above) and grandson of both brothers, Thomas and John Robertson, was born on November 14, 1798, in Bardister in Walls Parish, Shetland.

Catherine and John were married on December 11, 1826, by Rev. John Brydon in Sandsting & Aithsting Parish. John Robertson was then twenty-eight years old, and Katie was twenty. They had six sons and a daughter, whose descendants still live in the Shetland Islands as well as England, Australia, and New Zealand.

John was listed as a joiner or carpenter. But according to their descendant Alice Drury, the family members had to work at many trades to find work and earn a living. Referring to an 1834 letter written by John Robertson to solicit employment, Alice noted that "Amongst the skills he offered were: all kinds of building and brick work; all kinds of joinery and woodwork; fishing and curing of fish; accounting and bookkeeping; teaching of reading, writing, arithmetic, music, piano, organ and singing. Quite an adaptable man!"

Catherine and John Robertson and their family lived in Stove in Walls Parish for almost twenty-two years. Apparently, the land in Stove, even supplemented by fishing and other work, was too poor to support the family. On October 1, 1848, they moved to an "outset" in Culswick in Sandsting Parish.[99] When Dr. Eddie Robertson visited Shetland in July 1982, he went to Culswick and found that only the stone walls of the small house—called "Glessieburn"—and those around the land were still standing.

About 1850, Catherine and John's three eldest sons immigrated to Australia and spent time in the Victoria gold fields. The oldest, Thomas, came home to Shetland about 1867, married in 1868, and settled permanently there. It appears that John, the second son, died in the South Sea Islands about 1873, and James, the third son, died in New Guinea in 1912.

In 1867, some nineteen years after moving to the outset in Culswick, John and Catherine Robertson moved to Westerskeld, a few miles away. There they lived with their fifth son, Erasmus, and their only daughter, Margaret—neither of those children having married—in a house named Crool. John and Catherine were both in their sixties by then. Alice Drury believes they had been evicted from their croft.

The youngest son, Magnus, joined his two older brothers in Australia about 1870. Later, Magnus fell ill in Australia and returned to Shetland for about a year, married in 1879 while in Shetland, and soon afterwards went back to Australia.

Catherine Robertson died on December 1, 1886, age eighty, in Westerskeld, Sandsting & Aithsting Parish, Shetland. John died there on December 20, 1887, at age eighty-nine. The death was registered by his son Erasmus.

**Children of John and Katie Robertson**[100]

IV. **Thomas Robertson**, born on December 8, 1827, in Stove, Walls Parish, Shetland. He married *Catherine Thomson*, and they had seven children. Thomas died on January 3, 1913, at age eighty-five, at Westerskeld, Sandsting & Aithsting Parish. (*SEE SECTION 4-A.*)

IV. **John Scott Robertson**, born on September 30, 1830, in Stove, Walls Parish, Shetland; he died in March of 1873 or 1874 in the South Sea Islands at the age of forty-three.

IV. **James Robertson**, born on June 1, 1834, in Stove, Walls Parish, Shetland; died on October 8, 1912, in New Guinea, age seventy-eight.

IV. **Robert Robertson**, born on November 2, 1836, in Stove, Walls Parish, Shetland; died at sea on May 29, 1869, age thirty-two.

IV. **Erasmus Johnson Robertson**, born on July 1, 1840, in Stove, Walls Parish, Shetland; died on April 4, 1925, in Ayres of Selivoe, Sandsting & Aithsting Parish, Shetland. He was a stone quarrier and never married.

IV. **Margaret Mouat Robertson**, born on April 17, 1843, in Stove, Walls Parish, Shetland; died on September 4, 1929, in Ayres of Selivoe, Sandsting & Aithsting Parish, Shetland, age eighty-six. Margaret was given the same name as the third wife of her uncle, Thomas Robertson, who also lived in Walls. She was a knitter and did not marry.

IV. **Magnus Jameson Robertson**, born on February 17, 1846, in Stove, Walls Parish, Shetland; died on September 18, 1897, in New Zealand. He married *Helen Manson* in Sandsting & Aithsting Parish, and they had two children. (*SEE SECTION 4-B.*)

## 3-B: MAGNUS ROBERTSON (1822-1901)
### Son of Thomas Robertson II

III. **Magnus Robertson**, son of Bessie Jamieson and Thomas Robertson (2-A above), was born on January 6, 1822, in Unifirth, Aithsting, Shetland. His great-grandson Charles Gifford has a copy of the birth certificate, prepared in December 1854 by the parish session clerk, stating that "Thomas Thomason and Bessy Jamieson, Unifirth, Parish of Aithsting, had a son born on the 6th day of January 1822, named, Magnus." Thus, the name of Magnus's father was recorded in the birth register in the patronymic form of Thomason, rather than Robertson. The child may initially have been known as Magnus Thomason but later used the surname Robertson.

Magnus Robertson was a fisherman. He married *Marion Hunter* in Whiteness, Tingwall Parish, Shetland, on either February 1 or July 1 of 1853.[101] His wife, Marion, daughter of Margaret Jamieson and Joseph Hunter, was born in Tingwall Parish. Marion and Magnus had at least six children.

Magnus Robertson died at the age of seventy-nine on September 16, 1901, in Houlland, Sandsting & Aithsting Parish. Marion died in Bridge of Walls, Shetland, on February 15, 1915. Her death certificate stated that she was eight-five years old, indicating that she was born in 1828.

## Children of Magnus Robertson

IV. **James Robertson**, son of Marion Hunter and Magnus Robertson, born on November 11, 1854.[102]

IV. **Margaret Robertson**, daughter of Marion Hunter and Magnus Robertson, born on October 9, 1857.[103]

IV. **A daughter, name unknown**, born on October 27, 1860, to Marion Hunter and Magnus Robertson.[104]

IV. **Thomas Robertson**, son of Marion Hunter and Magnus Robertson, was born on February 17, 1862, in Unifirth, Sandsting & Aithsting Parish, Shetland. He was a seaman in the merchant service and apparently worked as a stone mason and artisan; his granddaughter Eileen Kelley recalls that one of his jobs was "sheep marker" helping to identify owners of the sheep that grazed the Shetland hillsides and byways.

Thomas married *Alison (Alice) Guthrie Jamieson*, daughter of Margaret Gray (whose parents were Lillias Henry and John Gray) and James Jamieson (whose parents were Mary Tait and James Jameson), on November 22, 1883, in Walls Parish.[105] Alice was born on September 4, 1856, in Claybottom, Walls Parish. Thomas and Alice had seven children. Alice died on February 22, 1897, at the Punds, Walls. Her death was possibly the result of complications in childbirth, as her last child was born (and died) that same year.

Thomas Robertson remarried in Lerwick on June 1, 1897. His second wife, *Elizabeth Jeromson*, was born in Ures of Vesquoy, Shetland, in 1861. She became stepmother to Thomas's six surviving children, ranging in age from one to twelve years, and she and Thomas later had twins. Elizabeth died on July 13, 1942, at Roadside Cottage, Punds, Walls Parish, at about eighty-one years of age. Thomas then moved to South Shields in Durham, England, to stay with his daughter Jemima, whose husband had been killed in the war. Thomas Robertson died on June 28, 1945, at 41 Salmon Street in South Shields; he was eighty-three.

Traveling to Edinburgh in 1935, Reuben Robertson Sr. made the acquaintance of a Mr. Murray, who was the Legal Assessor of the Land Court for crofters that was held in Shetland every year. Mr. Murray knew Thomas Robertson because he was assigned work projects by the Land Court from time to time. He reported that Thomas was regarded as efficient in his work but a bit "pugnacious." Once, Mr. Murray said, Thomas was fined thirty shillings after he "dotted the eye" of a local troublemaker; he paid the fine gladly, commenting that it was well worth the money.

### Children of Thomas Robertson

V. **Margaret Robertson**, first daughter of Alice Jamieson and Thomas Robertson, was born on October 5, 1884, in West Houlland in Walls Parish, Shetland. She married *Magnus Williamson*, and they had six children. Margaret died on July 27, 1966, in Lerwick. (*SEE SECTION 5-A.6.*)

V. **Marion Robertson**, second daughter of Alice Jamieson and Thomas Robertson, was born on June 4, 1886, in West Houlland, Walls Parish, Shetland. She married *James Mann* on February 22, 1918, at St. Ringan's Manse in Lerwick, Shetland. James was born on September 30, 1883, in Brough, Setter, Twatt, Sandsting & Aithsting Parish, Shetland. They had two sons. James Mann died on March 31, 1974, in Skeld, Sandsting & Aithsting Parish, Shetland. Marion died three years later on April 1, 1977, in Brevik Hospital, Lerwick, Shetland.

### Children of Marion Robertson

VI. **James Mann**, born about 1919. He married *Jemima Jean Moar* in the Methodist Church in Lerwick on June 17, 1942. Jemima, called "Mimie," was born on July 4, 1920, in Easter Skeld, Sandsting & Aithsting Parish, Shetland. James, a renowned fiddler, reportedly died in Shetland.

VI. **John Thomas Mann**, born on June 23, 1921, in Stove, Walls Parish, Shetland. He died on Christmas Day in 1940, in District Hospital, Cairns, Queensland, Australia. He was nineteen.

V. **Eliza Catherine Robertson**, third daughter of Alice Jamieson and Thomas Robertson, was born on August 21, 1888, in Bridge of Walls, Walls Parish, Shetland.[106] She married *Scott Williamson*, and they had seven children. After his death she married *William Leask* and had one more child. Eliza died in 1945 in Lerwick, Shetland. (*SEE SECTION 5-A.7.*)

V. **James Robertson**, oldest son of Alice Jamieson and Thomas Robertson, was born on August 29, 1891, in Bridge of Walls, Shetland. Jim apparently left Shetland at an early age. He settled for a while in Saskatchewan, Canada, and afterward lived in Nanaimo, Vancouver Island, British Columbia. He owned a fishing boat, a 32-foot gill-netter called *Omianan* (Nanaimo spelled backwards), which later caught fire and sank.

Jim Robertson ultimately returned to Shetland, married a woman named *Peggy* (maiden name unknown) about 1958, and settled into a small farmstead in Mucklure in Walls Parish. Jim's niece Eileen Kelley and her husband visited him and Peggy in Mucklure during a trip to Shetland in 1973. Prior to their return in 1978, he had died.

In December 1961, Jim wrote to his "Dear Brother Mack" (Magnus), urging him to return to Walls from Canada and move into the Punds, the homestead where their parents had lived and raised children. "There is no one in the Punds at present or has been for some time now. . . . If you will come here and take it over, I will move lock, stock and barrel to come in with you, so you wouldn't need to buy any stock or furniture. However, I don't suppose you are interested, but if you are I could easily make enquiries for you and find out all about it." Jim went on to describe his own farming at Mucklure. "We never had to feed the sheep last winter and the lambs were never inside, but it sure looks different this winter. Of course we are not fully stocked yet as we just started in a small way and are trying to increase as we go along. We shipped 6 wether lambs this fall to the south market and got £26 - 5/ for them clear, so if a fellow had the length of 30 to sell it would be all right."

V. **Magnus Robertson**, second son of Alice Jamieson and Thomas Robertson, was born on December 12, 1892, in Bridge of Walls, Shetland. In 1935, Magnus Robertson's sister Margaret Williamson wistfully wrote to Reuben Robertson Sr.: "I have a brother Magnus Robertson in America. He lives in Beatty, Saskatchewan, Canada, and is farming. But it is a most barbarious climate, and we would gladly know him out of it; only he cannot get back here as the value of stock (cattle, sheep) etc. is too little to raise the passage money for himself and his family. So unless he could get shifted somewhere else in America, I suppose there's nothing for it but to remain where he is."

Research help from cousins in Shetland recently allowed us to identify and contact the descendants of Magnus Robertson in Canada. We now know that Magnus Robertson immigrated to Canada as a young man and that he married *Violet Ludella Dryborough* in the province of Saskatchewan. They had six children. Magnus died in 1964 in Victoria, Vancouver Island, British Columbia. (*SEE SECTION 5-C.5.*)

V. **Alice Robertson**, fourth daughter of Alice Jamieson and Thomas Robertson, was born on September 16, 1895, in the Punds, Walls Parish, Shetland. She married *George Gifford*, and they had five children. Alice died in Lerwick in September 1979. (*SEE SECTION 5-A.8.*)

V. **Robina Robertson**, fifth daughter of Alice Jamieson and Thomas Robertson, was born on February 7, 1897, in the Punds, Walls Parish, Shetland. She died as a baby that same year.

V. **Thomas Robertson** was born on September 14, 1899, in the Punds, Walls Parish, Shetland, one of the twins born to Elizabeth Jeromson and Thomas Robertson. He moved to South Shields, England, where he first married *Dorothy Gray,* and they had three children. Dorothy died in childbirth, and Thomas then married *Caroline Richardson*. Thomas Robertson died about 1982 in South Shields, England. (*SEE SECTION 5-A.9.*)

V. **Jemima Robertson** was the other twin born to Elizabeth Jeromson and Thomas Robertson on September 14, 1899, in the Punds, Walls Parish, Shetland. She married *Laurence Coutts*, and they had four children. (*SEE SECTION 5-A.10.*)

IV. **Catherine Robertson**, daughter of Marion Hunter and Magnus Robertson, was born on June 4, 1865.

IV. **Magnus Robertson**, son of Marion Hunter and Magnus Robertson, was born on April 26, 1868.

## 3-C: THOMAS ROBERTSON (1796-1873)
### Son of Jerom and Umphray Robertson

III. **Thomas Robertson**, eldest son of Umphray and Jerom Robertson (2-B above), was born on September 8, 1796, in Bardister, Walls Parish, Shetland.[107] He settled nearby in Stove, an area in the village of Walls, where he became a well-to-do merchant. He was also a leader in the Methodist Church and active in the affairs of his community and parish.

Thomas Robertson's son James once commented that the tradition in the Robertson family was to marry within "the clan"—like Thomas's parents, to marry cousins—but that his father broke with the custom and three times married "strangers." He married his first wife, *Ursula Smith*, (born May 20, 1800) on April 21, 1828, in Lerwick, Shetland.[108] She died in Walls on October 28, 1831, and was buried in Walls Churchyard. They evidently had no children. Although information from the SFHS suggests there may have been a son named Thomas, born in 1828, this has not been verified. Thomas remained single for almost six years after Ursula's death.

At the age of forty, Thomas married his second wife, *Christina Dumbreck*, who was twenty-five. They were married in Walls Parish on August 8, 1837, by Rev. William Bryden. Christina died a year and a half later, on March 14, 1839, at their home in Stove, Walls. Her death was just eight days after the birth of her only child, Charles Dumbreck Robertson. She was buried in the Walls Churchyard.

Christina Dumbreck was born on March 31, 1812. It was long thought that she had a French mother and was born in France, but Dumbreck is a Scottish name, not French. Christina's son, Charles, was given a watch and chain and an Episcopal prayer book that had belonged to her, but he knew very little about his mother or where she came from.

As an elderly man in his late seventies, Charles wistfully wrote to his daughter-in-law Hope about Christina:

> *My father made her acquaintance in Shetland, where she was visiting at the rectory of an Episcopal Church minister; her home was then in or near Edinburgh. She had a sister who visited her in Shetland after her marriage. The Town of 'Dumbreck' near Edinburgh I was told was named after my mother's father; all I ever heard of my mother's family came to me through my step mother. My mother's*

*ancestors were said to have been among those followers and admirers of 'Mary' and migrated with her from France to Scotland. About 20 years ago I tried to trace the Dumbreck family and found one who was a Barrister in Edinburgh and one lady who was a cousin of mine—my mother's sister's daughter; she was a teacher in Edinburgh. About a month ago, I got sent from New Zealand a clipping showing her death in Edinburgh. I got the impression that the family had been influential and highly regarded. That's about all I know of my ancestry on my mother's side. Not much, is it?*

Two decades later, Charles's son Reuben Robertson Sr. attempted again to solve the mystery of grandmother Christina Dumbreck's origins by having research done in the Old Parish Records in Edinburgh, but without success.

We believe the mystery is now solved. Help from our friend Stuart Robertson has turned up evidence from the OPRs that Christina Dumbreck was born in Edinburgh, Scotland, and that she was the daughter of Mary Cromar and Charles Dumbreck (which would well explain the family's choice of those names for Christina's son). The Walls Parish records reflect the death of a Mrs. Dumbreck in Stove, Walls Parish, in June 1840—apparently, Christina's mother, Mary. If her husband was deceased, it is not unlikely that Mary Dumbreck would have been living near or with her daughter in Shetland or moved there to help with the baby.

Thomas Robertson and his family lived in Stove, an area in or near the village of Walls. The official census taken in 1841 recorded that the following persons were living in Stove Cottage No. 4 on June 5, 1841:

Thomas Robertson, aged 46 years (Merchant)

Charles Dumbreck Robertson, aged 2 years

George Georgeson, aged 15 years (Shopkeeper)

Margaret Mowat, aged 25 years (Housekeeper)

Agnes Hughson, aged 30 years (Female servant)

Next door, in Stove Cottage No. 5, the listed residents on June 5, 1841, were Thomas's mother, Umphray Robertson, then seventy years of age, and another Thomas Robertson, aged thirteen. The younger Thomas was apparently Umphray's grandson, the child of John and Katie Robertson, who was born in December 1827 and, therefore, was thirteen years old in 1841.

The Margaret Mouat who was staying in Thomas Robertson's household in 1841 was a well-educated young woman from Unst, the northernmost island of Shetland. She was hired by Thomas as a governess for his young son but soon became his third wife. Margaret was a daughter of Elizabeth Gray and Captain John Mouat of Brook Point, near Haroldswick, Unst.[109]

Thomas married *Margaret S. Mouat* (or *Mowat*), on June 28, 1842, in Walls Parish.[110] She was born in Brook Point, Unst, Shetland, on April 6, 1815. In addition to raising his first son, Margaret and Thomas had eight more children—three boys and five girls.

## Good Times and Hard Times in Walls

Thomas travelled extensively on business to Scotland, England, and on the European continent, and he owned a number of sailing vessels. For example, he had 75 percent ownership interest in the *Thomas*, a 42-foot sloop, according to the official certificate of registry dated April 6, 1839. (The other 25 percent was held by someone named Mitchell Reid; Magnus Thompson was listed as Master, or captain of the ship.) In early September of 1840, Thomas was in mainland Scotland on business and became concerned that he might not get home in time to appear for service on a jury court, scheduled for the middle of the month; he wrote to a lawyer in Lerwick, asking that this situation be explained to the court if he was unable to make it back.

Thomas Robertson later acquired a 44-foot sloop, (a type of single-masted sailing vessel), the *Charles*, named after his first son. That vessel was built in Walls Parish and registered in the Port of Lerwick on June 2, 1842, when little Charles Dumbreck Robertson was three years old. Magnus Thompson was listed as Master of the *Charles*, and a new Master replaced him on the *Thomas*. Although Thomas Robertson was the initial registered owner of the *Charles*, official records indicate that he must have transferred it at some point to his son: Charles D. Robertson was listed as owner after the boat was broken up as unseaworthy in 1863 and when the registration was cancelled in 1867. A 39-foot vessel, called *Seafield*, was built in Walls in 1847 and registered to Thomas Robertson as owner on August 26 of that year.

Active and energetic in his business affairs, Thomas was generous in extending credit and, evidently, had more than a little difficulty collecting what was owed to him. Here is a letter he sent to the law firm of James Greig & Son in October 1839:

*Gentlemen,*

*As you were kind enough to honour me with one of your circulars just as I was making ready for the South Shore, I had not time to thank you till now.*

*You will, I doubt not, suffer me herein to state a few facts relative to Shetland lawyers and Shetland law. A good few years ago I applied to one of them who kindly wrote a few letters to bad debtors. He obtained nothing and kindly charged nothing. Some time afterwards, I applied to another graduate which, in my opinion, ought to have for his motto an ass's head and a pig's tail. He at last obtained, of a good many bad or outstanding debts, 20 shillings sixpence – his charge on me was 12 shillings sixpence – I never to this day saw the balance, so I concluded in my own mind that justice had perished from the poor unfortunate Shetlanders.*

*However sometime afterwards I employed another which I considered more judicious, and he too postponed the matter so long that, to present appearance, I expect little or nothing from a just debt of near twenty pounds sterling. Now from all those circumstances and many more of a similar nature, the rogues may as well get off with the debt without putting us to more trouble. After all, if you will undertake to do a little for me, you will please to say what percentage you will require or demand for trying to obtain balances of signed accounts or otherwise. Of course one does not like to pay out money where nothing can be obtained, and besides it appears to me those wicked creatures who put us to the trouble and expense of prosecutions should pay all charges.*

*It also appears to me very strange and unlike the customs in Scotland that we cannot have permissions to ordain a proxy or mandate to answer in court for us when sometimes it is impossible for us to attend in consequence of bad weather and length of journey.*

*I am, Gentlemen,*

*Yours most respectfully*

*Thomas Robertson*

The Shetland Archives contain documents pertaining to several lawsuits brought by Thomas for collection of debts. In June 1839, for example, he sued John Adie and Magnus Smith of Greenland, Walls Parish, described as "carrying on a joint business as fishcurers," for the sum of slightly over twenty pounds sterling owed to him on account, plus interest and court costs. The debtors, rather than paying, hired a lawyer who raised numerous nitpicking and baffling arguments in defense. Thomas's representative apparently did nothing further to pursue the case. A later court entry noted that, after the passage of a year and a day with no action, the process had "fallen asleep," and it was up to the pursuer "to have the said process wakened, and insisted in, begun where it had left off, and justice administered therein, until the end and conclusion thereof." Whether that was done, and whether Thomas ever obtained a judgment or settlement from Adie and Smith, is not known.

In 1843, shortly after he married Margaret Mouat, Thomas Robertson purchased a house called "Seafield" on the waterfront of Vaila Sound, near the center of the village of Walls.[111] Possibly the oldest house in Walls today, it is still occupied as a residence.[112] The walls of Thomas Robertson's former fish-curing shop adjacent to the house were still standing in 1994, but the roof long ago went off. It was once thought that Charles D. Robertson was born at Seafield in 1939. However, as is clear from the 1841 census noted above that the family was still living in Stove Cottage No. 4 then. Charles was actually four when his father bought Seafield. The official tax rolls for Walls Parish reflect that Thomas Robertson still owned Seafield in 1856; a tax of fifteen pounds was levied on the house and shop that year.

Life in Shetland had a rough quality, even in the years when Thomas's business ventures were flourishing. Records in the Shetland Archives include a letter from Thomas Robertson in May 1838 complaining about a theft of some of his supplies and equipment by a seaman named George Georgeson from the Island of Papa Stour. This man came ashore from his boat and went into Thomas Robertson's warehouse, where he stole "a fine piece of Highland oak" that Thomas had put aside for a new sloop. When Thomas's employees challenged Georgeson, he responded rudely and offered a few potatoes to let him take away some other property. All attempts to stop Georgeson and to get the valuable oak back were unsuccessful. Thomas urged the authorities to prosecute the crime with diligence, hopefully stimulated by "a sense of your duty and a love to your parish."

Thomas was the victim of another theft in January 1844, when one Jerom Cheyne, "having secreted himself within a cellar, or a loft adjoining to and in connection with the shop in Stove in the parish of Walls occupied by Thomas Robertson" got into the shop while Thomas and his shopkeeper were away. There he "did wickedly and feloniously and theftivously [sic] away take from out of a drawer in the counter . . . twelve shillings sterling or thereby and a French five franc piece." The villain was swiftly apprehended and confessed his crime.

Still another episode occurred on October 13, 1852, when two seamen named Thomas

Fraser and Scott Sinclair barged into Thomas Robertson's shop. According to the criminal charges later pressed by the law enforcement authorities, these louts "conducted themselves in a violent and outrageous manner and by the noise and disturbance which they made collected a considerable crowd of persons in and around" the shop. After throwing off his jacket, Fraser then "attacked and assaulted James Georgeson, shopman to the said Thomas Robertson, by striking him on the head or face with his clenched fists, all the time cursing and swearing and using violent and abusive language."[113]

Meanwhile the second ruffian, Sinclair, was also cursing and swearing loudly. When Thomas walked into the shop, "he thumped upon the shop counter with his fist, bawling out 'there's the old grey headed buggar. Let us pitch it in to him' . . . or other similar threatening language expressive of an intention to assault the said Thomas Robertson."

Margaret Robertson quietly told her husband to leave the shop at once, and he did so. But the intruder Fraser struck Margaret in the face and "made use of the most fearful imprecations and threats of further personal violence to her and her said husband." Fraser also assaulted a local seaman, George Georgeson, who happened to be in the shop at the time and was coming to Margaret's aid—possibly, the same George Georgeson who was shopkeeper for Thomas Robertson and lived in his house eleven years earlier, as reported in the 1841 census. Sinclair finally left when Margaret turned out the lights and threatened to lock him in for the night. Fraser was removed from the premises but returned a while later and commenced "a violent attack on the back door of the house with his hands and feet threatening at the same time to break it in."

At the time, Thomas Robertson was fifty-six years of age, and his wife, Margaret, was thirty-seven. The rowdies were later arrested and charged with assault and breach of the peace. Sinclair pleaded guilty. Fraser was tried, convicted, and sentenced to thirty days in jail.

A later brush with the law, documented in the court records in the Shetland Archives, shows how fierce and fearless Margaret could be—especially in the defense of her husband. In 1865, Margaret was charged with assault for dumping a pail of water over a woman named Mary Neill, who was then living in rented quarters in Stove. Miss Neill and another woman, Christina Garriock, were sitting together and sewing before the fireplace in her second-floor room when "Mrs. Robertson came to the door carrying a pail of water. . . . The door was open and as soon as she got to the top of the stairs, she lifted the pail of water she had in her hand and plunged the water over my neck and shoulders. . . . Before I had time to rise off my seat, she lifted the pail over her head and gave me a severe blow on the left arm." Miss Neill finally got Margaret out the door, but not before being hit on the leg when the pail came hurtling out of Margaret's hand. Margaret then beat loudly on the door with the pail as if to break it down, threatening murder "if she could only get in."

Once Margaret was out of the house, Miss Neill recollected, "I heard her then call me a bad woman in the broadest language she could call it, and threatening to murder me— saying 'She's calling out murder' (referring to me) 'but murder she shall have if my life should be taken for it.'" Jemima Irvine, daughter of sailmaker James Irvine of Stove, testified that, "I was sitting in our house, when I heard cries of murder, and on going outside to see what was the matter, I found the cries proceeded from Mary Neill. . . . I met Mrs. Robertson when I came outside, and asked her what was going on. She replied that she had been 'sluicing' down that vagabond Mary Neill with some soap suds, with whom she had been hot (meaning angry) for some days back. Mrs. Robertson appeared to be in an awful rage." Margaret admitted dousing Mary Neill but claimed that the pail (which she said was just a toy bucket belonging to her children) had slipped from her hands; she did not actually intend it to strike the woman and did not think that it really had.

What could have provoked such anger? Under judicial examination, Mary Neill finally admitted that she had gotten into a tiff with Thomas Robertson over some peat (the mossy turf that Shetlanders cut from the ground, dry, and burn for heating and cooking). Thomas, by that time an elderly man approaching seventy, had cut and stacked some peat, which Miss Neill had the effrontery to throw into a ditch. "He afterwards came to my house and gave me some words, and I retaliated," she testified, "but previous to this assault nothing had passed between the husband and me for a day or two." Christina Garriock recalled hearing Margaret say "she would be revenged on Mary for what she had done to her husband's peats." She had been in Margaret's house about two days earlier when, "speaking of what Mary had done to her husband's peats, she told me that she would 'skelp' Mary if God gave her strength to do it." Margaret Robertson had to pay a fine; Mary Neill—who obviously chose the wrong woman's man to abuse—moved away in fear that Margaret really would do her in.

$\backsim$

By the 1860s, Walls was no longer thriving. The fishing industry of Shetland had been in decline for years due to competition from other countries; also, terrible storms at sea caused the loss of several fishing boats and the death of many fishermen. Men were leaving Shetland to join the Merchant Navy or to immigrate to Canada, the United States, Australia, and New Zealand (which was offering free emigration and subsidized passage for Shetlanders interested in settling there). Boat building ceased in Walls. The Fishermans Bank in Lerwick had closed, making it almost impossible to obtain needed credit for working capital.

Thomas Robertson and his family in Walls fell on very hard times in the waning years of his life. His business ventures may have been doomed by general economic conditions. Thomas and Margaret had to sell their home, Seafield, to pay debts. At some point it appears they moved across the Voe to take up residence in "Gwen Haven," a house Thomas had built for his son James David Robertson.

Thomas Robertson, age seventy-six, died on January 9, 1873, in Walls and was buried in the cemetery of St. Paul's Church in Walls.[114] By then many of his children had left or were planning to leave Shetland to seek better opportunities elsewhere. Charles, the oldest son, had settled in America, was married with several children, and was building a successful career as a lawyer in Cincinnati, Ohio. None of the other children—the oldest then being twenty-nine years of age and the youngest, a daughter not yet thirteen—were married.

The house called Gwen Haven was also sold after Thomas's death to help pay debts. James Robertson arranged shelter for himself, his mother, and the younger children at Happy Hansel, the former schoolhouse on the hill overlooking Vaila Sound. The modest structure had four rooms, but the partitions inside were collapsing due to age and poor maintenance. James worked on repairs whenever he had time.

James Robertson and his mother lived at Happy Hansel until her death at the age of ninety-three. Margaret Mouat Robertson died on August 30, 1908, in Walls, Shetland. She was buried in the Walls Churchyard.

**Children of Thomas Robertson**

IV. **Charles Dumbreck Robertson** was born on March 6, 1839, in Walls, Shetland, the only child of Christina Dumbreck and Thomas Robertson.[115] He immigrated to America in 1863 and married *Cynthia Buck (Hillman)*, a young widow. They had five children, two of whom lived to maturity and had families of their own. (*SEE SECTION 4-C.*) Charles died on August 28, 1919, at age eighty, in Cincinnati, Ohio.

IV. **Thomas Robertson**, born on July 7, 1843, at Seafield in Walls, Shetland, was the first child of Thomas Robertson and his third wife, Margaret Mouat.[116] He was baptized in Walls by a Rev. Peterson, evidently a Methodist minister. Thomas never married and died in Cincinnati, Ohio, in 1900, about fifty-seven years of age.

Thomas apparently left home and went to Cincinnati in 1876, about three years after the death of his father. Almost certainly, he was sponsored there by his half-brother, Charles, four years older than Thomas, who at the time was building a successful law career and raising a family of his own in Cincinnati.

Abstracts of the Hamilton County, Ohio, citizenship records reflect that a Thomas Robertson, age thirty-eight, filed a declaration of intention to naturalize on April 4, 1882, having arrived in New York from Scotland on April 16, 1876.[117] This individual would have been the right age for "our" Thomas, who was thirty-eight years old during April 1876. Ten years later, in 1886, a Thomas Robertson was listed in the Williams' Cincinnati Directory as a printer. He was later listed in the city directory as a "copy holder."

According to Ann Margaret Cheyne of New Zealand, the grand-niece of Thomas who visited Robertson kin in Cincinnati, Thomas Robertson was regarded as something of a recluse.[118] Apparently, Thomas spent much of his time alone, writing poetry and studying astronomy, ornithology, and other branches of zoology. He also collected and stuffed birds, toads, and small animals. His nephew William Hillman Robertson received part of Thomas's collection after Thomas died.

IV. **James David Mouat Robertson**, son of Margaret Mouat and Thomas Robertson, was born on July 26, 1845, at Seafield in Walls, Shetland, and baptized by Rev. Alfred Abbott.[119] He became a merchant seaman as a young man and sailed to New Zealand and the South Sea islands. Because of a serious back injury, he had to give up the seafaring life and return home to the Shetlands.

When James left home for a seafaring life, his father was prosperous. In those days it was very difficult if not impossible for seamen in the merchant marine to correspond with family and friends at home, so James did not hear that his father's businesses were failing. When he returned to Shetland in the early 1870s, it was a shock to find his father broken in health and spirit and the family in severe financial straits.

Among a variety of occupations, James Robertson served as a school teacher. In 1883, he was elected by the crofters (tenant farmers) of Walls Parish to defend their interests and express their grievances before the Royal Napier Commission (which met in Lerwick) against unfair rents, and lack of security of tenure imposed upon them by the lairds (property owners), also to complain of the lack of roads and inadequate upkeep of existing roads and the need for fair compensation for property improvements made by crofters. He became the civil registrar for Walls Parish, and his fine handwriting can still be seen in the local register. He also served at times as a substitute minister, although he later expressed skepticism about organized religion.

Another job James held was Inspector of the Poor for Walls Parish. In early 1916, with his eyesight failing and no longer able to continue the required travel, he wrote to his niece Greta Robertson in Ohio that he had to retire from that job "but got the Old Age Pension which is payable from 70 years and up."

In his later days, James lived in Riskaness, farther down the Voe from Gwen Haven. His old rolltop desk is said to still be in Riskaness.

James David Robertson never married, but throughout his life he helped keep our Robertsons in various parts of the world in contact with one other. In September 1921, with the First World War just over and Germany defeated, James wrote a thoughtful letter to his sister-in-law Cynthia Robertson, Charles's widow, reporting that he had not been well but expressing opinions on a variety of topics and giving a flavor of Shetland life:

*Yesterday brought your letter. . . . I was glad to see by it you were as well as could be at your age. Since I wrote I have been far from well. Commencing with heavy heartburn, it continued till about two weeks ago when a boil burst in the stomach.*

*The Doctor was in attendance and did what he could – said it was "ulsurated stomach" and beyond his power. I am glad that I am now so far recovered as to be out and about again. He (the doctor) may or may not be right, I have always thought 'no man will pass away till his time comes.' So I am taking things easy.*

*No use talking about peace terms or League of Nations. All nonsense. If you want peace be ready for war. Germany, as is well known, is only making ready for revenge and England is making ready also. The public cry here is 'Be ready.' . . .*

*I am gathering in the harvest and not behind any neighbours yet. The herring fishing is over for this season and a very successful season it has been. Prices of goods coming down gradually and things will slowly come back to pre-war times. As for Ireland, it seems to puzzle our best statesmen what to do. The great trouble is – it is divided against itself. The Christian religion whether Catholic or Protestant has not proved an unmixed blessing – and Ireland is no exception. Even in Shetland Sunday is not looked upon as a sacred day and even church attendance is falling gradually away. . . .*

*I need say little more but would wish a communication was kept up between us while life lasted.*

*Affectionately, James*

Five years later, on December 6, 1926, James D. Robertson died in Riskaness, Walls, at eighty-two years of age. He was buried near his father, Thomas, in the Walls churchyard. James was remembered long as a man of character, intelligence, and wit.

Margaret Robertson Williamson was James's housekeeper for many years and looked after him in his later years. She stayed in Riskaness in Walls, in James's home, was married there, had several children there, and continued to live in the homestead in Riskaness with other family members after James died. The widow of Margaret's son Magnus Williamson still lives there.

Visiting Shetland in 1935, Reuben Robertson Sr. heard a number of amusing tales about his uncle James. While serving as Inspector of the Poor for Walls Parish, James was once called to testify in a legal proceeding against a local woman charged with keeping her home in a filthy condition. Asked by the presiding official whether he had found her home to be filthy, James said no—he thought it was just "comfortably dirty."

Another story recounted that James was once arrested for hunting without a license, hauled into court, and fined ten pounds. Lecturing James on complying with the law, the judge pointed out that a license would have cost him only one pound a year, but the fine was ten times that much. James responded, with all due respect, "I wish to differ with Your Lordship on that score, as I have been hunting without a license for 40 years, and this is the first time I've been fined."

IV. **Christina Dumbreck Robertson**, first daughter of Margaret Mouat and Thomas Robertson, named for her father's deceased wife, was born on January 27, 1847, at Seafield in Walls, Shetland.[120] She was baptized by Rev. James Kendall, Wesleyan Methodist minister in Walls. Christina married *Robert Thomas Cheyne* and had four children by him. She died on September 21, 1934, age eighty-seven, in Woodville, New Zealand. (*SEE SECTION 4-D.*)

IV. **Ann Elizabeth Mouat Robertson**, second daughter of Margaret Mouat and Thomas Robertson, according to her father's record was born at 9:00 a.m. on Thursday, June 28, 1849, at Seafield in Walls, Shetland; her birthday is listed as June 26 in the IGI.[121] She was baptized by Rev. Hesk, a Wesleyan Methodist minister.

Ann Elizabeth became a schoolteacher. A few years after the death of her father, her aunt and uncle Elizabeth and James Georgeson decided to leave Shetland with their family and look for better opportunities in New Zealand, and they invited Ann Elizabeth to go along with them. They departed from Shetland in November 1876 and arrived in Wellington, on New Zealand's North Island, aboard the *Hurunui* on February 18, 1877. Ann Elizabeth was twenty-seven years old and single. Her younger sister Agnes went over and joined Ann Elizabeth a few years later.

On or just before her thirty-fifth birthday, Ann Elizabeth married her first cousin *George Georgeson*. The wedding was in Wellington on June 26, 1884. George's parents were Elizabeth Mouat and James Georgeson, and he had been on the trip to New Zealand as a teenager. Born about 1860 in Walls, George was about ten years younger than Ann Elizabeth. Not long after getting married, Ann Elizabeth and George returned with her sister Agnes to Shetland—possibly because of the illness and premature death of their sister Eliza.

Ann Elizabeth and George Georgeson had two children, at least one a girl born at Happy Hansel, the former schoolhouse in Walls, Shetland, where her mother and other family members had been living. Both children evidently died very young and tragically: one was scalded and the other died of scarlet fever.

Around 1888, Ann Elizabeth and her husband again left home—this time to move to Ohio, where they would be near Ann Elizabeth's half-brother, Charles D. Robertson, who had become a prominent lawyer, her two full brothers, John and Andrew, and other Georgeson family members who were then living in Ohio. Her sister Agnes also went with them on this voyage. However, Ann Elizabeth was widowed when George Georgeson died in Ohio during the mid-1890s. After that, Ann Elizabeth and Agnes again returned to Shetland, where she helped take care of their mother Margaret, who lived until 1908.

Around 1919, when she was about seventy years of age, Ann Elizabeth Georgeson was traveling once more. Again, she left Walls and immigrated to New Zealand, spending the last sixteen years of her life there. She died in her eighty-sixth year on March 1, 1935, in Wadestown, a suburb of Wellington, where she and Agnes were living.

Margaret Fowlds (born O'Brian) writes of her grand aunt:

*"Aunt" Annie entered my life by some kind of osmosis; I cannot remember the first appearance, it seems she was always there – she and her sea chest. The two were inseparable. Where she went, it went; it was her alter ego. To understand one, you would have to rumble through the other. She had no permanent home. She moved from one family member to the other trailing clouds of glory.*

*She had been an Art Teacher at Clifton Terrace School in Wellington, she had been educated at College in Edinburgh, she was a lady of substance – she had bought herself an ANNUITY! And, she subscribed to Arthur Mee's Children's Encyclopedia!!*

*Aunt Annie was certainly someone to be treated with deference. Those around her definitely thought so. They spoke of her in hushed tones to anyone prepared to listen. She didn't drift about in old clothes like her sister Charlotte. Each day she spent hours adorning herself. Face plastered with white starchy substance, and dyed brown hair carefully arranged she could attract anyone's attention.*

*That she was a widow who had lost husband and two children was never mentioned.*

*In the late 20ies she moved into a private hotel at Island Bay, Wellington. "The Blue Platter" was situated on rocks overlooking Cook Strait. The bleak outlook could well have been a replica of her native home, Shetland. From there, when she became ill, she moved into her niece's home, the arrangement being Margaret (Galbraith) would become her sole heir. Margaret looked after her faithfully till her death.*

### Children of Ann Elizabeth Mouat Robertson

V. **Elizabeth Ann Georgeson**, daughter of Ann Elizabeth and George Georgeson, was born at Happy Hansel in Walls, Shetland, on February 1, 1887. The birth certificate lists her father as a merchant and also records that her mother's sister Agnes was present at the birth. She died young.

V. **A baby, name unknown**, born to Ann Elizabeth and George Georgeson, possibly in Shetland.

IV. **Charlotte Umphray Robertson**, third daughter of Margaret Mouat and Thomas Robertson, was born on December 28, 1851, at Seafield in Walls Parish, Shetland, and baptized by the Wesleyan minister there, Rev. Farquhar.[122] She also immigrated to New Zealand, where she married *Francis O'Brian*, and they had eight children. Charlotte died there on September 12, 1941, at the age of eighty-nine. (*SEE SECTION 4-E.*)

IV. **Andrew Umphray Robertson**, son of Margaret Mouat and Thomas Robertson, was born on April 10, 1854, at Seafield in Walls Parish, Shetland,[123] and baptized in the Wesleyan church by a Rev. Foster. He married *Esther Bosworth Hillman* and they had eight children. Andrew died on April 5, 1915, in Cincinnati, Hamilton County, Ohio, just short of his sixty-first birthday. (*SEE SECTION 4-F.*)

It is worth noting that another child with the identical name of Andrew Umphray Robertson was born to another Robertson family in Walls Parish five years earlier. The older boy was born on October 2, 1848, to Mary Irvine and Scott Robertson of Grutquoy. We have found no link between the Robertsons of Grutquoy and our Robertsons, despite the use of such a distinctive name.[124]

IV. **<u>Eliza Nichol Robertson</u>**, fourth daughter of Margaret Mouat and Thomas Robertson, was born on October 8, 1856, at Seafield in Walls, Shetland.[125] Eliza did not marry and was the only member of the family who never traveled far from home. She died of tuberculosis on June 9, 1886, at age twenty-nine, at Happy Hansel in Walls, where she lived with her mother and her brother James.

IV. **<u>Agnes Catherine Scott Robertson</u>**, fifth daughter of Margaret Mouat and Thomas Robertson, was born on January 29, 1860, at Seafield in Walls, Shetland.[126] The youngest of the family's eight children, Agnes was not yet thirteen years old when her father died in 1873.

Agnes travelled widely during her life, following generally the same paths as her sister Ann Elizabeth. Both immigrated to New Zealand as young women to join their Aunt Elizabeth and Uncle James Georgeson. Passenger list records preserved in the New Zealand National Archives in Wellington show that an Agnes Robertson, age nineteen, arrived in Wellington on October 17, 1879, on the ship *Zealandia,* after an ocean voyage of three months. Her sister had arrived with the Georgeson family in early 1877. A few years later, Agnes went with her sister Ann Elizabeth and new brother-in-law George Georgeson back to Shetland and afterwards went with them to Ohio. After George died in Ohio, Agnes accompanied her sister in returning to Shetland in the 1890s.

At the age of thirty-six, Agnes married *<u>James Thomas Arthur Thomson</u>* in Edinburgh, Scotland, on October 7, 1896 (by special license). He had been born on Unst, the most northern of the Shetland Islands. They lived in Glasgow for a while, where James ran a hotel. They had one daughter, Margaret.

In 1907, Agnes again immigrated—this time with her husband and their young daughter—to New Zealand. There, they settled in Wadestown near Wellington.

Agnes Robertson Thomson died on January 28, 1940, in Wellington, New Zealand, one day short of her eightieth birthday. James Thomson had died five years earlier in Wellington. Her great-niece Tina Cheyne Rankine described Agnes as very attractive, fairly short, and of dark complexion, with brown eyes and a beautiful voice.

**Child of Agnes Catherine Scott Robertson**

V. <u>**Margaret Mouat Thomson,**</u> born in 1900 in Glasgow, Scotland; died on September 18, 1967, in Wellington, New Zealand. She married *Normal Malcolm Galbraith* in Wellington, New Zealand, on June 8, 1924. Normal was born about 1903 in Paisley, Scotland. They adopted a daughter, Ann.

**Child of Margaret Mouat Thomson**

VI. <u>**Ann Thomson Galbraith**</u>, who was living in Melbourne, Australia, when her mother died in 1967.

## 3-D: JAMES GREIG ROBERTSON (1806-1876) AND HELEN TWATT (1802-1901)

III. <u>**Helen Twatt**</u>, daughter of Agnes Robertson and James Twatt (2-D above), was born on October 25, 1802, in Burraland, Walls Parish, Shetland.[127] In 1834 she married her first cousin, *James Greig Robertson* (below):

III. <u>**James Greig Robertson**</u>, born on May 8, 1806, in Stove, Walls Parish, Shetland.[128] He was the fifth and youngest son of Umphray and Jerom Robertson (Section 2-B above).

Helen and James were married on March 11, 1834, in Tingwall Parish, Shetland.[129] They had eight children: Mary Ann, Thomas, Helen, Sarah, Jean, Ann Eliza, James John, and Jessie Margaret. The family apparently lived for a while in Lochend, Northmavine Parish, in the northern part of Mainland Shetland, where the first three children were born. Sometime before 1840, they relocated to Scalloway, Tingwall Parish, in the southern portion of mainland Shetland, as that was where the fourth child and the later children were born.[130]

James G. Robertson was a merchant and druggist in Scalloway; he also described himself as a "medical practitioner" and was referred to at times as "Dr." Robertson. He may have had interests in shipping and fishing, as well. Ship registry records in the Lerwick Customs Office indicate that a 35-foot sailing ship called *Fame*, originally built in Banff County of mainland Scotland in 1811, and registered in Lerwick, Shetland, in 1838, was transferred to a James G. Robertson (75 percent interest) and John Inkster (25 percent interest) on February 15, 1844.

James was a most colorful character, based on court records and other documents in the Shetland Archives. He filed legal cases against a number of persons, generally to collect moneys owed but—on more than one occasion—for slander or other personal disputes. He also was on the receiving end of numerous lawsuits filed by others.

For example, in June 1841, James brought suit against an Elizabeth Thomson of Northmavine Parish, who owed him money and, worse yet, had called him "a thief and a liar" and refused to take it back. The defendant failed to show up in court, and James won the suit by default. Two decades later, in 1861, James sued one John Halcro for money owed on account of services that James had rendered a year earlier but was never paid for. According to the court papers, the work performed included removal of the dead body of Mr. Halcro's brother from a bed in the Halcro house "to his last abode," disposal of the bedding, and fumigation of the house. The amount owed was nine shillings.

In May 1844, James G. Robertson had criminal charges brought against a fisherman named Moar from the Island of Yell, who was working on a sloop out of Lerwick. The charge was that Mr. Moar stole James's property from a beach near Scalloway, consisting of "two split salted and partly dried cod." When brought before the court, Mr. Moar confessed and was sent to the jail in Lerwick for twenty days.

James was ardent and outspoken in trying to get help for the needy. In July 1854, for example, serving in the official capacity of Inspector of the Poor for several parishes of Shetland, he commenced several formal legal action against various persons. In one suit, he complained about the lack of financial support provided to an impoverished man who had fallen ill and whose wife had recently died. With obvious passion and outrage, James stated in the court papers, "I would not have thought a Parochial Board could be found in the United Kingdom that would have refused to pay for saving the life of a man who had so resantly [sic] lost his wife and was unable to pay a farthing for a Doctor." A couple of years later, James wrote to the owners of the Union Bank of Scotland asking for their help in a tragic situation that had occurred in Shetland a few weeks earlier. "Painful indeed is the tale on which my remonstrance is founded," he wrote.

> *About the middle of January 1857, a large boat left Lerwick having on board ten men and one female, also a valuable little cargo, bound for Dunrossness, the Southmost Station in Shetland. But sad indeed to relate she never reached her destination . . . They were swallowed by the grate Atlantic!*
>
> *The sole owner of the boat and Skipper <u>Robert Leslie</u> had had a comfortable home: was kind, active, and careful. His wife <u>Ann</u> knew how to make him happy. On this fatal voyage his oldest son (21 years) was with him, and the balance of their years earnings was paid to them . . . in Union Bank notes to the amount of near £30. These alas are forthcoming no more at all in this world! A disconsolate widow with seven children of all ages under eighteen refuses to be comforted! as more genuine love is found at the humble fireside of the peasant than in the <u>Chateau</u> of the Nobleman.*
>
> *Gentelmen [sic] I hope I do not over estimate your Honour if I suspect you will forward a <u>ten pound note</u> on order in favor of this poor widow. Not to say that the lost notes are a direct profit to the Bank nor to say that any have a right so to ask. But your nobler finer feelings must be touched. . . .*
>
> *Gentelmen this is a graver sadder reality, and without daring to prescribe a thought I trust you will telegram to your office at Lerwick – what you are to give to this poor widow. . . .*
>
> *I have the honour to remain, Gentlemen, Your obt. servt*
>
> *James G. Robertson, <u>Medical Practitioner</u>*

James was not above asking help for his own family members. In 1858, he wrote to a friend, George Leisk, on the Island of Unst, whom he and his wife, Helen, had apparently seen on a recent visit. After expressing appreciation "for the kindness of the Ladies and others" there, and wishing for "another walk over the delightful island with you" James's letter noted that "we got a splendid passage to Lerwick" on the way home and reported with pleasure that his wife had not been seasick. Then James seized the opportunity to put in a plug for his oldest daughter, Mary Ann, then twenty-three and possibly in need of employment. "I think after all," James wrote Mr. Leisk,

> *. . . you would greatly add to your own comfort in latter days to take unto yourself Mary Ann. Not one shilling of patronage will I ever be able to give but all [my children] have had the excellent training of one of the best Mothers. My great wish is to see them happy, for wealth and happiness [are] certainly*

*not intermarried. . . . Most people are fond of their offspring, but I must beg to say when my third daughter had been only six weeks in a gentleman's family in Edinburgh, I have received from him the welcome present of the whole works of Lord Byron.*

Whether she got the job is unknown—or was James actually recommending his oldest daughter as a possible wife for Mr. Leisk?

James G. Robertson died on September 12, 1876, in Scalloway, age seventy. Helen Twatt Robertson died in 1901 at the age of ninety-eight.

## Children of James Greig Robertson and Helen Twatt

IV. **Mary Ann Clarke Robertson**, was born on October 19, 1834, in Lochend, Northmavine Parish, Shetland, and baptized in Tingwall.[131] At the age of thirty-six, she married *James Mitchell* in Tingwall Parish, Shetland, on March 12, 1871.[132] Her husband was born on August 23, 1818, and died on January 6, 1912. They had a daughter, born some five years after their marriage, when Mary Ann was forty-two. The Shetland parish records indicate that Mary Ann also had an older daughter, born when she was thirty-three. Mary Ann died on August 24, 1915, age seventy-nine.

### Children of Mary Ann Clarke Robertson

V. **Agnes Jean Robertson**, born on November 6, 1867, in Tingwall Parish, Shetland.

V. **Helen Eliza Shand Mitchell**, daughter of Mary Ann Clarke Robertson and James Mitchell, born on May 9, 1876.

IV. **Thomas Robertson**, born on January 18, 1836, in Lochend, Northmavine, Shetland.[133]

IV. **Helen Robertson**, born on December 24, 1837, in Lochend, Northmavine, Shetland.[134]

IV. **Sarah Smith Robertson**, born on January 1, 1840, in Scalloway, Tingwall Parish, Shetland.[135] She married *Robert Scott* on December 20, 1866, in Tingwall Parish.[136] He was born on November 10, 1840. They had seven children, at least three of whom died young.

**Children of Sarah Smith Robertson**

V. **Sarah Elizabeth Scott**, born on August 10, 1867; died barely a month after her eighth birthday, on September 4, 1875.

V. **Helen Ellen Scott**, born on March 27, 1869.

V. **Ann Louise Mary Scott**, born in 1870, died about age eleven on September 11, 1881.

V. **James Gideon Scott**, born on February 24, 1877.

V. **Robert Scott**, born on November 24, 1880.

V. **Sarah Gertrude Scott**, born on March 21, 1884; she died as a young child on December 31, 1885.

V. **Alice Mary Scott**, born on June 15, 1885.

IV. **Jean Robertson**, born on June 5, 1841[137] or November 17, 1841,[138] at Scalloway, Tingwall Parish, Shetland; died on April 26, 1903.

IV. **Ann Eliza Umphray Robertson**, born on June 5, 1845, in Scalloway, Tingwall Parish, Shetland;[139] died on May 22, 1929.

IV. **James John Robertson**, born on February 10, 1849, in Scalloway, Tingwall Parish, Shetland. (There are two conflicting IGI records concerning his birth: the first states the year of birth as 1847; the second lists 1849.[140])

IV. **Jessie Margaret Grace Robertson**, born on September 8, 1850, in Scalloway, Tingwall Parish, Shetland.[141] She married *William Hay Tulloch*, who was born on November 5, 1857. He died on April 24, 1914.

### 3-E: MARGARET TWATT (1796-1876)
Daughter of Agnes Robertson:
Matriarch of the Jeromson Branches

III. **Margaret Twatt**, daughter of Agnes Robertson (or Johnsdaughter) and James Twatt (2-D above), was born on September 25, 1796, in Bardister, Walls Parish, Shetland.[142]

On December 14, 1820, Margaret married *James Jeromson*.[143] Born in 1798, he was the son of Elizabeth Wishart and Jerom Manson (1769 – 1836).[144] They resided in Walls and had five children. James died on September 21, 1865, and Margaret died on April 17, 1876, at about eighty years of age.

**Children of Margaret Twatt**

IV. **Jerome Jeromson**, born in 1821, died on November 15, 1848. On November 20, 1844, he married *Hannah Umphray*, who was born in 1818 and died in 1890. They had two children.

**Children of Jerome Jeromson**

V. **Barbara Jeromson**, born in 1845.

V. **James Jeromson**, born in 1847.

IV. **Helen Jeromson**, born on May 27, 1824; died on November 9, 1913. On November 25, 1847, Helen married *Hay Williamson*, who was born in 1825. They had four children.

**Children of Helen Jeromson**

V. **John Williamson**, born in 1848.

V. **Margaret Williamson**, born in 1852. She married *Magnus Leask* and had six daughters.

**Children of Margaret Williamson**

VI. **Margaret Leask**, born on March 29, 1876.

VI. **Elizabeth Helen Leask**, born on March 8, 1878.

VI. **Jemima Harriet Leask**, born on October 24, 1879.

VI. **Williamina Leask**, born on June 8, 1885.

VI. **Jean Leask**, born on January 13, 1887.

VI. **Barbara Jane Spence Leask**, born on October 13, 1892.

V. **Helen Williamson**, born on 1854.

V. **James Williamson**, born on 1858.

IV. **John Thomson Jeromson**, born on July 23, 1827, died on June 8, 1902. On November 19, 1853, he married *Elspeth Jamieson*, born in 1828. They had five children. Elspeth died on August 8, 1881. About a year later, John married his second wife, *Catherine Fraser*, who was born in 1838.

### Children of John Thomson Jeromson

V. **Jeromina Jeromson**, born about 1854; married *Robert Tait*, born about 1850. They had one child.

### Child of Jeromina Jeromson

VI. **John Scott Smith Tait**, born in 1879.

V. **Gideon Jeromson**, born in 1861.

V. **Barbara Jeromson**, born in 1864.

V. **Catherine Jeromson**, born in 1868.

V. **John Robert Jeromson**, born in 1872, married *Catherine Diack Mouat*, born in 1871.

IV. **Isabella Lesevie Jeromson**, born on October 2, 1833. She married *Thomas Halcrow* about 1855. He was born on April 3, 1823. They had five children.

### Children of Isabella Lesevie Jeromson

V. **Charles Halcrow**, born in 1856.

V. **Margaret Halcrow**, born in 1858.

V. **Agnes Isobella Halcrow**, born in 1860.

V. **James Jeromson Halcrow**, born in 1867.

V. **Thomas Jeromson Halcrow**, born in February, 1872.

IV. **Robert Jeromson**, born on July 3, 1836. His wife was *Elizabeth Leask* (called "Betty"), who was born on November 11, 1834. They were married on March 6, 1858, and had at least one child. Robert died in 1909.

**Children of Robert Jeromson**[145]

V. **Jeremiah Jeromson**, born in 1858. He married *Margaret Young*, born about 1860. They had one child.

**Child of Jeremiah Jeromson**

VI. **Robert Jeromson**.

V. **Helen Jeromson**,, born in 1860.

V. **Catherine Jeromson**,, born in 1862.

V. **Robert Jeromson**, born in 1864. Married Ms. *Johnson*, (first name unknown), who was born about 1868, and they had one child.

**Child of Robert Jeromson**

VI. **Elizabeth Jeromson**, born about 1890; she married *John Robb Hamilton* .

V. **James Jeromson**, born in 1868.

V. **John Jeromson**, born in 1871.

V. **Charles Jeromson**, born on June 25, 1875. He married *Christian Thomason*, born about 1873, and they had one child.

**Child of Charles Jeromson**

VI. **Robert Jeromson**, who married *Christine Arthur*, and they had a son.

**Child of Robert Jeromson**

VII. **Robert Hugh Jeromson**, born on July 13, 1942.

## 3-F: JAMES TWATT (1798-1876)
### Son of Agnes Robertson

III. **James Twatt**, first son of Agnes Robertson (or Johnsdaughter) and James Twatt (2-D above), was born on August 12, 1798, in Bardister, Walls Parish, Shetland.[146]

James married *Andrina Robertson* in Walls Parish on January 31, 1822.[147] Andrina was born in 1806 and baptized on April 14, 1806. She was the daughter of Olla Robertson of Northmavine. It is unknown whether her father's family had any kinship to our Robertsons. James and Andrina had four children, and Andrina died in 1851, at about forty-five years of age. The following year, James married *Margaret Williamson* on March 18, 1852. His second wife was born in 1801 and died on July 20, 1875. They had no children. James Twatt died on September 9, 1876, just over a year after losing his second wife. He was about seventy-eight.

**Children of James Twatt**

IV. **Elizabeth Twatt** (called "Betty"), daughter of Andrina Robertson and James Twatt, was born on May 29, 1822, and baptized by Rev. David Thomson, minister of the gospel in the Church of Scotland in Walls, according to the Walls Parish Register of Births. About 1850, she married *Fraser Walterson*. He was born on October 28, 1821, and died in 1889. We have identified five possible children of this marriage. Betty died on November 19, 1879, age approximately fifty-four.

**Children of Elizabeth Twatt**

V. **Ann Walterson**, born on April 27, 1853, in Walls Parish, Shetland. We are not certain if this is the same or a different person than the child of the same name born on August 27, 1853, in Walls.[148] Ann married *Laurence Moffat*, who was born in 1853; they had six children.[149]

**Children of Ann Walterson**

VI. **George Moffat**, born in 1880.

VI. **Frederick Moffat**, born in 1882. He married *Mary Slater*, who was born in 1884. They had a daughter. Frederick later married *Margaret Irvine*, born on January 3, 1875.

**Child of Frederick Moffat**

VII. **Barbara Freda Moffat**, born in 1907. She married *Magnus Coutts*, born on October 28, 1902. They had one child.

**Child of Barbara Freda Moffat**

VIII. **Thomas Peter Coutts**, born on February 25, 1931.

VI. **Andrew Moffat**, born on May 5, 1886.

VI. **Elizabeth Moffat**, born on October 25, 1889.

VI. **Laurence Moffat**, born on September 11, 1891. He married a woman named *Isabell,* born about 1895, maiden name is unknown.

VI. **Thomas Moffat,** born on August 28, 1893.

V. **James Walterson**, born on January 6, 1855, in Walls Parish, Shetland.[150]

V. **Thomas Walterson**, born on July 1, 1858, in Walls Parish, Shetland.[151] According to SFHS, he married *Barbara Coutts*, born in 1849, and they had a son.

**Children of Thomas Walterson**

VI. **Thomas Walterson**, born in 1880. He married *Christina Smith*.

V. **Jane Walterson**, born on September 9, 1860, in Walls Parish, Shetland.[152] A family tree from SFHS places her birth in 1851, which would make her the oldest child of this family.

V. **William Walterson**, born on December 18, 1860, in Walls Parish, Shetland.[153]

IV. **James Twatt**, first son of Andrina Robertson and James Twatt, was born in 1826. He married *Robina Coutts* in Walls Parish, Shetland,[154] and they had five children. (*SEE SECTION 4-H.*) James died on July 28, 1884, age approximately fifty-eight.

IV. **Thomas Twatt**, second son of Andrina Robertson and James Twatt, was born on February 2, 1828, in Burraland, Shetland, and baptized by Rev. Thomson of the Church of Scotland. He married *Janet Coutts* in Walls Parish,[155] and they had eight children. (*SEE SECTION 4-I.*) Thomas died in 1898, at approximately seventy years old.

IV. **William Twatt**, fourth child and third son of Andrina Robertson and James Twatt, was born in 1833. On November 24, 1853, he married *Jean Abernathy*, who was born in 1827. The had eight children. Jean died in 1908, and William died two years later in 1910.

**Children of William Twatt**

V. **Mary Twatt**, born on July 25, 1853, in Walls Parish, Shetland.[156]

V. **Margaret Twatt**, born in 1856, according to information from the Shetland Family History Society. She must have died young, as another daughter was given the same name a few years later.

V. **Jemima Twatt**, born in 1858, according to information from the Shetland Family History Society.

V. **Peter Twatt**, born on August 7, 1860, in Walls Parish, Shetland.[157]

V. **William Twatt**, born on June 15, 1863, in Walls Parish, Shetland.[158] The Shetland Family History Society information places his birth in 1862.

V. **Robert Twatt**, born in 1865, according to SFHS.

V. **Andrina Twatt**, born on September 16, 1868, in Walls Parish, Shetland.[159]

V. **Margaret Twatt**, born on August 15, 1871, in Walls Parish, Shetland.[160]

## 3-G: ROBERT TWATT (1805-1869)
### Son of Agnes Robertson

III. **Robert Twatt** was born in 1805, the second son of Agnes Robertson and her second husband, James Twatt (2-D above). He married _Jean Anderson_ in June 1835—either on June 15, according to the IGI records for Northmaven Parish,[161] or June 16, as reflected in the record for Walls Parish.[162] Jean was born on December 17, 1809, on the island of Bressay, the daughter of Ann Christie and Magnus Anderson.

Robert and Jean had twelve children. All but two of the children were listed in the Walls Parish birth register under the patronymic surname Robertson, based upon their father's first name rather than their father's surname Twatt; several were also recorded with a middle initial "T," which probably stood for Twatt. Perhaps the children were given both names, i.e. "Twatt Robertson." Evidently, Robert and his family left the Church of Scotland and joined the Wesleyan Methodist church, as most of the children were baptized by Wesleyan ministers.

In March 1845, Robert bought the "manor house" of Voe and attached lands from the trustees of the late Henry Robertson, a merchant who had died the year previous. This

Henry, apparently unrelated to our Robertsons, had owned the property since 1784, according to his descendant Stuart Robertson. Immediately after acquiring the property, Robert Twatt commenced an action for eviction by having a "Summons of Removing" issued and served upon Henry's son Robert Robertson, who was listed as a cooper (or barrel-maker) in Voe, to have him removed from occupancy of the property. Afterwards, Robert Robertson went to live with a brother named Scott Robertson in Grutquoy.

Robert Twatt was a merchant in Voe. He died on September 9, 1869, approximately sixty-four years old. Robert's widow, Jean, died seventeen years later, on October 11, 1886. She was seventy-six.

**Children of Robert Twatt**

IV. **John Twatt or Robertson** was born on April 23, 1836, in Voe, Walls Parish, Shetland,[163] and baptized by Rev. Mr. Binns. According to family sources, he married *Jessie Robertson*, who was born about 1826 and died on February 23, 1897. (We note that the IGI lists a marriage of John Twatt to *Barbara Robertson* on December 4, 1860, in Walls Parish,[164] so the wife's given name may actually have been Barbara rather than Jessie.) We do not know whether she was related to our Robertsons or who her parents were. John Twatt died on February 4, 1879.

IV. **Catherine Twatt or Robertson**, born on August 3, 1837, in Voe, Walls Parish, Shetland.[165] She was baptized by Mr. Clarke, the Wesleyan minister. In 1856, she married *John Georgeson*, who was born on June 10, 1833. They had twelve children.[166] Her husband died on February 12, 1897, and Catherine died in 1905.

**Children of Catherine Twatt or Robertson**

V. **John Georgeson**, born in 1857 (possibly a twin with Peter).

V. **Peter Georgeson**, born in 1857.

V. **Jane Georgeson**, born in 1859.

V. **Mary Charlotte Georgeson**, born in 1863. She married *James Charleson*, and they had three children.

**Children of Mary Charlotte Georgeson**

VI. **Catherine Jane Charleson**, born on August 27, 1895. She married *Laurence Arthur*, who was born about 1895.

VI. **James Charleson**, born on January 10, 1897.

VI. **Thomas Stanley Charleson**, born in 1903.

V. **George Robert Georgeson**, born in 1865.

V. **Daniel Georgeson**, born in 1873 (with Helen, another possible set of twins).

V. **Helen Georgeson**, born in 1873.

V. **Lilias Georgeson**, born in 1874.

V. **James Georgeson**, born around 1876. He married *Mary Ann MacKenzie*, who was born in 1880.

V. **Joseph Georgeson**, born in 1880.

V. **David Georgeson**, born in 1882. He married *Evangentine G. Inkster*, born on November 28, 1884.

IV. **Helen Twatt or Robertson**, born on March 20, 1839, in Voe, Walls Parish, Shetland;[167] baptized by Mr. Clarke, Wesleyan minister.

IV. **Robert Twatt or Robertson**, born on September 16, 1840, in Voe, Walls Parish, Shetland;[168] baptized by Mr. Clarke, Wesleyan minister.

IV. **William Henderson Twatt**, born on February 12, 1842, in Voe, Walls Parish, Shetland; baptized by the Wesleyan minister.[169]

IV. **Jane T. Robertson** (Twatt), born on November 20, 1843, in Voe, Walls Parish, Shetland; baptized by the Wesleyan minister.[170] Although the information is not confirmed, she may be the Jane Twatt who married *Laurence Sinclair* on December 19, 1867, in Walls Parish.[171]

IV. **Thomas T. Robertson** (Twatt), born on July 25, 1845, in Voe, Walls Parish, Shetland;[172] baptized by Wesleyan minister Mr. Hesk. Thomas died on May 26, 1870, at the age of twenty-four.

IV. **Mary T. Robertson** (Twatt), born on September 9, 1847, in Walls Parish, Shetland;[173] baptized by the Wesleyan minister Mr. Hesk. On September 17, 1891, she married *James Magnus Manson*, who was born in 1834. He died on November 10, 1921, and Mary died on July 6, 1927.

IV. **Adam T. Robertson** (Twatt), born on September 13, 1849, in Walls Parish, Shetland.[174] He died on December 22, 1888.

IV. **Agnes T. Robertson** (Twatt), born on July 3, 1851, in Walls Parish, Shetland;[175] baptized by Rev. Mr. Farquhar, Wesleyan minister.

IV. **Daniel T. Robertson** (Twatt), born on April 15, 1853, in Walls Parish, Shetland;[176] baptized by Rev. Mr. Farquhar, Wesleyan minister.

IV. **Lilias Twatt**, born on March 8, 1855, in Walls Parish, Shetland.[177] On November 7, 1878, she married *George Georgeson*, who was born in 1846. They had two children.

**Children of Lilias Twatt**

V. **Jane A. Georgeson**, born in 1861.

V. **Charlotte M. Georgeson**.

# Part II

# THE FAMILY SPANS THE GLOBE

During the nineteenth century, economic conditions in Shetland became more severe as a result of various factors. These included actions on the part of some landowners to clear tenants off their lands in favor of sheep grazing, disastrous conditions in Shetland's traditional industries of fishing and fish curing, disasters at sea caused by fierce storms which resulted in the loss of many fishermen and merchant sailors and left families without support, and the potato blight which wiped out a large portion of the people's food supply in Shetland, as well as in Ireland and Scotland.

Emigration became a very attractive possibility during these years, and many branches of our Robertsons chose to leave Shetland to search for better opportunities abroad. Government and private programs in New Zealand and Australia actively encouraged Shetlanders to come and settle in those developing colonies and often provided financial support to do so. By the 1880s, perhaps a quarter of the population of Shetland had immigrated to Australia, New Zealand, Canada, and the United States. Our Robertsons thus began in the mid-1800s to spread out to make new lives for themselves and their families in those far-away lands.

# Chapter 4

# THE FOURTH GENERATION



IV. **Thomas Robertson**, first child of Catherine "Katie" Robertson and her husband, John Robertson (3-A above), was born on December 8, 1827, in Walls, Shetland. As a young man in his early twenties, Thomas went off to Australia. His great-granddaughter Irene Jones has written of Thomas:

> . . . *about the year 1850 he set sail for Australia where he dug for gold. He had heard of big "strikes" by the 49ers and he wanted money quickly to be able to return to Shetland to buy a piece of land and build a new home. Thomas managed to save 100 gold sovereigns which was a lot of money in those days. He returned to the Shetlands and bought his piece of land known as "North Dykes" and it became the family home of the Robertsons. My great-grandfather worked the land and gave up the sea which he loved.*

Some years ago, Alice Drury, another great-granddaughter, on a trip to Australia, succeeded in finding remains of the actual gold diggings Thomas had worked on.

On February 6, 1868, Thomas Robertson married *Catherine Thomson* in Sandsting & Aithsting Parish, Shetland. She was born in 1840 in Sandwick, Dunrossness, Shetland, daughter of Grace Irvine and Robert Thomson, a fisherman who lived in Garderhouse. Catherine and Thomas had seven children. Thomas died on January 3, 1913, age eighty-five.

Alice Drury visited "North Dykes," the house Thomas built in Westerskeld, some years ago. "I must say it gave me a strange feeling of empathy to think of my ancestor actually building the house with his own hands. I walked all over the surrounding acres of rough land which was tilled by the family using a team of oxen. Thomas actually built the house for his parents, who were being evicted from their croft, but he later lived there with his wife Catherine and they brought up their family there."

Magnus Robertson, one of the sons of Thomas and Catherine, years afterward lived in the North Dykes home with his family and died there at the age of ninety-three.

Alice and others have heard the story that Thomas for many years kept a large gold nugget from Australia on display on top of the sideboard in North Dykes. "One day some children took it out into the garden to play with it and they lost it. Somewhere amongst the stones of North Dykes, there is a gold nugget worth many hundreds of pounds!"

**Children of Thomas Robertson**

V. **Catherine Robertson**, born on November 18, 1868, in Skeld, Westerskeld, Sandsting & Aithsting Parish, Shetland.[178] She married *John Johnson* of North Huxter, Shetland, in December 1891, and they had ten children. Catherine died in 1941, age seventy-two. (*SEE SECTION 5-A.1.*)

V. **John Robert Thomson Robertson**, born on April 18, 1871, in Sandsting & Aithsting Parish, Shetland.[179]

V. **Williamina Ann Thomson Robertson**, born on September 1, 1873, in Sandsting & Aithsting Parish, Shetland.[180] She married *Robert Thomson*, a first cousin on her mother's side, and they had three children. (*SEE SECTION 5-A.2.*)

V. **Thomas Thomson Robertson**, born on April 20, 1876, in Sandsting & Aithsting Parish, Shetland. He married *Andrina Johnson*, and they had two children. Thomas died on December 29, 1909, in an accident in Kent, England. (*SEE SECTION 5-A.3.*)

V. **Magnus Jameson Robertson**, born on July 5, 1878, at North Dykes, the homestead his father built in Westerskeld, Sandsting & Aithsting Parish, Shetland.

On February 22, 1917, Magnus Robertson married *Mary Charlotte Urqhurt Robertson*. Mary was born on October 28, 1893, at "Swarthoull," the house opposite North Dykes where her husband grew up. Although she had the same surname, Mary evidently came from a family unrelated to our Robertsons. Her parents were Williamina Jamieson and Laurence Robertson (born on October 10, 1851, in

Westerskeld[181]), who had six children. Several of Mary's uncles immigrated to the United States, according to her granddaughter Margaret Ridland.[182]

Magnus and Mary lived in North Dykes. They had one son, who died at sea in World War II, and two daughters, who have produced twelve grandchildren.

Magnus Robertson died on August 25, 1965, in Westerskeld, Sandsting Parish, Shetland. He was ninety-three. His widow, Mary Robertson, died on May 2, 1976, age eighty-two.

### Children of Magnus Jameson Robertson

VI. **Christina Helen Robertson** (called "Tina") was born on September 28, 1916, in Shetland; died on June 2, 1994, at the age of seventy-seven. She married *Laurence Peter Garrick*, and they had seven children. (*SEE SECTION 6-A.3.*)

VI. **Robertha Catherine Robertson** was born on January 8, 1919, in Shetland. She married *Archibald Neilson*, and they had five children. (*SEE SECTION 6-A.4.*)

VI. **Peter James Robertson** was born on November 17, 1920. He was in the merchant navy. Peter never married; he died on December 5, 1940, at age twenty, a casualty of World War II. His ship, MV *Empire Statesman*, apparently was torpedoed and sunk by the German Navy in the North Atlantic. A photograph of Peter is in the Shetland Roll of Honor.

V. **James Greig Robertson**, born on October 13 (or November 13), 1880, in Sandsting & Aithsting Parish, Shetland; died in 1974, age ninety-three. He married *Williamina Arthurson*, and they had three children. (*SEE SECTION 5-A.4.*)

V. **Alexander Inkster Robertson**, born on August 22, 1883, in Westerskeld, Sandsting Parish, Shetland. He married *Margaret Catherine Anderson* (called "Maggie"), and they had two children. He died in 1965, approximately eighty-one years of age. (*SEE SECTION 5-A.5.*)

## 4-B: MAGNUS JAMESON ROBERTSON (1846-1897)
### Son of John Robertson and Catherine Robertson

IV. **Magnus Jameson Robertson** was born on February 17, 1846, in Stove in Walls Parish, Shetland. The youngest of six children, his parents were Catherine (called "Katie") and John Robertson (3-A above). He is the forebear of many of our Robertsons living today in New Zealand.

A merchant seaman, Magnus went to Australia about 1870, when he was around twenty-four years old, apparently to join his brothers John and James. Magnus later returned to Shetland for about a year due to illness. There he married *Helen Manson* in Sandsting Parish, Shetland, on February 6, 1879. The daughter of Catherine Jamieson and Mitchell Manson, Helen was born on January 1, 1845, in the hamlet of Twatt, Sandsting & Aithsting Parish, Shetland.

Magnus and Helen Robertson immigrated shortly after their marriage to Australia, where their two children were born. They all later moved to New Zealand, arriving in Dunedin in 1890.

Magnus Robertson died seven years later, at the age of fifty-one, on September 18, 1897, in Dunedin, New Zealand, and was buried in the Southern Cemetery. His widow, Helen, died in 1927 in Wanganui.

**Children of Magnus Jameson Robertson**

V. **John Robert Robertson**, was born on February 1, 1884, in Sydney, Australia, the son of Helen Manson and Magnus Jameson Robertson. He arrived with his parents in Dunedin, New Zealand, in 1890, at the age of six. His career was spent with the New Zealand Railways, where he was chief clerk upon retirement in 1940.

At the age of thirty, John Robertson married *Nora Isabella Walker* on June 24, 1914, in Masterton, New Zealand. Born on June 30, 1889, in Masterton, New Zealand, Nora was the daughter of Alexander Walker and Anne Bonthorne. John and Nora had four children. They are the ancestors of many of our Robertsons in New Zealand and Australia.

John died at the age of seventy on May 15, 1954, in Lower Hutt, New Zealand; he was cremated at Karori Cemetery in Wellington, New Zealand. His widow, Nora, died some twenty-nine years later in Lower Hutt, just before her ninety-fourth birthday, on June 26, 1983.

**Children of John Robert Robertson**

VI. **John Maurice Robertson**, born on October 31, 1916, in Petone, New Zealand. He married *Rebecca Joy Anderson*, and they had four children. (*SEE SECTION 6-B.1.*)

VI. **Edwin Ian Robertson**, born on January 21, 1919, in Petone, New Zealand. He married *Claude Sinclair Chalk*, and they had two daughters. (*SEE SECTION 6-B.2.*)

VI. **Enid Honorah Robertson**, born on April 2, 1921, in Petone, New Zealand. She married *John Roy Gibson*, and they had two children. (*SEE SECTION 6-B.3.*)

VI. **Leonard Hector Robertson**, born on November 14, 1923, in Petone, New Zealand; died on March 30, 1993, in Wellington. He married *Margaret Helen Virtue*, and they had three children. (*SEE SECTION 6-B.4.*)

V. **Catherine Robertson**, born on May 10, 1887, in Sandwell, Adelaide, Australia, daughter of Helen Manson and Magnus Jameson Robertson. In 1890, as a small child, Catherine was taken with her parents to Dunedin, New Zealand. In 1928 or 1929, she married *Ernest Butler Robinson* in Wanganui, New Zealand. They had no children.

Catherine died on September 14, 1977, age ninety, in Auckland, New Zealand, and was cremated at Purewa Cemetery.

## 4-C: CHARLES DUMBRECK ROBERTSON (1839-1919)
### First Son of Thomas Robertson

IV. **Charles Dumbreck Robertson**, a product of Shetland culture and education in the mid-nineteenth century, left as a youngster of eighteen to explore the far reaches of the world. During his lifetime, this engaging Shetland expatriate pursued interests and opportunities in an amazing variety of professions, including engineering, journalism, medicine, insurance, and law. The virtues of hard work, resourcefulness, and integrity that were ingrained during his upbringing brought him recognition as a distinguished lawyer, jurist, civic leader, and man of letters in his adopted land of America.

The only child of Christina Dumbreck and Thomas Robertson (3-C above), Charles was born on March 6, 1839, in Stove in Walls Parish, Shetland, and was baptized there by Rev. Clarke, a Wesleyan Methodist minister. His mother died within a few days after his birth.[183] His father, Thomas Robertson, was a merchant in Walls, where he owned a small fleet of fishing boats and operated a fish-curing and -smoking business that required frequent travel to mainland Scotland and the European mainland. Following Christina's death, Thomas employed a young woman from Unst named Margaret Mouat to live in the home and help take care of the child. Three years later, Margaret and Thomas were married; they eventually produced eight offspring of their own.

The first of many members of his family to emigrate from Shetland, Charles D. Robertson set out from Shetland to explore the world at the age of eighteen. He sailed first to India, where he found work as a surveyor and civil engineer on railway- and bridge-construction projects. Later, he made his way to the United States, arriving there in September 1863. Within four years, he had married _Cynthia Ann Buck (Hillman)_ and started a family. They settled in the bustling city of Cincinnati, Ohio, in the early 1870s, and there Charles forged a preeminent legal career. He died in 1919 at the age of eighty.

## Early Adventures

When young Charles was finishing his high school years, sailors home from the sea told of the discovery of gold on Canada's Vancouver Island off the western coast of British Columbia. Some showed off gold nuggets they had brought back. Charles knew it was time for him to leave the comforts of home, braving the dangers of the high seas and the voyage around Cape Horn, to explore the Vancouver gold fields for himself. But money would be needed to make the trip. In 1842, when Charles was three, his father had built a 42-foot sailing sloop named the _Charles_ and put the legal title in Charles's name. The boat would have to be sold to pay for his passage to the New World.[184]

With his father's reluctant approval, C.D. Robertson left home in 1857, armed with the Episcopal prayer book and watch that had belonged to his late mother. There was still a baby at home, born to his father and stepmother less than a year before; another half-sister was born three years later. It was the last time Charles would ever see his father.

When Charles arrived in mainland Scotland to board the ship for Vancouver, he learned that the scheduled departure had been delayed for several weeks. This gave him a chance to visit friends and relatives in Edinburgh in a "whirl of social enjoyment," as he later described it. But then another delay of the sailing date was announced, and his money began to run out. He was able to talk the ship's agent into refunding most of the ticket price and found work in Edinburgh to replenish dwindling funds. But the job—door-to-door sale of subscriptions for an illustrated Bible being published in installments—proved unrewarding, as Charles discovered how tough it was to separate skeptical Scots from their money for such a scheme.

Running out of options in Scotland, Charles made his way to London to seek advice and help from a business acquaintance of his father, who was a Member of Parliament.[185] His father's friend recommended that Charles get on the next ship to India, where he could find work on rail-construction projects then being undertaken by the British government. Charles took the advice and soon was on a clipper ship bound for India. The young man arrived in Bombay, the largest city of India, in May 1857. This was the beginning of five years of hard work, exotic life, and wild adventure. On the first night ashore in this turbulent and lawless environment, the captain of his ship was killed in a hotel brawl.

India at that time had fallen into political and military turmoil which soon led to the collapse of the East India Company that had controlled the subcontinent for over 250 years. A few days before Charles's ship landed, a bloody uprising that became known as the Sepoy Rebellion had broken out throughout India in protest against foreign cruelty and domination of the Indian people. Hundreds of European men, women, and children were butchered by rioters and mutinous troops. Just before Charles landed, a secret plot had been hatched in Bombay to kill all European residents:

> *There were only a handful of European soldiers in the city. . . . Native detectives in the employ of the government had revealed the secrets, and were active with the real conspirators. The plans were complete, and the day and hour for the rising appointed; on the day preceding the appointed time, under pretext of some sort of*

> *a religious holiday and ceremony, most of the European women and children were taken on board the ships in the harbor. That night the European officers broke in on the conspirators, and the three leaders were captured and blown away from cannon mouths. They might have been shot or put out of existence by other more usual methods, but blowing them into eternity from a cannon had a wholesome influence on the natives. It cooled their ardor, and struck terror into their religious souls.*

Despite this upheaval, Charles was accepted for employment in the civil service. He was assigned to stay in Bombay for a few months and worked to master the basics of Hindi, the official language of northern India. He was then sent to the interior to assist in the surveying, tunneling, grading, bridge building, and other work necessary for construction of the first rail lines across the Indian subcontinent.

A newspaper feature article many years afterward described C.D. Robertson's work experience during his time in India:

> *He entered the engineering service of the British government, and in the unsettled state of the country the life of a British government employee there was one of adventure and almost continuous peril of death. Young Robertson became a civil engineer and helped to push the first railroads through the jungles and plains of the Indian continent. He became especially proficient in the building of bridges, and within five years rose to the head of that branch of the service. Many of the bridges of India were constructed under his direction.*

There were many adventures and dangers during Charles's years in India. One that stands out started when the young man heard one afternoon that there was a tiger lurking in a culvert a mile or two from the camp. He grabbed a rifle and some ammunition, jumped on a horse, and raced off to look for the tiger. It was not to be found, but he saw and shot at a pair of hyenas that disappeared, sneering, into the jungle. Then he glimpsed a large antelope through a clearing. Charles tied his horse to a tree and went charging after it on foot, hoping to get a shot. Running through the jungle, the young man finally realized that he had lost his bearings and night was falling fast; panic began to set in. "Well," he thought, "here you are, lost in an Indian jungle, miles from any human habitation, with only the stars overhead, and surrounded with wild and ferocious animals." He ended up spending the night in the jungle, seated on a pile of stones with gun in hand, his imagination fired by visions of "the glaring eyes of the hyena from every bush, the crunching bloody jaws of the wolves from every rustling, falling leaf, and the wailing of the jackal, like that of lost spirits in Dante's Inferno." Fortunately, he survived to tell the tale fifty years later.

Charles Robertson continued working in India until 1862, when he became severely ill with malarial fever that quinine medication did not relieve. He had to get away from the interior's unhealthy tropical climate at once or die. So Charles headed back to Bombay, first by ox cart and then by train, so weak and sickly that he had to be carried on a stretcher—"a shivering, shaking, bronze skeleton," by his later self-description.

He was able to book passage on a steamship across the Indian Ocean to Suez, where he would connect with another ship to England, planning then to return home to Shetland. At sea, his health rebounded. Charles became acquainted with a fellow passenger from America on his way home to Boston, who told of great opportunities in the United States. By the time his ship reached England, Charles had decided to continue on to America instead of going back to Shetland.

He landed in New York on September 19, 1863, and began looking for work. At that time Abraham Lincoln was President of the United States, and the nation was engulfed in a civil war between northern and southern states. Having an aptitude for writing, Charles was hired to work on the editorial staff of the *New York Tribune*, run by the renowned newspaperman and anti-slavery crusader Horace Greeley. Impressed by the adventurous young Shetlander, Greeley employed him to help in the preparation of a running chronicle of the Civil War, titled *The History of the American Conflict*.

In New York, Charles became friends with a family who invited him to stay in their home in Brooklyn Heights. This family had wealthy relatives in northern Ohio who met the agreeable young Shetlander on a visit and, impressed with his capability and charm, offered him employment in their business. Following Horace Greeley's famous advice—"Go West, young man"—C.D. Robertson accepted the invitation and moved to Norwalk, Ohio.

Norwalk was a small but flourishing town near the shores of Lake Erie, less than fifty miles from Cleveland. Charles later recalled Norwalk as "One of the ideal villages of the West with its broad and spacious Main Street for miles shaded with magnificent maples, and fringed on both sides with handsome, and sometimes elegant residences, interspersed with artistic churches and commodious schools." He was offered room and board with

Judge and Mrs. Samuel Worcester in Norwalk, in a home that Charles considered "the most refined and aristocratic in that part of the State."

Perhaps influenced by Judge Worcester, Charles developed a strong interest in the law and considered a possible career in that profession. To pursue it, however, Charles felt he needed more formal education or training in other disciplines. He therefore enrolled in the Cleveland Medical College in Cleveland, Ohio. There, he became acquainted with another medical student, Jirah Dewey Buck, who introduced Charles to his recently-widowed sister, Cynthia.

## Cynthia Ann Buck

One of the two children of Reuben and Fanny Morton Buck, Cynthia Buck was born on May 21, 1836, in the village of Fredonia, in Chautauqua County, in the far western corner of New York State. (Because Fanny Morton and Reuben Buck also appear to be common ancestors of virtually all of the known descendants of "Our Robertsons" born in the United States, a brief discussion of their lives and origins appears in the Notes.[186]) Life had not been easy for her: Cynthia was only seventeen when her father died, leaving debts unpaid and few assets for his family. Her first husband, William Hillman, had died in 1864, leaving Cynthia with a young child. One other daughter born to Cynthia and Mr. Hillman had died as a baby. By the time Cynthia was twenty-eight—with the United States still embroiled in Civil War—she was a single mother forced to make her own way in life.

Charles D. Robertson and Cynthia Buck were married in December 1867 and took up residence in the town of Sandusky, Ohio, near the shore of Lake Erie.[187] A woman of strong character and physique, Cynthia Robertson was dedicated to literary and academic pursuits and to the interests of women. She was an avid reader, and her home became a center of culture where friends and neighbors would come together for discussion and for lectures by distinguished guests from the fields of science, literature, and philosophy.

Cynthia was very active in women's organizations committed to broadened educational and cultural opportunities for women. She was one of the organizers of the Cincinnati Women's Club, which still exists in that city, and within that organization, she led a group devoted to Greek literature and philosophy. In 1894, she helped found the Ohio Federation of Women's Clubs, in which she served in various positions and for several years as its general secretary. A memorial tribute called her the "soul of Plato in a woman's frame."

## Professional and Public Life in Cincinnati

While still living in northern Ohio, C.D. Robertson decided to get into the business of insurance. Starting as an apprentice, he went to work with a prominent insurance company in Sandusky and soon was promoted to the job of actuary (an expert who calculates insurance and annuity premiums, dividends, etc.) for the company. That position in turn led to an offer of employment from an insurance company in Cincinnati—a bustling city on the banks of the Ohio River in the southwestern part of the state.

About 1870, Charles and Cynthia moved to Cincinnati. In 1871, a city directory listed him as Vice President of the Cincinnati Mutual Insurance Company. But there remained his interest in the law. Enrolling in the Cincinnati Law School, he obtained his degree in 1872, was admitted to the bar, and began to practice. He soon became a respected trial attorney and counsellor for insurance firms in the area.

With his intellect, professionalism, and engaging personality, Charles D. Robertson's star was rising at a time when that of his father in Shetland was falling. By the time Thomas Robertson died in 1873, he had lost his business and fallen into virtual poverty, while his son in Ohio had become a practicing lawyer with a supportive, loving wife, and a growing family.

A fine writer and an avid student of history, C.D. Robertson was elected to membership in the prestigious Cincinnati Literary Club in 1872, the same year he was admitted to the bar. This organization, limited to one hundred members, held weekly meetings for reading and discussion of original papers prepared by the members. This brought Charles into regular contact with some of the leading lights of the Cincinnati business and intellectual worlds.[188] He was an active, prolific member of the Literary Club for more than forty years, holding numerous leadership positions, including the office of president. Fortunately, many of the scholarly and historical papers presented by C.D. Robertson to the Cincinnati Literary Club between 1886 and 1916 have been preserved in the collection of the Cincinnati Historical Society.

Training in mathematics, engineering, medicine, insurance, and general law equipped Charles Robertson to become an outstanding member of the bar and a respected community leader. Within a few years, he was appointed to the board of trustees of the University of Cincinnati, serving from 1876 until 1883. In 1883, he was elected Judge of the Court of Common Pleas of Hamilton County, Ohio, and took office on the first Monday of December in that year.

Judge C.D. Robertson's introduction to his new position could literally be called a trial by fire. Like other growing cities in America in the late nineteenth century, Cincinnati had a rough, often violent edge. Crime was a matter of great concern, and there was public outcry against what some perceived as excessive delay in bringing criminals to justice, followed by inadequate punishment for those convicted.

Matters got completely out of hand, however, barely three months after the new judge was raised to the bench. In March of 1884, an uproar arose when the jury in a homicide case against a man named Berner returned a manslaughter verdict. Many people thought it was cold-blooded murder. The presiding judge sentenced Berner to twenty years in prison, the maximum sentence for manslaughter, but strongly criticized the jury for not returning a verdict of murder in the first degree. A public assembly was convened to discuss problems in the criminal justice system and to protest the verdict, but passions were inflamed, and the assembly turned into a full-scale riot. The mob stormed the city jail, intent upon applying its own justice to the inmates there, but was turned away by the police. The rioters then turned to the courthouse in downtown Cincinnati, which was set on fire. The courthouse burned to the ground overnight. So much for law and order.

Despite this inauspicious beginning, Judge C.D. Robertson served with distinction on the bench of the Common Pleas Court, presiding over a number of dramatic and colorful cases. One of the most sensational involved a proceeding for the disbarment of attorney Thomas Campbell on charges of bribery, fraud, and corruption of the judicial process. Campbell was, in fact, the attorney who had represented Berner in the murder trial that led to the courthouse riot and fire. Immediately afterward, a committee of the Bar Association of Cincinnati had conducted its own investigation of the attorney's conduct in that case and others, resulting in a formal petition to the court for Campbell's disbarment. Among the allegations were that Campbell had attempted to bribe a juror in the Berner case and had allowed two others to be seated as jurors without disclosing that they were clients of Campbell's. Although the case had been pending for some time, Judge Robertson was appointed in 1885 to a panel of three judges assigned to hear the matter. Many of the city's most powerful and best-known lawyers were involved in the proceedings. The legal team against Campbell was led by William

Howard Taft, an aggressive young prosecutor who later became President of the United States and was appointed Chief Justice of the U.S. Supreme Court.

After five years on the bench, Charles Robertson decided not to seek another term as Common Pleas Court judge and instead went back into private practice. Together with another retired jurist, he opened the law firm of Robertson and Buchwalter in 1888, where he practiced for the rest of his life. Even as a private lawyer, however, he continued his involvement in public affairs and his opposition to corruption in politics.

In the late nineteenth century, politics and public administration in the United States were dominated by two organized political parties, Republican and Democratic, which amassed much greater power than the counterparts of today. C.D. Robertson was a Democrat and committed to political reform and civic integrity. The 1880s and 1890s saw the rise of a ruthless political machine in Cincinnati and Hamilton County, dominated by a saloon keeper named George B. Cox. Boss Cox was one of the most notorious of the American big-city bosses of the time. He seized and asserted almost dictatorial power, able to control the granting of public contracts, the outcome of elections, appointments to important offices—even, it was rumored, outcomes of cases in court. Many years later, Charles Robertson's son reminisced about the bad old days of Boss Cox and his father's opposition to the corrupt machine politics:

*When the City decided to build a new water works system, complete with filter plant and everything—citizens had complained that when residents of Pittsburgh [upstream on the Ohio River] ate asparagus, the folks in Cincinnati could tell it—a non-partisan committee was selected to supervise the building of the water works and Father was chosen as Legal Advisor. Later a dispute arose between the Commission and the prime contractor, which resulted in a long drawn out legal battle.*

*The Judge in the case was a friend and neighbor of my father, but of opposite political faith. When he had decided to run for the position of Judge, he enlisted the aid of George B. Cox and was elected. As the trial was reaching its climax, late one night this Judge came to Father as a friend and told him that George B. had sent him "orders" to decide the case in a way favorable to the defendant contractor, regardless of law and facts. Inasmuch as he had accepted the support of the Cox gang to get into office, he was torn between conflicting obligations—loyalty to his oath and loyalty to one who had helped him politically. My father's advice to him, of course, was to comply with his oath of office. And that is what the Judge did, but he considered it wise not to reappear on the political scene thereafter.*

Judge C.D. Robertson pursued his commitment to good government even at the state level. Running as a reform candidate in 1897, he was elected to the Ohio Senate, where he was chosen chairman of the Democratic Steering Committee and Democratic floor leader. As a member of the Ohio Senate, he continued to oppose the powerful political boss of northern Ohio, Mark A. Hanna. In those days, members of the United States Senate from each state were selected by the state's legislature, not popularly elected as they are today. When Boss Hanna sought to have himself appointed to the U.S. Senate, Charles Robertson put up a valiant but losing fight to block his power grab. His effort was warmly praised by many, including the *Cincinnati Times-Star* newspaper which wrote, "Judge Robertson played good politics . . . and almost prevented the selection of the Cleveland statesman."

When the Mayor of Cincinnati named C.D. Robertson to an important public position in 1910, the appointment was hailed as one that pleased "even the opposition," the *Cincinnati Times-Star* wrote, because he "is known throughout the city as a staunch Democrat and is liked by everybody." The paper continued in its praise of Charles Robertson: "No member of the Hamilton County bar is held in higher esteem by his associates and none has a larger circle of friends. Judge Robertson deeply sympathized with the struggles of young men in their fight to make their way in the world and there are many who could tell interesting stories of how he reached forth a helping hand."

Charles Robertson was again proposed for an important public trusteeship in 1914. The *Cincinnati Times-Star* endorsed his selection in glowing terms:

*The position . . . needs men of the caliber of Judge Robertson – men of sound judgment, of sober thought, of progressive ideas along the lines on which true and abiding progress alone can be built; men of affairs and men of action; men who know Cincinnati and appreciate her best interests; men with the right grasp of civic affairs; men of experience in matters affecting the city of Cincinnati – and of that class of men Judge Robertson is an honored illustration. His services on the bench of the Common Pleas Court were distinguished not alone for a knowledge of the law and its right application, but for courtesy, high judicial bearing and a seeking after justice in all things.*

*None stands higher on the roll of a judiciary distinguished throughout Ohio than Judge Charles D. Robertson, and the reputation he gained on the bench and at the bar is a reputation based on high character and unimpeached probity.*

## Family Life

Charles and Cynthia Robertson had five children—in addition to Cynthia's daughter from her first marriage—but only two of the five survived to maturity. Their first child, Thomas Walter Robertson, was born in 1868 and died of blood poisoning in 1884 when he was less than sixteen years old. The second child, Georgia Dumbreck Robertson, was born in October 1870, grew up to marry and raise a family, and lived to the age of eighty-one. Two of the following children fell victim to scarlet fever within a month of each other in 1878. Charles and Cynthia's youngest child, Reuben Buck Robertson, was born in June 1879; he lived to the age of ninety-three, raised three children, and had an outstanding career of his own.[189]

After their father, Thomas Robertson, died in 1873, two of Charles's younger half-brothers followed him to settle in Cincinnati, Ohio. Thomas, who never married, arrived in the United States in April 1876. He was listed in the city directory as a resident of Cincinnati in 1886. He died in 1900. Andrew Umphray Robertson, the sixth child of Margaret and Thomas Robertson, immigrated to America around 1880; in 1881, he married Cynthia Robertson's daughter Esther Hillman (called Etta for short). Etta and Andrew lived for a while with Cynthia and Charles, and Etta helped care for the young children.

When they first moved to the Cincinnati area, Charles and Cynthia were living across the Ohio River in Covington, Kentucky, which was accessible by a newly constructed suspension bridge. By 1875, the family was residing at 221 Auburn Avenue in the Mt. Auburn section of Cincinnati and for a time resided at 1510 Eastern Avenue. They finally bought a large, beautiful home on Ridgeway Avenue in Avondale, which was then a separate municipality but was later annexed to become part of the city of Cincinnati.[190] The house on Ridgeway Avenue was also home to numerous other relatives from time to time. In later years, Cynthia's granddaughter Greta Robertson, the daughter of Etta and Andrew, lived on Ridgeway Avenue and worked as Charles's secretary in the law firm.

C.D. Robertson and his wife enjoyed seeing the world and traveled extensively. In 1885, they visited Scotland and Shetland, and Charles again was able to see his aged stepmother,

Margaret Mouat Robertson, and to visit with his half-brother James D. Robertson. Later, they travelled to the St. Lawrence Seaway, Toronto, Quebec, and Montreal in Canada, to the Grand Canyon in Arizona, Yosemite and Coronado Beach in California, and to Hawaii, where they went to the rim of the volcano Kilauea.

Charles Dumbreck Robertson died in his sleep on the night of August 28, 1919. Distinguished leaders of the bench and bar wrote of him, "It may safely be said that Judge Robertson had no enemy. He never spoke unkindly to anyone. His sunny, genial disposition; his guileless frankness, ready humor and warm heart; his deep sense of justice, personal honor and courage; his thoughtful consideration for others; his clear sense, ability and habits or industry gave him a life of happiness, usefulness and distinction. . . . He never denied any man his due, and he left to those he loved the priceless heritage of an untarnished name."

Cynthia Buck Robertson lived for four years after the death of her husband. She died in Cincinnati on November 16, 1923, at eighty-seven years of age. She was honored by her peers as an exceptional but unassuming woman who was instrumental in the women's club movement, a civic leader in arts and education, and a kind, charitable, and loyal friend. Cynthia Buck and Charles D. Robertson, all of their children, the children's spouses, and some of the grandchildren and their spouses are buried in the Robertson lot in Spring Grove Cemetery in Cincinnati (Section 79, Lot 1).

**Children of Charles Dumbreck Robertson**

V. **Thomas Walter Robertson**, oldest son of Cynthia Buck and Charles D. Robertson, was born about September 1868 in Sandusky, Ohio. He died of blood poisoning in Cincinnati, Hamilton County, Ohio, on May 18, 1884, when he was fifteen years and eight months old.

V. **Georgia Dumbreck Robertson**, oldest daughter of Cynthia Buck and Charles D. Robertson, was born on October 7, 1870,[191] in Covington, Kentucky. She married *Lyman Perin*, and they had four children. She died on April 20, 1952, age about eighty-one, in Cincinnati. *SEE SECTION 5-C.1.)*

V. **Charles Dumbreck Robertson Jr.**, second son of Cynthia Buck and Charles D. Robertson, was born on September 19, 1872, in Cincinnati, Hamilton

County, Ohio. He died of scarlet fever on his sixth birthday, September 19, 1878, in Cincinnati.

V. **<u>Grace Robertson</u>** was born on August 9, 1874, in Cincinnati, Hamilton County, Ohio. The second daughter of Cynthia Buck and Charles D. Robertson, Grace died in Cincinnati at the age of four, also of scarlet fever, on October 9, 1878, less than a month after her older brother Charlie.

V. **<u>Reuben Buck Robertson</u>** was named for his maternal grandfather, Reuben Buck. Born on June 11, 1879, in Cincinnati, Hamilton County, Ohio, he was the fifth child and third son of Cynthia Buck and Charles D. Robertson (although two of his siblings died before his birth). Reuben married *Hope Lindenberger Thomson*, and they had four children. He died at age ninety-three on December 26, 1972, in Asheville, North Carolina. (*SEE SECTION 5-C.2.*)

## 4-D: CHRISTINA DUMBRECK ROBERTSON (1847-1934)
### Daughter of Margaret Mouat and Thomas Robertson:
### Matriarch of the Cheyne Branches

IV. **<u>Christina Dumbreck Robertson</u>**, the oldest daughter of Margaret Mouat and Thomas Robertson (3-C above), was born on January 27, 1847, at Seafield in Walls, Shetland, and named in the memory of her father's second wife.

Christina married *Robert Thomas Cheyne* on June 4, 1874—about a year after her father died—in South Voe, Walls Parish.[192] She was then twenty-seven years old. Her husband was born about 1844 in Ellon, Aberdeenshire, Scotland, not far from the major port city of Aberdeen, and was living in Stapness, Walls, Shetland, at the time of the wedding.

Christina and Robert Thomas Cheyne took advantage of the free emigration offered by the New Zealand government. Soon after their marriage in 1874, they set sail for New Zealand, taking with them Christina's twenty-two-year-old sister, Charlotte. They arrived in Blenheim on the northeastern side of the South Island of New Zealand.

Christina and Robert Cheyne established their home on a sheep farm in Blink Bonnie in the lower Wairau Valley, a few miles southwest of Blenheim. In 1880, they moved to

Blenheim, where Robert worked as a milkman and shopkeeper. Around 1882, with three small children in their growing family, they moved to Picton, a few miles to the north of Blenheim, and another child was born there. Robert Cheyne died in Picton a few years later, about 1884, leaving a widow and four young children: James, Ann Margaret, Charlotte, and Robert.

In 1893, some nine years after Robert's death, Christina remarried in Blenheim, New Zealand. Her second husband was _James Beauchop_. They soon moved to Newtown, a suburb of Wellington on the North Island of New Zealand. After her son James's wife died in 1907, she had the two grandchildren come and live with her and her oldest daughter, Ann Margaret Cheyne. In 1911, Christina, her daughter, and the two grandchildren moved from Newton to Woodville, about 120 miles north of Wellington, where they would be near another daughter, Mary Charlotte Cheyne Fraser.

That is where Christina stayed for the rest of her life. She died at the age of eighty-seven in Woodville on September 21, 1934, two days after the death of her beloved niece Elizabeth O'Brian Lyver (_SEE SECTION 5-B.3._)

### Children of Christina Dumbreck Robertson

V. **James Cheyne**, son of Christina Dumbreck Robertson and Robert Cheyne, was born on April 27, 1875, in Blink Bonnie in the lower Wairau Valley, near Blenheim, New Zealand; died on April 8, 1937, age sixty-one, in Wellington, New Zealand. He was the father of two children by his first wife, _Jesse Skilling_. (_SEE SECTION 5-B.1._)

V. **Ann Margaret Cheyne** (sometimes called "Aunt Sis" by her nephews and nieces) was the oldest daughter of Christina Robertson and Robert Cheyne. She was born on September 27, 1877, in Blink Bonnie in the lower Wairau Valley, near Blenheim, on the beautiful South Island of New Zealand.

In 1914, while living with her mother in Woodville, Ann Margaret and her first cousin Agnes O'Brian, who lived in the South Island of New Zealand, made an extensive tour to Canada, Ohio, Scotland, and the Shetlands, visiting many friends and relatives. She helped her mother keep in close contact with all the relatives, and she was greatly loved by her family at home.

She was around sixteen years old when her mother married her second husband, James Beauchop, and she moved with the family to the North Island of New Zealand. There she lived part of the time with her mother and part of the time with Georgeson relatives. Starting around 1919, she lived for about eight years with her mother, Christina, who had moved to Woodville, about 120 miles north of Wellington, and since around 1907, she had helped her mother take care of Tina and Laurie Cheyne, the two children of her widowed brother, James Cheyne. Tina and Laurie were moved to Woodville, but in 1919 Ann Margaret, with the two children, moved back to the Wellington area to live with her brother until he remarried in 1922.

After that, Ann Margaret moved to Remuera, a suburb of Auckland, where she worked and supported herself. A dress designer, she never married.

Ann Margaret Cheyne died in Remuera, New Zealand, on October 31, 1947, thirteen years after her mother passed away and just two months after the death of her youngest brother, Robert. She was seventy.

V. **Mary Charlotte Agnes Cheyne**, born on June 17, 1880, in Blenheim, South Island, New Zealand; died on May 19, 1958, at age seventy-seven, in Te Awamutu, New Zealand; she married *John Smith Fraser,* and they had four children. (SEE SECTION 5-B.2.)

V. **Robert Andrew Thomas Cheyne**, youngest son of Christina Dumbreck Robertson and Robert Thomas Cheyne, was born on September 9, 1882, in Picton, New Zealand. He was only two when his natural father died, and when he was about eleven, about 1893, his mother remarried and the family relocated to Wellington on the North Island, across the strait that divides the two parts of New Zealand.

Robert Cheyne married *Olive Geraldine Boielle* in Wellington on September 4, 1912. They lived in Wellington until the early 1930s, when they moved to Dunedin, New Zealand, in the southern part of the South Island. They had no children. Robert Cheyne died on August 26, 1947, at age sixty-four, in Dunedin in the southern part of the South Island, New Zealand.

## 4-E: Charlotte Umphray Robertson (1851-1941)
### Daughter of Thomas Robertson and Margaret Mouat:
### Matriarch of the O'Brian branches

IV. **Charlotte Umphray Robertson**, born at Seafield in Walls, Shetland, on December 28, 1851, was the fifth child of Thomas Robertson and Margaret Mouat (3-C above). When she was twenty-two years old, Charlotte immigrated to New Zealand, along with her oldest sister, Christina, and Christina's husband, Robert Cheyne. They landed at Blenheim, on the South Island, and Charlotte lived in that area for the rest of her life.

Charlotte Robertson married *Francis O'Brian* (called "Frank") in Blenheim, New Zealand, on July 31, 1875.[193] Born on November 9, 1851, at Robin Hood Bay, Port Underwood, New Zealand, Frank was the son of John O'Brian and Metapere Kawhe, a member of the Ngati Toa Tribe of the Maori people of Wairau, New Zealand. Charlotte and Frank had eight children.

Frank O'Brian worked as a shepherd in the Awatere Valley, a large valley south of Blenheim in Marlborough Province, which extends into the heart of the Southern Alps of New Zealand's South Island. First, he was at Molesworth,[194] near the head of the valley. Kate Mitchell reports that Frank also worked at some point as a shepherd at the Dungree Station in the Lower Awatere Valley. Later on, he worked at the nearby Muller Station, first as a shepherd and later as station manager. Founded in 1851, the Muller Station was situated on a vast amount of high, rugged land lying between the Tone and Yeo Rivers. The land was very isolated and difficult to farm, much of it being under snow in the winter, and the men had to struggle to keep the hordes of rabbits under control. Prices for meat and wool were generally poor.

Because of the severe conditions, the runs in the Upper Awatere were pretty much a man's world. While Frank was there working in the sheep business, Charlotte O'Brian lived in the city of Blenheim, where she worked as a machinist. The family's address in 1879, when their first son was born, was listed as 3 Mause Road, Blenheim, although it seems unlikely that Frank actually spent much time there.

However, Kate Mitchell's research indicates that Charlotte probably did move up to the Muller Station to be with Frank by 1881. A daughter, Maud, was born there in March of that year. It is not clear whether living at Muller Station was a temporary arrangement or how long Charlotte stayed in that rugged environment. The younger children were born in Blenheim.

Charlotte's grandchildren remember her as an extremely strong character, a great story-teller, with a wonderful sense of humor. Her namesake, Charlotte Gibson, has a snapshot of Grandmother Charlotte leading a pony on which a small lad is mounted. "Mum's mother," she recalls, "was a honey. She used to teach children to ride horses, and it was always said there wasn't a horse in Blenheim that would go fast enough for her. Those days she used to ride side saddle." Another granddaughter, Violet Thomas, recalled that "Grandmother was so funny. She was a real comedian. She would make you as mad as anything but you would still have to laugh." Charlotte never lost her Shetland Islands accent, which Violet thought "sounded like a different language." Margaret Fowlds (nee O'Brian) remembers her grandmother as a "Woman of Spirit" and offers this tribute:

*At the time of my birth in May 1912, Charlotte Robertson, of the Shetland Isles, had already survived a hazardous journey across the world's oceans, overcome the trauma of being an unwed mother, plunged into marriage with a man who would have been an anathema to many of her relatives, brought up eight children under difficult circumstances, lost her eldest to peritonitis in adulthood, and become grandmother to Violet Collett, Olive Liver, and Frances Georgeson.*

*What worth another granddaughter?*

*My father, her eldest son, Francis Robert O'Brian, was soon to take himself off to war, leaving my mother and me to flounder in life's tide. He sailed away February, 1915, never to return, our stability departing with him. My mother could not manage. I hate to think what might have become of me, without Charlotte's sanctuary to shelter in. For eighteen years we floated in and out of my grandparents' home with sickening regularity. Never once were we rebuffed. I never heard Grandma O'Brian utter a harsh word; she was "unflappable."*

*When her youngest daughter, a baby, developed diphtheria, the doctor said she would die. Die? Never! At the crisis Charlotte put her fingers down the child's throat and dragged out the obstruction.*

*I grew up hoping some of Grandma's character would rub off on me. I cherished everything she did and said, reveling in her impudent approach to life. This tall strong blonde woman with a soldierly bearing commanded attention when she strode down the street.*

*How she put up with me and my mother, I'll never know. With my mother steeped in Catholicism, and me at a Convent School she must have been sorely tried. Yet she handled it with aplomb. Her approach to religion was extremely liberal. Grandma, a true Christian in her ways, had long abandoned going to church, yet daily she consulted her Bible for some guiding phrase. Around her she had collected a coterie of people devoted to probing fringe beliefs. Weekly they gathered at her place for a sing-a-long. Hymn books of all descriptions, except Catholic, sat on the organ which filled a corner in the parlour. And I used to play accompaniment, glorying in Moodie and Sankey, Salvation Army, and Pentecostal tunes.*

*If the nuns at school had but known!!*

*In spite of being a heretic of sorts, Grandma treated Sunday with great respect. Arising early, her first self-appointed duty was a session at the organ. The clarion call of "What a friend we have in Jesus" would echo through the house. Keeping the Sabbath holy was an obligation. If one wanted to play tennis, one had to resort to subterfuge to sneak the racquet away secretly.*

*Scarcely in the door, Agnes put down her bags, and the pantomime began.*

*"Mother! Mother!" (hands raised high threshing the air.) "Mother! Mother!"*

*"What's the matter, Agnes?"*

*"That coat!" (more pantomime).*

*"Harry's girl-friend gave me this coat!" (Harry was her youngest son who was killed in 1915, at Gallipoli.)*

*More explosions and fizzing from the doorway! Agnes had become almost speechless.*

*"Harry didn't HAVE a girl-friend!" she spluttered.*

*Unperturbed, Grandma claimed sentimental attachment to the garment.*

*Her home was an excellent backdrop to this drama. Like Grandma it had its quirky twists and turns. Nothing was quite where you might expect it to be. A stranger would seek in vain, the front door – there wasn't one. At an earlier period, part of the house had been transformed into a photographer's studio. Thus, living there now subjected the occupants to seasonal intense heat and cold. A large spacious room was constructed almost entirely of glass, roof as well as wall.*

*The whole place reflected Grandma's personality, sewing and knitting machines dumb witness to her industrious nature. In the earlier days their constant use brought much needed money to the family. Her Scottish upbringing enabled her to knit tartan socks for the local pipe band without referring to a pattern. Homemade rag mats graced the linoleum covered floors.*

*Of course, Charlotte and Frank had not always lived in this house. They began life together living and working on the Muller Station many miles from town, high up in the mountainous region of Marlborough, 4806' above sea level. Life for workers on such vast property, often in primitive conditions, was very hard. Some actually lived under canvas and cooked over open fires. Several of the O'Brian children were born there.*

*When schooling became imperative, they moved to Blenheim, and Grandfather worked closer to town, riding home each weekend. He was a shepherd. For some years when the children were young, they lived in Manse Road (now Main Road). Later when the family was older they shifted to upper Maxwell Road.*

*At the time my life became entangled with theirs, and all the fledglings had left the nest, my grandparents were residing in Earl Street (now Seymour Street). I loved that place intensely. A straight path from gate to front door divided the garden into two equal plots, a red camellia tree centered in one, a white camellia in the other. Real fairy-tale land.*

*Inside, my grandmother daily regaled me with stories from her own youth, tales she had learned in Shetland from an itinerant story teller, one who visited her home regularly. How I adored the "Bremen Town Singers" and "Cinderella."*

*There, I was centre of attention while my mother's life hung in the balance after catching the 1918 plague. Grandma would not allow my mother to be taken to the emergency hospital in the Town Hall. She insisted on looking after my mother herself. From Earl Street I went to school for the first time.*

*In 1921 we found them settled in this quaint old house (with an organ in the parlour) in Maxwell Road, where they eked out their remaining years, among the flotsam and jetsam of a lifetime.*

*My parting memory of this unique couple is a sunny one. On a summer's day in February 1931, we all were in the garden. I was seated by a lilac tree when the leaves began rustling. There was no wind.*

*"Earthquake!" I shouted.*

*"So it is," said the indomitable Charlotte, hastening to the back verandah and seating herself, feet on the earth. "Sit down Frank," she called to Grandfather, patting the floor of the verandah beside her. "Sit down and get the good of it!"*

> *Obligingly, he sat beside her, and I assume – got the good of it.*
> *This was the day of the Napier earthquake where much of that city was reduced to rubble.*
> *There they are still, seated in my heart.*
> *Oki oki ra, e Nana! Oki oki ra e Koro! Oki oki ra korua!*
> *Haere ki te po! Haere! Haere! Haere!*

As for Charlotte's husband, Kate reports, "Francis O'Brian seems to have been a quiet, peaceful gentleman, who was very methodical in the way he worked. My grandmother [Elizabeth O'Brian] recalls him drying between every prong of a fork with his tea-towel." Frank remained a shepherd most of his life—although at some point he must have been employed as a mail carrier, because that was listed as his occupation on the birth certificate of one of his sons. Apparently, Frank could not read or write, raising some question about how he could have delivered mail.

Violet Thomas recalled of her grandfather that "He was very quiet. I only heard him speak once. He used to just sit in a corner and watch everyone. I don't think many people heard him speak, but everyone liked him."

Margaret O'Brian relates a story told to her by her grandmother:

> *When Charlotte first arrived in New Zealand, she worked as barmaid in the Duke of Edinburgh Hotel, Wellington, before heading for Marlborough. Her daughter Anne was born in Picton. One day when visiting the Blenheim A&P Show, she met bluff red haired Irishman John O'Brian, father of several part-Maori children. Hankering for his son Frank to marry other than a Maori, noting Charlotte's pleasant appearance (and predicament possibly), he suggest she marry his son.*
> *She agreed.*

When Kate Mitchell interviewed Margaret Fowlds about the family history, Margaret remembered Francis taking some potato cakes that Charlotte had made, apparently once too often, "and nailing them to the wall"—leading to Kate's wry observation that she must have been "no culinary master."

Margaret Fowlds remembered Frank speaking of the family's Maori connection, which later in life helped to spark a deep interest in her to discover those roots.

Charlotte Robertson O'Brian died on September 12, 1941, in Picton, Marlborough Province, on the South Island of New Zealand. She was eighty-nine years old. Her husband,

Frank O'Brian, had died four years earlier, also at the age of eighty-nine, on December 24, 1937, at Wairau Hospital in Blenheim and was buried at Owaka Cemetery (where Frank's father, John, was also interred).

**Children of Charlotte Umphray Robertson**

V. **Kora Annie O'Brian** was born on July 28, 1876, in New Zealand, the oldest daughter of Charlotte Robertson and Francis O'Brian. She married *Donald McLean* on June 11, 1910. Kora died on October 8, 1910, at the age of thirty-four.

V. **Francis Robert O'Brian** (called "Bob"), first son of Charlotte Umphray Robertson and Francis O'Brian, was born on April 12, 1879, in Blenheim, New Zealand. He married *Margaret O'Shea* on June 8, 1908. They had one daughter. Bob was a casualty of the First World War. At the age of thirty-eight, he was killed in action in Palestine on September 20, 1917. His younger brother Harry had been killed in the fighting on the Gallipoli Peninsula in Turkey two years earlier.

**Child of Francis Robert O'Brian**

VI. **Margaret O'Brian**, born on May 8, 1912, in Saint Helen's Maternity Hospital, Wellington, New Zealand, to Francis Robert O'Brian and Margaret (Maggie) O'Shea. She was only five years old when her father died. She married *John Fowlds*, and they had two sons and two daughters. (*SEE SECTION 6-B.8.*)

V. **Unst Mouat Eliza O'Brian** (called "Maud"), daughter of Charlotte Robertson and Frank O'Brian, was born on March 31, 1881, at Muller Station, near Blenheim, New Zealand. She is remembered as beautiful and stylish as a young woman. On May 20, 1919, at the age of thirty-eight, Maud married her second cousin, *Peter Currie McErchern Georgeson*, a lawyer and a skilled calligraphist. Born in Walls, Shetland, about 1866, Peter was the son of Elizabeth Mouat and James Georgeson, a tailor. Peter had come to New Zealand with his parents and other Georgeson relatives at the age of ten, arriving on the ship *Hurunui*, which landed at Wellington on February 18, 1877, after a journey of ninety days.

Maud and Peter Georgeson lived in Wellington and had one daughter. Maud died on January 29, 1960, in New Zealand, at the age of seventy-eight.

**Child of Unst Mouat Eliza O'Brian**

VI.  <u>**Frances Elizabeth Mouat Georgeson**</u>, born about 1920 in New Zealand. Frances died of tuberculosis at the age of thirty. She was unmarried.

V.  <u>**Agnes Cawthron Scott Robertson O'Brian**</u>, daughter of Charlotte Robertson and Francis O'Brian, was born on August 18, 1883, in Blenheim, New Zealand. Agnes never married. She taught school at Greymouth and at Christchurch on the South Island of New Zealand. According to Kate Mitchell, she was a well-known nanny and children's nurse around Picton and Blenheim.

Agnes was remembered by her niece and namesake, Agnes Lyver Beere, as "a very strong family character, whom everyone respected but didn't always like. She was a domineering, class-conscious woman and ashamed of her half-Maori father, Francis. When he died, she destroyed all his papers, photographs, correspondence and other records in a fire. This is very sad for us now but it has been done, and there is no point in dwelling on it."[195]

Agnes traveled around the world two times and kept in touch with her cousins Greta and Willie (William Hillman) Robertson and other Robertson relatives in America. "On receipt of American news," she wrote to one of her cousins in 1920 (when she was thirty-six), "I always feel like flying back and having a good talk with everybody again. . . . I hope to return to America some day and will not miss a place where a relative is stationed.

"America is a wonderful country," she added. "How grand to think that intoxicating liquor has been thrown from every town. On that account alone, America will dictate to the World. The curse of Great Britain is the intoxicating drink, and must have a weakening influence on the whole nation. In New Zealand we came very close to expulsion of drink and hope in the near future to rid the country of the evil."

Agnes O'Brian died in Wellington, New Zealand on October 4, 1967, at eighty-four years of age.

V.  <u>**Christina O'Brian**</u>, daughter of Charlotte Umphray Robertson and Francis O'Brian, was born on December 30, 1885, in Blenheim, New Zealand. On or about

August 4, 1905, she married *Alfred Collett*, a native of Liverpool, England. They had one daughter, Violet, and lived in Wellington, New Zealand. Christina died in Wellington, New Zealand, on March 31, 1948. She was seventy-two.

### Child of Christina O'Brian

VI. **Violet Elfreda Collett**, born on January 10, 1910, in New Zealand. She married *Leonard Shutler Thomas* (called "Lenn"), who was born on July 28, 1908, the son of Maude Mary Shutler and Harold William Thomas. They lived in Khandallah, near Wellington, New Zealand, and had one daughter, Jennifer. Violet died in May 1997 in New Zealand.

### Child of Violet Elfreda Collett

VII. **Jennifer Thomas**. She married *Kevin Purdom*, and they have two children.

### Children of Jennifer Thomas

VIII. **Marie Purdom**.

VIII. **Stephen Purdom**.

V. **Charles Francis O'Brian** (called "Charlie"), son of Charlotte Robertson and Francis O'Brian, was born on October 24, 1887, in New Zealand. On May 20, 1919, he married *Margaret Cecilia Tandy* in Wellington, New Zealand. They had one daughter. Charlie O'Brian died on April 14, 1945, and his widow died some thirty years later, in May 1975.

### Child of Charles Francis O'Brian

VI. **Patricia Elizabeth O'Brian**, born on November 19, 1926. She married *Andre Franz Schleicher* on December 18, 1954, in Wellington, New Zealand. He is a native of Zurich, Switzerland. They lived in Karori, Wellington, New Zealand, and had two children before they separated.

### Children of Patricia Elizabeth O'Brian

VII. **Franz Andre Schleicher**, born on January 28, 1965.

VII. **Mary Ann Schleicher**, born on September 8, 1967.

V. **Elizabeth Georgeson O'Brian**, youngest daughter of Charlotte Robertson and Francis O'Brian, was born on July 27, 1890, in Blenheim, New Zealand. She died on September 19, 1934, in Wellington. She married *Robert Jamieson Liver* (later spelled "Lyver"), and they had eight children. (SEE SECTION 5-B.3.)

V. **Harry O'Brian**, youngest son of Charlotte Robertson and Francis O'Brian, was born in New Zealand on June 19, 1895. He became a soldier with the Australian and New Zealand Army Corps (ANZAC), which fought valiantly with Allied troops in the First World War. On August 12, 1915, barely past his twentieth birthday. Harry was killed in action at Gallipoli on the Dardanelles strait in Ottoman Turkey. He was unmarried.

## 4-F: ANDREW UMPHRAY ROBERTSON (1854-1915)
### Son of Thomas Rovertson and Margaret Mouat

IV. **Andrew Umphray Robertson**, born at Seafield in Walls, Shetland, on April 10, 1854, was the sixth child of Margaret Mouat and Thomas Robertson (3-C above). He was eighteen years old when his father died in 1873. After staying with his mother in Walls for several years, Andrew immigrated to the United States around 1880 under the sponsorship of his older half-brother, Charles D. Robertson, in Cincinnati, Ohio. He was around twenty-six years old at the time. Charles, by then, was an established lawyer and respected member of the community.

Within a couple of years after settling in America, Andrew married *Esther Bosworth Hillman*. The wedding was held in Cincinnati on Christmas Day in 1881. Esther (called Etta for short) was twenty-three years old, and Andrew was twenty-seven. Born in Crystal Lake, Wisconsin, on November 22, 1858, Etta was the daughter of Cynthia Buck Robertson and her first husband, the late William Hillman, and also was the stepdaughter of Charles D. Robertson.

Esther and Andrew had four sons and four daughters, two of whom died as infants. They spent most of their married life in Cincinnati. An Andrew U. Robertson was listed in the 1885 Williams' Cincinnati Directory as a "shoe maker" and residing at 16 Yungbluth Avenue in the Columbia section of Cincinnati. The next year, and thereafter, he was listed as a clerk with the Union Central Life Insurance Company, a major Cincinnati insurance firm. In 1887, the home address was listed as McDowell Street, Cottage Hill (i.e., College Hill); later, the family moved to Shattuck Avenue, Linwood, a suburb of Cincinnati.

Esther and Andrew Umphray Robertson also lived for a brief period in the mountains of western North Carolina. Andrew's nephew Reuben Robertson had moved there in 1906 to help build and operate a large wood-pulp mill in Canton known as the Champion Fibre Company. Andrew's son William Hillman Robertson worked for Champion in Canton for his entire career, spanning some forty-six years. One of his grandchildren is James Boyd Robertson, a co-author of this family history, and several of Andrew's other descendants still live in the Canton area.

Andrew Umphray Robertson died of heart disease in Cincinnati, Ohio, on April 5, 1915, five days before his sixty-first birthday. After her husband died, Esther resided in a house on Windisch Avenue in Cincinnati that was owned by Charles D. Robertson. When Charles died in 1919, his will left the house to Esther and her daughter Daisy. Esther Hillman Robertson died in Cincinnati on December 27, 1929, at the age of seventy-one.

**Children of Andrew Umphray Robertson**

V. **Charles Andrew Robertson**, oldest son of Esther Hillman and Andrew Umphray Robertson, was born in Cincinnati, Hamilton County, Ohio, on October 7, 1882. He died in Cincinnati on March 20, 1923, at age forty. He was married twice and was the father of seven children. (*SEE SECTION 5-C.3.*)

V. **Marguerite Esther Robertson** (called "Greta") was born in Cincinnati, Hamilton County, Ohio, on July 31, 1884. She was the second child and oldest daughter of Esther Hillman and Andrew Umphray Robertson.

For a time Greta assisted her uncle Charles D. Robertson as a secretary in his law office.[196] Later, around 1935, Greta moved to Columbus, Ohio, where she had a job at the State Office Building, working for the Ohio State Employment Service. On September 25, 1935, she wrote that she was living in "an immense brick house" in a little park "across the street from the old governor's mansion." She commented that she was getting well acquainted in Columbus now and liking it better. "I like my work and the people for whom I work. The position pays well, and there's a life pension attached."[197] Her room was in a beautifully furnished home, where she was treated like a daughter of the family.

Among numerous friends and relatives visiting Greta in Columbus were her niece Elsie Robertson Crowder and Elsie's two small daughters, Phyllis (then age six) and Dorothy (known as "Dodo", then age three), who stayed nearly a week. Greta wrote, "Dodo and Phyllis had a wonderful time playing with the tame squirrels on the lawn of the State Capitol Building. They run right up one, and take nuts from one's hand. The children had never seen any, and were wild about them. . . . Neither of the children wanted to go home, and [they] said that Elsie could go and they would stay with me. . . . Both of the children were very good while here, and Mrs. Chandley (my landlady) wants them to come back."

Greta later moved to Asheville, North Carolina, where she worked for a while at The Norburn Hospital. Greta Robertson never married. She died at the age of sixty-eight in Asheville, Buncombe County, North Carolina, on August 3, 1952, and was buried in nearby Canton in Haywood County.

V. **William Hillman Robertson** (named for his maternal grandfather), second son of Esther Hillman and Andrew Umphray Robertson, was born in Cincinnati, Ohio, on June 21, 1886. He died on March 22, 1963, in Waynesville, North Carolina, at age seventy-six. He married *Sarah Rebekah Leisher*, and they had ten children. (*SEE SECTION 5-C.4.*)

V. **Albert Dewey Robertson**, third son of Esther Hillman and Andrew Umphray Robertson, was born on September 6, 1890, in Cincinnati, Ohio. A career military officer, he played in military bands in various parts of the world. Albert was stationed at Fort Monroe, Virginia, where he died on May 1, 1938, at age forty-seven.

On September 27, 1915, he married *Edith Emma Signor*, who was born on May 25, 1890, in Watertown, New York. They had three daughters. Edith taught grade school and survived for another thirty-one years after Albert passed away. She died in Tampa, Florida, on November 19, 1969.

**Children of Albert Dewey Robertson**

VI. **<u>Alice Ruby Robertson</u>**, eldest daughter of Edith and Albert Robertson, was born on June 11, 1917, in Fort Monroe, Virginia. She married *<u>William Degyansky</u>* of Pennsylvania, a career military officer with the United States Army. They had one son. Alice died at the age of sixty-four in February, 1982. (*SEE SECTION 6-C.13.*)

VI. **<u>Alberta Daisy Robertson</u>**, second daughter of Edith and Albert Robertson, was born on April 18, 1921, in Fort Monroe, Virginia. Bertie married *<u>Carl Joseph Bender</u>*, and they had four sons. (*SEE SECTION 6-C.14.*)

VI. **<u>Edith Emma Robertson</u>**, born on February 7, 1920; never married; she is deceased.

V. **<u>Agnes Georgia Robertson</u>** (called "Daisy"), fifth child of Esther Hillman and Andrew Umphray Robertson, was born in Cincinnati, Hamilton County, Ohio, on June 27, 1892. Daisy suffered severe brain damage as the result of a childhood fall and was institutionalized at the Longview Hospital in Cincinnati until her death at the age of forty-eight. She died on June 1, 1941, after being struck by another inmate at the institution.

V. **<u>Levi Morton Robertson</u>**, fourth son of Esther Hillman and Andrew Umphray Robertson, was born on June 7, 1895, in Cincinnati, Hamilton County, Ohio.[198] Known as Morton, he served as a seaman in the US Navy in World War I. Later, he was an officer with the Cincinnati Police Department, a detective for the Baltimore and Ohio Railroad, and a yard conductor for the Pennsylvania Railroad.

Morton married *<u>Annie Pearl Munsey</u>* on November 8, 1915, in Muncie, Indiana. The daughter of Emma and William Munsey, Pearl was born on October 20, 1897. They had two children, Esther and Bud.

Morton Robertson died in Cincinnati, Ohio, on August 12, 1964, at the age of sixty-nine. Pearl died almost ten years later, on June 23, 1974, at the age of seventy-seven.

**Children of Levi Morton Robertson**

VI. <u>**Esther Lois Robertson**</u>, daughter of Pearl Munsey and Morton Robertson, was born in Cincinnati, Ohio, on November 7, 1924. She first married *Joseph Hancel Hamilton*, with whom she had two children, and after a divorce, married *Richard C. Winkelbach* and adopted another child. (*SEE SECTION 6-C.15.*)

VI. <u>**Albert Jirah Robertson**</u> (called "Bud"), son of Pearl Munsey and Levi Morton Robertson, was born in Cincinnati, Ohio, on March 19, 1927. He married *Laura J. Corell*, and they had three children. He died in November 1996. (*SEE SECTION 6-C.16.*)

V. <u>**Rose Robertson**</u>, seventh child and third daughter of Esther Hillman and Andrew Umphray Robertson, was born in Cincinnati, Hamilton County, Ohio, in 1888. She died the same year.

V. <u>**Violet Robertson**</u>, eighth child and fourth daughter of Esther Hillman and Andrew Umphray Robertson, was born in Cincinnati, Hamilton County, Ohio in 1897. She died the same year.

## 4-G: ROBINA ROBERTSON (1821-1876)
### Daughter of Robert Robertson and Margaret Fraser
### Matriarch of the Jamieson Branches

IV. <u>**Robina Robertson**</u> was born in Elvister, Walls Parish, Shetland, on December 8, 1821, according to the IGI[199]—or on that same date in 1822, according to an entry in a family Bible written by her husband. She was the daughter of Margaret Fraser and Robert Robertson (2-C above).

Robina married *Thomas Gifford Jamieson* on January 27, 1848, in Lerwick, parish of Lerwick & Gulberwick, Shetland. Rev. Peter McGuffie presided at the ceremony. Thomas was born on March 28, 1821, in Brae, Delting Parish, Shetland. He was the son of Janet Robertson and Peter Jamieson (or Jameson), a fisherman and crofter. He became a teacher in Scalloway under the Scottish Society for the Propagation of Christian Knowledge by appointment on April 5,

1844, earning a salary of fifteen pounds per year. It seems he stayed in that position at least until 1853, about five years after his marriage, when his annual salary was eighteen pounds. He apparently left the teaching job to become an Inspector of the Poor, an important job under the Parochial Board. In August 1856, Thomas was listed as an Inspector of the Poor on the birth certificate when a daughter was born in Lerwick. But he must have been looking for greater opportunities elsewhere, as it was not long before he left Shetland altogether, bound for Australia, where gold had been discovered and was actively being mined.

An obituary for the teacher who succeeded Thomas at Scalloway, a Mr. Smith, stated that his predecessor Mr. T. Jamieson had left the position upon appointment as Inspector of the Poor. The rugged conditions under which Thomas must have worked as a schoolteacher in Scalloway are evident from the obituary for Mr. Smith years later, when it was observed that, "When one looked at the small and mean apartment in which [the teacher's] school work was carried on . . . it can only be a matter of surprise that educational results of any value were possible. Such, however, was not the case, for besides children, young men and married men attended school primarily to acquire navigation. As a matter of fact a large number of [Mr. Smith's] students are at the present moment in good positions at home and abroad. . . . Shetland has been much indebted to her old Parochial & Society Teachers!"

The family immigrated to Australia in late 1856 or in 1857 with four children under nine years old—the youngest being not yet two. They must have arrived at or near Melbourne, the capital of Victoria, in the south of Australia, as another child was born in Emerald Hill, not far from Melbourne, in November 1857; five more children were born in Victoria within the next seven years. Thomas obtained employment with the government of Victoria as a schoolteacher, traveling around the gold fields of Victoria; in fact, every time a new child was born, it was at one of the places where gold had been discovered. In 1869, he was listed in a post office directory as schoolmaster at Bubingyong Rural School; later, he was listed as teacher in Corop, Victoria, in 1880, 1884, 1888 – 1889, and 1891 – 1892, meaning that he was over seventy and apparently still teaching.

Robina and Thomas had a total of twelve children born in Shetland and Australia, but six of them died as babies or young children. Their great-great-granddaughter Delphine Slattery writes, "It must have been very hard to make the decision to leave the Shetlands, as they had buried two of their children there. In the end they buried another four at different places in

Victoria. We can only imagine what life must have been like for Robina, having to move around so much with all of those children, and the conditions would not have been easy."

Robina Robertson Jamieson died in Corop, Victoria, on March 23, 1876, age either fifty-three or fifty-four, depending on the year of her birth. Her husband, Thomas, remembered her fondly as "Highly beloved in life and deeply lamented in death." Thomas lived until September 21, 1894, when he died in Victoria, Australia, at the age of seventy-three.

**Children of Robina Robertson**

V. **Mary Elizabeth Irvine Jamieson** was born on December 31, 1848, in Scalloway in Tingwall Parish, Shetland. She married *John Greaves* in Corop, Victoria, in 1873; they had two children. (SEE SECTION 5-B.4.) Mary Elizabeth died on January 22, 1922, in Queensland, Australia, at the age of seventy-three.

V. **Peter Jamieson** was born on April 16, 1850, in Scalloway, Tingwall Parish, Shetland. He married *Louisa Ridgewell* in Stawell, Victoria, Australia, with whom he had five children and, after her death, married *Ellen Lynch* (or *Jenkins)*, with whom he had one more child. (SEE SECTION 5-B.5.) He died in Victoria, Australia, in 1902.

V. **Robert Andrew Jamieson**, born on August 2, 1851, in Scalloway, Tingwall Parish, Shetland; died as an infant on May 4, 1852, in Scalloway.

V. **Robert Andrew Jamieson**, born on May 5, 1853, in Scalloway, Tingwall Parish, Shetland; died in his twelfth year on February 7, 1865, in Victoria, Australia.

V. **Thomas Gifford Jamieson**, born on December 12, 1854, in Tingwall Parish, Shetland. He married *Mariea Elizabeth Schmidt* in 1897 in Natimuk, Victoria, Australia, and they had one child. He was a wheat merchant.

**Child of Thomas Gifford Jamieson**

VI. **Robina Mariea Jamieson**, born in 1898 in Buelah, Victoria, Australia.

V. **Jessie Margaret Jamieson**, born on August 28, 1856, in Lerwick, Shetland; died as an infant on October 7, 1856, in Lerwick.

V. **Elizabeth Jessie Margaret Jamieson**, born on November 28, 1857, in Emerald Hill, Victoria, Australia, not far from Melbourne; she died as an infant on January 26, 1858, in Victoria.

V. **Robina Charlotte Jamieson**, born on January 25, 1859, in Rokewood, Victoria, Australia. She was a school teacher. She married *William James Bishop* in Corop, Victoria, on February 8, 1886. He was born in Fryers Creek, Victoria, in 1857.

V. **Arthur Henry Jamieson** born on November 1, 1860, in Italian Gully, Victoria, Australia; died as a small child on October 1, 1862, in Victoria.

V. **James Jamieson**, born on January 1, 1863, in Staffordshire Reef, Victoria, Australia; died as an infant on July 24, 1863, in Victoria.

V. **William Campbell Wallace Jamieson**, born on October 10, 1864, in Staffordshire Reef, Victoria, Australia. In 1895, he married *Elizabeth Catherine Wright* in Victoria, and they had two children.

### Children of William Campbell Wallace Jamieson

VI. **Helen Robina Jamieson**, born in 1898 in Buelah, Victoria, Australia.

VI. **Kathleen Jamieson**, born in 1901 in Geelong, Victoria, Australia.

V. **Eliza Margaret Jamieson** (called "Lill"), born on May 16, 1869, in Buningyong, Victoria, Australia. She married *Robert Crawford Miller* in Corop, Victoria, on September 6, 1897. Robert was born in 1844 in Saltcoats, Ayrshire, Scotland, and he died in 1914 in Bendigo, Victoria, Australia. She died in 1941 in Fitzroy, Victoria. They had one child.

### Child of Eliza Margaret Jamieson

VI. **Aubrey Gifford Miller**, born in 1900 in Rochester, Victoria, Australia; died on September 10, 1981, in Barter, Victoria. In 1934, he married *Muriel Edith Ethel Symes* in Camberwell, Victoria. They had no children.

### 4-H: JAMES TWATT (1826-1884)
First Son of James Twatt and Andrina Robertson

IV. **James Twatt**, born in 1826, was the son of Andrina Robertson and James Twatt (3-F above). James married *Robina Coutts* on December 4 or December 26, 1850, in Walls Parish.[200] Robina, the daughter of Janet Jacobson and Robert Coutts, was born in Walls on September 4, 1824.[201]

James and Robina apparently joined the Wesleyan Methodist Church, as did a number of Robertson cousins in Walls about that time. Five children born to them have been found in our research. James Twatt died on July 28, 1884, and Robina died in 1891.

**Children of James Twatt**

V. **John Twatt**, born on July 17, 1852, in Voe, Walls Parish, Shetland; baptized by Rev. Farquhar, Wesleyan minister in Walls.[202]

V. **Janet Twatt**, born in 1854, according to SFHS information.

V. **James Twatt**, born on May 21, 1857, in Walls Parish, Shetland.[203] He married *Andrina Cumming*, and they had four children.

**Children of James Twatt**

VI. **Joan Twatt**, born on May 24, 1886.

VI. **Robina Jane Twatt**, born on June 4, 1887.

VI. **James Twatt**, born on February 27, 1888.

VI. **Robert Andrew Twatt**, born on May 6, 1891.

V. **Lillias Twatt**, born on February 9, 1860 in Walls Parish, Shetland.[204] She married *James Laurenson*, who was born on March 19, 1867.

V. **Robina Twatt**, born on October 27, 1862, in Walls Parish, Shetland.[205] She married *Peter Tait*, who was born in 1865. They had five children.

**Children of Robina Twatt**

VI. <u>**William Tait**</u>, born on July 10, 1889.

VI. <u>**Jessie Ann Tait**</u>, born on May 10, 1891.

VI. <u>**Thomas Tait**</u>, born on July 16, 1894.

VI. <u>**James Tait**</u>, born on February 5, 1897. He married *Georgina B. Johnson*, who was born on June 20, 1912. They had four children.

**Children of James Tait**

VII. <u>**Peter Tait**</u>, born in 1945.

VII. <u>**Andrew Tait**</u>, born in 1949. Married *Christine Helen Tait*, and they had four children.

**Children of Andrew Tait**

VIII. <u>**Angela Marie Tait**</u>, born on March 6, 1977.

VIII. <u>**Graham Tait**</u>, born in 1979.

VIII. [Name of child not available.]

VIII. [Name of child not available.]

VII. <u>**Bertha Rose Tait,**</u> married *Laurence William Tait*, who was born on September 25, 1939; they had two children.

**Children of Bertha Rose Tait**

VIII. <u>**Michael Tait**</u>, born in 1974.

VIII. <u>**Richard Tait**</u>, born in 1978.

VII. <u>**James Brian Tait**</u>, born in 1950. He married *Joy Elizabeth Bound*.

VI. <u>**Peter Tait**</u>, married *Ruth Laura Jamieson*.

V. <u>**Andrew Twatt**</u>, born on July 13, 1866, in Walls Parish, Shetland.[206]

## 4-I: THOMAS TWATT (1828-1898)
### Second Son of James Twatt and Andrina Robertson

IV. **Thomas Twatt** was born on February 2, 1828, in Burraland, Shetland, and baptized by Rev. Thomson, minister of the Church of Scotland in Walls Parish. He was the second son of Andrina Robertson and James Twatt (3-F above).

Thomas married *Janet Coutts* on May 22, 1851, in Walls Parish.[207] She was born on January 13, 1830, in Walls Parish, the daughter of Ann Laurenson and William Coutts.[208] They had at least eight children. Thomas died in 1898, and Janet died in 1915.

**Children of Thomas Twatt**

V. **Catherine Twatt**, born on June 4, 1850, in Walls Parish, Shetland.[209] She married *Laurence Fraser*, and they are believed to have had two children, whose names are unknown.

**Children of Catherine Twatt**

VI. [Name of first child not available], born on October 22, 1878.

VI. [Name of second child not available], born on November 16, 1880.

V. **James Twatt**, son of Janet Coutts and Thomas Twatt, was born on September 22, 1853, in Walls Parish, Shetland.[210] He married *Elizabeth (or Eliza) Williamson*, born in 1854. They had two children.

**Children of James Twatt**

VI. **Jemima Twatt**, born in 1879.

VI. **James Twatt**, born in 1881. He lived in Scalloway, Shetland.

V. **Thomas Twatt**, son of Janet Coutts and Thomas Twatt, was born on October 27, 1856, in Walls Parish, Shetland.[211] He married *Catherine Nicolson*, and they had nine children. (*SEE SECTION 5-A.11.*)

V. **Ann Twatt**, daughter of Janet Coutts and Thomas Twatt, was born on May 12, 1859, in Walls Parish, Shetland.[212] She married *James Flaws*, and they had one child.

**Child of Ann Twatt**

VI. **<u>Jemima Ann Twatt</u>**, born on May 25, 1887. According to Beryl Smith, she married *Thomas Laurenson* of Bigton, and they had two children.[213]

**Children of Jemima Ann Twatt**

VII. **<u>James Thomas Laurenson</u>**, born in 1919. He was a casualty of World War II, lost at sea on the *Andorra Star* in 1941.

VII. **<u>Edna Laurenson</u>**. She married *James Leask* of Scalloway, Shetland. They reportedly had two daughters, one of whom is deceased.

V. **<u>William Twatt</u>**, son of Janet Coutts and Thomas Twatt, was born on September 11, 1862, in Walls Parish, Shetland.[214] He married *Barbara Fraser*, who was born in 1859, and they had two children.

**Children of William Twatt**

VI. **<u>Thomas A. Twatt</u>**, born on February 8, 1885.

VI. **<u>John W. Twatt</u>**, born on September 12, 1886.

V. **<u>Jessie Twatt</u>**, daughter of Janet Coutts and Thomas Twatt, was born on April 10, 1865, in Walls Parish, Shetland.[215] She had a daughter, according to information from SFHS, and married a Mr. *Cheyne*.

**Child of Jessie Twatt**

VI. **<u>Catherine Twatt</u>**, born on October 29, 1886. She married *William Raden*, and they lived in Lerwick.

V. **<u>John Twatt</u>**, son of Janet Coutts and Thomas Twatt, was born in 1868, according to SFHS information.

V. **<u>James Twatt</u>**, son of Janet Coutts and Thomas Twatt, was born on April 20, 1872, in Walls Parish, Shetland (the IGI lists the birth of a male child but does not give his name).[216] According to Beryl Smith, he was married in Scalloway and had one son.

**Child of James Twatt**

VI. <u>**James Twatt**</u>.

V. <u>**Andrina Twatt**</u>, daughter of Janet Coutts and Thomas Twatt, was born on August 28, 1873, in Walls Parish, Shetland.[217] She married *James Cutt* in Lerwick, who was born about 1870. They reportedly had six children, but we do not have their names or birth information.

# THE U.K. BRANCHES, GENERATION FIVE

## 5-A.1: CATHERINE ELLEN ROBERTSON (1868-1940)
### Daughter of Thomas Robertson: The Johnson Branches

V. **<u>Catherine Ellen Robertson</u>**, oldest of the seven children of Catherine Thomson and Thomas Robertson (4-A above), was born on November 18, 1868, in Skeld, in Westerskeld, Sandsting & Aithsting Parish, Shetland.[218]

On December 9, 1891, Catherine married *John Johnson*, her cousin. John was the oldest son of Catherine Rose Moodie and her cousin, Captain Peter Johnson, who were married on February 9, 1860, in Sandsound, Sandsting & Aithsting Parish. Their son John Johnson was born on October 24, 1862, in North Huxter in Weisdale Parish, the family home and croft farmed by the Johnson family for almost one hundred years.

Catherine and John were a dashing couple. They left the Shetland Islands to find work in Glasgow on the Scottish mainland, where John eventually became a journeyman shipwright. He worked in the Glasgow shipyards, which at one point were the largest in the world. Economic conditions were very difficult, but Catherine and John raised ten children. Their daughter Williamina remembered her mother bringing up the family on very little money but always having an open door for people worse off than herself. "She was a lovely lady, a real 'lady' in the purest sense," Williamina's daughter Alice Drury recalls of her grandmother. "She was tall and stately, very handsome and with a lovely soft voice. I can see her now, wearing her long Queen Mary-type coat with a large fur collar. I used to think she *was* Queen Mary when I was little."

John Johnson died at the age of fifty-nine on January 11, 1927, in Glasgow. The cause of death was listed as myelogenous leukemia. Catherine died on March 10, 1941, at age seventy-two, at the family home on Govan Road in Glasgow, Scotland.

**Children of Catherine Ellen Robertson**

VI. <u>**Catherine Ellen Johnson**</u>, (called "Kate"), daughter of Catherine Robertson and John Johnson, was born on April 28, 1892. "This Catherine was a great beauty," her niece Alice McAdam Drury recalled. "She was the 'Sleeping Beauty' on the Ovaltine tins and 'Nell Gwynn' on Chiver's Marmalade." Kate Johnson married a Mr. *Robin*, and they had one son. She died about 1955.

**Child of Catherine Ellen Johnson**

VII. <u>**Raymond Johnson Robin**</u>, born in 1921. According to family members, he immigrated to Australia as a young man, later moved to South Africa and England, and is believed to be deceased. He reportedly married and had a son.

**Child of Raymond Johnson Robin**

VIII. <u>**Raymond Robin**</u>.

VI. <u>**Isabella Margaret Johnson**</u> (called "Isa") was born in 1894, the second daughter of Catherine Robertson and John Johnson. She married *Richard McAdam*, whose brother Stephen became the husband of Isa's younger sister, Williamina. Richard and Isa had at least eight children.

**Children of Isabella Margaret Johnson**

VII. <u>**James McAdam**</u>, son of Isabella Johnson and Richard McAdam. As a young man, he immigrated to Tasmania, Australia, for reasons of health, and settled in Hobart.

VII. <u>**Catherine McAdam**</u>, daughter of Isabella Johnson and Richard McAdam. She married *James Sprint*. They had three children and resided in Glasgow, Scotland.

**Children of Catherine McAdam**

VIII. <u>**Rosemary Sprint**</u>. She may have immigrated to Canada.

VIII. <u>**Isabel Sprint**</u>. Said to live in Glasgow.

VIII. <u>**James Sprint**</u>. Also possibly living in Glasgow.

VII. **John McAdam**, son of Isabella Johnson and Richard McAdam, born about 1929. He married *Cathie* (whose maiden name we do not have), and they reportedly had twin daughters.

### Children of John McAdam

VIII. [Name of first child not available.]

VIII. [Name of second child not available.]

VII. **Isobel McAdam**, daughter of Isabella Johnson and Richard McAdam. She married *Jack Bulloch*. They reportedly had two sons and a daughter and lived in Drumchapel, Glasgow, Scotland.

### Children of Isobel McAdam

VIII. [Name of first child not available.]

VIII. [Name of second child not available.]

VIII. [Name of third child not available.]

VII. **Richard McAdam**, son of Isabella Johnson and Richard McAdam. Married *Nan*, whose maiden name is unavailable.

VII. **David McAdam**, son of Isabella Johnson and Richard McAdam, born about 1934. Unmarried, he lives in Glasgow.

VII. **Stephen McAdam**, son of Isabella Johnson and Richard McAdam and twin brother of Wilson. He married *Joan*, whose maiden name is unavailable.

VII. **Wilson McAdam**, a twin son of Isabella Johnson and Richard McAdam. He married *Ann*, whose maiden name we have not found. Said to be a resident of Strathaven in Lanarkshire, Scotland.

VI. **Williamina Alice Johnson**, third daughter of Catherine Robertson and John Johnson, was born on June 1, 1896, in Glasgow, Scotland. She married *Stephen McAdam*, the brother of her sister Isabella's husband, and they were the parents of three sons and a daughter. Williamina died on April 9, 1970, in Gourock, Scotland. (*SEE SECTION 6-A.1.*)

VI. **Peter John Johnson**, son of Catherine Robertson and John Johnson, was born in 1898. He married *Isabella McShane*, and they had two children.

**Children of Peter John Johnson**

> VII. **Catherine Johnson**.

> VII. **Peter Johnson**.

VI. **John James Johnson**, son of Catherine Robertson and John Johnson, was born in 1900. He married *Molly*, and they had two children. A seaman, John was lost at sea and drowned.

**Children of John James Johnson**

> VII. **John Johnson**.

> VII. **Mary Johnson**, married and divorced a Mr. *Abraham*.

VI. **Christina Agnes Johnson**, fourth daughter of Catherine Robertson and John Johnson, was born in 1902. She spent much of her youth looking after her mother and her unmarried brother Robert. About 1950, she married *George Wilson*. They had no children, and both are deceased.

VI. **Thomasina Mary Johnson** (called "Ina"), sixth daughter of Catherine Robertson and John Johnson, was born in 1905. She married *Thomas Fraser*, and they had three children.

**Children of Thomasina Johnson**

> VII. **Rose Fraser**. She died as a young child.

> VII. **Stanley Fraser**.

> VII. **John Fraser** (called "Jackie"). Lived in Glasgow, Scotland.

VI. **Jemima Jean Johnson** (called "Jean"), fifth daughter of Catherine Robertson and John Johnson, was born on February 24, 1908, in Glasgow, Scotland. She married *Alexander Picken MacLachlan*, who was born in Ayrshire, Scotland, on Christmas Day 1906. They lived in Glasgow and had one daughter and two sons. Jean died in Glasgow in 1994.

**Children of Jemima Jean Johnson**

VII. <u>**James MacLachlan**</u>, born in Glasgow, Scotland, on September 15, 1929. He is unmarried and lives in Carrdonald, a suburb of Glasgow.

VII. <u>**Irene Fiona MacLachlan**</u>, born in 1934. She married *Brian Edwin Jones*, and they had one son. Irene lives in Shrewsbury, Shropshire, England. Brian, who served as Chief Clerk of Works for Shrewsbury, died there after a long struggle with cancer on April 2, 1999.

**Child of Irene Fiona MacLachlan**

VIII. <u>**Allister David Jones**</u>, born on November 28, 1954, in Glasgow, Scotland. He died in December 1994.

VII. <u>**David Jenkins MacLachlan**</u>, born on October 23, 1939, in Glasgow, Scotland. Now retired, he was a commissioned officer in the merchant navy and later worked for Rolls-Royce. In December 1950, in Glasgow, he married *Margaret Bell*, who was born on January 1, 1939. They have two sons and two daughters and reside in Moss Park, a suburb of Glasgow.

**Children of David Jenkins MacLachlan**

VIII. <u>**David Jenkins MacLachlan**</u>.

VIII. <u>**Steven James MacLachlan**</u>.

VIII. <u>**Lynda MacLachlan**</u>.

VIII. <u>**Lorraine MacLachlan**</u>.

VI. <u>**Robert David Johnson**</u>, son of Catherine Robertson and John Johnson, was born in 1910. Unmarried, he died without issue.

VI. <u>**Joseph Magnus Johnson**</u>, youngest of the ten children of Catherine Robertson and John Johnson, was born on July 12, 1912, in Govan, near Glasgow in Lanarkshire, Scotland. He married *Martha McKie*, and they had two sons. Joseph and his family immigrated to New Zealand, where Joseph died at the age of sixty-five in December 1977. (*SEE SECTION 6-B.14.*)

## 5-A.2: WILLIAMINA THOMSON ROBERTSON (1873-19??)
### Daughter of Thomas Robertson: The Thomson branch

V. **<u>Williamina Thomson Robertson</u>**, second daughter of Catherine Thomson and Thomas Robertson (4-A above), was born on September 1, 1873, in Sandsting & Aithsting Parish, Shetland.[219]

Williamina married her first cousin, *Robert Thomson*, and they had three children. We have not found information concerning her death.

**Children of Williamina Thomson Robertson**

VI. **<u>Ursula Catherine Thomson</u>**, born on March 6, 1906; she died on May 11, 1916, only ten years old.

VI. **<u>Williamina Alice Thomson</u>** (called "Alice"), born on August 18, 1908. She never married and lived in Roeness, Reawick, in Shetland.

VI. **<u>James Robert Thomson</u>** (called "Bobby"), born in Shetland on January 20, 1911. He never married. He shared a home with his sister Alice in Roeness, Reawick, Shetland. He died at home on May 8, 1998, aged eighty-seven.

VI. **<u>Thomas Thomson</u>**, born on January 9, 1914. He married *Mabel Ann Umphray*, who was born on October 4, 1903, daughter of Mary Peterson and James Umphray of Reawick, Shetland. They had one child. Thomas worked as a joiner. He died on August 19, 1991, age seventy-seven.

**Child of Thomas Thomson**

VII. **<u>Emma Williamina Mary Thomson</u>**, born on September 23, 1941. On April 23, 1959, she married *David Watt* of Lerwick, Shetland. They had three children and divorced in April 1985. She then married *Lubin Poulton* on September 8, 1985. Born on November 20, 1949, he is a computer operator.

**Children of Emma Williamina Mary Thomson**

VIII. **<u>Thomas Alexander Watt</u>**, son of Emma Thomson and David Watt, was born on August 11, 1959. He works as a museum curator and lives in Sandwick, Shetland.

VIII. **Alison Mabel Watt**, daughter of Emma Thomson and David Watt, was born on October 28, 1960. She married *John Warham* on May 26, 1990. They live in Liverpool, England, where John works as a construction area manager. They have two children.

**Children of Alison Mabel Watt**

IX. **Matthew John Warham**, born on November 21, 1991.

IX. **Danielle Amy Warham**, born on September 30, 1996.

VIII. **Robert James Watt**, son of Emma Thomson and David Watt, was born on May 3, 1962. On May 23, 1986, Bobby married *Marion Beesly*, and they had one child. Marion died on February 5, 1990. Bobby married *Tracy Louise Cole* on July 12, 1997, at the English Church in Lerwick. He works as an offshore wire line operator.

**Children of Robert James Watt**

IX. **Jake Watt**, born on July 2, 1989.

## 5-A.3: THOMAS THOMSON ROBERTSON (1876-1909)
### Son of Thomas Robertson

V. **Thomas Thomson Robertson**, born on April 20, 1876, was a son of Catherine Thomson and Thomas Robertson (4-A above). He worked as a merchant seaman.

Thomas married *Andrina Johnson*, who was born on May 8, 1880. Her parents were Elizabeth Thompson (who was born on September 23, 1859, and died in 1942 in Lerwick, Shetland; daughter of Catherine Johnson and James Thompson), and George Johnson, a grocer, of Westerwick, Sandsting, Shetland. Andrina and Thomas lived in Westerwick in Sandsting and had two children.

Thomas Robertson died at the age of thirty-three on December 29, 1909, in Rochester, Kent, England. He was killed in an accident while employed by William Cary & Son, Ltd., which, after protracted legal dispute, paid a sum in compensation to his survivors. His death meant very hard times and severe financial deprivation for the young family, which relocated to Stove in Walls Parish in 1910. Despite living in near poverty, the family was close and supportive. Andrina was remembered as a capable, resolute, and cheerful woman, and the household was a happy and hospitable one. She died about 1948 after a long illness. The older son became a merchant seaman like his father. The quiet, reserved, younger son pursued academic interests and became a teacher, as well as Shetland's premier poet in the ancient dialect of the islands.

**Children of Thomas Thomson Robertson**

VI. **George William Johnston Robertson** was born on October 29, 1904, in Westerwick, Sandsting Parish, Shetland; he died at the age of seventy-eight on July 24, 1983, in Waterloo, Walls Parish, Shetland. George married *Maggie Dalziel*, and they had five children. (*SEE SECTION 6-A.2.*)

VI. **Thomas Alexander Robertson** was born on March 6, 1909, in Westerwick Village, in Skeld, in Sandsting Parish, Shetland. He was raised in Walls following the death of his father when Alex was only six months old. The family had to struggle to survive, but Alex overcame these severe financial deprivations to achieve an outstanding education and become a distinguished poet, linguist, and teacher.

By nature the young Alex Robertson was a very shy and reserved boy who often took refuge in silence. After completing studies at the Happy Hansel school in Walls, Alex went off to the Anderson Educational Institute in Lerwick, a transition that was very difficult for him. A friend later recalled that Alex was so homesick that he had to return to Walls during his first term "and only returned, after what must have been a fierce inner struggle, at the beginning of the second term. With his first big hurdle surmounted, he made rapid headway and soon began to show his ability both in the classroom and on the playing field." In his fourth year of school in Lerwick, 1926 – 1927, Alex was awarded the coveted prize as the school's best scholar-athlete. He was especially skilled in the high jump and long jump events, in which he established several records, and was an accomplished swimmer. Most of Alex Robertson's free time during these years were spent rambling around the beloved precincts of Walls (Waas) with a lifelong friend, who later reminisced:

*At weekends we used to go for long walks around the shores of the voe. On such walks Alex rarely conversed beyond saying "Yes" or "No," "Look at dat," or "Does du see yun?" He was intensely observant and loved to explore the countryside in detail. It all had great meaning for him. I think we investigated every old building and watermill around Waas. We tramped through the hills and visited most of the lochs which abound on the west side. I still recall an occasion, referred to by Alex in one of his poems, when we went to see the water-lillies in Lunga Water. The best blooms were farthest out and we found that by using the lily-pads as stepping stones we were able to get out to them. The hazards of our situation did not occur to either of us.*

Continuing in his quest for higher education, Alex Robertson was awarded a master of arts by Edinburgh University in 1932, where he concentrated in English and history. Although he hoped to become a teacher, no positions were then available in Shetland, and he had to work in a variety of temporary jobs for five years after getting his degree. Finally, in 1937, he was able to get a job teaching English and history at Lerwick Central School, later known as Anderson High School, and he stayed there until his retirement in 1970.

At the age of forty-four, Alex married <u>*Martha Andrew*</u> (called "Pat") on New Year's Eve 1953, in Edinburgh, Scotland. Pat, born in August, 1908, was the daughter of the late Rev. Robert Andrew, who served as minister of the Church of Scotland in Walls Parish for forty years. She also grew up in Walls and, like Alex, attended the school there called Happy Hansel. Later, they attended the same school in Lerwick, but they were not romantically linked in those school years, and Pat went on to pursue a civil service career away from Shetland. It was not until their middle years that they came back together, got to know each other well, and decided to marry, establishing a deep and abiding bond of companionship and collaboration. Pat and Alex had no children.

Writing under the pen name "Vagaland," Alex Robertson was a renowned poet both in the Shetland dialect and in English. He was a regular contributor to *The New Shetlander*, which first appeared shortly after World War II, and he served on the editorial committee of that periodical. John J. Graham, an editor of *The New Shetlander*, wrote of Vagaland's poetry that, "His constant passion for maintaining the local tradition . . . was no mere antiquarian indulgence. It was fixed by a real conviction, founded on personal experience, that the past revealed true insights into the art of living; that out of the lives of ordinary folk engaged in their daily tasks and sustained by the warmth of close community ties, there emerged basic truths about the human situation. And his poems were evocations of that life and affirmations of those truths."

Another admirer wrote, "The concrete word, the precise phrase, the exact observation, the clear image are, with richness of imagination and purity of diction, the stones and mortar of the poet; and we find them constantly in the Vagaland poems. In the simplest words, such as might be used by any countryman, T.A. Robertson could evoke the landscape of Shetland so intensely that the nostrils twitched with its remembered fragrance."

An example is one of the poems he wrote as an anniversary present for his wife each New Year's Eve:

### *WIDWICK*

*The wind-blown mist drove in o'er widwick,*
  *Over the strand where wreckage lay –*
*Planks and logs and spars and battens,*
  *Storm-spoil gathered many a day.*

*Nothing stirred in the lonely hollow*
  *But a heron, startled into flight;*
*The great grey crag rose high above us,*
  *Looming up in the misty light.*

*We lay on the green turf there and rested,*
  *Watching the fitful sunlight shine,*
*And climbed to look for garnets, sprinkled*
  *Over the rock like drops of wine.*

*And summer winds that blow o'er Houlland*
  *Will see us come again, us three,*
*Down the sheep-track into Widwick,*
  *You and the Susie dog and me.*

In collaboration with his friend John Graham, Alex Robertson prepared *Grammar and Usage of the Shetland Dialect* in 1952, *Nordern Lichts—An Anthology of Shetland Verse and Prose,* in 1964, and several volumes of *Shetland Folk Life.* Alex also served for almost three decades as secretary of the Shetland Folk Society. He and Pat edited a book of traditional Shetland folk songs, titled *Da Sangs at A'll Sing ta Dee,* which was published the month before his death in 1973. Two volumes of his poetry were published during his lifetime, *Laeves fae Vagaland,* in 1952, and *Mae Laeves fae Vagaland,* in 1965. A posthumous work compiled and edited by Pat Robertson, *The Collected Poems of Vagaland,* was published by the Shetland Times, Ltd. In 1975 and reprinted in 1980, but is now out of print.

Pat regrets that her husband's teaching responsibilities left him so little time to pursue his poetic muse. "Over a long period of years, classes were abnormally large, often over forty in number, and, with homework as the rule, there was always a mass of correcting work to be done. At examination time, and, indeed, frequently throughout the school term, our sitting-room floor would of an evening be strewn with papers! There was thus less time than one could have wished for him to pursue private interests and develop his undoubted gifts."

Pat Robertson was herself a writer, a linguist, and an expert on Shetland dialect. A book written by her in the late 1970s, titled *Night-Scented Stock in Bloom?,* was published in 1993 by The Pentland Press Ltd. In Durham, England. This most interesting work grew from Pat's fascination with paranormal coincidences she encountered in her life, which she believed may provide clues to the unseen world. Pat commented that, "The book still sells a few copies now and then, but there is an unwillingness among the scientifically minded to see any significance in 'coincidences,' and it may be that in this world we will never know their relevance!" Pat's book also includes a number of vivid thoughts and memories about her husband, as well as her own emotional struggles.

Of Vagaland and the gift of his work, she recalled, "His poetry—mostly in the Shetland dialect—from my first reading of it, after we became engaged in 1952, seemed to proceed from perceptual gifts not available to more ordinary mortals. I remember that on reading those early manuscripts, I was moved to tears, which psychiatry might possibly attribute to the fact that I was at that time on the verge of a very severe breakdown. But my own unaltered view is that I was given, through the poetry, an insight into the spiritual quality of the mind behind it."

Vagaland's widow thought his Scottish heritage had an important influence in the development of his poetic style and sensibility. Pat wrote:

> It is, perhaps, not generally known that on his father's side Vagaland (T.A. Robertson) was of Scottish descent, his antecedents, as members of the Robertson clan (Clan Donnachaidh), being understood to have fought at Culloden and escaped northwards. Because of the old custom through many generations of giving patronymic surnames in Shetland, the tracing of ancestry is no easy matter, but relatives in England and America are still pursuing lines of inquiry. In Scotland's Magazine, April 1966, A.D. Mackie wrote: "the language in which Robertson writes is a mixture of standard Scots and Norn. The Scots in it is, in fact, closely akin to the dialect of Perthshire. . . ." I have often felt that Vagaland's lyrical gift was to a great extent Scottish. Much of it had something of the quality of the historical ballads of which he was so fond.

Vagaland's poems and songs are quoted in almost every chapter of Pat's book. One of these, possibly his last, is a poem named for the flowers that Alex Robertson raised in his garden during his final illness during 1973:

## NIGHT-SCENTED STOCK

On soundless wings the voyagers of night-time
Who need no guiding light upon their way
Steer through uncharted air to find a haven
    Of rest at dusk of day.

The scent of flowers, by unseen pathways carried,
Has brought them safely through a deep of gloom,
To find, within the quiet of the garden,
    Night-scented stock in bloom.

When we are growing old, and deepening shadows
Blot out the path where we have wandered far,
When we know not the place to which we journey,
    Unlit by moon or star;

The thoughts of others who have truly loved us
May flow towards us on the channelled air,
Guiding us to a place beyond the darkness,
To find a garden there.

Thomas Alexander Robertson died on December 29, 1973, in Lerwick, Shetland. He was sixty-four. A former headmaster and warm friend gave this tribute:

*I had the privilege during most of his teaching career of being able to assess and appreciate the many qualities that Mr. Robertson had, both as a teacher and as a person. I think I am safe in saying that it would be very hard to find anywhere a person or a teacher who came to his work in such a conscientious spirit, who gave sympathetic consideration to the children under his charge, and who gave such a loyalty both to this authority, to the school and to his colleagues. His overriding concern was always the welfare and progress of his pupils. The community will remember Mr. Robertson as one of Shetland's most outstanding poets. His love of Shetland, his profound knowledge of the Shetland dialect, his awareness of the beauties of nature, and of nature in all its moods, is very ably expressed and vividly illustrated in all his poems.*

## 5-A.4: JAMES GREIG ROBERTSON (1880-1974)
### Son of Thomas Robertson

V. **James Greig Robertson** was born on October 13, 1880, in Sandsting Parish, Shetland. He was the son of Catherine Thomson and Thomas Robertson of Westerskeld (4-A above). He was the second of our Robertsons to bear the same name, as an earlier James Greig Robertson (whose father was also named Thomas) was born in Walls Parish some seventy-four years earlier (3-D above).

James G. Robertson married *Williamina Arthurson* on March 13, 1913. She was born on June 19, 1879, and died on November 15, 1952. They lived in Toogs in Reawick, Shetland, and they had three children. James died in the summer of 1974, age ninety-three.

**Children of James Greig Robertson**

VI. **James Greig Robertson**, born on May 13, 1914, in Shetland. He never married and stayed with his parents until their deaths. James died on March 8, 1980, at the age of sixty-five.

VI. **John Arthur Robertson**, born on July 12, 1919, in Shetland. He was a merchant seaman and never married. He died on February 12, 1976, age fifty-six.

VI. **Lillian Robertson**, born on July 9, 1925. She married *Laurence Tait* of Aith, Sandsting & Aithsting Parish, Shetland, on August 6, 1952. They lived in Dykeside, Aith, and had two daughters. Lillian died on October 20, 1978. She was fifty-three.

**Children of Lillian Robertson**

VII. **Wilma Tait**, born on April 15, 1953. She married *Allan Moncrieff*, son of James Moncrieff, on September 2, 1983. They reside in Tumlin, Bixter, Shetland, and have one daughter. Allan works with his brother Jim in the agricultural fencing business.

**Child of Wilma Tait**

VIII. **Kerry Moncrieff**, born on September 29, 1984, in Lerwick, Shetland.

VII. **Lorna Tait**, born on December 31, 1954. On February 11, 1977, she married *James Moncrieff*, son of James Moncrieff, whose brother Allan later married Lorna's older sister, Wilma. Jim and his brother have a contracting business specializing in agricultural fencing. Lorna and Jim have four children and live in Southtown, Aith, Shetland.

**Children of Lorna Tait**

VIII. **Lewis Moncrieff**, born on December 6, 1977, in Lerwick, Shetland.

VIII. **Lillian Moncrieff**, born on November 4, 1978, in Lerwick, Shetland.

VIII. **<u>Jon Moncrieff</u>**, born on May 24, 1980, in Lerwick, Shetland.

VIII. **<u>Mhari Moncrieff</u>**, born on April 14, 1983, in Lerwick, Shetland.

## 5-A.5: ALEXANDER INKSTER ROBERTSON (1883-1965)
### Son of Thomas Robertson

V. **<u>Alexander Inkster Robertson</u>**, son of Catherine Thomson and Thomas Robertson (4-A above), was born on August 22, 1883, in Westerskeld, Sandsting & Aithsting Parish, Shetland. He married *Margaret Catherine Anderson* (called "Maggie") of Westerskeld, who was born on November 25, 1885, and they had two children. She passed away in 1946. Alexander died almost twenty years later, in 1965, approximately eighty-one years of age.

**Children of Alexander Inkster Robertson**

VI. **<u>Williamina Ann Robertson</u>** (called "Annie"), oldest child of Maggie Anderson and Alexander Inkster Robertson, was born on December 23, 1909, in Westerskeld, Sandsting Parish, Shetland. In 1937, Annie married *John William Cheyne*, who was born on March 19, 1907, in Skeld, Shetland, the son of Jemima Goodlad and Joseph Cheyne. John worked as a merchant seaman, and they had a son and a daughter. Annie died in 1980 at the age of seventy.

**Children of Annie Robertson**

VII. **<u>John Cheyne</u>**, born on September 7, 1938, in Skeld, Shetland. He died on June 10, 1997. He was unmarried and lived with his father in Westerskeld.

VII. **<u>Irene Cheyne</u>**, born on July 20, 1941, in Skeld, Shetland. She worked in Edinburgh, Scotland, for a while and married *William Young* there on September 10, 1966. They have three daughters. The family moved back to Shetland in the early 1980s and now live in Skeld. Irene worked as a salmon processor at the Shetland Smokehouse with her second cousin Margaret Ridland. Bill was a postman.

**Children of Irene Cheyne**

VIII. <u>**Avril Young**</u>, born on November 2, 1967, in Edinburgh, Scotland. On September 7, 1990, in Walls, Shetland, she married *Brian Isbister*, who was born on March 20, 1965. They have two sons. Brian works as a secretary, and Avril is at home with the children.

**Children of Avril Young**

IX. <u>**Magnus Isbister**</u>, born on January 20, 1993, in Lerwick, Shetland.

IX. <u>**Robert Isbister**</u>, born on October 30, 1995, in Lerwick, Shetland.

VIII. <u>**Fiona Young**</u>, second daughter of Irene Cheyne and William Young, was born on January 3, 1970, in Edinburgh, Scotland. She works as a shop assistant in Aberdeen, Scotland.

VIII. <u>**Gillian Young**</u>, third daughter of Irene Cheyne and William Young, was born on May 3, 1973, in Edinburgh, Scotland. On September 6, 1997, in Aberdeen, Scotland, Gillian married *Graham Henry*, who was born on January 25, 1973. She has returned to Shetland and works as a dental nurse.

VI. <u>**Alexander Inkster Robertson**</u>, second child of Maggie Anderson and Alexander Inkster Robertson, was born on October 22, 1919, in Westerskeld, Sandsting Parish, Shetland. In 1958, he married *Denise Broderick* in Sunderland, County Durham, in the northeastern part of England. They had one son. Alexander died in 1970, approximately fifty years old.

**Child of Alexander Inkster Robertson**

VII. <u>**Mark Robertson**</u>, born on March 13, 1962, in Sunderland, County Durham, England. Unmarried, he lives at home in Sunderland with his mother, Denise.

## 5-A.6: Margaret Robertson (1884-1966)
### Daughter of Thomas Robertson: A Williamson Branch

V. **Margaret Robertson** (called "Maggie") was born on October 5, 1884, in West Houlland, Walls Parish, Shetland. She was the oldest daughter of Alice Jamieson and Thomas Robertson (3-B above). A single parent with a son born in 1905, Margaret became the housekeeper for her father's cousin James David Robertson (3-C below), who then lived in Riskaness in Walls Parish.

On January 1, 1914, Maggie married *Magnus Williamson* in Riskaness. (The record of their marriage is in the script of James David Robertson, who was the civil registrar for Walls.) Magnus was born on March 1, 1882, in Stensland, Walls Parish, son of Christian Williamson. Margaret and Magnus had six children in addition to raising her first child.

Like many of our Robertsons, Maggie was very interested in family history. In July 1935, she met Reuben B. Robertson (5-C.2 below) on his visit to Shetland. They continued to exchange cordial letters after the visit, and she sent Reuben a photograph of his paternal grandfather, Thomas Robertson. "I had treasured these old photos," Maggie wrote, "as I had wanted photos of the Clan Robertson as far back as I could trace them. So when you get a duplicate or painting, will you kindly send the photo back to me, as I value the same very greatly." On the back of the picture of Thomas were some notes that Reuben's mother, Cynthia Robertson, had made. Cynthia, according to Margaret, "was greatly interested in Shetland, and wrote a book about her visit, part of which I have read. But Mr. J.D. Robertson mutilated the same, by taking out all the most personal pages. It was very interesting." Neither the book nor Margaret's collection of photos have been found.

Maggie kept in touch with our Robertsons in New Zealand. She wrote to Reuben Robertson in 1935, "I have not had any letters from the friends in New Zealand, as the only two who wrote me are now laid to rest, Mrs. Cheyne and Mrs. Georgeson. The latter being very kind, all these long years, and many a time sent me a pound in her letters. But they are gathering home, one by one. And I trust we will all meet again when our little bit of work is over." A few months later, she wrote, "I am thankful I got a letter from the friends in New Zealand with particulars about Mrs. Georgeson's death. I had been worrying about not hearing from them. But they have been too upset to write letters. So many deaths crowded into one year, and now there's just Mrs. Thomson and Mrs. O'Brian left.[220]

Maggie continued living in the house in Riskaness long after James D. Robertson died. Her daughter-in-law Kathleen Williamson is still living there. Margaret Robertson Williamson died in Lerwick on July 27, 1966. She was eighty-one.

## Children of Margaret Robertson

VI. **John Thomas Robertson**, son of Margaret Robertson, was born on November 3, 1905, in Walls Parish, Shetland. He immigrated to New Zealand as a young man of nineteen. Johnny married *Myrtle Irene Cook* of Christchurch, and they had three children. (SEE SECTION 6-B.15.)

VI. **Christina Williamson** (called "Tina") was born in 1915 in Riskaness in Walls Parish, Shetland, the first daughter of Margaret Robertson and Magnus Williamson. In 1933, she married *Andrew Brown*, who was born about 1913. They had three children. Tina resides in Germatwatt, near the village of Walls.

### Children of Christina Williamson

VII. **Margaret Brown**, born about 1933 in Walls Parish, Shetland. She married *James Thomas Manson* on August 4, 1952, at the Church of Scotland in Sand. Her husband was born on April 23, 1931. They have two children.

### Children of Margaret Brown

VIII. **Catherine Manson**, born in Lerwick, Shetland, in 1953. She married *Oliver Henry*.

VIII. **James Manson**, born in Lerwick, Shetland, in 1955.

VII. **Freda Brown**, born in 1936 in Germatwatt, Walls Parish, Shetland. On July 1, 1959, she married *Norman James Irvine* at the Manse of St. Paul's Church in Walls. He was born in 1938 in Bardister, Walls Parish, Shetland. They have three children.

### Children of Freda Brown

VIII. **Norma Irvine**, born after 1959.

VIII. **Margaret Irvine**, born after 1961.

VIII. **Elizabeth Catherine Irvine**, born on June 10 in Hillcrest, Bardney, Lincoln, England.

VII. **Christopher Brown**, born on May 31, 1954.

VI. **Margaret Alice Williamson**, second daughter of Margaret Robertson and Magnus Williamson, was born on July 10, 1917, in Riskaness in Walls Parish, Shetland. She married *Peter Twatt* on November 15, 1950, in the Congregational Church Manse in Lerwick. Peter was born in 1909 at Happy Hansel in Walls Parish, where they lived and raised their daughter. Margaret died at Happy Hansel on June 25, 1973.

**Children of Margaret Alice Williamson**

VII. **Patricia Rose Margaret Twatt**, born in 1951 at Happy Hansel in Walls Parish, Shetland. She married *Alistair James Couper* on September 4, 1970, at St. Paul's Manse in Walls. He was born in Bevlah, Westerskeld, Shetland. They have four daughters.

**Children of Patricia Rose Margaret Twatt**

VIII. **Angela Couper**, born in 1973 in Walls, Shetland. She married *Ian Anderson*, who was born in Gonforth, Delting, Shetland. They have two daughters.

**Children of Angela Couper**

IX. **Amy Anderson**, born in 1993.

IX. **Iona Anderson**, born in 1997.

VIII. **Leanne Couper**, born in 1975. On August 18, 1995, Leanne married *John Phillip Johnson* in the Methodist Chapel in Westerskeld in Sandsting. He was born in Skeld, Sandsting, Shetland. They have one child.

**Child of Leanne Couper**

IX. **Garry Johnson**, born in 1998.

VIII.  **Pauline Couper**, born in 1978.

VIII.  **Kirsten Couper**, born in 1983.

VI.  **Jemima Ann Williamson** (called "Mimie"), third daughter of Margaret Robertson and Magnus Williamson, was born after 1920 in Riskaness in Walls Parish, Shetland. She married *William Gilbert Scott* on February 6, 1942, in the Congregational Church in Walls. Her husband was born in Sand, Shetland, on June 15, 1908, and died on March 6, 1989. They had three children.

### Children of Jemima Ann Williamson

VII.  **James Magnus Scott**. Married *Josephine*, whose maiden name is unavailable; they had three children.

### Children of James Magnus Scott

VIII.  **Karl Scott**.

VIII.  **Gary Scott**.

VIII.  **Richard Scott**.

VII.  **Peter Scott**. Married *Alice* (whose maiden name is unavailable); they had three children.

### Children of Peter Scott

VIII.  **Heather Scott**, born after 1966.

VIII.  **Phillip Scott**, born after 1968.

VIII.  **Lynn Scott**, born after 1970.

VII.  **Mary Ann Scott**. She married *William Morrison*.

VI.  **Magnus Arthur Williamson**, son of Margaret Robertson and Magnus Williamson, was born on July 8, 1919, in Riskaness in Walls Parish, Shetland. He married *Kathleen Gribbin*, who was born in South Shields, Durham, England. They were married on June 2, 1941, in South Shields, and adopted a daughter. Magnus died about 1984 as a result of an automobile accident, and his widow is still living in Riskaness.

**Child of Magnus Arthur Williamson**

VII. **Laureen Williamson**, born after 1945. She married *Thomas Andrew Jamieson*. He was born in Burra, one of the Shetland Islands off the mainland near Scalloway, and is involved in commercial fishing. They have three children.

**Children of Laureen Williamson**

VIII. **Magnus Jamieson**.

VIII. **Callum Jamieson**.

VIII. **Josie Jamieson**.

VI. **Martin Edward Williamson**, born on August 23, 1927, in Lerwick, Shetland, was the second son of Margaret Robertson and Magnus Williamson. He was married on May 10, 1951, in Walls to *Laura Helen Jamieson*. Born on Christmas Eve 1933, in Mucklure in Walls Parish, Shetland, she is the daughter of Mary Henry and Laurence Jamieson, who was the caretaker for Vaila Island.

Martin and Laura have two daughters and live in Sunnybank, Walls. Martin worked as a roadbuilder for the Shetland Islands Council.

**Children of Martin Edward Williamson**

VII. **Christine Williamson**, born in 1951 in Sunnybank, Walls, Shetland. She married *Frederick Georgeson*, who was born in 1948 in Lochside, Walls, Shetland. They were married in St. Paul's Manse in Walls on October 25, 1968. They have three children and live in Walls. Fred works as the caretaker of the Island of Vaila, across Vaila Sound from the village of Walls, which entails various duties, including running the boat and looking after the sheep.

**Children of Christine Williamson**

VIII. **Fiona Marion Campbell Georgeson**, born on March 13, 1969, in Sunnybank, Walls, Shetland.

VIII. **Marina Jane Georgeson**, born on June 1, 1971, in Lerwick, Shetland.

VIII. **Kevin Georgeson**, born in 1981 in Walls, Shetland.

VII. **<u>Caroline Margaret Williamson</u>**, born in 1953 in Sunnybank, Walls, Shetland. She married *Leonard Rodney Bryan Georgeson* (called "Lenny") on April 10, 1974, in St. Paul's Church, Walls. Lenny, brother of Frederick Georgeson, who married Caroline's sister, was born in 1951 in Lochside, Walls, Shetland. He works at the Sullom Voe Oil Terminal, and Caroline works at the bakery in Walls. They have two sons, who live with them at Lochside House in Walls.

### Children of Caroline Margaret Williamson

VIII. **<u>Bryan Edward William Georgeson</u>**, born on July 23, 1978, in Lerwick, Shetland. He works in salmon farming.

VIII. **<u>Garry Lawrence Georgeson</u>**, born on August 13, 1981, in Lerwick, Shetland.

VI. **<u>Peter Henry Williamson</u>**, youngest son of Margaret Robertson and Magnus Williamson, was born in 1925 at the Waddle, Walls Parish, Shetland. On October 16, 1956, he married *Lillias Irvine* in Lerwick. She was born in Staneydale, Walls Parish. Peter worked as a postman; he and Lillias had no children. Peter died on February 19, 1995, in Lerwick, Shetland.

## 5-A.7: ELIZA CATHERINE ROBERTSON (1888-1945)
### Daughter of Thomas Robertson: Another Williamson Branch

V. **<u>Eliza Catherine Robertson</u>**, third daughter of Alice Jamieson and Thomas Robertson (3-B above), was born on August 21, 1888, in Bridge of Walls, Shetland.[221] She married *Scott Williamson*, and they had seven children. After his death, she married *William Leask* and had one more child. Eliza died in 1945 in Lerwick, Shetland.

**Children of Eliza Catherine Robertson**

VI. **<u>Alice Jane Elizabeth Williamson</u>**, oldest daughter of Eliza Robertson and Scott Williamson, was born on April 13, 1909, in Setter, Walls Parish, Shetland. On February 25, 1926, Alice married *Robert Andrew Fraser* in Walls. Just sixteen years old at the time, her husband was almost thirty, having been born on October 6, 1896, in

Scarpigarth, Walls. They immigrated to New Zealand in 1934, settling in the South Island. Robert died on May 19, 1966, in Dunedin, New Zealand. Alice then married *Eric Treweek* in New Zealand; he is deceased. Now approaching her ninetieth birthday with energy and enthusiasm, Alice resides in Waikouiti, Dunedin. She has no children.

VI. **Marion Margaret Williamson**, second daughter of Eliza Robertson and Scott Williamson, was born on January 10, 1912, in Uphouse, Setter, Walls Parish, Shetland. She died there at the age of ten on April 19, 1922.

VI. **Adeline Agnes Williamson** (called "Ada"), third daughter of Eliza Robertson and Scott Williamson, was born on November 2, 1913. She married *Maxwell Robert Smith* in Lerwick on December 12, 1934. Maxwell was born on September 26, 1910. They had four children. Adeline died on April 24, 1993, at age seventy-nine.

### Children of Adeline Agnes Williamson

VII. **Ivor Smith**, born after 1934 in Veensgarth, Tingwall, Shetland.

VII. **Edith Smith**, born after 1934 in Veensgarth, Tingwall, Shetland.

VII. **Alistair Smith**, born after 1934 in Veensgarth, Tingwall, Shetland.

VII. **Susan Smith**, born after 1934 in Veensgarth, Tingwall, Shetland.

VI. **Christine Ann Williamson**, fourth daughter of Eliza Robertson and Scott Williamson, was born on November 20, 1916, in Setter, Walls Parish, Shetland. She died there at the age of five on May 6, 1922, less than two weeks after the death of her older sister.

VI. **Magnus James Phillip Williamson** (called "Mag"), first son of Eliza Robertson and Scott Williamson, was born on August 4, 1917, in Walls Parish, Shetland. At a very young age, Mag and his brother John immigrated to New Zealand on their own. On November 8, 1940, he married *Lorna Munro* in the Anglican Church in Caversham, Dunedin, New Zealand. Lorna was born in Caversham before 1920. They had four children and then divorced. Magnus then married *Rona Patiki* in New Zealand about 1948, and they had seven children, whose names and ages we have not learned. Magnus worked as a carpenter and resided in Balclutha, New Zealand.

### Children of Magnus John Phillip Williamson

VII. **<u>Vaila Williamson</u>**, eldest daughter of Magnus Williamson and Lorna Munro, was born in 1941 in New Zealand.

VII. **<u>Wynis Williamson</u>**, second daughter of Magnus Williamson and Lorna Munro, was born in 1942 in New Zealand. She died in 1995.

VII. **<u>Robin Williamson</u>**, third daughter of Magnus Williamson and Lorna Munro, was born after 1943 in New Zealand.

VII. **<u>Niare Williamson</u>**, fourth daughter of Magnus Williamson and Lorna Munro, was born after 1945 in New Zealand.

VI. **<u>John Scott Williamson</u>**, second son of Eliza Robertson and Scott Williamson, was born on October 26, 1919. John immigrated to New Zealand as a very young man with his brother Magnus. There he married *Morag MacLeod*, who was born about 1922, and they had three children. John was a farmer.

### Children of John Scott Williamson

VII. **<u>Scott Williamson</u>**, born after 1942 in New Zealand.

VII. **<u>Donald Williamson</u>**, born after 1944 in New Zealand.

VII. **<u>Maven Williamson</u>**, born after 1945 in New Zealand.

VI. **<u>Edith Kathleen Williamson</u>**, fifth daughter of Eliza Robertson and Scott Williamson, was born on May 5, 1920, in Setter, Walls Parish, Shetland. On April 10, 1941, in Lerwick, she married *Andrew MacDonald Brian Lawrie*, who was born on August 22, 1920, on Glasgow Road in, Dumbarton, Scotland. They had three children.

### Children of Edith Kathleen Williamson

VII. **<u>Wendy Lawrie</u>**, born on May 25, 1946. She has two children.

**Children of Wendy Lawrie**

VIII. <u>**Grant David Anthony Dyble**</u>, born on August 6, 1973.

VIII. <u>**Scott David Stanley Dyble**</u>, born on October 22, 1976.

VII. <u>**Inga Allison Lawrie**</u>, born on December 4, 1947. She married *Michael De Wolf* in London, England, in 1979. They have two children.

**Children of Inga Allison Lawrie**

VIII. <u>**Gerard Emil Henry De Wolf**</u>, born on April 19, 1983.

VIII. <u>**Claudia Joan Eliza De Wolf**</u>, born on March 26, 1985.

VII. <u>**Magnus Fraser Lawrie**</u>, born on January 14, 1953. He married *Patricia James* on August 6, 1982, in London, England. They have two children.

**Children of Magnus Fraser Lawrie**

VIII. <u>**Stuart Fraser John Lawrie**</u>, born on May 10, 1982.

VIII. <u>**Graeme Magnus Lawrie**</u>, born on May 6, 1987.

VII. <u>**Angus MacDonald Lawrie**</u>, born on October 7, 1955. He married *Joyce MacLeod Adam* in April 1979. They have one child.

**Child of Angus MacDonald Lawrie**

VIII. <u>**Angus MacLeod Lawrie**</u>, born on April 19, 1980.

VI. <u>**Bertie Leask**</u>, son of Eliza Robertson and her second husband, William Leask, was born in 1930.

## 5-A.8: ALICE ROBERTSON (1895-1979)
### Daughter of Thomas Robertson: The Gifford Branch

V. **Alice Robertson**, fourth daughter of Alice Jamieson and Thomas Robertson (3-B above), was born on September 16, 1895, in the Punds, Walls Parish, Shetland.

On September 16, 1915, Alice married *George Gifford* (known as Joe) in Lerwick, Shetland. Her husband was born in Lerwick in 1882. They had five children. Alice died in Lerwick in September 1979.

**Children of Alice Robertson**

VI. **Alice Marion Gifford**, daughter of Alice Robertson and George Gifford, was born about 1916 in Shetland. She married *Sydney Ian Hamilton Robertson* in Lerwick, Shetland, and they had two children.

**Children of Alice Marion Gifford**

VII. **Cynthia Robertson**, daughter of Alice Gifford and Sydney Robertson, was born on March 21, 1943, in Lerwick, Shetland. She first married *Kenneth Mackintosh* of Glasgow, Scotland; they divorced. Cynthia later married *George Allan*, a stonemason, and they live in Lerwick. She has two children.

**Children of Cynthia Robertson**

VIII. **Karen Robertson**. She married *John Leask* and lives in Lerwick.

VIII. **Kerry Jane Mackintosh**, daughter of Cynthia Robertson and Kenneth Mackintosh, was born about 1979.

VII. **Ian George Hugh Robertson**, son of Alice Gifford and Sydney Robertson, was born on February 25, 1948, in Lerwick, Shetland. He married *Alice Matthew* in Bucksburn, Aberdeen, Scotland. Alice was born on January 26, 1950, in Bucksburn. Becoming the fourth Alice Robertson by marriage, she was the daughter of Amelia Forest and Alexander Matthew, a farmer. Ian and Alice are the parents of two sons and live in Bucksburn, near Aberdeen, Scotland, where Ian works in a paper mill and Alice manages a doctor's office.

**Children of Ian Hugh George Robertson**

VIII. **Steven George Robertson**, born in Bucksburn, Aberdeen, Scotland, on March 26, 1976.

VIII. **Kevin Stuart Robertson**, born in Bucksburn, Aberdeen, Scotland, on March 31, 1979.

VI. **George Magnus Gifford**, oldest son of Alice Robertson and George Gifford, was born in Lerwick, Shetland, on January 27, 1920. In World War II, George volunteered for infantry service and was sent to North Africa with the 57th Battalion, Gordon Highlanders. He was killed by mortar fire on October 24, 1942, in the courageous infantry assault against German and Italian positions at the outset of the battle of El Alamein in Libya. The battle proved to be a decisive victory for the Allied forces. He was twenty-two years old and is listed in the Shetland Roll of Honour.

VI. **Thomas Gifford**, son of Alice Robertson and George Gifford, was born about 1922. He married *Bertha Davidson*, and they had two children. They resided in Lerwick.

### Children of Thomas Gifford

VII. **Hazel Gifford**, born after 1954. She lives in Lerwick and works for Shetland Enterprise.

VII. **Thomas Gifford**, born after 1956.

VI. **Charles Gifford**, son of Alice Robertson and George Gifford, was born on September 4, 1924, in Lerwick, Shetland. He married *Williamina Anderson*, known as Winnie, who was born on March 29, 1928, on Out Skerries, one of the Shetland Islands. They had five children and lived in Lerwick.

### Children of Charles Gifford

VII. **Kenneth Gifford**, born in 1948 in Lerwick, Shetland. He married *Carol Stewart*, who was born on Burra Isle, near Scalloway, Shetland, on April 16, 1951. They have one child and live in Lerwick. Kenneth works in the salmon farming business, in which he is a supervisor of diving operations.

### Child of Kenneth Gifford

VIII. **David Gifford**, born on April 13, 1983, in Lerwick, Shetland.

VII. **Barbara Alison Gifford**, born in 1949 in Lerwick, Shetland. She married *James Robertson* of Yell. He was born on September 20, 1942, son of Lexie Gray and William Robertson. They have three children.

**Children of Barbara Alison Gifford**

VIII. **Marvin James Robertson**, born on June 16, 1971, in Lerwick, Shetland.

VIII. **Avril Alexis Robertson**, born on March 13, 1974, in Lerwick, Shetland.

VIII. **Carolyn Marie Robertson** (called "Lyn"), born on October 6, 1978, in Lerwick, Shetland.

VII. **Marion Isobel Beatrice Gifford**, born in 1951 in Lerwick, Shetland. She married *Donald Gunn Leslie*, who was born in 1946. They have two children and live in Lerwick, where Don owns and operates a shop and pub near the waterfront.

**Children of Marion Isobel Beatrice Gifford**

VIII. **Richard Leslie**, born in 1972.

VIII. **John Leslie**, born in 1975.

VII. **Caroline Grace Gifford**, born in 1954 in Lerwick, Shetland. She married *Alan Fordyce Smith*, who was born in 1948. They have two children.

**Children of Caroline Grace Gifford**

VIII. **Ian Smith**, born in 1974.

VIII. **Brian Smith**, born in 1977.

VII. **John Alexander Gifford**, born in 1954 in Lerwick, Shetland. He married *Angela Cumming* from Burra Isle, Scalloway, Shetland, who was born in 1955. They have four children and live in Lerwick.

**Children of John Alexander Gifford**

VIII. **Joanna Gifford**, born in 1975.

VIII. **Stephen Gifford**, born in 1977.

VIII. **Jonathan Gifford**, born in 1980.

VIII. **Daniel Gifford**, born in 1989.

VI. **Greta Isobel Beatrice Gifford**, born about 1930. She married *Alan Hourie*, and they live in Whiteness, Shetland.

## 5-A.9: THOMAS ROBERTSON (1899-1982)
### Son of Thomas Robertson

V. **Thomas Robertson** was one of the twins born to Elizabeth Jeromson and Thomas Robertson (3-B above). He was born on September 14, 1899, in Punds, Walls Parish, Shetland. Like many others in his family, Thomas settled in South Shields, Durham, a merchant shipping center and port area in northern England.

Thomas first married *Dorothy Gray*, who was born in South Shields, daughter of Dorothy Wilkinson and William Gray. They had a son and two daughters, one of whom immigrated to the United States. Dorothy died on January 24, 1939, while giving birth to her third child. Thomas later married *Caroline Richardson* about 1955. Caroline was born on January 29, 1914, in Gateshead, Durham, England.

Until his retirement, Thomas worked for the U.K. Customs and Excise department as a launch pilot. He died about 1984 in South Shields at the age of eighty-four. His widow, Caroline, resides in South Shields.

**Children of Thomas Robertson**

VI. **Thomas Robertson**, born about 1926 in South Shields, England, was the son of Dorothy Gray and Thomas Robertson. He was married three times, lastly to *Margaret Mallows*, with whom he had three children. Thomas long suffered from kidney disease; he died in South Shields about 1976.

**Children of Thomas Robertson**

VII. **Dorothy Wilkinson Robertson**.

VII. **Alda Candida Robertson**.

VII. **Frederick Robertson**.

VI. **<u>Dorothy Wilkinson Robertson</u>**, first daughter of Dorothy Gray and Thomas Robertson, was born about 1930 in South Shields, England. Dorothy first married *Al Ezrow*, an American serviceman whom she met in London. They had a son, and she and the child went with her husband to New Jersey in the United States. There she spent the rest of her life. After Dorothy and her first husband divorced, she married *Richard "Dusty" Petroski*, who legally adopted her son. They later divorced, and Dorothy had a third husband whose name is not known to us. She died about 1974 in New Jersey, approximately forty-four years of age.

### Child of Dorothy Wilkinson Robertson

VII. **<u>Peter (Ezrow) Petroski</u>**, born on April 6, 1949, in London, England, was the son of Dorothy Robertson and Al Ezrow. He moved to America with his parents as a young child and took the surname of his stepfather, Richard Petroski. Disabled in an automobile accident some years ago, Peter resides in St. Petersburg, Florida. He is divorced from *Trudy Celucci.* They had no children.

VI. **<u>Margaret Robertson</u>**, born on January 24, 1939, in South Shields, Durham, England, was the second daughter of Dorothy Gray and Thomas Robertson. Her mother died at the time of her birth, and Margaret was raised by her maternal grandmother until she was in her teens and her father remarried.

On July 4, 1959, Margaret married *William Jeromson* in South Shields, England. Bill was born there on October 8, 1934, the son of Catherine Hayton and William Jeromson, a seaman from Shetland. Prior to retirement, Bill worked as a machinist. They have two daughters and live in South Shields.

### Children of Margaret Robertson

VII. **<u>Lynne Jeromson</u>**, born on August 4, 1962, in South Shields, Durham, England. She married *Anthony Carr*, son of Joan Whitfield and Peter Carr, on September 26, 1987, in South Shields. He was born on October 14, 1963, in South Shields. They have two sons and live in South Shields, England. Tony is a joiner and is employed by the Newcastle City Council.

**Children of Lynne Jeromson**

VIII. <u>**Michael Anthony Carr**</u>, born on March 5, 1991, in South Shields, England.

VIII. <u>**David William Carr**</u>, born on May 4, 1995, in South Shields, England.

VII. <u>**Lorna Jeromson**</u>, born on May 8, 1964, in Jarrow, near South Shields, England. She married *Geoffrey McKay* about 1985; they divorced about 1994. Lorna lives in Gosforth, near Newcastle, England.

## 5-A.10: JEMIMA ROBERTSON (1899-1963)
### Daughter of Thomas Robertson: The Coutts Branch

V. **Jemima Robertson** (called "Mimie") was one of twins born on September 14, 1899, in Punds, Walls Parish, Shetland, to Elizabeth Jeromson and Thomas Robertson (3-B above).

Jemima married *Laurence Coutts* on January 16, 1919, in St. Ringan's United Free Church in Lerwick, Shetland. Son of James Coutts, Laurence was born on June 20, 1895, at Melaquilse, a croft in Walls Parish, Shetland. They had four daughters and a son. The family at first lived in Shetland and then, about 1929, moved to South Shields, a major shipbuilding and shipping port area in northern England where the River Tyne enters the North Sea. Many Shetland Islanders went to South Shields because it was known as the best place to find work in merchant shipping and related fields of employment.

Another of our family who became a casualty of World War II, Laurence Coutts died at sea while serving as a carpenter on the S.S. *Harpagus*, which was sunk south of Greenland in the North Atlantic by a German torpedo on May 20, 1941. Jemima Robertson Coutts died in 1963 in South Shields.

**Children of Jemima Robertson**

VI. <u>**Ruby Beatrice Coutts**</u>, daughter of Jemima Robertson and Laurence Coutts, was born on July 30, 1920, in Lerwick, Shetland. She remembered being taken to South Shields with her family as a child of nine. She married *Geoffrey Brian Mullens* in London, England, on May 26, 1945. Brian was born on April 19, 1923, in Wales. They had one son and lived in Forest Hill, London, England.

**Child of Ruby Beatrice Coutts**

VII. <u>**Peter Michael Mullens**</u> (called "Michael"), born on March 7, 1946. He received a degree in economics from the University College of Wales, Aberystwyth, and later became qualified as a chartered accountant. Michael retired from the accounting profession in 1988 and became a consultant to municipal authorities.

Michael married <u>*Salima Monani*</u> on December 28, 1968, in St. Mary's Church, Ladywell, London, England. His wife, called Sally, was born on February 20, 1948, in Lahore, Pakistan, daughter of Sherali Monani, a native of Pakistan, and an English woman named Lylie. Sally's parents had met during the 1930s at Oxford University. Sally and Michael had two sons and adopted a daughter. They divorced in 1987. Michael then married <u>*Teresa Isabella (Copper) Stearn*</u> on December 10, 1988, in Maidstone, Kent, England. They divorced in March of 1994, with no children.

On April 8, 1995, Michael married <u>*Paula Jane (Clitheroe) Baldock*</u> in Sittingbourne, Kent, England. She was born in Dover, Kent, on September 26, 1958. Paula Jane and Michael live in Sittingbourne. Michael describes himself as a born-again evangelical Christian.

**Children of Peter Michael Mullens**

VIII. <u>**Peter Marc Mullens**</u>, born on October 10, 1970, in Bromley, Kent, England. Qualified as an under-five teacher, Marc is attending Bible college; he, like his father, is a born-again Christian and plans on becoming a missionary in Central America.

VIII. <u>**Gavin Siward Mullens**</u>, born on March 17, 1972, in Lewisham, London, England. Unmarried, he is in social work in North Wales.

VIII. <u>**Lara Rachel Mullens**</u>, born as Rachel Carli Hinch on March 21, 1974. She was adopted by Sally and Michael as an infant. Lara lives in Hereford, England.

VI. **<u>Laurence Coutts</u>** (called "Laurie"), born on February 10, 1923, in Lerwick, Shetland. He was the only son of Jemima Robertson and Laurence Coutts.

Laurie Coutts spent some forty years at sea. He started as a messroom boy, was soon promoted to seaman, and worked up to the position of petty officer. He then attended classes to qualify for his master's papers. Laurie served as a shipping captain for over twenty years. He commanded very large crude oil tankers for Shell, including ships of up to 360,000 tons capacity, and retired from seafaring in 1980. During World War II, he served in the British supply convoy to Malta. Two of his ships were sunk by German torpedoes, including the S.S. *Harpagus* on which his father went down in 1941.

On November 26, 1949, he married *Catherine Joyce Lapping*, the daughter of Elizabeth Muldoon and Richard Lapping. Joyce was born in Bramton, Cumbria, on July 9, 1926. Joyce and Laurie Coutts have three daughters and live in Sunderland, England.

### Children of Laurence Coutts

VII. **<u>Mona Lauraine Coutts</u>**, born on January 1, 1951, in Bramton, Cumbria, England. She is manager of a healthcare facility that treats Alzheimer's patients. Lauraine married *John Robinson*; they had two children and divorced. She lives in Sevenoaks, Kent, England.

### Children of Mona Lauraine Coutts

VIII. **<u>Helen Robinson</u>**, born on September 20, 1981.

VIII. **<u>John Robinson</u>**, born on October 13, 1983.

VII. **<u>Marlene Carol Coutts</u>**, born on July 12, 1954, in South Shields, Durham, England. She married *Michael Rennie*. They immigrated to Australia and live in Northcote, Victoria, near Melbourne. They have no children.

VII. **<u>Catherine Maureen Coutts</u>**, born on November 28, 1962, in Sunderland, England. She received a PhD in archeology from Sheffield University. Unmarried, Catherine lives in Sheffield and works as chief archeologist for the local authority in Warwick.

VI. **Catherine Coutts**, second daughter of Jemima Robertson and Laurence Coutts, was born about 1925 in Lerwick, Shetland. She died at the age of sixteen in 1941.

VI. **Margaret Rose Coutts**, third daughter of Jemima Robertson and Laurence Coutts, was born on October 28, 1926, in Lerwick, Shetland. Her family moved to South Shields in England when she was a young child of three or four, and Rose recalled returning to Shetland with her mother for a week's holiday when she was about ten.

On November 13, 1950, in South Shields, England, Rose married *Thomas Gutcher Harrison*. He was born in South Shields on September 25, 1921, son of Jane Ann Moore and John Harrison, and served for many years in the Navy and later worked in merchant shipping. They had five daughters and lived in South Shields.

### Children of Margaret Rose Coutts

VII. **Heather Harrison**, born on January 24, 1951, in South Shields, Tyne and Wear, England. She married *George Heron* at St. Stephen's Anglican Church in South Shields on April 26, 1980. He was born there on July 29, 1952. Heather and George have two sons and live in South Shields, where he works as a joiner.

### Children of Heather Harrison

VIII. **Stephen Heron**, born on September 21, 1980, in South Shields, Tyne and Wear, England.

VIII. **Michael Heron**, born on June 5, 1986, in South Shields, Tyne and Wear, England.

VII. **Joan Harrison**, born February 29, 1952 (1952 was a leap year), in South Shields, Tyne and Wear, England. She married *Eamon Mahoney* at St. Stephen's Church in South Shields on September 8, 1979. Eamon, a native of Ireland, was born there on May 27, 1956. They have two sons and live in Birmingham, England.

**Children of Joan Harrison**

VIII. **Kierin Mahoney**, born on March 29, 1982.

VIII. **Ryan Mahoney**, born on November 28, 1983.

VII. **Leah Harrison**, born on November 18, 1953, in Jarrow, Tyne and Wear, England. She is married to *John Errington*, who was born on July 10, 1959, and works in insurance sales. They have two children.

**Children of Leah Harrison**

VIII. **Rachel Errington**, born on March 12, 1990, in South Shields, Tyne and Wear, England.

VIII. **Gary Errington**, born on May 13, 1992, in South Shields, Tyne and Wear, England.

VII. **Patricia Harrison**, born on October 16, 1959, in Jarrow, Tyne and Wear, England. She married *Ralph Donnelly* in 1980. They had one son and divorced. Second, Patricia married *Alan Robertson* on August 22, 1992, in South Shields, England. Alan was born on July 3, 1957. Patricia works in municipal government in South Shields.

**Child of Patricia Harrison**

VIII **Neil (Donnelly) Robertson**, son of Patricia Harrison and Ralph Donnelly, born on December 29, 1980. He has taken the Robertson surname of his stepfather.

VII. **Ann Harrison**, born on September 26, 1964, in South Shields, Tyne and Wear, England. She married *Richard Harrison* in South Shields on March 30, 1991. He was born on September 29, 1956. They have two daughters.

**Children of Ann Harrison**

VIII. **Elizabeth Rose Harrison** (called "Beth"), born on June 8, 1993, in South Shields, England.

VIII. **<u>Sarah Ann Harrison</u>**, born on March 16, 1996, in South Shields, England.

VI. **<u>Adaline Maureen Coutts</u>** (called "Reenie"), the fourth daughter of Jemima Robertson and Laurence Coutts, was born on January 17, 1931, in South Shields, Tyne and Wear, England.

In October 1951, Maureen married *Reginald William Robson*, who was born on April 15, 1927. They had two children and lived in Boldon, England. Maureen died on June 6, 1998, in Sunderland, England.

### Children of Adaline Maureen Coutts

VII. **<u>Fred Laurence Robson</u>** (called "Laurie"), born on June 17, 1952, in South Shields, Tyne and Wear, England. After university, he pursued a seafaring life in the merchant navy and was qualified as a chief engineer on both steam and diesel vessels. After being injured in a serious accident in Mexico, Laurie went back to school at Liverpool University and became a chartered marine surveyor. He now owns and operates a retirement home in Liverpool.

On December 15, 1974, Laurie married *Philamena Meldrum*. She was born in Liverpool, England, of Irish parents, on August 28, 1953. They have four children and live in Liverpool, England.

### Children of Fred Laurence Robson

VIII. **<u>Melissa Robson</u>**, born on August 12, 1975, in Liverpool, England. She is studying dentistry at the University of London.

VIII. **<u>Helena Robson</u>**, born on March 5, 1976, in Liverpool, England. She attended University College of Wales, Aberystwyth, from which she obtained her teacher's certificate.

VIII. **<u>Laura Robson</u>**, born on September 14, 1979, in Liverpool, England.

VIII. **<u>Stuart Robson</u>**, born on March 12, 1983, in Liverpool, England.

VII. **June Allyson Robson**, born on June 17, 1954, in South Shields, Tyne and Wear, England. She married *Andrew Ward* on June 1, 1977, in Keighley, West Yorkshire, England. He was born on August 23, 1946, in Jarrow, Tyne and Wear, England. They had one son in addition to Andrew's daughter from a previous marriage, Maxine Ward. June and Andrew divorced on August 10, 1995.

On September 26, 1998, June married *Michael Frank Rhodes* in Christ Church, Keighley. He was born in Keighley on March 10, 1950.

### Child of June Robson

VIII. **Richard Andrew Ward**, son of June Robson and Andrew Ward, born on August 3, 1979, in Keighley, West Yorkshire, England. He is a student of interactive media at Sunderland University.

## 5-A.11: THOMAS TWATT (1856-19??)
### Son of Thomas Twatt

V. **Thomas Twatt**, oldest son of Janet Coutts and Thomas Twatt (4-I above), was born on October 27, 1856, in Walls Parish, Shetland.[222] He married *Catherine Nicolson*, who was born in 1862. They had two daughters and seven sons, three of whom settled in the United States. Great-granddaughter Beryl Nicolson Smith recalls a favorite family anecdote about Thomas: when told by a neighbor that there was no such place as Hell, Thomas replied, "That's the best news I've heard yet."

### Children of Thomas Twatt

VI. **Margaret Twatt**, daughter of Catherine Nicolson and Thomas Twatt, was born on September 12, 1885. She married *James Ganson*, and they had one child. Margaret died about 1913 in Sandwick, Shetland. (*SEE SECTION 6-A.5.*)

VI. **John Thomas Watt (Twatt)**, first son of Catherine Nicholson and Thomas Twatt, was born before 1890 in Shetland. He immigrated to Brooklyn, New York, where he married *Winifred McCann*. They had two daughters, Catherine and Winifred. (SEE SECTION 6-C.20.)

**Children of John Thomas Twatt**

VII. **Winifred Twatt**. She died in 1997 and is survived by her second husband.

VII. **Catherine Twatt**. Reportedly married and living next door to her late sister's home in Boston, Massachusetts.

VI. **Jessie Ann Twatt**, second daughter of Catherine Nicolson and Thomas Twatt, was born on February 16, 1890. She married *John Johnston*, and they had one daughter.

**Child of Jessie Ann Twatt**

VII. **Catherine Johnston**, born on June 6, 1920, in Shetland. She married *Peter Goodlad*, who had children from a previous marriage. Catherine died about December 1995, age seventy-five, and Peter resides in Lerwick.

VI. **Robert Twatt**, second son of Catherine Nicolson and Thomas Twatt, was born on June 17, 1892. He married *Margaret Fraser*, and they had one child. (*SEE SECTION 6-A.6.*)

VI. **Andrew Watt**, son of Catherine Nicolson and Thomas Twatt, was born on January 28, 1895. Never married, he lived in Brooklyn, New York.

VI. **Thomas Watt**, son of Catherine Nicolson and Thomas Twatt, was born on July 25, 1897, in Walls, Shetland. Thomas became a seaman in the merchant navy. He married *Annabella Moir*, from Kirkwall, Orkney, and they settled in Grangemouth, Scotland, where Thomas found employment. They had three children.

**Children of Thomas Watt**

VII. **Mary Wardrop Brownlee Watt**, born on June 23, 1923, in Camelon, Stirlingshire, Scotland. She had one son, who was raised by her mother. In about 1945, Mary married *Roy Jewell*, and they had two sons. After her first husband died, she married *Arthur Jewell*, Roy's brother; they had no children. Arthur died of a stroke in March, 1999. Mary died a few days later on March 21, 1999.

**Child of Mary Watt**

VIII. **Brian Watt**, son of Mary Watt, was born on March 30, 1940, in Grangemouth, Stirlingshire, Scotland. He married *Agnes Russell Brennan* (called "Nancy"), who was born on July 9, 1941, in Glasgow, Scotland. They have two children (twins) and live in Grangemouth.

**Children of Brian Watt**

IX. **Bryan Kemp Watt**, born on May 20, 1967, in Edinburgh, Scotland. Unmarried, he is a freelance designer and photographer in London, England.

IX. **Denise Mary Watt**, born on May 20, 1967 in Edinburgh, Scotland. On August 26, 1994, she married *Derek Jamieson*. They have one daughter and live in Aberdeen, Scotland.

**Child of Denise Mary Watt**

X. **Lesley Avril Jamieson**, born in Aberdeen, Scotland, on August 15, 1996.

VIII. **Raymond Edwin Jewell,** son of Mary Watt and Roy Jewell, was born about February 2, 1946, in Stirlingshire, Scotland. He is unmarried and lives in Melbourne, Australia.

VIII. **Norman Trevor Jewell,** son of Mary Watt and Roy Jewell, was born about July 16, 1949, in Stirlingshire, Scotland. He married *Angela King*, who has two daughters from a previous marriage, Marnie and Carla. They live in Victoria, Australia, near the border with New South Wales.

VII. **Thomas (Twatt) Watt**, born in Grangemouth, Stirlingshire, Scotland, about 1926. He was known as Tom. He changed his surname to Watt. He married *Wilma Smith*, and they had one son. Tom is deceased and his widow resides in Grangemouth.

**Child of Thomas Watt**

VIII. **Christopher Watt**.

VII. **James (Twatt) Watt**, born in Grangemouth, Stirlingshire, Scotland, on May 27, 1929. In October 1952, he married *Rose Allan* in Grangemouth. Rose was born on October 18, 1932, in Glasgow, Scotland. They have three children and reside in Grangemouth.

**Children of James Watt**

VIII. **Alan Watt**, born on July 30, 1952, in Stirling, Scotland. On August 13, 1977, in Liverpool, England, he married *Marion Foley*. They have two sons.

**Children of Alan Watt**

IX. **Stuart Watt** born on March 7, 1991.

IX. **Graeme Watt** born April 4, 1996.

VIII. **James Alistair Watt**, born in Falkirk, Scotland, on May 4, 1956. He married *Kathleen Mary Flynn*, and they have a son and a daughter.

**Children of James Alistair Watt**

IX. **Aimee Watt**, born on July 15, 1985.

IX. **Callum Watt**, born on June 21, 1988.

VIII. **Moira Watt**, born on March 5, 1966, in Grangemouth, Stirlingshire, Scotland. She married *William Lapsley* on September 24, 1990. They have no children.

VI. **James William Watt**, son of Catherine Nicolson and Thomas Twatt, was born on March 26, 1900. Unmarried, he lived in Brooklyn, New York. He worked as a painter and later had a restaurant in New York. He died in the United States around the early 1970s.

VI. **Peter Twatt**, son of Catherine Nicolson and Thomas Twatt, was born in 1903. He worked the family croft in Brebister, Walls Parish, Shetland, and never married. He died about 1969.

VI. **George Arthur Twatt**, son of Catherine Nicolson and Thomas Twatt, was born on April 13, 1907, in Brebister, Walls Parish, Shetland. He married *Jemima Catherine Fraser*, called "Mimie", on April 30, 1942, in Lerwick, Shetland. She was born in Dale of Walls, Walls Parish, Shetland, on January 14, 1919, daughter of Catherine Walterson and William Fraser. They had three children. For about eighteen years the family lived in Grangemouth, Scotland. During that period, they used the surname Watt, but upon returning to Shetland, they reverted to Twatt.

George died in 1982 in Aberdeen, Scotland, after which Mimie lived at the family croft in Brebister, Walls with her two sons.

**Children of George Arthur Twatt**

VII. **George Twatt** was born on April 3, 1943, in Brebister, Walls, Shetland. Unmarried, George and his brother have been working the family croft in Brebister since the early 1960s.

VII. **Catherine Margaret Ann Twatt** was born on April 2, 1944, in Brebister, Walls Parish, Shetland. She married *Charles Glennon*. They live in Halifax, Yorkshire, England, and have four children.

**Children of Catherine Margaret Ann Twatt**

VIII. **Peter Andrew Glennon**, born on October 6, 1972. He married *Lisa Marley*. They reside in Halifax, Yorkshire, England.

VIII. **Jacqueline Glennon**, born in Halifax, Yorkshire, England, on March 1, 1975.

VIII. **Catherine Glennon**, born on November 8, 1978, in Halifax, Yorkshire, England.

VIII. **Susan Glennon**, born on June 28, 1982, in Halifax, Yorkshire, England.

VII. **William Frank Twatt** (called "Frank"), born on April 30, 1945, in Brebister, Walls, Shetland. Frank is a crofter in Brebister and is not married.

Chapter 5-B

# THE SOUTH PACIFIC BRANCHES, GENERATION FIVE

## 5-B.1: JAMES CHEYNE (1875-1937)
### Son of Christina Dumbreck Robertson

V. **James Cheyne**, son of Christina Dumbreck Robertson and Robert Cheyne (4-D above), was born on April 27, 1875, in Blink Bonnie in the lower Wairau Valley, near Blenheim, South Island, New Zealand. James was around nine years old when his father died. At about seventeen, he moved with his mother and stepfather to Wellington. He lived in that area for the rest of his life.

James Cheyne married *Jessie Skilling* on January 15, 1902, in Ashburton, which is located in the east central part of South Island, New Zealand. Jessie was born in 1879 in Elgin, Canterbury, New Zealand, the daughter of Ellen Cochrane and her husband, James Skilling, who were sheep farmers. James and Jesse had two children, Tina and Laurie.

Only twenty-eight years old, Jessie died in Wellington, New Zealand, about 1907, leaving a daughter of four and a son about two years old. After her death, the children were taken in and raised by their grandmother, Christina (Cheyne) Beauchop and their father's sister Ann Margaret, often known as "Aunt Sis." When Christina and Aunt Sis moved from Wellington to Woodville, Tina and Laurie went with them. Around 1919, Aunt Sis brought the children back to stay with their father, James, in the Wellington area. According to his daughter, Tina, James had fair skin and curly golden hair.

James later married *Edith Mary Jones* around 1922 in Palmerston North when his children were in their late teens. There were no children in the second marriage. James Cheyne died on April 8, 1937, at age sixty-one, in Wellington, New Zealand.

**Children of James Cheyne**

> VI. **Christina Helen Cheyne** (called "Tina"), born on December 31, 1903, in Wellington, New Zealand. She married *Leslie Marshall Rankine* in 1929, and they had one son. (*SEE SECTION 6-B.5.*)

> VI. **Lawrence James Alexander Cheyne** (called "Laurie"), born in 1905 in Wellington, New Zealand; died in 1982 in Auckland, New Zealand. Twice married, he was the father of two sons. (*SEE SECTION 6-B.6.*)

## 5-B.2: MARY CHARLOTTE AGNES CHEYNE (1880-1958)
### Daughter of Christina Dumbreck Robertson: The Fraser Branches

V. **Mary Charlotte Agnes Cheyne** (called "Lottie"), was born on June 17, 1880, in Blenheim, South Island, New Zealand. She was the youngest daughter of Christina Dumbreck Robertson and Robert Cheyne (4-D above).

Lottie married her distant cousin *John Smith Fraser* (called "Jack") on July 17, 1906, in Wellington, New Zealand. The son of Bruce Fraser, Jack was born about 1874 in Walls, Shetland. Lottie and Jack had four children.

At the time of their marriage, Jack Fraser was a seaman on the S.S. *Mapourika*. He gave up the sea about two years later and went to work for the Harbour Board in Wellington. Around 1911, he left that job to become a farmer, and the family moved to a farm near Woodville on the North Island. The same property is still being lived on and farmed by their granddaughter Joyce Henson and her husband.

Jack Fraser died in 1952, about seventy-eight years of age, near Woodville, New Zealand. Mary Charlotte died on May 19, 1958, in Te Awamutu, a few miles south of Hamilton, New Zealand. She was seventy-seven.

**Children of Mary Charlotte Agnes Cheyne**

> VI. **Winifred Mary Fraser**, born about 1907 in Wellington, New Zealand; died about 1939 of tuberculosis, in Woodville, New Zealand, when she was approximately thirty-two. She never married.

VI. **<u>Lillias Mancrefe Fraser</u>**, born about 1909 in Wellington, New Zealand; died in infancy, about 1911.

VI. **<u>Iris Moncrieff Fraser</u>**, born on March 24, 1911, in Woodville, New Zealand. Iris married *<u>Oliver Frederick Bridges</u>*, and they had three children. She died in October 1997, age eighty-six. (*SEE SECTION 6-B.7.*)

VI. **<u>John Malcolm Fraser</u>**, born in 1917 in Woodville, New Zealand; son of Jack Fraser and Mary Charlotte Agnes Fraser. His first wife was named *<u>Joan</u>* (maiden name not available). His second marriage was to *<u>Georgia Ethel May Conroy Robinson</u>*. She was born in Charter Towers, in the north part of Queensland, Australia, daughter of Alfred Herbert Conroy and Georgia May Lukes.

Georgia and John Malcolm Fraser live in Wellington, New Zealand.

## 5-B.3: ELIZABETH GEORGESON O'BRIAN (1890-1934)
### Daughter of Charlotte Umphray Robertson: The Lyver Branches

V. **<u>Elizabeth Georgeson O'Brian</u>** was born on July 27, 1890, in New Zealand. She was the youngest daughter of Francis O'Brian and Charlotte Umphray Robertson. (4-E above.) Many of the recollections and perceptions that follow are taken from a family history written by Sonja Mitchell, Elizabeth's great-granddaughter, based in part on interviews of her grandmother "Ness" Beere, Elizabeth's fourth daughter.[223]

Elizabeth married *<u>Robert Jamieson Lyver (Liver)</u>* on March 20, 1913, in Springlands, Wairau, New Zealand.[224] He was born on November 1, 1886, in Killearn, Stirling, Scotland. They had eight children. Robert Lyver worked for the New Zealand Post Office. For a while, until about 1922, the family lived in a small house in Bealey, about one hundred miles inland from Christchurch on the South Island of New Zealand, where Robert was the post-master. Bealey is situated beside the Waimakariri River, with a view up the wide, braided river and surrounded by the gorgeous high peaks of the Southern Alps. Today, a bridge spans the river, but in those days the river was a formidable barrier, and the town grew up as a staging post to cross the river.

Every week or so, Elizabeth would pile the children onto a horse-drawn cart and cross the river to go into the nearby township of Arthur's Pass to do their shopping. This could be dangerous, as the depth and width of the water often changed, depending on weather conditions, and the river was impassable after heavy rain.

In addition to his duties as postmaster in Bealey, Robert Lyver would go hunting for keas—brownish-green parrots native to the New Zealand mountains, which have a nasty habit of attacking sheep and pecking them to death. The government paid a bounty of two shillings for every kea beak brought in from the field. Robert also hunted for wild pigs, and sometimes, the pig bladders were blown up and used for footballs.

As Robert received promotions in the post office, the family had to move several times. About 1922, the family relocated to Christchurch, the major city of the South Island. Ness remembered as a small child playing in the paddocks which then surrounded their house and making little forts out of kerosene tins. "I used to hide behind my fort. My mother would be calling me, wanting me for something, and I would hide down underneath these tins. There was a coal box at the back door, and she'd pick up a piece of coal and fling it, and it would hit one of the tins which would fall down on me. I would then decide she meant business." Next, the growing family moved to Ashburton, where more children were born. About 1928, an earthquake hit Ashburton. Ness was then about nine years old but still vividly remembered the concrete on the school playground starting to roll and ripple like waves while the children were out playing.

About a year later, the Lyvers were on the move again. This time it was a transfer to Lower Hutt on the North Island, where they rented a house while they waited for their own to be built in nearby Waiwhetū. The house in Lower Hutt was "chocolate-colored" and surrounded by a beautiful garden containing many kinds of colorful bushes and plants—azaleas, bulbs, verbena, freesias, grape hyacinths, violets, pansies—and a vegetable patch with a big asparagus bed. The children were first introduced to electricity while living in Lower Hutt. Until then, they had used gas mantles. "A rather well-to-do family were the first to get it," Ness remembered. "Everyone in the neighborhood went to their homes and flicked the switches. It was quite exciting really."

The new home on Cambridge Terrace in Waiwhetū was finally completed about 1929. While Robert continued working for the post office, Elizabeth stayed home and tended to her large family. Ness recalled, "There wasn't much talk about women's rights in those days. Couples worked as a team, and women never questioned their role as homemaker." Times grew tough for the family as the Great Depression of the 1930s grew worse. But everyone in the community was in the same boat, and in a sense the financial hardships led neighbors to grow closer and help each other out whenever possible. In a sense, the Depression made for a closer community and greater sharing. Fortunately, Robert kept his job and was an expert gardener, so the family never went hungry.

During these lean years, the children's clothes were made and repaired by their parents. Elizabeth used flour bags to make tea towels, pillow cases, and even underwear and linings for the boys' pants. Almost nothing was thrown out. Ness recalled, "As a young person, I was very conscious of holes in my shoes and tried desperately to hide them from view. Our father would buy sheets of leather to repair our shoes and there was no question of putting them into the shop for repair. Shoes were passed down from one child to another, which was not good for our feet. At least we did have shoes, though, while some other children would go around barefoot."

Elizabeth O'Brian Lyver died suddenly on September 19, 1934, in Wellington, New Zealand. Only forty-three years old, she suffered a fatal stroke, apparently caused by undiagnosed high blood pressure. Her death came as a terrible shock to the family, leaving several young children without a mother.

Charlotte, who had recently turned seventeen, took up the role of mother for the younger children, doing a lot of the housework and cooking. She left school early to go home and prepare meals but still worked as an usher at a local movie theater at night.

As the children grew, they pursued various employment opportunities and hobbies. Ness was encouraged by her father to learn secretarial skills so she could get a position in a government office. This was not of much interest to her, but as a matter of necessity, she succeeded in getting a job at the Transport Office for three pounds a week (considered not bad pay at the time). The family members were also involved in sports and outdoor activities, including tennis, cricket, and hiking with the New Zealand Tramping Club.

Robert Lyver died a decade after Elizabeth, on August 14, 1945, when he was fifty-eight. Although he had remarried, the new wife was not close to his children.

**Children of Elizabeth Georgeson O'Brian**

VI. **<u>Olive May O'Brian Lyver</u>** was born on May 2, 1910, in Wellington, New Zealand. Olive married *Frederick Charles Newlyn* in Lower Hutt, New Zealand, in February 1938. Frederick was born on March 22, 1901, in London, England, son of Mary Ann Stubbles and Frederick Charles Newlyn.

Olive and Fred had three children, and he had two daughters by a previous marriage, Ruth Newlyn and Doris Newlyn. Fred died on December 14, 1971, at age seventy. Olive died on May 9, 1989, in Lower Hutt, New Zealand. She was seventy-eight.

**Children of Olive May Lyver**

VII. **<u>Margaret Joy Newlyn</u>**, born on May 5, 1938, in Wellington, New Zealand. She married *William Robert O'Leary* on October 14, 1961, in Lower Hutt, New Zealand. Bill was the son of Annie Evelyn Johnson and William Matthew O'Leary and was born on September 13, 1938, in Lower Hutt. They have three children.

**Children of Margaret Joy Newlyn**

VIII. **<u>Neil Craig O'Leary</u>**, born on August 22, 1962, in Lower Hutt, Wellington, New Zealand. Unmarried, he lives in London, England, and works as an accountant there.

VIII. **<u>Susan Jane O'Leary</u>**, born on June 7, 1965, in Lower Hutt, Wellington, New Zealand. Susan married *Raymond Ian Webster* in London, England, on September 1, 1995. He was born in London on August 13, 1959, the son of Lillian Evelyn Finch and Joseph Herbert Webster. Ray is a self-employed contractor and painter. They have two children and are in the process of moving to New Zealand.

**Children of Susan Jane O'Leary**

IX. **<u>Matthew Joseph Webster</u>**, born on February 21, 1996, in London, England.

IX. **<u>Amy Louise Webster</u>**, born on November 29, 1997, in Lower Hutt, Wellington, New Zealand.

VIII. **<u>Christine Anne O'Leary</u>**, born on September 25, 1971, in Lower Hutt, Wellington, New Zealand. Unmarried, she works as a hairdresser in Brighton, England.

VI. **<u>Jessie Cameron Lyver</u>**, daughter of Elizabeth O'Brian and Robert Lyver, was born on February 19, 1914, in Waiwhetū in Lower Hutt, Wellington New Zealand. She married *Edward Thomas Claude Smith* (called "Claude"), who was born on December 26, 1908, in Balclutha on the South Island of New Zealand. They had two children. Jessie died at the age of sixty-five on April 6, 1979, at their home in Lower Hutt. Claude died there on November 28, 1985. He was seventy-nine.

### Children of Jessie Cameron Lyver

VII. **<u>Edward Thomas Claude Smith Jr.</u>**, born on March 9, 1941, in Lower Hutt, Wellington, New Zealand. Eddie married *Glenys Lorraine Orr* on March 19, 1964. She was born on July 19, 1942, the daughter of Elizabeth Frances Douhett and James Ernest Orr. They had five children.

### Children of Edward Thomas Claude Smith

VIII. **<u>Gary Raymond Smith</u>**, born on March 19, 1965. He married *Carla Nancy Anderson*, daughter of Nancy Margaret Thompson and John Arthur Anderson, in Lower Hutt on March 25, 1995. Carla was born on March 10, 1967, in Lower Hutt, Wellington, New Zealand.

VIII. **<u>Darryl Edward Smith</u>**, born on October 18, 1966. He married *Annette Allen,* daughter of Tony Allen, on February 26, 1994. They have one child.

### Child of Darryl Edward Smith

IX. **<u>Cory Darryl Smith</u>**, born on December 13, 1987, in Lower Hutt, Wellington, New Zealand.

VIII. **<u>Craig Allen Smith</u>**, born on September 22, 1968.

VIII. **<u>Antony Claude Smith</u>** (called "Tony"), born about 1970.

VIII. **<u>Janelle Smith</u>**, born on April 4, 1972. She died as an infant.

VII. **<u>Eunice Doreen Smith</u>** (called "Doreen"), was born in Lower Hutt, Wellington, New Zealand, on November 25, 1946. Gifted with special musical talent from an early age, Doreen was trained in England for a career as a concert pianist. Instead, she chose a spiritual course and joined the Dominican Order in New Zealand to become a Catholic nun. She later went into nursing. After qualifying as a nurse, she spent time working on a hospital theater team at a Saudi military base in the high southern mountains of Saudi Arabia. That was an exciting and rewarding time for Doreen, during which she learned Arabic, explored the countryside, and enjoyed snorkeling and relaxing in the Red Sea. After that experience, she settled in Australia and worked in key hospital staff positions in surgery and related skills.

Doreen lives in Sydney, Australia. Music remains an important part of her life, and she continues to practice on her grand piano.

VI. **<u>Robert James Lyver</u>**, oldest son of Elizabeth O'Brian and Robert Lyver, was born in Bealey, Ashburton, New Zealand, on February 24, 1916. As a big brother to many, Bob was looked up to by the others and took a responsible role in the family from a tender age. He took up a paper run so that he could buy his own clothes as well as help pay for things for the family, such as carpet for the home. Later in life he, as the ship's radio operator, was the last person to leave the *Wahine* when it sank during a terrible storm in Wellington Harbor in 1968.

Bob married *Muriel Gray* in Lower Hutt, Wellington, on April 4, 1942. She was born in Martinborough, Wellington, New Zealand, on February 28, 1916, daughter of Grace Allen and Walter Henry Gray. Muriel and Bob had three children. She died on June 25, 1983, at Whakatane Hospital, and Bob died on January 20, 1987, at Lowry Bay, Wellington, New Zealand. Both are buried at Tauranga Lawn Cemetery.

### Children of Robert James Lyver

VII. **<u>Robert John Lyver</u>** (called "John") was born on February 4, 1943, in Howick, Auckland, New Zealand. He married *Lesley Ann Hicks* in Brooklyn,

Wellington, New Zealand, on October 11, 1969. She was born on July 23, 1945, in Wellington, daughter of Beatrix Mary Lucre and Stanley George Hicks. John, who is an information technology manager, has graciously supplied us much of our information on the Lyvers and related branches.

VII. **Bruce Cameron Lyver** was born on April 12, 1946 in Rarotonga, Cook Islands. He married *Lorraine Pollard*. They have one child.

### Child of Bruce Cameron Lyver

VIII. **Geoffrey Lyver**.

VII. **Pamela Joan Lyver** was born in Lower Hutt, Wellington, New Zealand, on December 27, 1952. She married *Tom Donnelly* in Pāuatahanui, Wellington, New Zealand, on March 15, 1986. He was born on April 1, 1936, son of Ellen Clark and Hugh Ringhard Donnelly. They have two children.

### Children of Pamela Joan Lyver

VIII. **Kieran Robert Hugh Donnelly**, born on July 24, 1987, in Lower Hutt, Wellington, New Zealand.

VIII. **Lauren Sioban Elyn Donnelly**, born on January 18, 1990, in Paraparaumu, Wellington, New Zealand.

VI. **Charlotte Robertson Lyver**, daughter of Elizabeth O'Brian and Robert Lyver, was born on July 26, 1917, in New Zealand. She married *Basil Adam Gibson*, and they had two sons. (*SEE SECTION 6-B.9.*)

VI. **Agnes Cawthron Lyver** (called "Ness"), daughter of Elizabeth O'Brian and Robert Lyver, was born on June 1, 1919, in Bealey, South Island, New Zealand. She married *Leonard Beere*, and they were the parents of two daughters.(*SEE SECTION 6-B.10.*)

VI. **Harry O'Brian Lyver**, second son of Elizabeth O'Brian and Robert Lyver, was born on August 2, 1921, in Linwood, Christchurch, New Zealand. He married *Norah Donkin*, and they had four children. Harry died on March 20, 1989. (*SEE SECTION 6-B.11.*)

VI. **James Lyver**, third son of Elizabeth O'Brian and Robert Lyver, was born about 1923 in New Zealand; he died on March 27, 1964, in Kaeo, North Auckland, New Zealand, age about forty.

Jim suffered from severe asthma throughout his life and required a lot of attention. Sometimes, his asthma attacks would get so bad that he would have to lean against a wall, struggling to get a breath. Olive, the oldest sister, was especially attentive and helpful in taking care of Jim as a child. He never married. His sister Charlotte recalls that Jim was a solicitor for the South Island cricket teams.

VI. **John William Lyver** (called "Jack"), fourth son and youngest child of Elizabeth O'Brian and Robert Lyver, was born on June 18, 1927, in Ashburton, New Zealand. He married *Olwen Joan Lloyd*. They have three children and live near Auckland, New Zealand. (*SEE SECTION 6-B.12.*)

## 5-B.4: MARY ELIZABETH IRVINE JAMIESON (1848-1922)
### Daughter of Robina Robertson: The Greaves Branches

V. **Mary Elizabeth Irvine Jamieson**, daughter of Robina Robertson and Thomas Gifford Jamieson (4-G above), was born on December 31, 1848, in Scalloway in Tingwall Parish, Shetland, where her father was the local schoolteacher. As a child she left Shetland and was taken to Australia with her parents and younger family members.

At the age of twenty-four, she married *John Greaves* at the family's home in Corop, Victoria, on June 26, 1873; the services were performed by Rev. David Renton, Presbyterian Minister. John, a native of Rawdon in Yorkshire, England, was born on October 22, 1829, and was almost twenty years older than his wife. They had two children.

John Greaves worked as a contractor in Victoria. He died on June 19, 1904, in Townsville, Queensland. Mary Elizabeth died on January 22, 1922, in Ingham, Queensland, where she had moved to live with her daughter's family after the death of her husband. She is buried in Ingham Cemetery.

**Children of Mary Elizabeth Irvine Jamieson**

VI. <u>**John Thomas Greaves**</u> (called "Jack") was born on November 18, 1873, in Corop, Victoria, Australia. Delphine Slattery, his great-grandniece, tells that Jack was involved in logging operations with the Hartwell family in northern Australia: "John Thomas came up to Queensland to work for the Hartwells, who had a sawmilling plant which they took all over the area around here cutting sleepers [railroad ties] for the Railway when it was being put through to the North. They were around Ayr (about an hour and a half south of Townsville by present day travel), and they were also around Townsville and went as far as Liverpool Creek which is just south of Innisfail. It was apparently a big concern and took a bit of moving."

In October 1900, Jack wrote in somewhat primitive prose about work and life in the logging camps in a letter to his mother: "I am so glad Father is getting better. I was longing to [know] how he was getting on, in fact how you all were getting. . . . I am getting on like a house on fire. Emily does all my washing & mending – I done no washing that not to bad for a new chum. . . . We have shifted [the sawmill plant] twenty two miles further up the line. It is a big plant to shift. . . . I am on the bench with Harry [Hartwell]. They put through between 6 to 7 hundred sleepers a day with one mill."

Jack's letter suggests that his sister Ruby wanted him to find out from Harry Hartwell (her future husband, as things turned out) whether the company might have a job opening for her, and he was concerned that the timing was not right to ask. He wrote, "in regards to Ruby question, [it's] a bit to strong to ask Harry just now as he [has] a trying time of it alright, [it's] enough to turn a saint off . . . There was seven men sacked because they would not get to work at the right time, they thought they had him under the whip, so things are not all honey being a Boss. He is real good tempered – if I was in his place I would be jumping on the chest of some of them. . . "

Another affectionate letter came from Jack in Ross River, Queensland, to his mother and his sister Ruby just before Christmas in 1900. He wrote:

*I just receive[d] your so loving letters. I was so glad that you are all well that dear old Dad is keeping so well. I would have written sooner only we were busy getting finish and moving our camp home, we are at the house at last but it is terribly dry at present. We are expecting rain every day but [it] blows off again. Harry caught a very bad cold but he is getting better now. We blew an alligator up in dynamite, he was eighteen feet long but we [were] waiting till he had decay[ed] to get his teeth but we was to late . . . I can't see no opening for you here yet but I will have a look round, as I am in town nearly every day. I receive[d] the pretty tie you sent – I thank you with all my heart. I am sending you some money down instead of a present as I think it will be more useful to you all. There is going to be federation sport in Townsville on New years day, it is going to be a big day. We will be starting the saw mill going after Xmas sawing house timber . . . I hope Ruby will get away for her holidays to Melbourne, it will do her good . . . Harry is sending Ruby a present . . . I remain your loving son & brother Jack.*

Never married, Jack Greaves died at the age of thirty-four on April 9, 1908, as the result of an accident in Townsville, Queensland. He is buried in the Townsville Cemetery.

VI. **<u>Robina Greaves</u>** (called "Ruby") was born on October 28, 1875, in Wanalta, Victoria. She married *<u>Harry Hartwell</u>* of Townsville, Queensland, and they had six children. Robina died on November 2, 1962, at the age of eighty-seven. (*SEE SECTION 6-B.13.*)

## 5-B.5: PETER JAMIESON (1850-1902)
### Son of Robina Robertson

V. **<u>Peter Jamieson</u>**, son of Robina Robertson and Thomas Gifford Jamieson (4-G above), was born on April 16, 1850, in Scalloway in Tingwall Parish, Shetland. As a child of about six, he was taken with his family to Australia, where he grew up and lived the rest of his life.

Peter Jamieson married *<u>Louisa Ridgewell</u>* in 1877 in Stawell, Victoria, Australia. She was born in 1858 in Gawler Plains, South Australia. They had five sons, at least one of whom died as a baby. Louisa died as a young woman on March 10, 1885, in Stawell, leaving four sons under eight years old. Second, in 1886, in Lubeck, Victoria, Peter married *<u>Eleanor Ellen Lynch</u>* (or *<u>Jenkins</u>*),[225] who became a stepmother to Peter's four children. They also had one child.

Peter Jamieson died at the age of fifty-one on January 26, 1902, in Yalaquil, Victoria. His occupation was listed as commission agent, probably in the sale of wheat or wool.

**Children of Peter Jamieson**

VI. **<u>Thomas Gifford Jamieson</u>**, first son of Louisa Ridgewell and Peter Jamieson, was born in 1878 in Mt. Pleasant, Victoria, Australia. He married *Mary Reid* in 1908 in Victoria, and they had three children.

### Children of Thomas Gifford Jamieson

VII. **<u>Louisa Bridget Jamieson</u>**, born in 1909 in Victoria, Australia.

VII. **<u>Peter John Jamieson</u>**, born in 1911 in Victoria, Australia.

VII. **<u>Mary Margaret Jamieson</u>**, born in 1913 in Victoria, Australia; she died as a small child in 1914 in Victoria.

VI. **<u>Alfred Peter Jamieson</u>**, second son of Louisa Ridgewell and Peter Jamieson, was born in 1880 in Mt. Pleasant, Victoria, Australia.

VI. **<u>Francis Herbert Jamieson</u>**, third son of Louisa Ridgewell and Peter Jamieson, was born in 1881 in Murtoa, Victoria, Australia.

VI. **<u>William George Jamieson</u>**, fourth son of Louisa Ridgewell and Peter Jamieson, was born in 1883 in Rupanyup, Victoria, Australia. He died there as an infant, age one month, twenty-one days.

VI. **<u>Edward Norman Jamieson</u>**, fifth son of Louisa Ridgewell and Peter Jamieson, was born in 1884 in Rupanyup, Victoria, Australia. In 1907, he married *Elizabeth Bridget McGinn* in Victoria. They had two children.

### Children of Edward Norman Jamieson

VII. **<u>Norman Edward Thomas Jamieson</u>**, born in 1908 in Horsham, Victoria, Australia.

VII. **<u>Noel Hanley Jamieson</u>**, born in 1912 in Rainbow, Victoria, Australia.

VI. **<u>Loyal Lubeck Jamieson</u>**, child of Peter Jamieson and his second wife Eleanor Lynch, born in 1886 in Lubeck, Victoria, Australia.

# THE AMERICAN BRANCHES, GENERATION FIVE

## 5-C.1: GEORGIA DUMBRECK ROBERTSON (1870-1952)
### Daughter of Charles Dumbreck Robertson: The Perin Branch

V. **<u>Georgia Dumbreck Robertson</u>**, daughter of Cynthia Buck and Charles Dumbreck Robertson (4-C above), was born in Covington, Kenton County, Kentucky, on October 7, 1870.[226] Covington is directly across the Ohio River from Cincinnati.

Georgia married *<u>Lyman Perin</u>*, who was born on January 10, 1863, in Bellefontaine, Ohio; his parents were Lyman C. Perin (born on March 6, 1826; died on February 4, 1905) and Mary Elizabeth Buchanan (born on March 16, 1838; died on June 5, 1922). Lyman owned and operated a grain mill on the Ohio River. They had four children.

Lyman Perin died at the age of seventy-three in Cincinnati, Ohio, on September 24, 1936. Following her husband's death, Georgia lived for many years in an apartment at the Alms Hotel in Cincinnati. She died of cancer on April 20, 1952, at Good Samaritan Hospital in Cincinnati, and was buried in the Robertson family plot in Spring Grove Cemetery. She was eighty-one years old.

**Children of Georgia Dumbreck Robertson**

VI. **<u>Reuben Robertson Perin</u>**, son of Georgia Robertson and Lyman Perin, born on November 22, 1900, and died two days later, on November 24, in Cincinnati, Hamilton County, Ohio.

VI. **<u>Gail Dumbreck Perin</u>**, eldest daughter of Georgia Robertson and Lyman Perin, was born on February 14, 1902, in Cincinnati, Hamilton County, Ohio. A gifted artist, Gail married *<u>Clifford Brand</u>* on August 7, 1939. He worked for the U.S. Post Office. They had two children. Gail died in 1956 in Cincinnati, Ohio.

She and Clifford Brand are buried in Spring Grove Cemetery, Section 79, Lot 1, in Cincinnati.

### Children of Georgia Gail Perin

VII. **Clifford Perin Brand** (called "Perry"), born in Cincinnati, Ohio, on August 6 (year unknown).

VII. **Georgia Gail Brand**, born in Cincinnati, Ohio. (Birthday September 19, year unknown). She married a Mr. *Lazarus*. They had two sons and divorced.

### Children of Georgia Gail Brand

VIII. [Name of first child not available.]

VIII. [Name of second child not available.]

VI. **Reuben Lyman Perin**,[227] son of Georgia Robertson and Lyman Perin, was born on June 8, 1904, in Cincinnati, Ohio; he died on September 23, 1983, in Scarsdale, New York. He married *Virginia Danson*, and they had four children. (*SEE SECTION 6-C.1.*)

VI. **Cynthia Perin**, ("called Bumpy") born on February 26, 1907, in Cincinnati, Hamilton County, Ohio, the daughter of Georgia Robertson and Lyman Perin. She died on May 12, 1973, age sixty-seven, in Green Valley, Arizona. She married *James Donald Mawhinney*, and they had three children. (*SEE SECTION 6-C.2.*)

## 5-C.2: REUBEN BUCK ROBERTSON (1879-1972)
### Son of Charles Dumbreck Robertson

V. **Reuben Buck Robertson Sr.** was born on June 11, 1879, in Cincinnati, Ohio, and given the name of his maternal grandfather, Reuben Buck. He was the son of Cynthia Buck and Charles Dumbreck Robertson (4-C above).

Reuben attended Walnut Hills High School in Cincinnati, where he starred on the football and track teams. In the fall of 1896, he entered Yale College in New Haven, Connecticut, the first member of his family to attend college. At Yale, he continued his interest in sports. Injuries kept him off the football field, but Reuben again starred at track, in which he specialized in the shot put and hammer throw. In those days, Yale, Harvard, and Princeton were regarded as the "Big Three" of college athletics in America and usually dominated the intercollegiate meets.

Reuben graduated from Yale College in the Class of 1900. Intending to follow his father's profession, he attended the Cincinnati Law School while working as a law clerk for his father. He received his law degree in 1903 and practiced as a young attorney in his father's law office from 1903 to 1906. Years later, he recalled those times in Cincinnati when he was a law student and a young attorney starting out in his father's law office, and the city was largely controlled by the corrupt political machine of "Boss" George B. Cox:

> *After graduating from Yale, I studied law at the Cincinnati Law School. The Law School was then located in the old Mercantile Library building on the East side of Walnut Street, between Fourth and Fifth Streets.*
>
> *On the opposite side of the street was a very ornate Beer Saloon, owned and operated by George B. Cox. We law students frequented it at lunch because, after careful "Research," we found that George B. served the biggest free lunch in town, if you purchased a stein of beer or a bowl of soup. The beautiful oil painting over the bar portrayed a lady of charming form, but quite devoid of garments. So far as I know, a room back of this bar was where the "gang" congregated, on call of George B. when important matters of business had to be discussed, and it was from this office that the Generalissimo issued his directives.*
>
> *I think you should understand clearly that George B. was a <u>thoroughly honest</u> political leader who never stole a penny from the city's till. However, he was admittedly a man of shrewdness and power and many people sought his advice. If a contractor wanted to secure a contract for paving a street, for building a City building, for selling supplies to the City, the <u>advice</u> of George B. always proved to be most helpful; and of course, for such advice, he was entitled to a suitable fee.*
>
> *Ambitious individuals who sought political preferment knew who to see to get the election machinery into smooth operating order and of course machinery to run smoothly must be greased. The saloon business must have been profitable, for George lived in a $300,000 mansion in the Mt. Auburn section and died a millionaire. Of course gambling joints, houses of prostitution and the like found it wise to see George if they were to avoid police interference. The gang followed the practice honored by Tammany Hall and the political organizations of such cities as Chicago,*

*with tightly organized and firmly disciplined captains in charge of every precinct, with favors and coercion as their tools.*

*At that time, traffic on the Ohio river was active, and many roustabouts and steam boat employees occupied boarding houses and flop houses (at 25 cents a night) on Water Street, facing the boat landing. These workmen were, like most river men, "comers and goers" and formed a fine reservoir of purchasable votes, when votes were needed by the gang. This was looked upon as a most important area and for its control, one of George B's most trusted and most politically wise lieutenants, Mike Mullen, was put in charge.*

*Mike believed that attainment of the objective was the thing, and the method of arriving at the objective was of no importance. The goon squad was called upon as needed to prevent a recalcitrant voter from reaching the polling place.*

*While I was in law school some restlessness began to develop regarding the autocracy maintained by George B., and an effort to check his power was organized. It was thought that some restraints might be accomplished if "watchers" were provided at each polling place, from among the younger voters who were not involved with the gang. Harry Hunt and I had volunteered to help and were assigned to Mike Mullen's water front, but we were just `babes in the woods' when we entered Mike Mullen's domain, and I'm sure that vote purchasing at $1.00 per head went merrily on just as though we hadn't been there, and George B.'s candidate won almost a unanimous approval.*

*Between classes at the Law School, I spent as much time as possible getting indoctrinated in the ways of a law office. My father, after completing his term as Judge of the Common Pleas Court, joined forces with Morris L. Buchwalter (who had also completed his term as Judge), to form the partnership Robertson and Buchwalter. Judge Buchwalter's son Robert, Yale '99, and I were the office neophytes, hoping ultimately to be accepted as full scale members of the firm. The Buchwalters were Republicans, the Robertsons Democrats, so Robert and I heard both sides of the political arguments. The Buchwalters looked the other way when the short-comings of Cox and his associates were mentioned.[228]*

On June 7, 1905, Reuben married twenty-one-year-old *Hope Lindenberger Thomson*. Hope was born on September 8, 1883, in Cincinnati, Ohio. She was the daughter of Laura Gamble[229] and Peter Gibson Thomson, a prominent publisher and the founder of a major pulp and paper enterprise now known as the Champion International Corporation.[230]

Following a nationwide financial panic and economic depression in 1905 – 1906, Reuben's father-in-law, Peter G. Thomson, encountered severe difficulties in his business ventures. To make matters worse, he was taken ill and ordered to bed by the doctor. Because Peter G.'s sons had other problems to cope with, and had no knowledge of the kinds of problems being encountered in the newly established Champion Fibre Company in Canton in the rugged mountain country of western North Carolina, the Thomsons asked Reuben Robertson to go down for thirty days and report on the conditions there.

Reuben agreed to the temporary assignment, arriving in Canton with his young bride and baby daughter in September of 1906. Little did they realize they would stay there for the rest of their lives. The first thirty days was extended to sixty, and soon, Reuben was put in charge of the entire logging and timber operations for the new company.

The situation was chaotic. As Reuben later wrote, "The executives at Canton had found many areas of disagreement and very few occasions for cooperation. Discords, frictions and jealousies were rampant." The problems among competing managers in the Canton operation became so acute that in November 1907, Peter G. Thomson granted the young lawyer complete control over the entire operation in a letter, stating: "Mr. Reuben B. Robertson is hereby given full authority to take entire charge of details of every kind at the plant of the Champion Fibre Co., to employ and discharge hands, and his decisions are to be absolute in all matters."

This mandate was sometimes referred to as Reuben Robertson's "Letter of Marque" because of the extremely broad powers it conferred upon him. He later recalled:

> *"[it] gave me a degree of organizational respectability and was never directly challenged. Obviously I was inexperienced in the problems of pulp and paper extract manufacturing; I was there because Champion's ox was in the ditch. One of the first moves made to establish a "cease fire" among the warring executives was to bring them all together for a daily luncheon meeting. These meetings proved to be most effective, not only in maintaining diplomatic relationships between the individuals but also in educating the undersigned in the techniques of mill operation. For the most part only "problems" were discussed, so the writer gained his familiarity with the company activities more from what was going wrong than from what was going right.*

When Hope and Reuben Robertson and six-month old daughter first arrived in western North Carolina, their home was a small slab cottage in the remote logging town of Sunburst, near the rugged Richland Balsam mountains, a dozen miles south of the pulp and paper mill which was being built in Canton. This beautiful area is now traversed by the Blue Ridge Parkway, which runs along the high ridges a few miles south of the old Sunburst logging village, but in those days it was still almost wilderness. There were no paved roads, and the dirt roads that did exist were rough and often impassible. A narrow-gauge logging train called "The Pea Vine" ran along the Pigeon River between Sunburst and the Canton mill.

It was a huge change for Hope, a young woman who had grown up in a well-to-do family in a large, sophisticated city, but she was tough and resourceful. In later years, she recalled it as a great learning experience and a happy time for her. She said she was never lonely or homesick, as she had no time to think about such matters. Like other women in the town, her days were spent caring for her baby, washing, ironing, cooking, and making clothes.

Around 1908, with a growing family, they moved to the West Asheville area of Buncombe County. In the 1940s, Reuben and Hope acquired a large, splendid country estate in Flat Rock, near Hendersonville, North Carolina, and after that they lived in a stone mansion on top of Town Mountain in Asheville. They also kept a home near the Atlantic shore in Ft. Lauderdale, Florida.

In 1912, Reuben Robertson was made general manager of the Canton mill. In 1916, he became vice president, and in 1925 he was made president and general manager. Reuben succeeded his late brother-in-law, Logan C. Thomson, as president of the combined Champion Paper and Fibre Company, Inc. on August 17, 1946.[231] He held that position until 1950, when he was appointed chairman of the Board of Directors, and his son, Reuben B. Robertson Jr., became president of the company. After his retirement in 1960, he was given the titles of Director Emeritus and Honorary Chairman of the Board.

After the pulp mill was constructed at Canton, the logging operations at Sunburst were phased out, and at Reuben's urging, a large dam was constructed to create a reservoir that could supply water for the mill in times of drought. The result was that about a mile of the upper Pigeon River valley, the rail line, and the small Sunburst station were flooded. A deep, clear, new lake was formed, called Lake Logan in honor of Hope's brother Logan Thomson, and looked very much like one of the lochs of Highland Scotland. Reuben Robertson Sr.

rebuilt one of the old cabins of Sunburst into a mountain lodge, which he called "Sit-N-Whittle," for a family retreat, and his children and other relatives built cabins for themselves. In its rugged, isolated mountain setting, Lake Logan became one of the most beautiful spots in America. The families spent many happy summers at Lake Logan, and numerous world leaders were entertained there by Reuben and his sons over the years.[232]

Reuben B. Robertson Sr. was honored as "Man of the South" in 1950, based on a consensus of regional business leaders. He received an honorary Doctor of Science degree from North Carolina State University in 1932, (and the Reuben B. Robertson Forestry Lab at that institution was later named in his honor), an honorary Doctor of Laws from Western Carolina College in 1956, the Human Relations Award given by the Society for the Advancement of Management in 1957, and the 1954 Conservation Award of the American Forestry Association, among many other honors. He received such accolades with characteristic modesty and humor.

Throughout his long life, Reuben Buck Robertson had an abiding passion for family history. He published a book called *Leaves of a Family Tree* that explored some of the roots of our Robertsons, as well as those of the Buck family, and he published a separate book on the Scottish Thomson family of his wife Hope. Reuben and Hope, together with their teenage son Logan, visited Shetland in the summer of 1935, a homecoming adventure that he often mentioned in later years.[233] Hope recorded her impressions and observations in an article in *The Log*, a Champion company magazine that was distributed to mill workers, executives, and friends of the company. Her article introduced the trip as follows:

> *A lifelong dream of my husband's came true last summer, when he, Logan and I went to the Shetland Islands and saw the home in which his father was born. We took the S.S. St. Sunniva at Aberdeen, Scotland, for the 150 mile boat trip over waters that are frequently* **very** *rough, but, fortunately for us, were quite calm this time. The only reservation we could get was one small cabin for the three, so small that when we walked in together we could not turn around so had to back out; the distance between the berths was just as wide as Mr. Robertson's shoulders. But after seeing the islands, the difficulties of getting there dwindled into insignificance.*

We know that Reuben and Hope visited Walls and other places of interest on their trip to Shetland in 1935. They met at least one member of our Robertsons in Shetland, Margaret

Robertson Williamson of Riskaness (5-A.6 above), with whom Reuben continued to correspond for some time.

Reuben Buck Robertson died at the age of ninety-three on December 26, 1972, in Asheville, Buncombe County, North Carolina, having lived most of his life in the Smoky Mountains of western North Carolina. A great and much beloved man in the eyes and hearts of the people of North Carolina, "Mr. Reuben" was a giant in the fields of forestry and papermaking.

Reuben's wife, Hope Thomson Robertson, had passed away some fourteen years earlier, on September 19, 1958, also in Asheville. She was seventy-five.

**Children of Reuben B. Robertson Sr.**

VI. **Hope Thomson Robertson**, born on March 31, 1906, in Cincinnati, Ohio; died on September 7, 1973, age sixty-seven, in Asheville, Buncombe County, North Carolina. She was first married to _Bertram Colthup_ and second to Dr. _Russell L. Norburn_, and had three children. (_SEE SECTION 6-C.3._)

VI. **Reuben Buck Robertson Jr.**, born on June 27, 1908, in Asheville, North Carolina; died on March 13, 1960, age fifty-one, in Cincinnati, Ohio. He married _Margaret Louisa Watkins_, and they had six children. (_SEE SECTION 6-C.4._)

VI. **Laura Thomson Robertson**, born in 1913 in North Carolina; she died during the influenza epidemic of 1919, at the age of five, on February 4, 1919, and was buried in Spring Grove Cemetery in Cincinnati, Ohio (Sec. 79, Lot 1).

VI. **Logan Thomson Robertson**, born on April 18, 1916, in Asheville, North Carolina; died on December 16, 1987, age seventy-one, in Bruges, Belgium. He was married three times and had four children. _SEE SECTION 6-C.5._)

## 5-C.3: CHARLES ANDREW ROBERTSON (1882-1923)
### Son of Andrew Umphray Robertson

V. **Charles Andrew Robertson**, son of Andrew Umphray Robertson and Esther Hillman (4-F above), was born in Cincinnati, Hamilton County, Ohio, on October 7, 1882.

He married _Ellen May Kuhn_ on June 22, 1904. The daughter of Priscilla Rophier and

George Kuhn, Ellen was born on April 29, 1886. The had two children, Elsie and Charles. Ellen died on October 28, 1912.

Charles Andrew Robertson's second marriage was to *Georgia Conner* on October 13, 1915. She was born on August 30, 1890, in Asheville, North Carolina. She had a daughter, Charlotte, by a previous marriage, who was adopted by Charles. They had four children of their own: Andrew, Grace, Marge, and Jim.

Charles died in Cincinnati, Ohio, on March 20, 1923, at age forty. His widow, Georgia, was then thirty-three years of age, with a four-month old baby, three other children under the age of seven, and a daughter not quite eleven. Charles's two oldest children were seventeen and fifteen. Georgia Conner Robertson lived to the age of ninety-two, passing away on June 17, 1982, in Cincinnati, Ohio. She is buried at Rest Haven Cemetery in Cincinnati.

**Children of Charles Andrew Robertson**

VI. **Elsie Marie Robertson**, daughter of Ellen Mae Kuhn and Charles Andrew Robertson, born on April 15, 1905, in Hamilton County, Ohio. She was only seven years old when her mother died and just seventeen when her father died. She first married *James Monroe Crowder*, with whom she had three daughters. After the death of her first husband, she married *Robert Bruce Robertson* (no relation). (*SEE SECTION 6-C.6.*) She died on February 3, 1992, in Milford, Clermont County, Ohio.

VI. **Charles William Robertson**, son of Ellen Mae Kuhn and Charles Andrew Robertson, born in Cincinnati, Ohio, on January 29, 1908; died on December 20, 1972, at age sixty-four. His mother died when he was only four, and his father died when he was fifteen. He married *Marion Lomatch*, and they had three children. (*SEE SECTION 6-C.7.*)

VI. **Charlotte Robertson**, born on March 26, 1912, the daughter of Georgia Conner, was adopted by Charles Andrew Robertson after his marriage to her mother when Charlotte was three years old. On December 31, 1934, she married *Morgan Pennington* in Cincinnati, Ohio. Morgan was the owner and co-founder of a well-known local bakery company in Cincinnati. They had no children.

Charlotte lived in the lovely Amberley Village neighborhood of Cincinnati. After her death, the house was purchased by her half-sister Grace Robertson Guidi, and it us now owned by Grace's son Alfred Guidi Jr.

VI. **Andrew Francis Robertson**, first son of Charles Andrew Robertson and Georgia Conner, was born on August 13, 1916, in Cincinnati, Hamilton County, Ohio. His father died when Andy was only six years old. Andy Robertson's first wife was *Margaret* (called "Marge," last name unknown), who was born on February 13, 1912. They had one child. Andy's second marriage was to *Jackie Wright*, who died in 1972. His third wife was *Dorothy Carpenter*; they divorced.

Andrew Francis Robertson lived in Cincinnati and, after military service in World War II, worked for the Pennington Bakery, which was owned by his brother-in-law Morgan Pennington. He died on October 6, 1981, in the Veterans Administration Hospital in Cincinnati, Hamilton County, Ohio. He was sixty-five.

**Child of Andrew Francis Robertson**

VII. **James Michael Robertson**, son of Marge and Andrew Robertson, was born about 1948 in Cincinnati, Hamilton County, Ohio. According to other family members, he ran away from home and went to California in 1966 at the age of seventeen. Jim has not been heard from for many years.

VI. **Grace Elizabeth Robertson**, daughter of Charles Andrew Robertson and Georgia Conner, born on May 20, 1918. She was four years old when her father died. Grace married *Alfred John Guidi,* and they had three sons. She died on February 21, 1995, in Cincinnati, Ohio. (*SEE SECTION 6-C.8.*)

VI. **Margaret Robertson** (called "Marge"), second daughter of Georgia Conner and Charles Andrew Robertson, was born on April 29, 1920, in Cincinnati, Hamilton County, Ohio. She was still a small child, not yet three, at the time her father passed away.

Marge first married *Trevon Taylor* in 1940. They divorced, having no children. Second, Marge married *Edward Franklin Burdett* (called "Fuzzy") in Cincinnati. He was born on September 3, 1928, in St. Albans, West Virginia. That marriage also ended in divorce. On August 22, 1969, in Cincinnati, Marge married *Howard Eddy Ballagh*, who was born in San Francisco, California, on October 5, 1917.

Howard Ballagh died on February 3, 1995, in Cincinnati, Ohio, and is buried there at Rest Haven Cemetery. Marge lives in the Amberley Village suburb of Cincinnati.

VI. **James Reuben Robertson**, youngest child of Georgia Conner and Charles Andrew Robertson, was born on November 13, 1922, in Cincinnati, a few months before his father died. He married *Dorothy Grosch*, and they had three children. He died in 1997. (*SEE SECTION 6-C.9.*)

## 5-C.4: WILLIAM HILLMAN ROBERTSON (1886-1963)
### Son of Andrew Umphray Robertson

V. **William Hillman Robertson** was born in Cincinnati, Ohio, on June 21, 1886. He was the son of Esther Bosworth Hillman and Andrew Umphray Robertson (4-F above), and the grandson of Margaret Mouat and Thomas Robertson of Walls, Shetland (Section 3-C).

Sometimes called "Willie" by his friends and family, William Hillman Robertson moved to western North Carolina in 1908 to work for the new Champion Fibre Company mill, which was then nearing completion at Canton. He was active in civic and industry organizations, including the American Pulp and Paper Superintendents' Association and the Knights of Pythias. He retired as a department superintendent in 1954, after forty-six years of service at the Champion mill. In all that time he never missed a day of work.

On June 15, 1911, he married *Sarah Rebekah Leisher* in Canton, North Carolina. Born on December 20, 1891, in Chambersburg, Franklin County, Pennsylvania, she was the daughter of Catherine Anna Hepfer (called "Katie Ann") and John Hoffman Leisher.

Sarah Rebekah Leisher and William Hillman Robertson had ten children. The family experienced the tragic deaths of two of the sons at an early age.

William Hillman Robertson died on March 22, 1963, in Waynesville, North Carolina, at age seventy-six. Just forty-nine days later, on May 10, 1963, Rebekah died. She was seventy-one. Both are buried at Locust Field Cemetery in Canton, North Carolina.

**Children of William Hillman Robertson**

VI. <u>**Charles Brailler Robertson**</u>, oldest son of Sarah Rebekah Leisher and William Hillman Robertson, and named for a Dr. Brailler of Chambersburg, was born on May 31, 1912, in Haywood County, North Carolina. He died on May 13, 1927. Only fourteen years old, he got into a dispute with a teacher about whether he could take some material home from school with him. Grabbing the object, he raced out of the school and ran home with the teacher in hot pursuit. The boy dashed into the house, for some reason picked up his father's gun, and somehow ended up shooting himself. He is buried in Locust Field Cemetery in Canton.

VI. **Marguerite Marie Robertson** (called "Marie"), first daughter of Sarah Rebekah Leisher and William Hillman Robertson, was born in Canton, Haywood County, North Carolina, on April 7, 1914. On May 30, 1943, in Buncombe County, North Carolina, she married *Lloyd Thomas Allen*. He was born on January 6, 1905, in Whitney, Spartanburg County, South Carolina, the son of Marion Madison Allen and Fairy Ellen Metcalf. Marie and Lloyd settled in Los Angeles, California, but after having one child, they divorced. Marie retired as a supervisor in the US Customs Service in Los Angeles.

### Child of Marguerite Marie Robertson

VII. <u>**Lloyd Thomas Allen Jr.**</u> (called "Tommy") was born in Los Angeles, California, on December 23, 1949. Tommy was married in 1972 to *Danielle Dorsch*; they divorced, with no children. On September 23, 1984, in the Wilshire United Methodist Church in Los Angeles, Tommy married *Clemencia Patricia Valencia*, born on January 15, 1952, in Quito, Ecuador. She is the daughter of Maria Elena Jaramillo and Jaime Oswaldo Valencia. Tommy and Clemencia live in Los Angeles. They have no children.

VI. <u>**Esther Kathryn Robertson**</u>, second daughter of Sarah Rebekah and William Hillman Robertson, and named for both grandmothers, was born in Canton, North Carolina, on October 20, 1915. She married *Ralph Schofner Crawford*, and they had two children. (*SEE SECTION 6-C.10.*)

VI. **William Davis Robertson**, second son of Sarah Rebekah Leisher and William Hillman Robertson, was born in Canton, Haywood County, North Carolina, on August 29, 1917. He married *Nettie Mae Robertson* (no relation), and they had four children. (*SEE SECTION 6-C.11.*)

VI. **John Andrew Robertson** (called "Andrew"), third son of Sarah Rebekah Leisher and William Hillman Robertson, was born on November 26, 1919, in Canton, Haywood County, North Carolina; a handsome young man, he died when he was only eighteen.

Andrew ran away from home when he was seventeen. Lying about his age, he enlisted in the US Army in Texas. There, he was accidentally kicked by an army mule and, when it was discovered that he was underage, he was sent home. Andrew returned to Canton High School that fall and went out for the football team. During football practice on a hot afternoon, Andrew became ill, sat down on the field to rest for a minute, and died. His mother felt that he must have had a head injury or blood clot from the mule kick which caused his death, but the exact cause of his death was not determined.

VI. **James Boyd Robertson**, fourth son of Sarah Rebekah Leisher and William Hillman Robertson, was born in Canton, Haywood County, North Carolina, on May 29, 1922. On August 29, 1964, he married *Blanche Roberts*, born on January 15, 1918, in Reems Creek Township, Buncombe County, North Carolina. She is the daughter of Mildred Lee "Minnie" Brank and Morris Adler Roberts.

Jim and Blanche live on a farm on Parker Cove Road near Weaverville, North Carolina. Both retired as auditors for the U.S. Post Office Department. No children. Blanche is an accomplished genealogical researcher, and Jim is an outstanding amateur photographer. They are co-authors of this family history.

VI. **Albert Edward Robertson** (called "Bert") was born in Canton, Haywood County, North Carolina, on April 28, 1924, a son of Sarah Rebekah Leisher and William Hillman Robertson.

While serving in the US Marine Corps, Bert married *Mary Romanchuk* on May 15, 1943, in Harrisburg, Dauphin County, Pennsylvania. Mary was born on October 2, 1923, in Emaus, Lehigh County, Pennsylvania. Her parents, Mary Farynick and

Theodore F. Romanchuk, both of Ukrainian heritage, were born in the same area on the border of Poland and Czechoslovakia but did not know each other there, and both immigrated to Allentown, Pennsylvania, where they met and were married. (A year and a half later, Mary's older brother Michael Romanchuk married Albert's sister, Dorothy Hope.)

Bert and Mary settled a few miles from her family home. They live in the country near Coopersburg, Lehigh County, Pennsylvania. They have four children.

Bert Robertson retired from a small company in Allentown, Pennsylvania, where he was a designer and maker of special-order upholstered furniture. One couch he designed and built, which was covered with tapestry and mohair, when put together, was the length of a football field. It was ordered by, and flown to, the head of an Arab state. Bert also made a leather couch for a bank in Tokyo and made furniture for the home of the famous bandleader Fred Waring, among other notable customers.

### Children of Albert Edward Robertson

VII. **Albert Edward Robertson Jr.**, born in Canton, Haywood County, North Carolina, on November 10, 1944. Bert Jr. is unmarried and lives in Charleston, South Carolina. Now retired, he formerly headed the computer section for a hospital there.

VII. **Mary Louise Robertson**, born on January 25, 1947, in Allentown, Lehigh County, Pennsylvania. She graduated from a business college but was institutionalized after a mental breakdown. She is unmarried.

VII. **Gloria Anne Robertson**, born in Allentown, Lehigh County, Pennsylvania, on May 11, 1954. On November 23, 1972, she married *Steven O'Shall*, who was born on November 23, 1954, the son of Robert O'Shall. They divorced.

Gloria then married *David Alan Romberger*, who was born on November 22, 1950, in Shamokin, Columbia County, Pennsylvania, the son of Joy Doreen Williams and Austin Charles Romberger. Gloria and David were married on May 15, 1995, in Gatlinburg, Tennessee, and now live in Bath, Northampton County, Pennsylvania. Gloria works as a computer expert for the Good Shepherd

Rehabilitation Center in Allentown, Pennsylvania. David works for a computer company. They have no children.

VII. **John Andrew Robertson**, born on July 31, 1957, in Allentown, Lehigh County, Pennsylvania. He was educated at the School for the Deaf in Philadelphia. He is unmarried and is hospitalized in an institution near Pittsburgh, suffering from schizophrenia.

VI. **Dorothy Hope Robertson** (called "Dodie"), twin sister of George Reuben Robertson, was born in Canton, Haywood County, North Carolina, on December 22, 1926. She married *Michael Romanchuk* (the older brother of her sister-in-law Mary, who had married Albert Edward Robertson). They had four children. (*SEE SECTION 6-C.12.*)

VI. **George Reuben Robertson**, twin brother of Dorothy Hope Robertson, was born in Canton, Haywood County, North Carolina, on December 22, 1926.

George first married *Zoë Russell Clayton* on March 12, 1949; they divorced. Second, he married *Hazel Blanche Franklin*, the daughter of Louise Henson and Hardy Randolph Franklin, on October 14, 1951, in Haywood County, North Carolina. Hazel was born on January 14, 1928, in Haywood County and graduated from Brevard College in Brevard, North Carolina, in 1948. She retired from Champion International Corporation.

In World War II, George served in the army of occupation in Germany. He later was in the North Carolina National Guard, retiring with the rank of major. George worked some forty years for Champion Papers. He and Hazel live in Canton, North Carolina. They have three sons, including second-generation twins. (Amazingly, George's twin sister, Dorothy, also produced second-generation twins.)

**Children of George Reuben Robertson**

VII. **George Merrill Robertson** (called "Merrill") was born on December 23, 1957, in Asheville, Buncombe County, North Carolina. While serving in the US military forces in Germany, he married *Maria-Rita Katharina Ott* on May 7, 1983, in Wurzburg. She was born on August 12, 1956, in Wiebelsberg, Germany, the daughter of Maria Paulina Weimann and Josef Michel Ott.

Merrill and Maria presently live in Haywood County, North Carolina. They have no children.

VII.  **<u>Donald Robert Robertson</u>** was born on July 16, 1965, in Asheville, Buncombe County, North Carolina. He married *<u>Janet Machelle Henson</u>* on July 5, 1994, in Gatlinburg, Tennessee. She was born on May 6, 1970, in DeKalb County, Georgia, daughter of Debrah June Miller and James McKay Henson Jr. They divorced, with no children. On June 12, 1998, Donald married *<u>Pamela Ledford</u>* at Davis Chapel Methodist Church in Haywood County, North Carolina. Donald is a deputy sheriff in Haywood County.

VII  **<u>David Bruce Robertson</u>**, Donald's twin brother, was also born on July 16, 1965, in Asheville, North Carolina. He obtained a degree in food management and is employed at Deer Park, a restaurant at the Biltmore Estate in Asheville. David is unmarried and lives in Asheville.

VI.  **<u>Thomas Leisher Robertson</u>**, born in Canton, Haywood County, North Carolina, on January 12, 1930. While in the US Air Force at Lackland Air Force Base in Texas, Tom married *<u>Evangeline Flores Fuentes</u>*, who was born on June 20, 1929, the daughter of Fermin Montemayor Fuentes and Ursula Flores. Their marriage took place in San Antonio, Bexar County, Texas, on February 5, 1952. They had two daughters and a son and lived in San Antonio.

Tom Robertson died of heart disease on July 16, 1992, at the age of sixty-two. He is buried in Fort Sam Houston Cemetery in San Antonio. Tom was an employee of Roy Akers Funeral Service and was a Sunday School teacher in the Christian Church.

### Children of Thomas Leisher Robertson

VII.  **<u>Eva Carol Robertson</u>**, born in San Antonio, Bexar County, Texas, on January 11, 1953. She lives in San Antonio and works as a registered nurse. On May 10, 1997, Eva married *<u>Paul David Charleson</u>* at the Marbach Christian Church in San Antonio.

VII.  **<u>Teresa Gay Robertson</u>**, born in San Antonio, Bexar County, Texas, on August 3, 1954. Teresa is a school teacher, unmarried, and lives in San Antonio.

While working on the security team at the 1996 Atlanta Olympics, Teresa and her cousin Jennifer Overcast were at Centennial Park and narrowly missed the bomb explosion there that killed and injured many people.

VII. **Thomas Leisher Robertson Jr.**, born in Waynesville, Haywood County, North Carolina, on August 25, 1956. He married *Elizabeth Lourdes Davis*, daughter of Isabel Guerrero and George W. Davis. Elizabeth was born on March 11, 1951, in Mission, Hidalgo County, Texas, near the Rio Grande River in the southern tip of Texas. The wedding was held on June 21, 1980, at Our Lady of Guadalupe Catholic Church in Mission. Tom and Elizabeth live in San Antonio, Texas, where he works for a school food service company, and she is a teacher at Harlandale High School. They have two children.

### Children of Thomas Leisher Robertson Jr.

VIII. **John Thomas Robertson**, born on October 22, 1982, in San Antonio, Texas.

VIII. **Karen Isabel Robertson**, born on August 5, 1987, in San Antonio, Texas.

## 5-C.5: MAGNUS ROBERTSON (1892-1964)
### Son of Thomas Robertson

V. **Magnus Robertson**, second son of Alice Jamieson and Thomas Robertson (3-B above), was born in Bridge of Walls, Sandsting & Aithsting Parish, Shetland, on December 12, 1892. He immigrated to Canada as a young man and became a farmer in the province of Saskatchewan.

After a visit back home to Shetland in the early 1920s, Magnus returned to his Canadian farm, which was comprised of a quarter section of land—160 acres—in Beatty, Saskatchewan. On June 12, 1923, he married *Violet Ludella Dryborough* in Punnychy, Saskatchewan. She was born on March 6, 1903, in Manitoulin District, Ontario, Canada, daughter of Florence and David Dryborough. Violet and Magnus had six children, all but one born in Saskatchewan. They separated in the 1950s.

Magnus (called "Mack") ultimately gave up farming in the frigid prairieland of central Saskatchewan, rented his land to a neighbor, and moved west to Vancouver Island in British Columbia. He worked at Arrowsmith Farms, a cattle operation in Qualicum Beach. His daughter Eileen Kelley recalls that Magnus trained sheep dogs to herd and guard the cows. The Saskatchewan property (described as the south-east quarter of Section 34 in Township 46, Range 20, west of the Second Meridian) was finally sold in 1962.

Magnus died on February 14, 1964, in Victoria, Vancouver Island, British Columbia. He was seventy-one. Violet died in February 1968 in Aldergrove, British Columbia.

**Children of Magnus Robertson**

VI. **Ivy Catherine Robertson** was born on January 31, 1924, in Kelliher, Saskatchewan. She first married *Karl Ludwig Lundgren*, and they had five children. She later married and divorced *Frederick Reisig* and *Al Hunter*, with whom she had no children. (*SEE SECTION 6-C.17.*)

VI. **Margaret Isabella Robertson** (called "Bella") was born on May 11, 1927, in Prince Rupert, British Columbia. She first married *Harold Martin Hyggen*, and they had five children. She later married *Paul Collett*. Bella died at age seventy on August 11, 1997, in Port Alberni, British Columbia. (*SEE SECTION 6-C.18.*)

VI. **Rubina Marion Robertson** (called "Ruby"), third daughter of Violet Dryborough and Magnus Robertson, was born on October 31, 1929, in Melfort, Saskatchewan. In 1961, she married *Anthony Skoro*, who was born on July 17, 1925. They had three children. She died in an automobile accident on August 6, 1981, in Hope, British Columbia. Anthony is a retired logger and resides in Aldergrove, British Columbia.

**Children of Rubina Marion Robertson**

VII. **Thomas James Colin Robertson**, first son of Ruby Robertson, was born on July 18, 1961. In 1984, he married *Colleen Haney* in Calgary, Alberta. She was born on September 15, 1961. They are divorced, with one child.

**Child of Thomas James Colin Robertson**

VIII. **Gail Patricia Robertson**, born on March 17, 1984, in Calgary, Alberta.

VII. **Bradley Glenn Skoro**, son of Ruby Robertson and Tony Skoro, was born on May 6, 1965, in Surrey, British Columbia. Unmarried, he works as a bookkeeper and lives in Aldergrove, British Columbia.

VII. **Kelleen Gale Skoro**, daughter of Ruby Robertson and Tony Skoro, was born on September 1, 1966, in Surrey, British Columbia. She married *Patrick Michael Bannon* in Surrey on November 11, 1994. They have one son and are separated. Kelleen attended Fraser Valley College and is now an insurance broker in Burnaby, British Columbia. She and her son reside in New Westminster, British Columbia.

**Child of Kelleen Gale Skoro**

VIII. **Brett Sheldon Bannon**, born on January 23, 1995, in Burnaby, British Columbia.

VI. **Eileen Della Robertson**, fourth daughter of Violet Dryborough and Magnus Robertson, was born on April 24, 1931, in Melfort, Saskatchewan. She married *James Douglas Kelley*, with whom she has three children. Eileen also has an older son from an earlier relationship. (*SEE SECTION 6-C.19.*)

VI. **Hazel Alice Robertson**, fifth daughter of Violet Dryborough and Magnus Robertson, was born on October 28, 1932, in Beatty, Saskatchewan. She married *William Leckay* at the Knox United Church in Prince George, British Columbia. William was born on April 1, 1919. He worked as a peeler in the Domtar lumber yard. They had three children and separated. Hazel died of a stroke in August 1988 at age fifty-four. William died on November 10, 1986, at age sixty-seven.

**Children of Hazel Alice Robertson**

VII. **David Leckay**, born about 1953 in Prince George, British Columbia.

VII. **Brian Leckay**, born in August 1964 in Prince George, British Columbia.

VII. **Donna-Mae Violet Leckay**, born on April 15, 1966, in Prince George, British Columbia. On May 28, 1988, at the Knox United Church in Prince George, she married *Murray Craig Stephen Tomchuk*. Murray, son of Moira Shane and William Joseph Tomchuk, was born in Pincher Creek, Alberta, on August 26, 1964. Donna-Mae is an assistant pharmacist. A man of many trades, Murray works as a glazer and metal fabricator and is also qualified as an operating engineer and finish carpenter. They reside in Langley, British Columbia. They have no children.

VI. **Thomas Duncan Robertson**, only son of Violet Dryborough and Magnus Robertson, was born on November 9, 1934, in Beatty, Saskatchewan. He and *Helen Barbara Markusich* were married in Port Alberni on Vancouver Island, British Columbia. She was born in Nanaimo, British Columbia, on June 18, 1938, daughter of Magda Simacac and John Ivan Markusich of Croatia, Yugoslavia. Tom and Helen had five children; they divorced in 1969. Tom was also the father of two other children. Tom died of cancer on October 26, 1998, in Abbotsford, British Columbia.

### Children of Thomas Duncan Robertson

VII. **Paulette Belinda Hall**, daughter of Thomas Duncan Robertson and Faye Marion Hall, was born on September 19, 1956, in Moose Jaw, Saskatchewan, Canada. She married *Richard Thomas McCullough*, who was born on October 25, 1956. Rich is an electrical designer-draftsman specializing in natural gas plants. They have one child and live in Calgary, Alberta.

### Child of Paulette Belinda Hall

VIII. **Erin Elizabeth McCullough**, born on May 26, 1982. She is a championship fiddler and musician.

VII. **Gordon Thomas Robertson**, born on May 8, 1957, in Port Alberni, Vancouver Island, British Columbia, son of Helen Markusich and Thomas Duncan Robertson. Gordie married *Jennifer Jane Nixon* on November 18, 1983, in Richmond, British Columbia. Jennifer was born in Vancouver, British Columbia, on April 14, 1960, the daughter of Gertrude Muriel Gatward and

Norman Nixon. Gordon adopted his wife's daughter, Crystal, and they have two other daughters. He is a marine engineer and heavy duty mechanic with BC Ferries, working on the large, modern, car and passenger ferries that operate between Nanaimo on Vancouver Island and mainland British Columbia.

### Children of Gordon Thomas Robertson

VIII. **Crystal Lynn Robertson**, born on November 29, 1978, in White Rock, Vancouver, British Columbia.

VIII. **Nichole Jean Robertson**, born on June 16, 1981, in Vancouver, British Columbia.

VIII. **Samantha Jane Robertson**, born on March 10, 1996. in Mission, British Columbia.

VII. **Julie Ann Robertson**, born on August 25, 1958, in Port Alberni, Vancouver Island, British Columbia, daughter of Helen Markusich and Thomas Duncan Robertson. She married *Glen Allen Stratford* on December 16, 1976, and they had a son. Glen was born on January 27, 1954, and died in 1982. Second, on June 26, 1982, Julie married *Peter Randall Wilson*, known as Randy, an inspector in the Royal Canadian Mounted Police, who was born on May 6, 1954. They have four daughters, including twins who died as infants. They reside in Casselman, Ontario.

### Children of Julie Ann Robertson

VIII. **Christopher Allen Stratford**, born on May 24, 1976, son of Julie Ann Robertson and Glen Stratford.

VIII. **Miranda Isabelle Wilson**, daughter of Julie Ann Robertson and Randy Wilson, born on February 24, 1983.

VIII. **Magdeline Barbara Wilson**, one of twins born to Julie Ann Robertson and Randy Wilson, born on July 25, 1985; died two days later, on July 27, 1985.

VIII. **Megan Athena Wilson**, twin sister of Magdeline Barbara Wilson, born on July 25, 1985; died two days later, on July 27, 1985.

VIII. **<u>Melanie Wilson</u>**, daughter of Julie Ann Robertson and Randy Wilson, born on June 13, 1996.

VII. **Laurie Helen Robertson**, born on October 5, 1959, in Port Alberni, Vancouver Island, British Columbia, second daughter of Helen Markusich and Thomas Duncan Robertson. On June 2, 1984, Laurie married *Douglas McRitchie*, who was born on July 27, 1954; they divorced in August 1991, with no children. Second, on June 6, 1992, Laurie married *Randall John Sliter*, known as John, who is an inspector in the Royal Canadian Mounted Police. John was born on November 30, 1957. They have two children and reside in Long Sault, near Ottawa, Ontario.

### Children of Laurie Helen Robertson

VIII. **<u>Jillian Helen Sliter</u>**, born on June 14, 1993.

VIII. **<u>Jack Donald Sliter</u>**, born on December 13, 1994.

VII. **<u>Nada Debra Robertson</u>**, born in Victoria, Vancouver Island, British Columbia, on September 2, 1960, third daughter of Helen Markusich and Thomas Duncan Robertson. On October 16, 1982, Nada married *Christopher Horton*, who was born on July 31, 1957. They had two children. They divorced in January 1997. Nada lives in Terrace, British Columbia.

### Children of Nada Robertson

VIII. **<u>Matthew Leslie Horton</u>**, born in Langley, British Columbia, on February 1, 1982.

VIII. **<u>Russell William Horton</u>**, born in Langley, British Columbia, on August 14, 1984.

VII. **<u>James Duncan Robertson</u>**, born on November 4, 1961, in Port Alberni, Vancouver Island, British Columbia, second son of Helen Markusich and Thomas Duncan Robertson. He and his partner *Doreen Louise Schafhauser* have three sons and live in Prince Rupert, British Columbia. In addition to working as a coal grader for the Canadian government, James has an independent business operating a charter boat for offshore fishing for salmon, halibut, and other deep-sea fish.

**Children of James Duncan Robertson**

VIII. **<u>Trevor James Robertson</u>**, born in North Vancouver, British Columbia, on August 20, 1984.

VIII. **<u>Michael Joseph Robertson</u>**, born in Prince Rupert, British Columbia, on September 1, 1994.

VIII. **<u>Liam James Robertson</u>**, born in Prince Rupert, British Columbia, on December 2, 1996.

VII. **<u>Darrel Wilson Vibert</u>**, son of Thomas Duncan Robertson, born on August 22, 1964. He married *<u>Heather Mabel Snow</u>*, who was born on November 22, 1965. They live in Calgary, Alberta. Darrel is in the landscaping business.

# Part III

# The Ever-Spreading Family Tree

This part covers major branches of Our Robertsons, commencing with the sixth generation of descendants of the original Robertson brothers. It is divided into three chapters that cover the principal parts of the world where our Robertsons have settled. Chapter 6-A follows the branches who stayed in the Shetland Islands, Scotland, and England; Chapter 6-B generally covers those who immigrated to New Zealand and Australia; and Chapter 6-C covers the North American branches. These lines are not perfect, as many of the branches have members who have gone elsewhere. Also, many members of the sixth and later generations are covered in previous chapters.

# THE U.K. BRANCHES
# GENERATION SIX AND BEYOND

## 6-A.1: WILLIAMINA ALICE JOHNSON (1896-1970)
### Daughter of Catherine Thomson Robertson

VI. **Williamina Alice Johnson** was born on June 1, 1896, in Glasgow, Scotland, one of ten children born to Catherine Thomson Robertson and John Johnson (5-A.1 above). She only kept in touch with a few of her siblings, and over time the family members drifted apart.

In 1920, she married *Stephen McAdam*, son of Mary and Stephenson McAdam, who was born on February 3, 1892, in Glasgow. They had four children, all of whom graduated with good university degrees and pursued academic and professional careers. The grandchildren have obtained university degrees in architecture, computer sciences, biology, the social sciences, and engineering.

Williamina's daughter Alice Drury recalls that life was not easy for her parents, especially during the Great Depression of the 1930s. She states:

> *They had to sell most of their valuables in order to live and bring up their four children. They were an intelligent pair, but too honest and unworldly to live in such circumstances. My father was an engineer but he and my mother bought a little general store and, with the Depression hitting everybody, my parents allowed people to have food etc. from the shop with no hope of ever receiving payment. In this way they gave the stock away. None of the money owing to them was ever recovered. This fact, along with having to sell their valuables, broke their spirit, and it is to their great credit that they managed to bring up four well-educated and well-looked-after children. My mother used to say that her priorities were a*

*roof over our heads, a fire in the grate, and food in our tummies. How I wish that they could have been rewarded in later life, but it wasn't to be.*

Stephen McAdam died on October 2, 1954, in Gourock, Scotland, not far from Glasgow on the River Clyde. Williamina Johnson McAdam died in Gourock on April 9, 1970, age seventy-three.

## Children of Williamina Alice Johnson

VII. **David McAdam**, born on May 14, 1921. On December 1, 1950, David married *Edith Logan,* the daughter of Mary and Robert Logan, born on April 4, 1926. David was a schoolmaster in Paisley, Scotland. They had no children.

VII. **Alice McAdam**, only daughter of Stephen McAdam and Williamina Alice Johnson, born on October 8, 1923, in Glasgow, Scotland. Alice married *Ronald J. Drury* on December 27, 1941. Her husband was born on July 28, 1916, in London, England, (son of Cassie and Louis Drury). Alice and Ronald raised two children and now have three grandchildren in Australia.

Trained as a librarian, Alice became an accomplished poet and writer of humorous verse and stories, "lucky enough" (as she puts it) to win "a few national competitions." Poems, short stories, and articles written by Alice have been published in many national magazines (including *The New Shetlander*), her poems have been included in the popular calendar "This England," and her work has been performed on radio and television. On Alice's seventy-fifth birthday, BBC Radio Devon announced on the air that she had won the county poetry competition for her humorous verse. Three of her poems were broadcast on the air, and she received some valuable prizes—quite an honor!

Alice provided this insight for those interested in genealogy and family history:

*In just ten generations we have 1,024 great-great-great-great-great-great-great-great-great-grandparents. In twenty generations the number of "greats" is 1,048,576. In thirty generations the number is 1,114,701,824.*

*Imagine this last number gathered together in one room and remind yourself that you are the descendant of everyone! It's a staggering thought, isn't it? And if even one had been different, you would have been a different person! And if you continue going back, the number of ancestors doubles with every generation, then in no time we find that everyone must have some common ancestry. I find facts like this quite fascinating and can't help thinking what a tiny bit of every ancestor has gone into creating us.*

*My daughter Pamela, who has a degree in the social sciences, has a keen interest in the study of genes and their make-up, and she informs me that even one different gene in one of our ancestors would have resulted in us being quite different people. It's all quite wonderful!*

Noting that by late 1995, research of "Our Robertsons" had identified about 700 members of the clan, Alice adds, "I wonder what the original Thomas and John would have thought about having so many descendants? And no doubt, in time, we shall have a good few descendants ourselves!"

Alice and Ronald Drury, together with their daughter, Pamela, live in Newton Abbot, Devon, England.

### Children of Alice McAdam

VIII. **<u>Ronald L. Drury</u>**, born on November 9, 1942, in West Kilbride, Scotland; died on January 15, 1978, and buried in Ballarat, Australia.

Ronald was a graduate mechanical engineer and won the Knox Bursary scholarship as the best student of his class in college. He worked initially as an experimental officer with the Hydraulics Research Centre (a government department) and later worked on the design of centrifugal pumps.

On October 9, 1971, Ronald married an Australian, *<u>Jillian Webb</u>*, and they settled in Australia and started a family. Jill was born on October 7, 1943, in Geelong, Australia, daughter of Doris and Don Webb. They had two daughters and one son, who are studying at the university in Adelaide.

Tragedy struck suddenly in January 1978, when Ronald and Jill, riding their tandem bicycle, were hit by a drunk driver. The accident killed Ronald and paralyzed Jill. She has been unable to walk since then but, according to Alice Drury, "managed to bring up the three children with the help of one cleaning lady." She recently married a financial counsellor, Vin Glen, who has three grown sons by a previous marriage.

**Children of Ronald L. Drury**

IX. **Iain David Drury**, born on August 24, 1973, in Castlemaine, Australia. David has a university degree in civil engineering and is doing postgraduate studies in computer sciences while teaching the same subject at Adelaide University.

IX. **Eleanor Drury**, born on September 12, 1975, in Castlemaine, Australia. She is studying child care sciences at Adelaide University.

IX. **Claire Drury**, born on July 25, 1977, in Castlemaine, Australia. She received a BS in applied sciences.

VIII **Pamela Drury**, born on October 5, 1948, in Reading, England. Unmarried, Pamela trained in the social sciences and works as a personal assistant.

VII. **Robert McAdam**, born on July 7, 1927, in Glasgow, Scotland. He attended the University of Glasgow and became the principal of James Watt College in Greenock, Scotland, from which he retired in 1990. He married *Lily Thomson*, who was born in 1928 in Port Glasgow, Scotland, the daughter of Sydney Thomson. They had one daughter and three sons.

**Children of Robert McAdam**

VIII. **Avril McAdam**, born on April 14, 1950, in Gourock, Scotland. On August 21, 1977, Avril married *Stephen Alexander*, a native of England. They have three children and live in Oxford, England. Avril works in medical research.

**Children of Avril McAdam**

IX. **Scott Alexander**, born on May 18, 1978, in Worcester, England.

IX. **Stephanie Alexander**, born on May 28, 1979, in Worcester, England.

IX. **Laura Alexander**, born on March 30, 1982, in Worcester, England.

VIII. **David McAdam**, born on April 13, 1952, in Gourock, Scotland. He married *Catriona Taylor* in Gourock on April 7, 1983. She was also born in Gourock, the daughter of Malcolm Taylor. David and Catriona have four children and live in Paisley, Scotland. He works as a computer scientist.

**Children of David McAdam**

IX. **Fiona McAdam**, born on July 2, 1984, in Paisley, Scotland.

IX. **Andrew McAdam**, born on July 10, 1986, in Paisley, Scotland.

IX. **Jennifer McAdam**, born on July 20, 1987, 1987, in Paisley, Scotland.

IX. **David McAdam**, born on July 16, 1993, in Paisley, Scotland.

VIII. **Robert McAdam Jr.**, born on June 10, 1956, in Gourock, Scotland. In 1978 in Gourock, he married *Sandra Reynolds*, also of Gourock. They have three children and live in Greenock, Scotland. Robert is a biology teacher.

**Children of Robert McAdam Jr.**

IX. **Karina McAdam**, born on August 15, 1983, in Greenock, Scotland.

IX. **Kevin McAdam**, born on August 16, 1985, in Greenock, Scotland.

IX. **Roseanna McAdam**, born on April 4, 1990, in Gourock, Scotland.

VIII. **Stephen McAdam**, born on June 26, 1958, in Gourock, Scotland. On June 26, 1982, he married *Susan Rennie*, who was born in Greenock, Scotland, daughter of W.J. Rennie. They have no children. They live in Colne, Lancashire, England. Stephen works in computer science.

VII. **Stephen McAdam Jr.**, born on March 11, 1929, in Glasgow, Scotland. Educated at the University of Glasgow, he became a consulting engineer. He married *Jean Anderson* on August 1, 1952. Jean was born in Greenock, Scotland, daughter of John Anderson. Stephen and Jean had four children. Stephen later married *Ica Lench*. She was born on July 16, 1947, in Romania, and they are living in Romania.

**Children of Stephen McAdam Jr.**

VIII. **Dawn McAdam**, born on November 26, 1953, in Gourock, Scotland. First, she married *Brian Drabner*, a native of Scotland, on June 1, 1976. Second, Dawn married *Geoff Turner* on November 26, 1991. They have no children.

VIII. **Stephen McAdam III**, born on June 8, 1955, in Glasgow, Scotland. On September 21, 1985, Stephen married *Kristina Norton*, who was born in London, England. Stephen and Kristina have two children. They both work as architects in London.

**Children of Stephen McAdam III**

IX. **Thomas McAdam**, born on August 27, 1987, in London, England.

IX. **Stephen McAdam IV**, born on February 19, 1990, in London, England.

VIII. **Deborah McAdam**, born on January 21, 1967, in Troon, Scotland. On August 28, 1989, she married *Paul Giles*. He was born in Torquay, Devonshire, England. They had one daughter and divorced. After a brief marriage to *Peter Lancaster*, Deborah and Paul Giles remarried and had a son.

**Children of Deborah McAdam**

IX. **Jasmine Giles**, born on August 23, 1990.

IX. **Grant Michael Giles**, born on November 10, 1996.

VIII. **Paul McAdam**, born on November 21, 1969. On May 13, 1995, he married *Kimberly Miles*, daughter of Gordon Miles. Paul and Kimberly have two children and reside in Paignton, England.

**Children of Paul McAdam**

IX. **Harrison McAdam**, born on July 8, 1996.

IX. **Benjamin McAdam**, born on September 2, 1998.

## 6-A.2: GEORGE WILLIAM JOHNSTON ROBERTSON (1904-1983)
### Son of Thomas Thomson Robertson

VI. **George William Johnston Robertson** was born on October 29, 1904, in Westerwick, Sandsting, Shetland, the son of Thomas Thomson Robertson and Andrina Johnston (5-A.3 above). When George was five years old, his father, Thomas, died in an accident in England. Following that, his mother moved with George and his baby brother, Alec, to Stove, Walls, where the family lived in difficult financial conditions, and the children grew to maturity.

On June 12, 1940, George married *Margaret Dalziel* (called "Maggie"), daughter of William Dalziel and Helen Barclay. Maggie was born on August 17, 1911, in Sandsound, Shetland.

George and Maggie Robertson lived at "Waterloo" in Walls, Shetland. They were the parents of five children: George, Sheila, Angus, Eleanor, and John. Four of the children are still living in the Shetland Islands; one immigrated to Queensland, Australia, and is raising a family there.

George Robertson was very interested in family history and provided Blanche and Jim Robertson much helpful genealogical information that has been used in this study of "Our Robertsons." He died on July 24, 1983, age seventy-eight, in Walls Parish, Shetland. His widow, Maggie, died eleven years later on September 28, 1994, in Lerwick, Shetland.

### Children of George William Johnston Robertson

VII. **George William Thomas Robertson**, born on May 9, 1941, in Stove, Walls Parish, Shetland, is the oldest son of Maggie Dalziel and George W.J. Robertson.

He married *Gaylynn Olive Groves* in Auckland, New Zealand, on December 5, 1964. Born in Auckland on May 6, 1944, Gay is the daughter of Nola Ann Fill (born on June 13, 1920, in New Zealand) and Charles Groves (born October 9, 1899, in London, England; died on September 7, 1977, in Auckland, New Zealand).

After their marriage, George and Gay lived in Mount Maunganui on the North Island of New Zealand until 1977. At that time they went to live in Shetland, deciding to do so after spending a three-month holiday there in 1976. In 1981, they moved to Australia, where George commenced work with P&O Shipping Lines as a foreman stevedore. He took early retirement in 1992 and now fills in for the company when needed.

George and Gay have three children, all born in New Zealand. They fondly recall the four years they lived in Shetland as a great learning experience in many ways, especially for the older children, who were in school there. They now reside in Aspley, near Brisbane, in Queensland, Australia. They travelled back to Shetland to visit with George's mother in 1992, a couple of years before she passed away.

**Children of George W.T. Robertson**

VIII. **Margaret Ann Robertson**, oldest daughter of Gaylynn Groves and George W.T. Robertson, was born on September 1, 1965, in Auckland, New Zealand. Margaret was married in Brisbane, Australia, on March 1, 1986. Her husband, *William F. Hannan*, was born on June 17, 1957, in New Guinea, the son of Vivian Aldridge and Bruce Hannan.

They live in Brisbane and have four children. In addition to raising her young family, Margaret has operated a childcare business and is now pursuing full time studies in Early Childhood Education.

**Children of Margaret Ann Robertson**

IX. **Shaun William Hannan**, born on August 3, 1988, in Sydney, Australia.

IX. **Mitchell George Hannan**, born on January 31, 1990, in Nowra, New South Wales, Australia.

IX. **Callum Bruce Hannan**, one of the twins, born on July 10, 1992, in Wollongong, Australia.

IX. **Thomas Edward Hannan**, another twin, and also born on July 10, 1992, in Wollongong, Australia.

VIII. **Andrea Gaye Robertson**, second daughter of Gaylynn Groves and George W.T. Robertson, was born on January 13, 1967, in Auckland, New Zealand. A qualified teacher and aerobics instructor, in 1993 Andrea earned a scholarship to study in Japan through her university. She is now an Education Officer in the RAAF, based in Victoria.

Andrea married *Robin Mark Orr* in Brisbane, Australia, on December 16, 1995. He was born on June 5, 1971, in Durban, South Africa, son of Marilynn Rosen and George Orr. Robin is a physical training instructor at the Australian Defence Force Academy. They have one daughter, Samantha.

**Child of Andrea Gaye Robertson**

IX. **Samantha Gaye Orr**, born on September 20, 1988, in Sydney, Australia.

VIII. **Iain George Robertson**, son of Gaylynn and George Robertson, was born on March 30, 1972, in Tauranga, New Zealand. Iain has a BA in Asian Studies and for several years taught English in Japanese high schools under a Japanese government program, enabling him to continue his long-standing interest in karate with further study of the art in Japan. A lieutenant in the Australian Army Reserve, Iain returned to Australia in 1996 and is now in the process of joining the RAAF as a ground defense officer. He is not married.

VII. **Sheila Robina Ruth Robertson**, born on August 12, 1942, in Shetland, is the oldest daughter of Maggie Dalziel and George W.J. Robertson. Sheila married *John Peter Johnson*. They live in Catwell, Eshaness, Shetland, and have three children.

**Children of Sheila Robertson**

VIII. **George Peter Johnson**. He married *Lynn Jamieson*, and they have two children.

**Children of George Peter Johnson**

IX. **Kylie Ann Johnson**.

IX. **Carl Johnson**.

VIII. **Erik Johnson**.

VIII. **Janice Margaret Johnson**. She has two children, whose names are not available to us.

VII. **<u>Alexander Angus Robertson</u>**, born on August 19, 1944, in Waterloo, Walls Parish, Shetland, is the second son of Maggie Dalziel and George W.J. Robertson.

Angus married *Lauretta Wishart* in Walls, Shetland, on October 24, 1973. She was born on September 24, 1945, in Whiteness, Walls, Shetland, the daughter of James Wishart (born on April 25, 1904, Sandsting & Aithsting Parish, Shetland; died in 1986) and his wife, Williamina Rose Fraser (born on November 2, 1908, in Gracefield, Sandsting Parish, Shetland).

Angus is a plant operator at the Sullom Voe Oil Terminal in Mainland Shetland. He is active in community affairs and has served as chairman of the Sandness-Walls Community Council since 1981. Angus and Lauretta have three children and live in Kirkigarth, Walls, Shetland.

### Children of Angus Robertson

VIII. **<u>Hamish William Alec Robertson</u>**, born on October 5, 1976, in Lerwick, Shetland. He is working as a heavy machinery operator in Brae.

VIII. **<u>Neil Laurence Robertson</u>**, born on December 1, 1977, in Lerwick, Shetland. He works in a fish farming operation in Walls and is residing in West Burrafirth, near Brindister.

VIII. **<u>Diana Jane Robertson</u>**, born on April 13, 1980, in Lerwick, Shetland. She is a business student at the University of Aberdeen in Aberdeen, Scotland.

VII. **<u>Eleanor Ann Robertson</u>**, second daughter of Maggie Dalziel and George W.J. Robertson, was born about 1951 in Waterloo, Walls, Shetland. Eleanor married *Peter John Hall*. They had one child, Melvin George Hall, and the family resided in Waterloo. Eleanor died on June 8, 1996.

### Child of Eleanor Ann Robertson

VIII. **<u>Melvin George Hall</u>**, born in December 1980 in Shetland. He is studying to become an electrician at a technical college in Edinburgh, Scotland.

VII. **<u>John Magnus Campbell Robertson</u>**, born in December 1955 in Waterloo, Walls Parish, Shetland, the third son of Maggie Dalziel and George W.J. Robertson. John is unmarried and farms and raises sheep in Walls.

## 6-A.3: Christina Helen Robertson (1916-1994)
### Daughter of Magnus Jameson Robertson

VI. **Christina Helen Robertson** (called "Tina"), oldest child of Mary and Magnus Jameson Robertson (5-A.3 above), was born on September 28, 1916, at "Swarthoull" in Westerskeld, Sandsting Parish, Shetland.

Tina married *Laurence Peter Garrick*, son of Helen Johnson and Laurence Garrick, on March 3, 1938. He was born on March 5, 1912, in Culswick, Shetland. For a couple of years they stayed with Tina's parents at the family home called "North Dykes" in Westerskeld. After that, they lived and farmed on a croft in Hestensetter in Westerskeld and raised their seven children. Laurence died at age sixty-eight on January 31, 1980, in Hestensetter. Tina lived another fourteen years. She died on June 2, 1994, at the age of seventy-seven, at the hospital in Lerwick, Shetland.

**Children of Christina Helen Robertson**

VII. **William Peter Garrick**, born on August 8, 1938, in North Dykes, Westerskeld, Shetland. He is a crofter in Norville, Sandness, Shetland. On November 10, 1965, he married *Florence Jane Sinclair* in Sandness, Shetland. Born on February 3, 1943, she is the daughter of Jessie Anderson and John Sinclair of Sandness. Florence and William have three children.

**Children of William Peter Garrick**

VIII. **Wilda Marie Garrick**, born on October 6, 1966, in Lerwick, Shetland. She married *David Nicolson* on August 1, 1986, at Sandness Church in Shetland. David, the son of Agnes Tait and Herbert Nicolson, was born in Lerwick on March 11, 1964. They have two children and live in Twatt, Bixter, Shetland. David works with his brother-in-law Raymond Garrick as an agricultural contractor in Shetland.

**Children of Wilda Marie Garrick**

IX. **Dawn Nicolson**, born on February 3, 1994, at Aberdeen Hospital in Aberdeen, Scotland.

IX. **<u>Edward Nicolson</u>,** born on December 3, 1996, at Aberdeen Hospital in Aberdeen, Scotland.

VIII. **<u>Anita Joan Garrick</u>**, born on November 26, 1968, in Lerwick, Shetland. She married *Michael Coutts* at Sandness Church on March 27, 1992. Born on October 18, 1968, Michael is the son of Jeanetta Smith and William Coutts. Michael works for the government in custom and excise taxation, and they live in Vivilea in Tresta, Bixter, where they have built a home. They have one child.

### Child of Anita Joan Garrick

IX. **<u>Craig William Coutts</u>**, born on October 20, 1997, in Aberdeen, Scotland.

VIII. **<u>Raymond Laurence Garrick</u>**, born on October 31, 1972, in Lerwick, Shetland. He is living on his parents' croft in Norville in Sandness. Raymond operates an agricultural contracting business together with David Nicolson, his brother-in-law.

VII. **<u>Marina Helen Garrick</u>**, born on April 26, 1940, in North Dykes, Westerskeld, Shetland. She married *James William Jeromson*, and they had one daughter. She died in Hestensetter, Westerskeld, on December 29, 1976, age thirty-six. Her husband, the son of Elizabeth Williamson and Thomas Jeromson, was born on June 6, 1938, in Gruting, Shetland. He died on February 18, 1996, in Lerwick hospital.

### Child of Marina Helen Garrick

VIII. **<u>Fiona Jeromson</u>**, daughter of Marina Garrick and James Jeromson, born on September 5, 1972, in Lerwick, Shetland. Fiona married *Colin McKearney* on September 14, 1996, in West Burrafirth, Shetland. Colin was born on October 11, 1962, in Lerwick, Shetland. They live in Stoneydale, Bridge-of-Walls, Shetland. Fiona has a daughter, Caitlin.

**Child of Fiona Jeromson**

IX. <u>**Caitlin McKearney**</u>, born on April 25, 1995, in Lerwick, Shetland.

VII. <u>**Robert Edward Garrick**</u>, born on November 28, 1941, in Hestenstetter, Westerskeld, Shetland. Unmarried, he stays at his parents' croft in Hestensetter and works with David Nicholson and Raymond Garrick in their agricultural business during the summer.

VII. <u>**Lorna Christina Garrick**</u>, born on May 28, 1943, in Hestenstetter, Westerskeld, Shetland. She is unmarried and lives in Bixter, Shetland.

VII. <u>**Margaret Catherine Garrick**</u>, born on January 18, 1945, in Hestenstetter, Westerskeld, Shetland. On December 16, 1966, in Sand Manse, Shetland. Margaret married *Jack Ridland*, son of Mary Isbister and James Ridland. Jack was born on April 10, 1937, in Westerskeld, and he works on pilot boats at the Sullom Voe Oil Terminal. Margaret works for the Shetland Smokehouse, which sells smoked salmon and other gourmet food products by mail order and internet. She and Jack have four children and live at Bri-Mar in Westerskeld, Bixter, Shetland.

**Children of Margaret Catherine Garrick**

VIII. <u>**Jacqueline Helen Ridland**</u>, born on February 27, 1967, in Lerwick, Shetland. She married *Erik Moar* on October 20, 1989, at Gulberwick Church in Shetland. Erik is the son of Linda Ganson and James Moar and was born on January 13, 1964, in Lerwick, Shetland. He works as an electrician at Sullom Voe Oil Terminal. They have three children and live in Tumlin, Bixter, Shetland.

**Children of Jacqueline Helen Ridland**

IX. <u>**Cheryl Margaret Moar**</u>, born on July 14, 1991, in Lerwick, Shetland.

IX. <u>**Lisa Helen Rose Moar**</u>, born on November 16, 1995, in Aberdeen, Scotland.

IX. <u>**Rhona Mary Moar**</u>, born on November 14, 1996, in Lerwick, Shetland.

VIII. **Brian Laurence Ridland**, born on February 6, 1970, in Lerwick, Shetland. He lives and works on the family croft at Bri-Mar in Westerskeld and also works as a welder in Lerwick.

VIII. **Kevin James Ridland**, born on July 19, 1972, in Lerwick, Shetland. He is an engineer officer in the merchant navy.

VIII. **Stuart Desmond Ridland**, born on April 24, 1974, in Lerwick, Shetland. He is an engineer on a floating oil-production platform in the North Sea.

VII. **John Magnus Garrick**, born on January 12, 1954, in Lerwick, Shetland. John is a charge hand on a Shetland Island fishing vessel. On March 15, 1975, he married *Caroline Jamieson* of Voe in Delting Parish, Shetland, the daughter of Margaret Mann and John Jamieson. She works as a health center nurse. They have two sons and live in Voe.

### Children of John Magnus Garrick

VIII. **Neil Laurence Garrick**, born on December 19, 1977, in Lerwick, Shetland. He works on a fishing boat with his father.

VIII. **Steven John Garrick**, born on May 24, 1979, in Lerwick, Shetland. Steven works as a marine engineer with the firm of Malakoff and Moore in Lerwick.

VII. **Linda Ann Garrick**, born on November 30, 1958, in Lerwick, Shetland. She married *Richard Leask* on June 22, 1979, at Weisdale Church in Shetland. The son of Christine Johnson and Laurence Leask of Nesting, Shetland, Richard was born on December 12, 1951, in Vidlin, Shetland. Richard works on jetties at the Sullom Voe Oil Terminal. They live in Nesting and have four children.

### Children of Linda Ann Garrick

VIII. **Gary Laurence Leask**, born on October 20, 1988, in Lerwick, Shetland.

VIII. **Grant Christopher Leask**, born on July 12, 1990, in Lerwick, Shetland.

VIII. **Lauren Emma Leask**, born on July 9, 1994, in Lerwick, Shetland.

VIII. **Leanne Helen Leask**, born on July 30, 1996, in Lerwick, Shetland.

## 6-A.4: ROBERTHA CATHERINE ROBERTSON (1919- )
### Daughter of Magnus Jameson Robertson

VI. **Robertha Catherine Robertson**, second daughter of Mary and Magnus Jameson Robertson (4-A. above), was born on January 8, 1919, at Swarthoull, her mother's family home in Westerskeld, Shetland. She worked as a nurse.

She married *Archibald Neilson*, a newsagent shop owner in Stirling, Scotland. He was born on April 21, 1917, the son of Janet Lamont, who worked as a shopkeeper, and John Neilson, a miner.

Robertha and Archibald had five children, who have produced twelve grandchildren. Archibald died on September 7, 1985, in Stirling. Robertha is now living with her son Christopher Neilson and his family in Dunblane, Scotland.

**Children of Robertha Catherine Robertson**

VII. **Johnathon Robertson Neilson** (called "Ian"), oldest son of Robertha Robertson and Archibald Neilson, was born on March 3, 1950, in Stirling, Scotland. He is an engineer. Ian married *Dorothy Boutts* of Perth, Scotland, daughter of Ann McLellan and George Boutts, who worked as an estate gardener. They have two children and live in Stirling.

**Children of John Robertson Neilson**

VIII. **Mark Neilson**, born on February 20, 1973, in Stirling, Scotland. He and his partner have one son.

**Child of Mark Neilson**

IX. **Shaun Ian Bruce Neilson**, born on November 11, 1997.

VIII. **Edward Neilson**, born on January 21, 1976, in Stirling, Scotland.

VII. **<u>Christopher Magnus Neilson</u>**, second son of Robertha Robertson and Archibald Neilson, was born on September 5, 1951. Chris married *Jenny Lamers* of Holland, the daughter of Jan Frederick Lamers, a farmer, and his wife, whose maiden name was Romyn.

Chris and Jenny live in Dunblane, Scotland. They have four children.

**Children of Christopher Magnus Neilson**

VIII. **<u>Art Christopher Archibald Neilson</u>**, born on March 20, 1986, in Stirling, Scotland.

VIII. **<u>Joni Robertha Lamas Neilson</u>**, born on November 2, 1987, in Stirling, Scotland.

VIII. **<u>Magnus Peter Robertson Neilson</u>**, a twin, born on July 5, 1990 in Stirling, Scotland.

VIII. **<u>Alison Rose Jennifer Neilson</u>**, the other twin, born on July 5, 1990 in Stirling, Scotland.

VII. **<u>James Charles Marshall Neilson</u>**, third son of Robertha Robertson and Archibald Neilson, was born on May 20, 1954. On September 23, 1978, Jimmy married *Margaret Ferguson*, daughter of Margaret Auchinvole and Alistair Ferguson. They have two children and live in Stirling, Scotland.

**Children of James Charles Marshall Neilson**

VIII. **<u>Jonathon James Neilson</u>**, born on May 26, 1986, in Stirling, Scotland.

VIII. **<u>Matthew David Neilson</u>**, born on April 2, 1991, in Stirling, Scotland.

VII. **<u>Charlotte Jennifer Neilson</u>** is one of a pair of twins born on December 12, 1955, in Stirling, Scotland, to Robertha Robertson and Archibald Neilson (their only daughter). She married *Bill Bowditch* in London, England. They have two children and reside in Farnham, England.

**Children of Charlotte Jennifer Neilson**

VIII. **Cameron Harold Bowditch**, born on April 1, 1989, in Farnham, England.

VIII. **Erin Muriel Bowditch**, born on July 18, 1991, in Farnham, England.

VII. **Andrew Archibald Neilson**, Charlotte's twin brother, born on December 12, 1955, in Stirling, Scotland, is the fourth son of Robertha Robertson and Archibald Neilson. He married *Rhona McCallum* from Thornhill, outside of Stirling. They live in Stirling with their two children.

**Children of Andrew Archibald Neilson**

VIII. **Loyd Andrew Neilson**, born on May 14, 1990, in Stirling, Scotland.

VIII. **Florence Neilson**, born on June 16, 1995, in Stirling, Scotland.

## 6-A.5: MARGARET TWATT (1885-1913)
### Daughter of Thomas Twatt

VI. **Margaret Twatt**, daughter of Catherine Nicolson and Thomas Twatt (5-A.11 above), was born on September 12, 1885, in Walls Parish, Shetland. She married *James Ganson* of Sandwick, Shetland. James, who was born on December 10, 1876, was an insurance agent and a fisherman.

Margaret died as a young woman about 1913 in Sandwick, apparently as a result of childbirth complications. She and James had one daughter, who survived her.

**Child of Margaret Twatt**

VII. **Mary Catherine Ganson**, born on September 24, 1911, in Cumbliwick, Shetland, was a small child when her mother died. She married *Robert Peter Nicolson* of Setter, Walls Parish, who was born on November 4, 1907, and was Mary's first cousin once removed. He was the son of Robina Sinclair and Peter Nicolson, the brother of Mary's grandmother Catherine Nicolson. Mary and Robert had two children. He worked as a seaman and later became a builder. Robert is deceased, and Mary stays with her daughter and son-in-law near Sandwick.

**Children of Mary Catherine Ganson**

VIII. **James Peter Nicolson** was born in Lerwick, Shetland, on July 28, 1946. On August 15, 1969, Jim married *Lillian Rosabel Sinclair*, daughter of Mary Ann Priest of Unst and Adam Sinclair of Levenwick. Jim is the Depute Head Teacher in Aith.

**Children of James Peter Nicolson**

IX. **Ingrid Marie Nicolson**, born in Lerwick, Shetland, on December 18, 1973. A nursery teacher in Aith, Ingrid has a B.Ed (with honours) in primary education.

IX. **Julie Anne Nicolson**, born in Lerwick, Shetland, on July 31, 1976. Julie has an honours degree in English from Strathclyde University in Glasgow, Scotland.

IX. **James Robert Sinclair Nicolson**, born in Lerwick, Shetland, on October 5, 1982.

VIII. **Margarette Beryl Nicolson** was born in Lerwick, Shetland, on March 30, 1948. Beryl received a diploma in child education and an associateship in that field at Aberdeen College of Education before earning a Master's in Science from Strathclyde University in Glasgow, Scotland. She also has a computing qualification from Paisley University.

On October 19, 1977, Beryl married *Maurice John Smith,* son of Janet Hughson of Unst and John A. Smith of Burra Isle, Shetland. Beryl teaches twelve-year-olds in primary level seven at Sandwick Junior High School. Maurice teaches in the same school and serves as the Depute Head Teacher there.

Beryl and Maurice live in Broonies Taing, near Sandwick, about a twenty-minute drive south of Lerwick on the Shetland mainland. They also maintain a large croft with several hundred sheep in Sandwick and in Walls.

## 6-A.6: ROBERT TWATT (1892-19??)
### Son of Thomas Twatt

VI. **Robert Twatt**, son of Catherine Nicolson and Thomas Twatt (5-A.11 above), was born on June 17, 1892. He married *Margaret Fraser* (called "Maggie"), who was born on October 27, 1889. They had one child.

### Child of Robert Twatt

VII. **Thomas Twatt**, son of Maggie Fraser and Robert Twatt, was born on October 6, 1923, in Walls, Shetland. On September 28, 1949, Tom married *Elizabeth Grace Malcolmson* (called "Betty") in Quarff, Shetland. Betty was born in Quarff on February 14, 1920, daughter of Annie and Alex Malcolmson. They had two sons. Betty is deceased, and Tom resides in Lerwick.

### Children of Thomas Twatt

VIII. **Thomas (Twatt) Watt** (called Tommy) was born on February 14, 1952, in Lerwick, Shetland. He changed his surname by dropping the first "T" to become Thomas Watt.

Tommy first married *Jane McKay* from Caithness, Scotland; they divorced. In about 1989, Tommy married *Rowena Santos*, a native of the Philippines, and he adopted two daughters from her previous marriage.

Tommy's career is in contract construction work for Shell Oil and other major oil companies around the world. As of mid-1999, he was working on a gas pipeline project in Muscat, Oman. The family lives in Oman but owns a home in Edinburgh, Scotland, where they ultimately plan to stay.

### Children of Thomas (Twatt) Watt

IX. **Melissa Watt**, born on December 18, 1982.

IX. **Lyka Watt**, born about March 1984.

VIII. **<u>Alexander Twatt</u>** (called "Alex") was born in Lerwick, Shetland, on January 2, 1955. He received a Diploma in Fine Arts in 1976 from the Edinburgh College of Art, now part of the University of Edinburgh, and taught art for several years in Shetland. He first married *<u>Margaret Liddle</u>*, who was also an art teacher, whom he divorced.

On August 22, 1989, Alex married *<u>Mary Theresa Godfrey</u>*, daughter of Theresa Turner and Kenneth Godfrey, who was born on October 1, 1952, in Enfield, Middlesex, England. With one daughter, they live in Harrogate, Yorkshire. Alex and Mary often use the combined surname Godfrey-Twatt.

Mary is creative director of Taylor's of Harrogate, a purveyor of fine teas, coffees, and other specialty products. Alex operates a prestigious fine-arts-and-crafts business, Godfrey & Twatt, in Harrogate, trading in ceramics, domestic pottery, glass, jewelry, and wood items. The company is a member of the Independent Craft Galleries Association of England.

### Child of Alex Twatt

IX. **<u>Lauren Godfrey-Twatt</u>**, born on April 6, 1989, in Harrogate, Yorkshire, England.

# The South Pacific Branches
# Generation Six and Beyond

## 6-B.1: John Maurice Robertson (1916- )
### Son of John Robert Robertson

VI. **John Maurice Robertson**, first child of Nora Isabella Walker and John Robert Robertson (4-B above), was born on October 31, 1916, in Petone, New Zealand. He received the Master's in Commerce from Victoria University in Wellington and served with the Royal New Zealand Air Force in World War II.

On October 18, 1941, John married *Rebecca Joy Anderson*. The daughter of Phyllis Walker and Frank Anderson, Rebecca was born in Dunedin, New Zealand, on December 18, 1918. They had three daughters and a son.

John Robertson is a retired accountant and company director. Rebecca died in Lower Hutt, Wellington, New Zealand, on November 11, 1996. He resides in Lower Hutt, has a home in Taupo, and enjoys traveling.

**Children of John Maurice Robertson**

VII. **Diane Joy Robertson**, eldest child of Rebecca Joy Anderson and John Robertson, was born on July 9, 1944, in Lower Hutt, Wellington, New Zealand. On October 1, 1966, she married *Murray Leonard Pearce* in Lower Hutt. He was born on July 14, 1942, in Christchurch, New Zealand, son of Eric Pearce and Lois Brown. Murray operates a pharmaceutical business. They have three children and live in Christchurch, New Zealand.

**Children of Diana Joy Robertson**

VIII. <u>**Kirsten Pearce**</u>, born on January 27, 1970, in Christchurch, New Zealand. She received a degree from Otago University and is a doctor and pharmacist.

VIII. <u>**Emily Pearce**</u>, born on July 15, 1972, in Christchurch, New Zealand. She is a lawyer practicing in Wellington, New Zealand.

VIII. <u>**Michael Pearce**</u>, born on March 17, 1976, in Christchurch, New Zealand. He is a lawyer in Wellington.

VII. <u>**Jacqueline Wendy Robertson**</u>, second daughter of Rebecca Joy Anderson and John Robertson, was born on January 8, 1948, in Lower Hutt, New Zealand. She married *Peter Kahu* on February 4, 1972, in Taupo, New Zealand. Peter was born on November 8, 1950, in Taumarunui, New Zealand, the son of Pikikotuku Te Kahu and Mihimamao Te Rangiita. They have no children. Peter is foreman in a lumber yard, and Jacqueline teaches primary school children in Taupo.

VII. <u>**Susan Lynette Robertson**</u>, third daughter of Rebecca Joy Anderson and John Robertson, was born on April 5, 1951, in Lower Hutt, New Zealand. Sue married *Donald Paul Saché* on August 11, 1973. Don was born in Wellington, New Zealand, on October 16, 1951, son of Margaret Taylor and David Saché. Don is a pharmacist and operates his own business. They have two children.

**Children of Susan Lynette Robertson**

VIII. <u>**Amanda Kate Saché**</u>, born on February 17, 1980, in Christchurch, New Zealand. She is a student at Canterbury University.

VIII. <u>**Anthony Paul Saché**</u>, born on March 18, 1982, in Christchurch, New Zealand.

VII. <u>**John Wayne Robertson**</u> (called "Wayne"), son of Rebecca Joy Anderson and John Robertson, was born on April 5, 1951, in Lower Hutt, New Zealand. A qualified accountant, Wayne is business executive with Mitsubishi in New Zealand. On December 30, 1981, Wayne married *Allison McConnochie*. She is a daughter of

Bruce McConnochie and Jill Davis and was born on March 19, 1958, in Napier, New Zealand. They have two children and live in Wellington.

**Children of John Wayne Robertson**

VIII. **Nicholas John Robertson**, born on February 8, 1987, in Christchurch, New Zealand.

VIII. **Kathryn Robertson**, born on December 18, 1988, in Christchurch, New Zealand.

## 6-B.2: EDWIN IAN ROBERTSON (1919- )
### Son of John Robert Robertson

VI. **Edwin Ian Robertson**, known by family and friends as "Eddie" and professionally as Dr. E.I. Robertson, was born on January 21, 1919, in Petone, New Zealand, the second son of John Robert Robertson and Nora Isabella Walker (4-B above). During World War II, Eddie served with the Royal New Zealand Navy as a degaussing officer.

Following the war, Eddie completed his education and became a renowned scientific researcher and administrator. He received his Master' in Science (M.Sc.) from Victoria University in Wellington, New Zealand, and was awarded a PhD in February 1948 from the University of London, England, in the field of geophysics. Now retired, Dr. E.I. Robertson served as the Director General of the New Zealand Department of Scientific and Industrial Research (DSIR) from 1970 to 1980. He was made a Fellow of the Royal Society of New Zealand in 1963. In 1981, he was awarded the CBE (Commander of the Most Excellent Order of the British Empire) for his outstanding services to science.

In the early 1980s, a large, modern building for the DSIR's Physics and Engineering Laboratory was commissioned in his name. The Robertson Building houses some of the country's most sophisticated scientific projects and equipment, including New Zealand's first silicon chip-fabrication facility.

Eddie married *Claude Sinclair Chalk* in Wellington, New Zealand, on March 14, 1941, in the midst of World War II. She was born on June 23, 1919, in Greymouth, New Zealand. She is the daughter of Ivy Cornwall (born on November 9, 1892, in Greymouth,

New Zealand; died on June 29, 1981, in Lower Hutt, New Zealand) and Claude Chalk (born on December 4, 1889, in Greymouth, New Zealand; died on November 14, 1918, in Palmerston North, New Zealand).

They reside in Tawa, New Zealand, and have two daughters, six grandchildren, and two great-grandchildren. Since his retirement, Eddie has been working with the New Zealand Futures Trust in Wellington, which describes itself as "an independent non-profit organization whose members aim to identify developments and changes affecting the lives and aspirations of New Zealanders, and to promote debate about possible futures."

**Children of Edwin Ian Robertson**

VII. **Helen Elizabeth Robertson**, eldest daughter of Claude Sinclair Chalk and Edwin Ian Robertson, was born on October 6, 1941, in Auckland, New Zealand.

She married *John Arthur Laurenson* on May 20, 1961, in Wellington, New Zealand. He was born on September 7, 1937, in Wellington, the son of Ruth Carrod and Arthur Laurenson.[234] He earned his law degree (LL.B.) from Victoria University in Wellington, became a barrister in Taranaki, New Plymouth, and was designated Queen's Counsellor (Q.C.) in 1989.

On July 17, 1997, John Laurenson became a judge of the New Zealand High Court. At his swearing-in ceremony before a packed audience in the main courtroom of the New Plymouth courthouse, Chief Justice Sir Thomas Eichelbaum praised the new justice. The New Plymouth *Daily News* reported on the proceedings as follows:

*"You have had a most distinguished career in the law," Sir Thomas told Justice Laurenson, referring to his lengthy period with leading Taranaki law firm Govett Quilliam and the fact that he was the third member of that firm to become a High Court judge.*

*Justice Laurenson had been Crown prosecutor for many years in Taranaki, said Sir Thomas. He had been president of the District Law Society and vice-president of the New Zealand Law Society, and chairman or member of many community and sporting bodies. In recent years he had practised as a barrister sole, and had then become Queen's Counsel. He had broad experience in many branches of legal work and tribunals.*

*Attorney General Paul East said that to become a High Court judge was the pinnacle of any legal career. Justice Laurenson had resisted the pressures to practise in one of the main centres and had served as a role model for those lawyers who practised outside the main centres.*

Helen and John Laurenson have three sons. After living in New Plymouth for some thirty-six years, they moved to Auckland in 1997.

### Children of Helen Elizabeth Robertson

VIII. **Peter John Laurenson**, born on November 2, 1962, in New Plymouth, New Zealand. He married *Julie Rowan* in New Plymouth on March 22, 1986. Julie was born on August 10, 1964, in New Plymouth, New Zealand, the daughter of Claude Rowan and Valda Bracegirdle. They have one son.

### Child of Peter John Laurenson

IX. **Ben Rowan Laurenson**, born on May 14, 1994, in Wellington, New Zealand.

VIII. **David Arthur Laurenson**, born on August 14, 1964, in New Plymouth, New Zealand. He married *Monique Dunnett* on March 12, 1994, in Wellington, New Zealand. She was born on June 20, 1965, in Wellington, New Zealand, daughter of David Dunnett and Marcia Lobb. They have no children.

VIII. **Andrew Richard Laurenson**, born on August 11, 1967, in New Plymouth, New Zealand. On January 9, 1993, in New Plymouth, he married *Jacqui Mann* (born on October 15, 1969, in Greymouth, New Zealand, daughter of Bruce Mann and Beverley Lynam). They have one daughter.

### Child of Andrew Richard Laurenson

IX **Elizabeth Laurenson**, born on June 23, 1994, in New Plymouth, New Zealand.

VII. **<u>Pamela Carol Robertson</u>**, born on March 22, 1950, in Wellington, New Zealand. Carol attended Victoria University in Wellington, earning the Bachelor's in Science (B.Sc.) in mathematics.

At the age of twenty, Carol married *Douglas Michael James Fleming* on August 8, 1970, in Wellington. Her husband was born on September 23, 1948, in Dunedin, New Zealand, the son of James Fleming and Anastasia McGrath. He is in the finance business. Carol and Douglas Fleming have three children and live in Auckland, New Zealand.

### Children of Pamela Carol Robertson

VIII. **<u>Nicola Ann Fleming</u>**, born on November 10, 1973, in Wellington, New Zealand.

VIII. **<u>Michael Ian James Fleming</u>**, born on November 20, 1975, in Wellington, New Zealand. He is pursuing a graduate degree in acoustics at the California Institute of Technology in Pasadena, California.

VIII. **<u>Rebecca Jane Fleming</u>**, born on May 4, 1982, in Auckland, New Zealand.

## 6-B.3: ENID HONORAH ROBERTSON (1921- )
### Daughter of John Robert Robertson

VI. **<u>Enid Honorah Robertson</u>**, only daughter of Nora Isabella Walker and John Robert Robertson (4-B above), was born on April 2, 1921, in Petone, New Zealand.

On October 10, 1951, Enid married *John Roy Gibson* in Australia. John, the son of William Gibson and Lilian Abbott, was born on January 31, 1910, in Hobart, Tasmania, Australia. He was managing director of a flour-milling business. They had two children, who have produced five grandchildren.

Enid worked as a private secretary. She is now retired and living in Hobart. Her husband, Roy Gibson, is deceased.

**Children of Enid Honorah Robertson**

VII. **<u>Harvey John Gibson</u>**, born on July 25, 1953, in Hobart, Tasmania, Australia. He is a chartered accountant. Harvey married *Elizabeth Colley Young* on October 18, 1980, in Hobart. She was also born in Hobart on June 12, 1956, and is the daughter of Mary Jaques and Aretas Young. They have three children.

**Children of Harvey John Gibson**

VIII. **<u>Thomas Gibson</u>**, born on May 6, 1982, in Hobart, Tasmania, Australia.

VIII. **<u>Diana Gibson</u>**, born on April 6, 1984, in Hobart, Tasmania, Australia.

VIII. **<u>Felicity Gibson</u>**, born on November 4, 1985, in Hobart, Tasmania, Australia.

VII. **<u>Pamela Kay Gibson</u>**, born on September 26, 1956, in Hobart, Tasmania, Australia. Her first marriage was in Hobart on January 21, 1978, to *Neil David Winter*. Later, she married *Greg Phair*, a school teacher, on May 27, 1989, in Lenna, Tasmania, near Hobart. He is the son of Nancy Pearce and Glenn Phair, and was born on November 3, 1956, in Longford, Tasmania. Pamela and Greg have two children.

**Children of Pamela Kay Gibson**

VIII. **<u>Jessica Kay Phair</u>**, born on June 19, 1990, in Hobart, Tasmania, Australia.

VIII. **<u>Andrew Roy Phair</u>**, born on November 16, 1993, in Hobart, Tasmania, Australia.

## 6-B.4: LEONARD HECTOR ROBERTSON (1923-1993)
### Child of John Robert Robertson

VI. **<u>Leonard Hector Robertson</u>**, fourth and youngest child of Nora Isabella Walker and John Robert Robertson (4-B above), was born on November 14, 1923, in Petone, New Zealand. He served in World War II with the New Zealand Army, and after the war he became general manager of an insurance company in New Zealand.

On December 9, 1950, at the age of twenty-seven, he married *Margaret Helen Virtue* in Wellington, New Zealand. She was born in Wellington on May 15, 1930, the daughter of John Virtue and Danena Clark. They had three children.

Leonard retired about 1990 and died in Wellington, New Zealand, on March 30, 1993, at the age of sixty-nine. His widow is living in Waikanae, New Zealand.

**Children of Leonard Hector Robertson**

VII. **Heather Anita Robertson**, born on March 29, 1954, in Wellington, New Zealand. On June 11, 1977, Heather married *Stephen Goodfellow Grant* in Wellington. Stephen was born on July 10, 1951, in Wellington, the son of Charles Grant and Peggy Campbell. He is a partner in an architectural business. Stephen and Heather Grant live in Plimmerton, New Zealand. They have two children.

**Children of Heather Anita Robertson**

VIII. **Aidan Goodfellow Grant**, born on February 7, 1982, in Wellington, New Zealand.

VIII. **Kate Fiona Grant**, born on June 21, 1984, in Wellington, New Zealand.

VII. **Jeanette Lynne Robertson**, born on July 12, 1955, in Wellington, New Zealand. On October 25, 1986, in Auckland, New Zealand, she married *Robert Paul Taylor*. He was born on September 20, 1953, in Auckland, son of Marie and Ron Taylor. They have one child, Alice Taylor, and a son by Rob's first marriage, Samuel James Taylor (who was born on June 9, 1982, in Auckland). Ron owns and operates a catering business.

**Child of Jeanette Lynne Robertson**

VIII. **Alice Taylor**, born on January 16, 1988, in Auckland, New Zealand.

VII. **Malcolm John Robertson**, born on February 3, 1957, in Wellington, New Zealand. On December 5, 1981, in Wellington, he married *Michelle Fairy Harkness*. The daughter of Michael Harkness and Lorraine Fairy, Michelle was born on September 16, 1956, in Te Kuiti, New Zealand.

Malcolm and Michelle have three children. Malcolm runs his own quantity surveying business.

### Children of Malcolm John Robertson

VIII. **Aaron Robertson**, born on July 3, 1985, in Auckland, New Zealand.

VIII. **Monique Sara Robertson**, born on October 3, 1987, in Paraparaumu, New Zealand.

VIII. **Scott Robertson**, born on December 16, 1990, in Paraparaumu, New Zealand.

## 6-B.5: CHRISTINA HELEN CHEYNE (1903-1992)
### Daughter of James Cheyne

VI. **Christina Helen Cheyne** (called "Tina") was the daughter of Jesse Skilling and James Cheyne (5-B.1 above). She was born in Kilbirnie, Wellington, New Zealand, on New Year's Eve 1903.

While growing up, Tina was told many stories by her Shetland-born grandmother Christina Robertson Cheyne and her grandmother's sister Ann Robertson Georgeson about life in the Shetlands and about their people who lived there. Those stories became such a part of their life that, when Tina and Laurie started to school, students and teachers asked how long they had lived in New Zealand and were surprised to learn the girls were born in New Zealand. Tina's grandmother Christina kept up correspondence with her brothers Charles and Andrew and with Andrew's daughter, Greta Robertson, in Cincinnati, Ohio. Tina said she often received postcards from her great-aunt Cynthia Robertson when Cynthia traveled, and Tina still has a folding postcard of Mount Mitchell and the scenic railway sent to her by her great-uncle Charles Dumbreck Robertson and great-aunt Cynthia Buck Robertson when they visited their son Reuben Robertson in North Carolina.

Tina's great-aunt Ann Margaret Cheyne ("Aunt Sis"), told her that the Struan Robertson branch of the clan came from the Central Highlands of Scotland, were a branch of the ancient Clan Donnachaidh, and were akin to the earls of Atholl and Stewart-Argyll. As she recalled the story told to her, the Duke of Argyll of that time took his two sisters and their Robertson kin out of Scotland for safety and sent them to the Shetlands during the fierce wars near Perthshire. On her last trip to Shetland, Aunt Ann had brought back a detailed book on the Robertsons of Struan, with notes in it, which she gave to Tina. Unfortunately, that book was lost when the home of Tina and her husband was destroyed during the Napier earthquake of 1930. Tina tried to find a book to replace it when she and her husband were in Scotland in 1951 but never found one as informative.

In 1929, at the age of twenty-five, Tina Cheyne married *Leslie Marshall Rankine* in Wellington, New Zealand. He was born on August 7, 1902, in Adelaide, Victoria, Australia, the son of Frederick William Rankine and Maude Sara, who moved from Australia to New Zealand about 1904 and lived in Wellington.

Tina and Leslie Rankine had one son, Ian. They first lived in Napier on Hawke's Bay, on the east coast of North Island, New Zealand. Around 1936, after the Napier earthquake in 1930, they moved to Lower Hutt. Leslie had a large importing business in Wellington. He died on December 24, 1961, at age fifty-nine, in Wellington. Tina died in 1992.

### Child of Christina Helen Cheyne

VII. **Ian Frederick Rankine**, born on March 29, 1930, in Napier, Hawke's Bay, New Zealand. He trained as an accountant and continued his father's import business for a number of years. Ian retired from business in 1996.

On April 10, 1952, at Khandallah Presbyterian Church near Wellington, Ian married *Margaret Euphemia Huffam*. They had met while riding horses at Paraparaumu Beach. Margaret was born on April 6, 1929, at "Rewa" in Roseneath, Wellington, the daughter of Kenneth Nelson Kingsford Huffam and Euphemia Agnes Catherine Gower ("Phemia").[235]

Ian and Margaret have three children. They live in the house that Ian's mother, Tina, owned in York Bay, Eastbourne, a suburb of Wellington.

### Children of Ian Rankine

VIII. **Bruce Marshall Rankine**, oldest son of Margaret and Ian Rankine, born on February 28, 1954, in Wellington, New Zealand. After working for a while as an accountant in Birmingham, England, Bruce returned home to New

Zealand. He married *Nancy Louise Cammell* on June 18, 1983, at St. Andrews Anglican Church in Taupo. She was born on October 13, 1956, the daughter of Douglas H. Cammell and Noeleen Kidd of Palmerston North, New Zealand.

Bruce and Nancy Rankine live in Heliers, Auckland, on the North Island of New Zealand. They have three children.

### Children of Bruce Marshall Rankine

IX. **Jonathan Kenneth Rankine**, born on August 10, 1985, in Auckland, New Zealand.

IX. **Samuel Douglas Rankine**, born on November 29, 1986, in Auckland, New Zealand.

IX. **Annaliese Margaret Rankine**, born on January 9, 1990, in Auckland, New Zealand.

VIII. **Robert Rankine**, second son of Margaret and Ian Rankine, was born on August 11, 1956. He died as an infant of six months in February 1957.

VIII. **Julie Margaret Rankine**, adopted daughter of Margaret and Ian Rankine, was born on October 4, 1958. Julie was educated as a school teacher.

On August 18, 1979, she married *Ross Church*, who was born on August 27, 1952. They divorced, with no children.

Her second marriage, to *Robert Marshall*, was on August 20, 1984, at "Craiglea," the home of her parents in York Bay. Robert was born on August 12, 1949, in Brisbane, Australia, (son of Hay Hobbs and Wallace Howard Marshall). Julie and Bob had two sons, and divorced. She later married *Stuart Gilmour*, a farmer. There were no children in that marriage. They live in Elsthorte, Hawkes Bay, near Hastings, New Zealand.

### Children of Julie Margaret Rankine

IX. **Benjamin Robert Marshall**, born on July 12, 1985, in New Zealand.

IX. **Michael Lloyd Leslie Marshall**, born on May 25, 1988, in New Zealand.

## 6-B.6: LAWRENCE JAMES ALEXANDER CHEYNE (1905-1982)
### Son of James Cheyne

VI. **Lawrence James Alexander Cheyne** (called "Laurie"), only son of Jesse Skilling and James Cheyne (5-B.1 above), was born in 1905 in Wellington, New Zealand. In 1927, Laurie married *Henrietta Lavinia Jakeman* (often called "Teddy"), in Wellington. She was born on January 6, 1912. They had two sons and divorced about 1948. Laurie later remarried, but the name of his second wife is unknown.

Laurie Cheyne worked for the Inland Revenue Department, the taxing authority of New Zealand, for some forty years, until retirement. He died in Auckland, New Zealand, in late 1982, about seventy-nine years of age. Teddy, his first wife, resides in Auckland.

**Children of Lawrence James Alexander Cheyne**

VII. **Kenneth James Cheyne**, born on September 26, 1928, in Wellington, New Zealand. He married *Gwendolyn Ruth Parsons* in Wellington. She was born in Wellington on December 28, 1933, daughter of Mabel Ruth Morris and Christopher Thomas Parsons. They raised two children. Gwendolyn died on January 27, 1981, at the age of forty-nine. A retired plumbing contractor, Ken lives in Paraparaumu.

**Children of Kenneth James Cheyne**

VIII. **Murray James Cheyne**, born on October 8, 1962, in Wellington, New Zealand. He lives in Timaru on New Zealand's South Island, where he works as an occupational therapist in a hospital. He is unmarried.

VIII. **Annette Ruth Cheyne**, born on January 15, 1964, in Wellington, New Zealand. Unmarried, she resides in Lower Hutt, Wellington, and is an assistant to a union secretary.

VII. **Malcolm Leslie Cheyne**, born on October 8, 1931, in Wellington, New Zealand. He married *Mary Brosnan* in Auckland, New Zealand, on February 26, 1955. She was born in Auckland on November 1, 1927, daughter of Annie Barnett and John Brosnan. Both her parents were Australians, but they married in Auckland. Mary and Malcolm have two children and live at Blockhouse Bay in Auckland.

**Children of Malcolm Leslie Cheyne**

VIII. **Anne Cheyne**, born on September 6, 1956, in Auckland, New Zealand. She first married *John Rudd*; they had a son and divorced. On November 24, 1988, Anne married *Geoffrey Raymond McGregor,* who was born on September 3, 1954. They live in Te Atatu, South Auckland.

**Child of Anne Cheyne**

IX. **Andrew Rudd,** born on July 28, 1984.

VIII. **Michael Cheyne**, born on November 9, 1958, in Auckland, New Zealand. On January 15, 1983, he married *Susan Louise Vial*, who was born on January 23, 1960. They lived in England for several years, where Michael worked as an accountant, before returning to New Zealand in the late 1980s. Michael is a financial controller, analyzing potential mergers and acquisitions for his employer. Susan and Michael have one son.

**Child of Michael Cheyne**

IX. **William Cheyne**, born on September 13, 1989, in Auckland, New Zealand.

## 6-B.7: IRIS MONCRIEFF FRASER (1911-1997)
### Daughter of Mary Charlotte Agnes Cheyne

VI. **Iris Moncrieff Fraser**, daughter of Mary Charlotte Agnes Cheyne and Jack Fraser (5-B.2 above), was born on March 24, 1911, in Woodville, New Zealand.

She married *Oliver Frederick Bridges* in Woodville on July 27, 1935. He was born in Woodville, New Zealand, on November 27, 1911, son of Isabella Mary McKenzie and Oliver Charles Bridges, both of whom were from New South Wales, Australia. Iris and Oliver had three children. They lived on and worked the farm near Woodville that her parents had owned, plus a few more acres they added. Oliver also worked on other farms and in forestry to help make ends meet.

Oliver Bridges died on February 11, 1974, at age sixty-three. Iris died at Palmerston North Hospital on October 6, 1997. She was eighty-six.

**Children of Iris Fraser**

VII. **Robert Malcolm Charles Bridges**, son of Iris Fraser and Oliver Frederick Bridges, was born in Woodville, New Zealand, on September 17, 1936. Bob married _Jocelyn Sylvia Harris_ in June 1959 in Pahiatua, New Zealand. They had three children and resided in Palmerston North. Bob Bridges died on August 5, 1989, at age fifty-three.

**Children of Robert Malcolm Charles Bridges**

VIII. **Raewyn Lynette Bridges**, was born on August 10, 1963, in Marton, New Zealand. On February 15, 1986, Raewyn married _Brian McGuinness_ in Palmerston North. They have three daughters and live in Wanganui on the North Island. Although she is a full-time mother, Raewyn still runs in marathons.

**Children of Raewyn Lynette Bridges**

IX. **Claire Jane McGuinness**, born on November 20, 1988, in Wanganui, New Zealand.

IX. **Kate Laura McGuinness**, born on September 22, 1991, in Wanganui, New Zealand.

IX. **Emily Joy McGuinness**, born on February 17, 1997 in Wanganui, New Zealand.

VIII. **Warren Craig Bridges**, born on January 31, 1965, in Palmerston North, New Zealand. He married _Sharyn Pearson_ on February 8, 1992, in Palmerston North. They have two children and live in Waiuku, near Auckland. Warren is a manager in a Kiwi fruit-growing operation.

**Children of Warren Craig Bridges**

IX. **Chantae Rose Bridges**, born on May 5, 1995, in Tauranga, New Zealand.

IX. **Brooke Ariana Bridges**, born on July 27, 1998, in Tauranga, New Zealand.

VIII. **<u>Mark Leslie Bridges</u>**, born on December 19, 1967, in Palmerston North, New Zealand. He married *<u>Ann Hodge</u>* in Inglewood, New Zealand, on January 30, 1993. They live in Manaia, near Wanganui, and have no children. Mark is a farming consultant.

VII. **<u>Murray McKenzie Bridges</u>**, born on July 11, 1939, in Woodville, New Zealand, was the second son of Iris Fraser and Oliver Bridges. He married *<u>Judith Jane Hunter</u>* in Danville, New Zealand. Judith was born on November 16, 1941, daughter of Jane Hind and Gerald Hugh Lester Hunter. They have two children and reside in Waekanae.

### Children of Murry McKenzie Bridges

VIII. **<u>Colin Ross Bridges</u>**, born on May 16, 1963, in Upper Hutt, New Zealand. On January 29, 1994, he married *<u>Karen Anne Woodgate</u>*, who was born on January 29, 1969, in Middlemore, South Auckland, New Zealand. They reside in Lyall Bay, Wellington, and have one daughter. Colin is a navigation systems engineer, a job requiring him to travel frequently.

### Child of Colin Ross Bridges

IX. **<u>Teagon Hunter Bridges</u>**, born on December 3, 1997, in Wellington, New Zealand.

VIII. **<u>Dianna Jane Bridges</u>**, born on June 23, 1966, in Lower Hutt, New Zealand. Dianna married *<u>Andrew van Olpen</u>* on May 8, 1993, but retained Bridges as her surname. Andrew was born on June 30, 1966, in Rangiora, near Christchurch, on the South Island of New Zealand. They live at Lyall Bay in Wellington. Dianna is a lawyer for Wespac Bank.

VII. **<u>Joyce Mary Bridges</u>**, born on October 18, 1949, in Woodville, New Zealand, daughter of Iris Fraser and Oliver Frederick Bridges. She married *<u>Alan Keith Henson</u>* in Woodville on June 3, 1972. The son of Ngaire Elizabeth Olsen and Kenneth John Henson, Alan was born on October 13, 1950, in Palmerston North, New Zealand.

Since 1977, Joyce and Alan have lived on a fifty-acre farm near Woodville, where they raise cattle, pigs, and about a dozen sheep. This is the same property that Joyce's grandparents and parents farmed, with each generation adding a few acres. Alan also does daily contracting work such as welding, fencing, spraying, topping horse paddocks, felling trees, and general farm work in the Woodville area. They have two children.

### Children of Joyce Mary Bridges

VIII. **Ivan Fraser Henson**, born on June 11, 1974, in Tokoroa, New Zealand. His partner is *Tracy Kinniburgh*. They have one son and live in Tokomaru. Ivan works as a cricket-park groundsman in Palmerston North.

### Child of Ivan Fraser Henson

IX. **Cameron Alan Kinniburgh Henson**, born on January 24, 1998, in Palmerston North, New Zealand.

VIII. **Tanya Ngaire Henson**, born on July 7, 1976, in Tokoroa, New Zealand. Tanya lives on the family farm in Woodville, helping with the animals in her spare time, and holds down a job in town.

## 6-B.8: MARGARET O'BRIAN (1912- )
### Daughter of Francis Robert O'Brian

VI. **Margaret O'Brian**, only daughter of Margaret O'Shea and Francis Robert O'Brian (4-E above), was born on May 8, 1912, in Saint Mary's Maternity Hospital, Wellington, New Zealand. She was only five years old when her father was killed in combat in Palestine, a casualty of World War I. Margaret became a schoolteacher. She married *John Fowlds* in New Zealand; he was born on September 20, 1915. They had four children.

Margaret wrote this brief autobiography:

My mother met my father in Blenheim where she worked as a barmaid; he was a shepherd. They were married in Wellington, 1907, and after residing a short period in the south Island, moved to Wellington, my mother's home town. He managed a farm on the out-skirts of the city. After my birth they moved to Feilding where he was employed installing electricity in that town.

War broke out in Europe between England and Germany in 1914 and my father volunteered to go overseas with the N.Z. Army. He sailed away February 1915. He served two and a half years on active service, first with the Mounted Rifles Brigade, then when that was disbanded, as Sergeant in charge of a Machine Gun Squadron, before he succumbed to wounds in the Sinai Desert, 20th August 1917. He is buried in Beersheba, in a country now known as Israel.

The tenor of my life was now set. I became a kind of refugee, a wanderer going aimlessly from one furnished room to another for the next twenty-five years. Apart from the brief period in Feilding, I never knew a home. I was always an out-sider in some other person's establishment.

In 1921 my mother and I settled permanently in Blenheim where life continued in the same manner but in a better environment. My paternal grandparents were always close at hand.

I attended St. Joseph's Parish School where I was conscious of being unlike the other children who had mothers and fathers as well as brothers and sisters. I was a very lonely little girl. My mother never let me associate with other children outside the school gate. School was an escape from an unhappy home life. There I coped well with lessons.

Thanks to a concerned teacher, Sister Mary Philomena, who put my name forward for the Trentham Scholarship, a bursary for children who had lost a father during the war, I was able to receive five years secondary education. My mother would not allow me to take up the scholarship at a city boarding school, so, in addition to attending St. Mary's College in Blenheim, a small Catholic establishment, I was able to study music and singing as well as the usual school subjects.

The irony of the situation does not escape me; my father's death enabled me to become a teacher.

In 1930 I became a probationer, and in 1931 proceeded to Teachers Training College in Wellington where I spent two years. By now N.Z. was in the grip of the Great Depression, many were out of work, but because I had no one to support me, I received constant employment. I travelled around N.Z. filling in, in a temporary capacity, at country schools.

I enjoyed every minute; it seemed idyllic, till in 1936 I was sent to a Maori School. Now, from 1866-1969 a dual system of education existed in New Zealand, one run by Education Boards whose members were voted for, the other Native (Maori) Schools which the Education Department, an arm of Government, operated. No one had prepared me for the difference. I gazed at my country through new eyes and did not like what I saw. I was changed forever!

I travelled up the Wanganui River by paddle-steamer to Pa Moana, at Koroniti. There I boarded with the Anglican Mission Sister, nurse as well as nun, Elsie Smith. As I trudged up the river's bank through silt and mud to the Mission House a new view of New Zealand opened up before me. I learned how the Mission Station worked hand in glove with Government to the complete exclusion of the Maori people.

Further up the river three priests, one I knew, conducted a Catholic Mission with the aid of a group of nuns. Seeing them running about in their pink singlets and learning that even though they possessed a launch which Catholic parishioners in Blenheim had help supply and they held services nowhere other than at their base, filled me with disgust.

I developed a deep dislike of Missions and have never put a cent in a Mission Box since!!

The now slightly militant Margaret O'Brian took up her first permanent teaching position in south Taranaki in September, 1938, where she encountered Maori children of spirit whose parents had not been subjected to Mission influence. And, oh, the relief!

In 1939 war broke out in Europe and the Maori Battalion was formed as a unit of the N.Z. Army – a gesture of goodwill which did not reach the die-hard "rednecks."

In 1941 I went to teach on the outskirts of Wellington close to the Trentham Military Camp. On the train I met my husband-to-be, John Fowlds, who worked in said camp as aide to Colonel Bown, head of N.Z. Ordnance. (The "Audience Corp" as it was nick-named.)

I never thought to marry; I had an incubus around my neck – my mother who wasn't adverse to water mixed with whisky, but had a deep dislike of it mixed with soap. John Fowlds also had an impediment to marriage – a young daughter. I loved his daughter on sight, he cheerfully tolerated my mother. We wed in May 1943 and quickly produced four children, two sons and two daughters.

Life in the Fowlds household was never dull with four offspring, a dog, a cat, a piano, and an entrepreneurial type salesman husband whose hobby was landscape painting. As the family grew, so, too, expanded the activities they pursued. The old piano succumbed to constant use and had to be replaced, the area where we lived resounded to the skirl of bagpipes, or the less cadent tones of the dance band assembled within when the tone-deaf saxophonist blew with abandon.

What happened on wet days you might ask? All became artists! The young folk gathered around the refectory table with paper and paint brushes. Dad, with enthusiasm took up the other kind of paint brush, dabbing it here, dabbing it there, even painting the lavatory seat.

In 1957 invited to help out at a local school, I went back to teaching. This proved a good move, because, when my husband died suddenly in 1966, I was able to support my children unaided. John, the eldest had just completed a lengthy five year apprenticeship in T.V. & radio. Robert was at the College of Education studying to be a teacher, Vivienne after studying at Wgtn School of Design had just obtained her first position in an Advertising Agency, Katherine was still at Secondary School aiming to go to the Otago Physical Education School in Dunedin.

I had my nose to the grindstone. I continued teaching till 1971, having been ST JC at Silverstream School and Senior Woman at Fergusson Intermediate School in the interim.

Here, chance, or fate, took a hand in my life. At a United Nations meeting (I'd been a member for some years) I was told the Correspondence School required an office clerk. I went along and was accepted. My job involved handling various bank accounts and making visits to Treasury and the Reserve Bank. I loved it and soon became proficient, so proficient, that when I had to leave the Correspondence School because of age, on my last trip to the Reserve Bank, two men came to the counter inviting me to join their department. I would have loved to do so, but I was committed to working in the Evening Post office. From there I transferred to "Castrol" because the pay was greater.

These were halcyon years. I commenced serious study of the Maori Language, something I felt impelled to do. I began evening classes at

Wellington High School before progressing to Wgtn Polytechnic. I moved to live in Palmerston North (1980) where I continued my lessons at Queen Elizabeth College sitting both School Certificate and University Entrance exam in that subject. Finally I attended Massey University. If I ever had an Alma Mater, this was it. Massey has a beautiful campus.

Again chance intervened; I saw an advertisement, somewhere or other, where Auckland University Education Dept. was commencing research into Native (later named "Maori") Schools of 1866-1969. I couldn't get to my pen fast enough. By return mail I received a reply from Dr. Judith Simon who headed the research. And so my acquaintance with her began. I went to Auckland (curiosity took me there) where I was interviewed by a man. All interviewees have to answer the same set of questions.

Before the questions began, I had to sign an oath that I would tell the truth, the whole truth and nothing but the truth.

This research has yet to be published. I of course am a very small part of the whole, but I like to think I have contributed something worthwhile to this volatile subject.

My life rolls inexorably onwards. Who knows what is ahead. "You never know what a day will bring forth," Grandma O'Brian used to say.

John Fowlds died at the age of fifty on June 11, 1966, in Lower Hutt, New Zealand. As of 1991, Margaret was living in Palmerston North.

## Children of Margaret O'Brian

VII. **John Fowlds**, first son of Margaret O'Brian and John Fowlds, was born on April 6, 1944, in Wellington, New Zealand. He first married *Linda Gorrie* in 1967. They had one son. He later married *Joanne Beckett*.

### Child of John Fowlds

VIII. **Jason Fowlds**, born on April 10, 1970. He died on February 10, 1991.

VII. **Robert Fowlds**, second son of Margaret O'Brian and John Fowlds, was born on April 15, 1946, in New Zealand. On May 12, 1969, he married *Joan Campbell*, and they had a daughter. On January 29, 1995, Robert married *Amanda Hartley*.

**Child of Robert Fowlds**

VIII. **Megan Fowlds**, born on April 11, 1973.

VII. **Vivienne Fowlds**, first daughter of Margaret O'Brian and John Fowlds, was born on December 14, 1947, in New Zealand. She married *Rob Roy Macgregor*, and they have two children.

**Children of Vivienne Fowlds**

VIII. **Lara Macgregor**, born on February 2, 1969.

VIII. **Duncan Macgregor**, born on June 30, 1972.

VII. **Katherine Fowlds**, second daughter of Margaret O'Brian and John Fowlds, was born on July 26, 1949. She married *Baye Riddell*, and they had a daughter. Katherine later married *Maurice Kidd*, and they had three children. Katherine's third husband is *Murray Cooper*.

**Children of Katherine Fowlds**

VIII. **Nicola Riddell**, born on July 30, 1971.

VIII. **Lauren Kidd**, born on October 26, 1977.

VIII. **Hannah Kidd**, born on October 4, 1979.

VIII. **Frances Kidd**, born on July 7, 1982.

## 6-B.9: CHARLOTTE ROBERTSON LYVER (1917-1999)
### Daughter of Elizabeth Georgeson O'Brian

VI. **Charlotte Robertson Lyver** was born on July 26, 1917, in New Zealand, daughter of Elizabeth O'Brian and Robert Lyver (5-B.3 above). Charlotte married *Basil Adam Gibson*, the son of Adam Gibson and Bessie Harris. They had two sons. Basil died on November 7, 1968.

Charlotte survived her husband by thirty years. She enjoyed keeping in touch with our Robertsons around the world and travelled extensively in North America to visit her son and his family as well as cousins in North Carolina. She died on June 12, 1999, at the age of eighty-one.

**Children of Charlotte Robertson Lyver**

VII. **Keith A. Gibson** was born on March 5, 1946, in New Zealand. About 1970, he married *Judy Chappell*, who was born on October 28, 1946, in Upper Hutt, New Zealand, the daughter of Iona and Peter Chappell. Keith received an honours degree in civil engineering and is a consulting engineer with the firm of Beca Carter Ferner & Hollings, which has branches around the world. Judy is an elementary school teacher. They have one son, Craig, and reside in Paremata, Wellington, New Zealand.

**Child of Keith Gibson**

VIII. **Craig Gibson**, born on November 25, 1972, in Wellington, New Zealand. An outstanding athlete and world-class pitcher, he plays fastpitch softball throughout the year with championship-level semipro teams in the United States and New Zealand. During the summer of 1997, he visited his cousins, the Reuben Robertson family, in Washington, D.C.

VII. **Wayne Basil Gibson** was born on October 23, 1949, in Te Kuiti, North Island, New Zealand. Wayne, according to his mother, Charlotte, was a champion ballroom dancer as a young man.

After spending some time in England, Wayne settled in Toronto, Canada, about 1974. He and his partner, *Nancy Olson*, have two children. Nancy was born in Toronto on August 12, 1949, and works as a bookkeeper.

Wayne was involved in custom carpentry work through a firm he owned in Toronto, Southern Cross Construction, and was active in recreational sailing on Lake Ontario. He built small sailboats for both children to help them learn the art of sailing. Wayne recently returned to New Zealand to be near his mother in her last years.

**Children of Wayne Basil Gibson**

VIII. **Karyn Melissa Sarah Gibson**, born on September 8, 1980, in Toronto, Ontario, Canada.

VIII. **Ryan Adam Gibson**, born on March 23, 1984, in Toronto, Ontario, Canada.

## 6-B.10: AGNES CAWTHRON LYVER (1919- )
### Daughter of Elizabeth Georgeson O'Brian

VI. **Agnes Cawthron Lyver** (called "Ness"), daughter of Elizabeth O'Brian and Robert Lyver (5-B.3 above), was born on June 1, 1919, in Bealey, on the South Island of New Zealand. She married *Leonard Beere* in Lower Hutt, New Zealand, shortly after his return from World War II. Len was born on August 3, 1908, in Bristol, England, and his family immigrated to New Zealand when he was a small child. He worked as a carpenter and died on March 13, 1980, in Nelson, on the South Island of New Zealand, at the age of seventy-one. Ness and Len had two daughters, Judy and Helen.

Reflecting a strong interest of "Our Robertsons" around the world in family history, Agnes is the subject of a detailed biography and memoir written by her granddaughter Sonja Mitchell. Sonja based her report on extensive interviews in which Ness recalled childhood memories and experiences growing up in difficult times. Much of the information that follows has been derived from Sonja's paper, titled "Ness's Story, a Personal Tribute."

Ness was the fifth child in a large family of four boys and four girls. Despite big gaps in their ages, she got along with all her siblings but was especially close to her older sister Charlotte. Ness attended Hutt Valley High School and was active in outdoor sports, tennis, choir, and other activities.

However, the family suffered through two major disruptions while Ness was still a teenager. The first was the sudden and unexpected death of her mother in 1934, when Ness was only fourteen years old, which came as a terrible shock to everyone. Charlotte had to take up the role of mother, doing a lot of the housework and cooking for the rest of the family.

The second problem was the effect of the Great Depression of the 1930s, which severely impacted New Zealand's economy. Despite the financial hardships experienced by the Lyver family and their neighbors and friends, Ness still thinks of the Depression years as a time of growth and generosity: "I think that neighbors grew closer to each other in the Depression, we were all in the same boat and people helped one another out whenever they could. The Depression made us a closer community and people shared more."

In the Lyver family, like many others in those times, clothing had to be recycled and passed from one child to another. Ness recalls:

*As a young person, I was very conscious of holes in my shoes and tried desperately to hide them from view. Our father would buy sheets of leather to repair our shoes and there was no question of putting them in the shop for repair. Shoes were passed down from one child to another, which was not good for our feet. At least we did have shoes, though, while some other children would go around barefoot. . . . You got your sister's old cast-offs and shoes as she grew out of them. I look back and see that we appreciated things when something new did come our way. I remember during the depression people going along the railway line picking up coal that had fallen from the locomotives. I remember too that the engineer or guard would occasionally throw off an extra shovel or two to help them out.*

Even people who had jobs, like Ness's father, were affected, because much of their wages were taken for special unemployment taxes. There was a great deal of social unrest, including marches and angry demonstrations by the unemployed in the larger cities like Wellington.

At her father's urging, Ness enrolled in the commercial course at the local technical school to learn clerical skills, although she had little interest in that kind of work. But through that connection she landed a government job in the Transport Office, earning three pounds a week.

She still had time and energy to pursue her love of outdoor sports. Ness was a top tennis player and became very active in "tramping," or cross-country backpacking. She joined the Hutt Valley Tramping Club, which went on outings most weekends. The club was a very close-knit group of young people who became lifelong friends. As Sonja noted, "Tramping was not easy in those days: the packs were cumbersome, the gear was heavy, there was no lightweight food, the huts were spartan, and the weather in the Tararua Ranges, where they often tramped, could be atrocious. But the group shared some of the best days of their lives during these years that they tramped together."

The club became the focal point for much of the social life of its members. That was how Ness met her future husband, Len Beere, who was a leader in the tramping club, ten years older than Ness, handsome, and charming. But in the late 1930s, war was breaking out in Europe and deeply impacted everyone's life in New Zealand.

Many of the Hutt Valley Tramping Club members left to serve in the war, and there were farewell functions for them. Len signed up for the Third Echelon of New Zealand, which was made up of men who had volunteered to serve. Ness objected to this and argued with

Len over whether he should go. She said, "To me it was like killing somebody you knew nothing about, who might be a marvelous person with a wonderful voice, or a pianist or a genius, someone really talented, someone that the world needs." Len, however, felt that someone had to stop people like Hitler from gaining power, so he stepped forward. But before he left, he and Ness became engaged.

Sent with the New Zealand forces to fight in the Mediterranean, Len was captured by the Germans and imprisoned on Crete, the largest of the Greek Islands. He managed to escape from the German prison camp and made his way into the rugged hills of Crete. There he hid out for almost three years, aided by a Cretan family named Vacachy, who provided food and shelter when German troops were not in the immediate area where they lived and farmed. When the Germans came into that area, Len would get away to the surrounding hills, where he hid in caves or other rudimentary shelters, sometimes for months at a time.

Ness remembers World War II as a terrible time:

> *The echelon would be marching down the streets of Wellington and everyone would be cheering. The last thing on earth you felt like doing was cheering. The men would go into camp for some time and there was always some uncertainty about whether they had gone or whether they were still here. Once they were overseas their mail was always censored. The censors cut out any reference to anything that could give the enemy any clues about where the troops were or what was happening. Len must have said a lot that he was not supposed to say because his letters were all chewed with these holes all over them where they had cut them to bits.*

Then came word that Len was missing and, after six months, presumed dead. That meant Ness no longer received his war-service pay.

During the war, many things in New Zealand were rationed. "You had ration tickets and you were only entitled to so much tea, sugar or butter. You received two ounces of butter each week and about the same amount of tea. There was never enough for what you needed. If you went out anywhere, you would take a bit of butter or tea with you to help out with the supper or meal because you knew the hosts would not have enough to cope." There were shortages of rice, tea, butter, and sugar, and marmite wasn't available. The butter was needed to send to Britain. Rice and sugar had to be imported, and imported foods were discouraged because of the danger to shipping.

Even with so many of its young men abroad, the tramping club stayed active during the war years and did many things for "the boys overseas." Ness recalls, "We all got together and had to write letters to the different ones who were away. Also we knitted socks. I couldn't count the number of khaki socks I made."

Ness was working in the Transport Office when the war started, but she had always been more interested in nursing. Finally, she enrolled in nursing school, which was very rigorous and required her to live in a spartan dormitory called the Nurses' Home—which was run like a tightly-supervised hostel—for three years.

Part of the training involved working on the wards of the Wellington Hospital, which was very hard work and could be very distressing. Because the windows of the hospital were bricked up as a wartime security measure, the wards were always very dark. Ness remembers once being left alone as a second-year nurse in a house that was being used to isolate patients during a laryngitis epidemic. Many of the patients were delirious with extremely high temperatures, and some were already dead but had not been removed—a very unnerving experience.

When Len returned home from the war, they got married. Still, the government manpower office would not let her leave her job at the hospital. Only when she became pregnant with her first child was she allowed to stop work. It turned out to be a difficult pregnancy, and Ness was confined to bed for many months. At the time, they were living in the gardener's cottage at the home of a doctor in Belmont, a hilly area above the Hutt Valley. The doctor let them stay there in exchange for odd jobs Len would do for him when Len wasn't working on a house he was building nearby on land that the doctor gave them.

The little wooden bungalow was finished just in time for the baby's arrival. But the house was located in an extremely windy and rainy area. The winds were so strong, Ness recalls, that "Len made a chain attached to the washing line to keep it still while the clothes were pegged on."

Eventually, Len and Ness began to look for a place to live that was more congenial for family life, and they settled on the area of Nelson on New Zealand's beautiful South Island. "We started looking at sunshine records, and that's what brought us to Nelson. Also, I had visited Nelson a long time ago while we were on a tramping trip and I fell in love with it then, I thought it was a beautiful place." Through some people they knew there, they found a property with a large cob louse—a building made of straw, clay and sand—and seven acres of land in a very rural part of Nelson called Mapua, which they bought in 1950 from the old man who had originally built it.

When the Beere family moved into their Mapua home, the property was remote and wild. Sonja Mitchell's paper describes what life was like in the family's new home:

> Scattered trees rose from the tussock covered slopes, and the closest thing to a garden was a lone lemon tree. Len named the place Strovles after the Cretan village he had stayed in during the war and he used the skills he had acquired while working on the farm in Strovles to make his own family fairly self-sufficient. He was determined that in the event of another depression or other times of shortage, the family would never go hungry.
>
> The lower section of the property was turned into paddocks where they grazed two cows. Ness milked these cows twice a day and separated the milk and cream in a machine called a separator the rhythmic sound of which would carry through the house. The milk was sent to the milk station in big metal cans and from the cream Ness made butter. She churned the butter by hand until the day she insisted Len do it, and from then on used the Kenwood beater which Len had gone straight out and bought.
>
> Len built a chicken run and so they always had plenty of eggs. They also grew a large vegetable garden, a flower garden, and had plum, apple, pear, citrus and feijoa trees planted around the property. Washing was boiled up in the wash-house in a copper which also cooked the Christmas ham. They did not have a refrigerator until . . . about 1956; until then Nessie draped muslin over perishable goods in a bowl of water.
>
> The town of Nelson was reached by bus after a journey more than an hour long over a winding clay road. Every time Nessie made this journey her daughter (my mother) was very motion-sick. It was not until 1958 that the family bought a car. It was an Austin 50 and Ness and Len were very proud of it. "We used it a lot, we thought we were just the cat's pajamas."

From 1950 to the present day the Beere family lived a full life in the Mapua community. At first it was a very small close community with its own little school, its clubs, and movies in the hall on Saturday night. But over the years it grew and the distance to Nelson became less of a barrier with better roads and more cars. Len worked at the local chemical works as their maintenance carpenter, using his bicycle for transport, while the children attended school just along the road.

The daily routine followed the pattern of Len's job, the seasons and school holidays. Everyone came home for the lunch hour when Nessie provided a cooked lunch. Her daily routine was governed by milking the cows, meal times, and the large garden. The cake tins were always full, the bottling was done in autumn and jam was made as the crops came in.

On Sundays there was the family drive exploring the countryside. Len continued to go tramping usually on his own or with the local club. During holidays relatives and former tramping club friends and their families came to stay. Nessie had a reputation for warm hospitality and the Mapua home became a retreat for relations and friends with problems or under stress. In the summer the family went on 3-week car and camping trips all over both islands.

In early 1980, Len died from a ruptured esophagus. For a while Ness lived alone at her remote home in Mapua, as her daughter Judy was living with her husband and children in Wellington, and daughter Helen was traveling abroad. However, Judy and her husband, David, decided later that year to return and make their home in Mapua. Ness moved into the cottage so Judy's family could live in the big house. Helen and her partner, John, later returned from their travels overseas and built an attic on top of the small cottage to live in.

Ness lives in the small cottage in Mapua, and her children and grandchildren are still living in the family home and the cottage with her.

**Children of Agnes Cawthron Lyver**

VII. **Judith Mary Beere**, first daughter of Agnes Lyver and Leonard Beere, was born on March 9, 1946, in Lower Hutt, Wellington, New Zealand. Judy studied at Victoria University in Wellington, where she received a BA in English language and literature in 1966. She later earned a diploma in Secondary Teaching and became a school teacher.

Judy married *David John Mitchell* on December 24, 1971, in the garden of the family home in Mapua. David is the son of Elizabeth Oakes Freeth and Frank Wyndham Mitchell, and was born on February 12, 1944, in Adelaide, Australia. He is a journalist and writer.

Since 1986, David has been the editor of the *Nelson Mail* in Nelson, a lovely coastal city on New Zealand's South Island. He is one of the longest-serving newspaper editors in the country. Judy notes, "He is still surviving his incredible hours and complexity of tasks editing the *Nelson Mail*, which is holding its own despite a severe economic downturn in Nelson, but has given notice that he will do it for only another year."

Judy and David Mitchell have two daughters and a son and live in the family compound in Mapua, with Judy's mother, her sister, and her brother-in-law as immediate neighbors. In 1997, Judy completed a Bachelor of Nursing degree and started a new career in psychiatric nursing. She has a permanent staff-nurse position "working with 'extended care' patients (i.e., people at the bottom of the heap with chronic schizophrenia/borderline personality disorder/forensic histories), who need twenty-four-hour cover although, theoretically, 'in the community' in a hospital-owned residence."

**Children of Judith Beere**

VIII. <u>**Katerina Eleni Mitchell**</u> (called "Kate") was born on June 14, 1975, in Christchurch, New Zealand. Kate's family research project succeeded in identifying the family's Maori roots (see 4-E above). She received a BA from Canterbury University in 1998 and a law degree (LL.B.) from Victoria University in 1999. Kate is working at Kensington-Swan, a large commercial law firm in Wellington, where she is involved in Maori land claims.

VIII. <u>**Sonja Lani Mitchell**</u> was born on August 27, 1978, in Christchurch, New Zealand. In 1997, taking time off from her educational interests, Sonja was employed as an au pair for a family in Albany, Georgia, in the Deep South part of the United States. This gave her a chance to widely explore America, including a visit with Robertson cousins in Washington, D.C. Sonja wrote a loving biography of her grandmother Ness from which we have quoted extensively. She is a student at Canterbury University.

VIII. <u>**James Julian Mitchell**</u> (called "Jamie") was born on March 14, 1981, in Nelson, New Zealand. He is a university student.

VII. **<u>Jennifer Anne Beere</u>** (called "Helen"), second daughter of Agnes Lyver and Leonard Beere, was born on January 18, 1950, in Lower Hutt, New Zealand. Helen qualified as a nurse and has pursued various other career interests as well as extensive travel to England and Europe. On July 24, 1998, in Auckland, New Zealand, she married her longtime partner and companion, *John Griffiths*, a native of Liverpool, England.

## 6-B.11: HARRY O'BRIAN LYVER (1921-1983)
### Son of Elizabeth Georgeson O'Brian

VI. **<u>Harry O'Brian Lyver</u>,** second son of Elizabeth O'Brian and Robert Lyver (5.B.3 above), was born on August 2, 1921, in Linwood, Christchurch, New Zealand.

Joining the military at the age of nineteen, Harry became a hero in World War II as a member of the 161st Squadron of the Royal New Zealand Air Force. He flew more than one hundred missions in Europe as an aircraft gunner and was awarded the Distinguished Flying Cross (DFC) for valor. He was involved in special operations of deception which were intended to confuse the enemy. These operations included dropping paratroopers to work with the French Resistance movement, which was working in the "underground" opposition to the German Nazi forces that had occupied France. At the same time, bombs were being dropped from the same aircraft as a smokescreen for the real purpose of the missions.

Harry was specially honored for his courageous work in support of the Resistance movement years later, during a visit to France in 1988, when he was given mayoral receptions at several villages in the Loire Valley, where many of the Resistance workers had been based.

On November 4, 1941, in York, England, he married *Norah Donkin*, whom he met while stationed in England during the war. Norah also served with Allied forces in the war as a member of the Women's Army Air Force (WAAF) of England. She was born on July 6, 1922, in York, England. Harry and Norah had a daughter and three sons: Annette and Ian, who were born in England during World War II, and David and Max, both born in New Zealand.

Following the war, Harry and Norah settled with their growing family in Hastings, New Zealand. Norah was a social worker, and Harry spent his working career in the meat-processing industry. He worked as a foreman with the Whakatū Freezing Works, where he started in 1962, until his retirement in 1978. He also was involved in the food-technology field. In addition, he did valuable work in marriage guidance, was a member of the Masons fraternal organization, and helped establish the New Zealand branch of the Bomber Command Association, of which he was a member.

A gregarious charmer, Harry became something of a celebrity because of a curious circumstance: his amazing resemblance to Norman E. Kirk, the popular former prime minister of New Zealand, often called "Big Norm." Harry was featured in an amusing 1977 newspaper article that contained large photos of both and described the fun and confusion that sometimes occurred:

> *The Prime Minister, Mr. Kirk, has a double—a Hastings man who gets a lot of fun and many free drinks out of his similarity to Big Norm.*
>
> *The similarity goes beyond looks—hair, build and height. Mr. Lyver is 52; Mr. Kirk is 50. Both were born at Linwood, Christchurch. They went to the same school—but they never met. Both have similar political views. Their wives are both social workers.*
>
> *It is only natural, therefore, that Mr. Lyver is known to his workmates as Big Norm, a label carried only by the Prime Minister.*
>
> *And it is only natural that Mr. Lyver, Big Norm No. 2, is sometimes mistaken for Big Norm No. 1.*
>
> *Take today, for instance, [during] a visit to nearby Hornby, Christchurch, when he was approached by an irate woman in a supermarket. Waving an adding machine strip of the cost of her purchases, she yelled: "You and your price freeze."*
>
> *But on the compensatory side, there have been handshakes and drinks all round.*
>
> *A group of farmers and stock agents were eyeing Mr. and Mrs. Lyver in a hotel lounge at Opotiki, whispering and nodding. One went to the couple, thinking they were the Prime Minister and his wife, and said: "Having a quiet time away from it all?" Mr. Lyver was, and said: "Yes." He was then invited to have a drink with the crowd.*

*At the Midland Hotel, Wellington, a group addressed Mr. Lyver as Mr. Kirk. They walked away disbelievingly when he said: "Mr. Kirk's not as good looking as me."*

*On another occasion, eyebrows were raised when Mr. Lyver walked among a group of people with Mrs. Lyver. "I could guess what they were thinking," Mrs Lyver said. "They thought Harry was Norm, and they realized I wasn't Ruth Kirk."*

Harry Lyver died at the age of sixty-seven on March 20, 1989, at his home in Havelock North, New Zealand. Norah is living in New Zealand.

## Children of Harry O'Brian Lyver

VII. **Ian James Lyver**, son of Norah Donkin and Harry Lyver, born on October 16, 1942, in York, England, was brought by his parents to live in New Zealand after World War II ended in 1945.

Ian married *Estelle Mary Leishman* (called "Pixie") about 1968 in New Zealand. She was born on September 1, 1943, in Bluff, New Zealand. Ian and Pixie had three children, who were still very young when Pixie was killed in an aircraft accident at the age of thirty-two. She died in Palmerston North, New Zealand, on July 27, 1976.

Ian then married *Elizabeth Katrina Field (Blincoe)*, a widow whose late husband had died in the same accident that claimed Pixie's life. Born on September 12, 1941, Elizabeth is the daughter of Lucy Ellen Tang and Geoffrey Arnold Field. Then thirty-five years old, she and Ian were married on February 12, 1977, in Woodville, New Zealand. She had two small children by her first marriage, whose names were changed to Lyver when they were adopted by Ian. The family lives in Hastings, New Zealand. Ian has a chartered accounting firm in Hastings.

### Children of Ian James Lyver

VIII. **Barry Charles (Blincoe) Lyver**, son of Elizabeth Field and her first husband, born on May 4, 1965, and adopted by his stepfather, Ian Lyver.

VIII. **Rachael Anne Lyver**, daughter of Ian Lyver and his first wife, Pixie, born on July 30, 1969, in Hastings, New Zealand. She is married to *Greg Barclay*, and they live in Hastings.

VIII. **Philip O'Brian Lyver**, son of Ian Lyver and his first wife, Pixie, born on May 16, 1971, in Hastings, New Zealand.

VIII. **Nicola Wendy (Blincoe) Lyver**, daughter of Elizabeth Field and her first husband, born on November 16, 1971, and adopted by her stepfather, Ian Lyver.

VIII. **Catherine Dulcie Lyver**, second daughter of Ian Lyver and his first wife, Pixie, born on May 21, 1975, in Hastings, New Zealand.

VII. **Annette Caraleen Joyce Lyver**, daughter of Norah Donkin and Harry Lyver, born on February 17, 1944, in York, England.

About 1961, in Hawke's Bay, New Zealand, she married *John Francis Wixon*, who was born on August 4, 1942, in Bluff, New Zealand, the son of Islay Mary Gerrard and Lewis Owen John Wixon. They are the parents of three grown children.

**Children of Annette Caroline Joyce Lyver**

VIII. **Karalyn Anne Wixon**, born on July 1, 1962, in Bluff, New Zealand. On January 7, 1984, in Clive, New Zealand, she married *Ron Van Deursen*, who was born on October 22, 1956, in Auckland, New Zealand. He is the son of Willamenia Maria Van Been and Johanus Antonius Van Deursen. They have two daughters.

**Children of Karalyn Anne Wixon**

IX. **Sophia Grace Van Deursen**, born on June 6, 1991, in Hastings, New Zealand.

IX. **Lucy Rose Maria Van Deursen**, born on August 22, 1993, in Hastings, New Zealand.

VIII. **Lynda Norah Wixon**, born on August 14, 1964, in Bluff, New Zealand. On June 24, 1995, she married *Jeffrey Paul Taylor* in Wellington, New Zealand. Born in Wellington on October 26, 1964, Jeffrey is the son of Joan Quade and Ernest Alan Taylor.

VIII. **Karl Francis Wixon**, born on May 17, 1967, in Bluff, New Zealand.

VII. **David O'Brian Lyver**, second son of Norah Donkin and Harry Lyver, was born on September 1, 1947, in Levin, New Zealand. He married *Meriana Mary Lewis*, daughter of Takutai Moana Pani and Manapouri Lewis, on March 28, 1980, in Napier, New Zealand. She was born on June 3, 1954, in Te Reinga, Wairoa, New Zealand. David and Meriana have two children and live in Napier, New Zealand, where they operate a fish-and-chips takeaway shop.

### Children of David O'Bryan Lyver

VIII. **James O'Brian Lyver**, born on October 3, 1979, in Napier, New Zealand.

VIII. **Rangilique Meriana Lyver**, born on May 16, 1982, in Napier, New Zealand.

VII. **Maxwell Harry Lyver**, youngest son of Norah Donkin and Harry Lyver, was born on January 3, 1951, in Levin, New Zealand. Max served with the New Zealand armed forces in Vietnam. He married *Alison Claire Budge*, daughter of Connie and Robert Budge, on August 25, 1973, in Christchurch, New Zealand. She was born in Greymouth, New Zealand, on June 22, 1953. Max and Alison are divorced, with four children. Max is a real estate broker with an international portfolio that includes ranches, forest lands, resort venues, and other high-value New Zealand real estate to buyers around the world. Max resides in the rural community of Cambridge, called "the Town of Trees," on the North Island.

### Children of Maxwell Harry Lyver

VIII. **Merryn Kay Lyver**, born on August 16, 1974, in Hastings, New Zealand.

VIII. **Raewin Alison Lyver**, born on April 14, 1977, in Hastings, New Zealand.

VIII. **Joanne Marie Lyver**, born on December 19, 1978, in Hastings, New Zealand.

VIII. **Robert James Lyver**, born on September 3, 1981, in Hastings, New Zealand.

## 6-B.12: John William Lyver (1927-)
### Son of Elizabeth Georgeson O'Brian

**VI. John William Lyver** (called "Jack"), fourth son of Elizabeth O'Brian and Robert Lyver (5-B.3 above), was born on June 18, 1927, in Ashburton, New Zealand. He and his siblings were brought up near Wellington, the capital of New Zealand. Like many others, the family struggled financially during the Depression years. The parents kept in touch with Robertson relatives in America, and Jack's sister Charlotte Gibson recalls that a relative in Cincinnati generously sent Jack birthday presents and summer suits every year when he was a child.

Jack still thinks of Wellington as "a diabolical place to live" because of the constant wind and fog for which it is known. "They should make it the wind turbine capital," Jack suggests wryly. "Perhaps all the wind has something to do with Parliament being situated here—all those politicians putting in their few pennies worth."

Jack married *Olwen Joan Lloyd*, on September 6, 1950, in Invercargill, New Zealand. Olwen, born in Marton, Shropshire, England, on July 10, 1924, is the daughter of Florence Annie Davies and Robert David Lloyd, who immigrated to New Zealand when she was a child. Jack met Olwen when he was working on a sheep station and she was working as a nurse in Clyde, New Zealand.

Jack and Olwen, along with Jack's brother Jim, acquired a 2,000-acre farm property in Keao in the far northern part of New Zealand's North Island, above the city of Auckland, in 1958, on which they started raising cattle and various agricultural crops. Jack and Olwen kept at it following Jim's death five years later and through hard effort were able to make their farming venture a success—while also raising their three children, who were very young when the family moved to the country. Jack and Olwen have retired from farming and are now living about twenty miles south of Auckland.

**Children of John William Lyver**

VII. **James William Lyver**, born on April 14, 1951, in Lower Hutt, Wellington, New Zealand, and moved with his family to the farm in Keao when he was about six years old. A professional airline pilot, Jim is a captain with Air New Zealand. He also owns and operates a number of smaller airplanes and engages in farming activities.

His wife, _Elizabeth Ivy Wright_ (called "Libby"), daughter of Lorna Jean McLean and Peter Day Wright, was born in Auckland on June 13, 1953. Libby and Jim were married in Auckland on February 16, 1974, and they have two children. They live near Auckland.

**Children of James William Lyver**

VIII.  **Michelle Ann Lyver**, born on September 10, 1979, in Papakura, New Zealand.

VIII.  **Jamie William Lyver**, born on March 14, 1980, in Papakura, New Zealand.

VII.  **Patricia Joan Lyver**, born on September 14, 1954, in Lower Hutt, Wellington, New Zealand. She was brought up in Keao, where the family moved when she was three or four years old. Patricia was seventeen when she married _Grant Charles Wolfe_ in Auckland, New Zealand, on December 3, 1971. Grant was born on March 31, 1953, in Rangiora, Christchurch, New Zealand, the son of Ethel Ernshaw and Lyall Wolfe. Patricia and Grant have a daughter and three sons.

**Children of Patricia Joan Lyver**

VIII.  **Stefan Charles Wolfe**, born on February 2, 1972, in Auckland, New Zealand.

VIII.  **Angela Wolfe**, born on April 25, 1973, in Auckland, New Zealand.

VIII.  **Liam Wolfe**, born on October 29, 1984, in Auckland, New Zealand.

VIII.  **Fremon Lloyd Wolfe**, born on December 3, 1994, in Auckland, New Zealand.

VII.  **William Stephen Lyver** (called "Billy"), born on September 4, 1956, in Lower Hutt, Wellington, New Zealand, and brought up in Keao, where the family moved when he was a child. He married _Ann Price_ in Kerikeri, Northland, New Zealand, on June 12, 1974. Ann, daughter of Muriel Keightly and George Price, was born on July 7, 1957. Billy and Ann divorced, with one son. Since about 1982, Billy's partner has been _Kerry Grace_. They have three children.

**Children of William Stephen Lyver**

VIII. **Jarratt Lyver**, son of Ann Price and William Lyver, born on April 12, 1975, in Kawakawa, New Zealand. His partner is *Leslie Lee Liddle*. The have two children.

**Children of Jarratt Lyver**

IX. **Hayden Rhys Liddle**.

IX. **Andrew Jack Liddle**, born on May 5, 1998, in Tokoroa, New Zealand.

VIII. **Stefanie Lyver**, daughter of Kerry Grace and William Lyver, born on August 27, 1984, in Gisborne, New Zealand.

VIII. **Jason Lyver**, son of Kerry Grace and William Lyver, born on October 3, 1987, in Gisborne, New Zealand.

VIII. **Brendon Lyver**, son of Kerry Grace and William Lyver, born on April 16, 1991, in Gisborne, New Zealand.

## 6-B.13: ROBINA GREAVES (1875-1962)
### Daughter of Mary Elizabeth Irvine Jamieson

VI. **Robina Greaves** (called "Ruby") was the only daughter of Mary Elizabeth Irvine Jamieson and John Greaves (5-B.4 above). She was born on October 28, 1875, in Wanalta, Victoria, Australia. On February 6, 1902, Ruby married *Harry Hartwell* at his father's home in Townsville, Queensland, in the far northern part of Australia, with Rev. Lewis Hudson, a Methodist minister, presiding. Harry was born on April 18, 1872, in Halifax, Yorkshire, England. They had six children.

Harry Hartwell's family had a substantial logging business in the early days of settlement and rail construction in northern Australia. Delphine Slattery of Townsville, a granddaughter of Robina and Harry, says the Hartwell business included a sawmilling operation, cutting ties for the railroad when the first lines were being put through the north. She writes:

*The Hartwells went up to Georgetown in the Gulf of Carpenteria looking for gold and did not have a great deal of success. They came back and bought land at Stone River, which is outside of Ingham (about two and a half hours drive north of here). That is where Robina Greaves had all her children and it was there that Mary Elizabeth Irvine Jamieson went after the death of her husband, John Greaves. . . . They must have come up to here from Victoria overland, as the railway was not through at that time. All of the Hartwell sons had a section of the big farm at Stone River and some of them are still farming there (sugar cane), and one of them still lives in the original house where Robina and Harry Hartwell lived and had their children (including my mother). When Harry got sick and they had to come to Townsville where he died, the other boys bought the farm off Robina, and they all moved to Townsville permanently.*

Harry Hartwell died in Townsville on June 3, 1924, at the age of fifty-two. Robina survived him by almost forty years. She died in Townsville on November 2, 1962, and was buried in the Townsville Cemetery with her late husband.

## Children of Robina Greaves

VII. **Harry Hartwell II**, born on September 8, 1903, in Ingham, Queensland, Australia. About 1931, in Townsville, Queensland, he married *Julia Petrina Jensen*, who was born on April 18, 1903. She died in childbirth on July 30, 1934, at the age of thirty-one. There was one child from that first marriage. Harry then married *Mary Elizabeth Fordyce* about 1937 in Townsville. She was born in Proserpine, Queensland, in 1911. They had four children.

Harry Hartwell II died in Townsville on January 25, 1961, age fifty-seven. His widow died in Townsville on June 19, 1974.

### Children of Harry Hartwell II

VIII. **Shirley Dawn Hartwell,** born on July 30, 1934, was the daughter of Julia Petrina Jensen and Harry Hartwell II. She married *Wilfred Burney* in June 1962. They had no children.

VIII. **Maureen Hartwell**, born on August 31, 1938, in Townsville, Queensland, Australia, is the daughter of Mary Elizabeth Fordyce and Harry Hartwell II. She married *John Walsh*, and they have two sons.

**Children of Maureen Hartwell**

IX. **James Walsh**, born in 1959.

IX. **John Walsh**, born in 1968. He is reportedly married with two children.

VIII. **Colin Hartwell**, born in 1943 in Townsville, Queensland, Australia, son of Mary Elizabeth Fordyce and Harry Hartwell II. He is unmarried.

VIII. **Brian Hartwell**, born in 1948 in Townsville, Queensland, Australia, son of Mary Elizabeth Fordyce and Harry Hartwell II. He married *Kathleen Dempsey* in 1973, and they had three children.

**Children of Brian Hartwell**

IX. **Monica Mary Hartwell**, born in 1975.

IX. **Ngari Joy Hartwell**, born in 1977.

IX. **Irene Patricia Hartwell**, born in 1980.

VIII. **John Hartwell**, born in 1952 in Townsville, Queensland, Australia, son of Mary Elizabeth Fordyce and Harry Hartwell II. In 1979, he married *Susan Flannery*, and they have a daughter and a son.

**Children of John Hartwell**

IX. **Evan Hartwell**, born in 1980.

IX. **Tracy Hartwell**, born in 1982.

VII. **John Leonard Hartwell**, born on November 29, 1905, in Ingham, Queensland, Australia. He married *Myrtle Hill* in Townsville, Queensland, in January 1931. John died on March 3, 1984, in Brisbane, Queensland, and his widow died there ten years later, in 1994. They had no children.

VII. **Robina Frances May Hartwell**, born on December 6, 1908, in Ingham, Queensland, Australia. She married *Frank Edward Hose* on December 26, 1931, in Townsville, Queensland. He was born in Cooktown, Queensland, on December 31, 1903. They had two children. Robina's daughter Delphine Slattery writes that

Robina "was a wonderful dressmaker. She began when she was about 14 and her mother bought her a treadle sewing machine. . . . Her sewing was beautiful and she never used a pattern—she just had to look at the design and then she would cut the pattern out of newspaper."

Delphine remembers the family's experience living in the far northern part of Australia, anticipating an invasion by Japanese forces in the Second World War:

*During World War II, when the Japanese looked like invading Australia, everything north of Brisbane was not given much consideration. A lot of people left Townsville and went south. My Dad was too old for the army but was an Air Raid Warden, and when the sirens sounded he would have to go off and leave Mum and my brother and me at home. When things got a bit close, the three of us plus grandma and [cousin] Shirley went to Rollingstone north of here to get away from the worst of it. My uncle John Hartwell and his wife were living there because he was in the Railway. There were soldiers stationed everywhere, and I can remember some of those around Rollingstone coming in at night, and there would be sing-alongs around the piano, because Aunty was a terrific pianist.*

*All around Townsville there were lots of Australian soldiers, and eventually a lot of Americans arrived, and the camps were not too far from my parents' house. There always seemed to be soldiers marching up the street. Everything was rationed. We all had ration cards, and there were queues for everything. When the Japanese were getting a bit too close the schools were closed as well.*

Frank Hose died in Townsville on May 29, 1967. Robina Hartwell Hose died on November 10, 1988, in Townsville, age seventy-nine. Her great-grandchildren may be the first of the tenth generation descended from Thomas and John Robertson of Shetland.

### Children of Robina Frances May Hartwell

VIII. **Clive Edward Hose**, born on March 28, 1935, in Townsville, Queensland, Australia. He married *Maureen Comerford* on November 29, 1958, at St. Joseph's Roman Catholic Church in Townsville. A carpenter by trade, he is active in restoration of old furniture, and Clive and Maureen now run an antique shop. They have four children.

**Children of Clive Edward Hose**

IX. **Terrence William Hose**, born on August 12, 1960, in Townsville, Queensland, Australia. He is unmarried.

IX. **Cathy Lou Hose**, born on January 25, 1962, in Townsville, Queensland, Australia. She married *Christopher Richard Mellerch* on January 29, 1983, at St. Joseph's Roman Catholic Church in Townsville. He was born on March 9, 1960, in Brisbane, Queensland. They have two children.

**Children of Cathy Lou Hose**

X. **Tremayne Alyse Mellerch**, born on July 9, 1987, in Townsville, Queensland, Australia.

X. **Brenna Alyse Mellerch**, born on May 3, 1992, in Townsville, Queensland, Australia.

IX. **Kylie Marie Hose**, born on November 14, 1968, in Townsville, Queensland, Australia. In November 1986, she married an American man, *Jaime Aquare*, in Townsville. They are separated, having no children. She is living in Cairns, Queensland.

VIII. **Delphine May Hose**, born on February 3, 1939, at the family home at Pimlico in Townsville, Queensland, Australia. She married *William John Launder Slattery* (called "John") on May 17, 1958, at St. Andrew's Presbyterian Church in Townsville. He was born on November 6, 1934, in Mareeba, Queensland, the son of Sarah Ethel Launder and Arthur Cornelius Slattery.

John, who retired in 1996, worked at various times as a motor mechanic on cars and tractors, as a boiler maker, and as an ambulance officer. Delphine worked as a secretary before her marriage and now enjoys caring for birds and animals, as well as grandchildren—and researching family history. She is an active member of the Shetland Family History Society. They have two children.

Delphine and John have lived in the same home in Mundingburra, Queensland, for forty years. This area is in the sub-tropical far northern part of Australia. Of their surroundings, idyllic except for the summer heat, Delphine writes: "At the moment all of the winter flowering native trees in our garden are in bloom & we have honeyeaters & parrots everywhere. We've got a birdbath just out the window, and they are all coming in for a bath as they do every afternoon. We have at least five different kinds of honeyeaters there, and it's a real pleasure to be able to see them at such close range."

**Children of Delphine May Hose**

IX.  **Debra Rose Slattery**, born on March 5, 1959, in Townsville, Queensland, Australia. On March 16, 1985, she married *Andrew Phillip Lee* at Central United Church in Townsville. Born on May 9, 1952, in Stanthorpe, Queensland, Andrew works as a butcher. They had two children and divorced in 1996. Debra married *Gavin Milton* on August 29, 1998, in Townsville.

**Children of Debra Rose Slattery**

X.  **Rebecca Jean Lee**, born on August 10, 1985, in Toowoomba, Queensland, Australia.

X.  **Georgette Rose Lee**, born on May 13, 1987, in Longreach, Queensland, Australia.

IX.  **Colleen May Slattery**, born on August 7, 1962, in Townsville, Queensland, Australia. On September 15, 1984, she married *Stephen Paul Barry* at St. Andrews Presbyterian Church in Townsville. Born on January 6, 1957, in Manchester, England, Stephen works as a nurse. They had a son and a daughter and divorced in 1995. Colleen also has a daughter with her former partner, *Terrance Michael Reeves*. She works part-time as a registered nurse in a doctor's office.

**Children of Colleen May Slattery**

X.  **William James Barry**, son of Colleen Slattery and Stephen Michael Barry, born on October 22, 1987, in Townsville, Queensland, Australia.

X. **Sarah Catherine Barry**, daughter of Colleen Slattery and Stephen Michael Barry, born on December 29, 1989, in Townsville, Queensland, Australia.

X. **Kathleen Valerie May Reeves**, daughter of Colleen Slattery and Terrance Michael Reeves, born on September 27, 1994.

VII. **Charles Aubrey Hartwell**, born on June 9, 1911, in Ingham, Queensland, Australia. He died in Ingham on August 31, 1921, at the age of ten.

VII. **Herbert Heaton Hartwell**, born on June 13, 1914, in Ingham, Queensland, Australia. Never married, he died in Townsville, Queensland, on January 7, 1982, age sixty-seven.

VII. **Leslie William Hartwell**, born on June 19, 1916, in Ingham, Queensland, Australia. He married *Marjorie Amelia Boyns*, and they had three children.

**Children of Leslie William Hartwell**

VIII. **Gary Leslie Hartwell**, born on October 18, 1941. On March 28, 1964, he married *Gwedolyn Dawn Cuddy*, and they had two children.

**Children of Gary Leslie Hartwell**

IX. **Treacey Lee Hartwell**, born on April 21, 1965. She married *Adrian Aaron Western* on April 1, 1981, and they have two children.

**Children of Treacey Lee Hartwell**

X. **Amie Paige Western**, born on December 5, 1993.

X. **Rachel Anais Western**, born on August 18, 1995.

IX. **Scott Andrew Hartwell**, born on March 23, 1968. He married *Joanne Mary Jean Mossop* on July 23, 1995.

VIII. **Gregory Alexander Hartwell**, born on January 3, 1945. He married *Carolyn Jean Keane* on April 9, 1966. They have two children.

### Children of Gregory Alexander Hartwell

IX. **Lisa Maree Hartwell**, born on July 19, 1968. She married *Tony Hogan* on July 10, 1993. They have one child.

### Child of Lisa Maree Hartwell

X. **Benjamin Gregory Hogan**, born on September 20, 1994.

IX. **Justin Gregory Hartwell**, born on March 9, 1978.

VIII. **Suzanne Hartwell**, born on November 26, 1955. She married *Cornelius Antonius Metz* on June 14, 1975, and they have two children.

### Children of Suzanne Hartwell

IX. **Jason Metz**, born on June 22, 1974.

IX. **Amanda Metz**, born on January 22, 1976.

## 6-B.14: JOSEPH MAGNUS JOHNSON (1912-1977)
### Son of Catherine Thomson Robertson

VI. **Joseph Magnus Johnson**, tenth child and fourth son of Catherine Robertson and John Johnson (5-A.1 above), was born on July 12, 1912, in Govan near Glasgow in Lanarkshire, Scotland. When he was seventeen, Joe worked as an apprentice boat-builder but was laid off because of lack of business. He became a journeyman joiner or carpenter and was admitted to membership in the Amalgamated Society of Woodworkers in 1934. He served in the British Army in World War II.

Joseph married *Martha McKie* on June 9, 1939, at Pollokshields West Church in Glasgow, Scotland. Martha was born on October 13, 1918, at Mull Farm in Kirkmaiden Parish, Wigtown, Scotland, the daughter of Mary McCracken and David McKie, whose occupation was listed as a "ploughman" on her birth certificate. Martha and Joseph had two sons.

In 1957, the family emigrated from Scotland to New Zealand on the steamship *Captain Cook*, which sailed on October 20, 1957. Their immigration papers listed Joseph Magnus Johnson as 5 feet 7 inches in height, with grey hair and brown eyes; his wife was described as 5 feet 2 inches tall, with brown hair and brown eyes. Initially, they settled in Ashburton, on New Zealand's South Island, where Joseph was able to transfer his membership in the Amalgamated Society of Woodworkers and work as a carpenter. After eight years there, they moved to Christchurch in 1965.

Joe Johnson died in Christchurch on December 4, 1977, after a heart attack. The following year, Martha sold her home and moved to Hamilton on the North Island to be near her children and their families.

**Children of Joseph Magnus Johnson**

VII. **Joseph Magnus Johnson** was born in Milliken Park Lochwinnoch, Renfrewshire, Scotland, on November 9, 1945. He immigrated to New Zealand with his family at the age of eleven.

Joe married *Coral Grace Moore* on December 14, 1968, at the John Knox Presbyterian Church in Rangiora, New Zealand. The daughter of Dorothy Knox and Wallis Frank Isaac Moore, Coral was born in Rangiora on April 2, 1950.

For the first two years of their marriage, Joe and Coral lived in Christchurch on the South Island. For the next six years, they were in Darfield, some twenty-five miles west of Christchurch. They have a son and a daughter.

Joe obtained his teaching certificate in Christchurch and in 1977 they moved to the North Island, where they settled into their present home in the city of Hamilton. For the past 21 years, Joe has been a mathematics teacher in the local high school in Hamilton. They enjoy outdoor life, especially boating and fishing. They keep a caravan at the campgrounds at Raglan Beach on the West Coast, not far from Hamilton, and most of their weekends during the summers are spent game fishing.

**Children of Joseph Magnus Johnson**

VIII. **Nicola Anne Johnson**, born on February 27, 1971, in Christchurch, New Zealand. She and her partner are living as "sharemilkers" on a dairy farm about twenty minutes' drive from her parents' home, coming into town about once a week.

VIII. **Richard Alan Johnson**, born on October 26, 1973, in Darfield, North Canterbury, on the South Island of New Zealand. He is attending university in Christchurch and is also involved in pottery.

VII. **David Alan Johnson**, born on August 12, 1951, in Barrhead, Renfrewshire, Scotland. At the age of twenty, he married *Sharyn Ann Hopkinson* on January 22, 1972, at the Church of St. John the Evangelist in Woolston, Christchurch, New Zealand. She was eighteen, having been born on April 6, 1953, in Christchurch, New Zealand, the daughter of Elizabeth Swinburn and Ian Everard Hopkinson. They have two sons and a daughter.

David qualified as a biology teacher, after which he and Sharyn spent a year in Britain. Since then, David has taught at Christ's College in Christchurch, punctuated by several sabbatical leaves to England, where he has taught at Harrow. Sharyn and David are avid skiers, and he is an accomplished photographer.

### Children of David Alan Johnson

VIII. **Andrew David William Johnson**, born on July 10, 1981, in Christchurch, New Zealand.

VIII. **Scott Michael Johnson**, born on August 11, 1984, in Christchurch, New Zealand.

VIII. **Kelly Ann Johnson**, born on February 15, 1991, in Christchurch, New Zealand.

## 6-B.15: JOHN THOMAS ROBERTSON (1905-19??)
### Son of Margaret Robertson

VI. **John Thomas Robertson**, first son of Margaret Robertson (5-A.6 above), was born on November 3, 1905, in Walls Parish, Shetland. As a young man, he worked as a caretaker on Vaila, the island near Walls, and immigrated to New Zealand in 1925. There he met and married *Myrtle Irene Cook*, daughter of Martha and Edwin Cook, who was born in Christchurch, New Zealand. They had three children. John was a gardener, serving at one time as foreman at the Wellington Botanical Gardens and, later, was the head gardener at Government House.

His son Paul recalls of John, "He was a quiet, sober, gentle, humble and very reliable man who kept pretty much to himself. He loved the outdoors and spent much of his spare time fishing and hunting. Needless to say, his sons and daughter became very interested in the same!"

**Children of John Thomas Robertson**

VII. **Donald John Robertson** was born on May 31, 1932, in Wellington, New Zealand. Now retired, he worked in Foreign Affairs for the New Zealand government and served in numerous posts abroad in the Foreign Service. Donald married a Japanese woman named *Taki*. They had two children and then divorced. Donald lives in Paraparaumu with his partner, *Betty Shrader*.

**Children of Donald John Robertson**

VIII. **Christine Robertson** (called "Tina"), born in Holland.

VIII. **David John Robertson**.

VII. **Janette Gayle Robertson** was born on August 12, 1937, in Wellington, New Zealand. She married *Peter Keegan*, whom she later divorced. They had three children. Janette lives in Camborne, near Wellington.

**Children of Janette Gayle Robertson**

VIII. **Ursula Keegan**.

VIII. **Leanne Keegan**.

VIII. **Steven Keegan**, born on December 14, 1963.

VII. **Paul Edward Robertson** was born on May 25, 1948, in Wellington, New Zealand. He graduated from Wellington Teachers College in 1970 as a trained primary school teacher. As a part-time student at Victoria University in Wellington, Paul later completed his undergraduate degree in 1980. In 1983, he received a post-graduate diploma in Educational Studies and, in 1984, a diploma in Teaching English as a Second Language, also from Victoria University.

Paul taught in primary and intermediate schools in the Wellington region for fifteen years, serving as Deputy Principal in three of the schools and Principal in another. Most of the schools he served in were in lower-socio-economic areas, and many of the children were Maori or Polynesian. In 1986, Paul joined the staff of Wellington College of Education and trained teachers until 1994. During that period, he was responsible for courses in Minority Group Education, teaching English as a Second Language, and General Classroom Practice. He was head of the Professional Studies department and, later, the Associate Director of Primary Education at Wellington College of Education.

In 1990, Paul was asked by one of the Samoan high chiefs to go to Western Samoa and was conferred with a chiefly title for his work with Samoan children and adults in New Zealand. His title, bestowed by High Chief Leoto of Solosol Village, Upolu, is "*Pule i a'ava*," loosely translated as "boss or guardian of the fires."

Earlier in 1990, he also travelled to Shetland and spent a month with his aunt Mimie Williamson Scott in Sand, Bixter. In 1994, Paul was invited to teach as a visiting professor at Edogawa University in Japan. What started as a one-year commitment has continued on, and Paul is still living in Japan and teaching English and Oceana Studies at Edogawa University.

On December 26, 1973, Paul and *Sally Rawnsley* were married at Our Lady of Lourdes Church in Palmerston North, New Zealand. Sally was born on December 16, 1950, daughter of Eva Gerson and John Morley Duret Rawnsley. They divorced in 1993, having had two children.

### Children of Paul Edward Robertson

VIII.  **Emma Louise Robertson**, born on April 29, 1978, in Wellington, New Zealand. She has completed a bachelor's degree at Victoria University in Wellington.

VIII.  **Jonathan Paul Robertson**, born on November 13, 1980, in Wellington, New Zealand.

# The American Branches
# Generation Six and Beyond

## 6-C.1: Reuben Lyman Perin Sr. (1904-1983)
### Son of Georgia Dumbreck Robertson

VI. **<u>Reuben Lyman Perin Sr.</u>** was born on June 8, 1904, in Cincinnati, Ohio, son of Georgia Dumbreck Robertson and Lyman Perin (5-C.1 above). Reuben married *<u>Virginia Frances Danson</u>* (called "Ginnie") on April 2, 1932. Ginnie was born on January 17, 1909, in Cincinnati, Ohio, daughter of Edward Bridge Danson and Ann Allen. Reuben and Ginnie lived in Scarsdale, New York, a suburb of New York City, where they raised four children.

Reuben Perin graduated with a BA from the University of Cincinnati in 1924, where he starred as tackle on the Cincinnati "Bearcats" football team. Following graduation, he went to work for the U.S. Can Company. Four years later, that firm merged into Continental Can Company. He rose quickly in the corporate ranks. In 1949, Reuben Perin became the General Sales Manager for the Metal Division of the company, and in 1950 he was promoted to Vice President and General Manager of the Eastern Metal Division. In 1956, he was elected to the board of directors and promoted to Executive Vice President and General Manager of the Metal Division. In 1962, he became Vice Chairman of the Board of this growing company, which is involved in forestry, papermaking, mining, and diversified packaging, with over 200 plants and offices and 48,000 employees around the world.

An article honoring Reuben Perin's career and accomplishments as "a modest industrial giant," published in the University of Cincinnati *Alumnus Magazine*, described him in glowing terms:

*The man who has had an important role in the emergence of this manufacturing giant from a simple can manufacturing company is a big, bluff, hearty man in his sixties, whose athletic bearing still dominates any gathering. He is sociable and humorous, and energetic.*

*When meeting Perin you are impressed by his bright blue eyes which have the penetrating, searching gaze of the hunter which he is, and he enjoys duck hunting. . . .*

*In addition to his many other civic and business responsibilities, Perin has remained a pillar of strength in the New York area for the University of Cincinnati. His efforts in fund raising, both as an alumnus and as a corporate executive, have been most successful, as have his activities in the field of student recruitment.*

In addition to his business endeavors, Reuben Perin was active in civic and charitable organizations. He served as President of the Greater New York Fund (one of the largest annual charity drives in the United States) and as President and Chairman of Keep America Beautiful, Inc., a nationwide nonprofit organization devoted to anti-litter efforts. In 1968, he authored a guest editorial in the monthly magazine *Reader's Digest* about the problems caused when people "carelessly throw away paper and bottles and cans that mar the beauty of forests, seashores, cities and highways," and describing the benefits and successes of anti-litter campaigns in various parts of the country. That same year, he was awarded the William Howard Taft Medal for Notable Achievement by the University of Cincinnati.

Reuben Perin Sr. died at the age of seventy-nine on September 23, 1983, in Scarsdale, New York. His widow, Virginia Danson Perin, died in Sewickley, Pennsylvania, on November 4, 1997. They are both buried in the Danson family plot at Spring Grove Cemetery in Cincinnati.

### Children of Reuben Lyman Perin Sr.

VII. **<u>Virginia Ann Perin</u>** (called "Annchen"), eldest daughter of Virginia Danson and Reuben Perin Sr., was born on July 11, 1934, in Cincinnati, Ohio.

Annchen attended Wheaton College in Norton, Massachusetts. She married *<u>Curtis Harrison Gager Jr.</u>* on September 8, 1956, in Scarsdale, New York. Curtis was born on December 10, 1928, in Jamestown, New York, the son of Marian Hendrickson and Curtis Harrison Gager Sr. Annchen and Curt had two daughters.

Curt was a graduate of the Wharton School of Business and Finance in Philadelphia, Pennsylvania. He served as a captain in the US Marine Corps in Korea during the early 1950s and, later, was aide to the commandant at Quantico Marine Base in Virginia. In the fall of 1953, after his military discharge, he pursued postgraduate studies in business at the Centre d'Etudes Industrielles in Geneva, Switzerland.

During Curt's career as a sales executive with Aluminum Company of America (ALCOA), the family lived in various places around the United States. In the late 1960s, he went into business for himself, becoming a partner in Ward Weller/ Torwell Industries in the Boston area, from which he retired in 1991. He died at the age of sixty-five on April 25, 1994, and is buried in Spring Grove Cemetery in Cincinnati.

Annchen has been active throughout her life in volunteer and community work. She lives in Wellesley, Massachusetts, and spends the summers on the island of Martha's Vineyard.

### Children of Virginia Ann Perin

VIII. **<u>Cynthia Ann Gager</u>** (called "Cindy") was born on September 6, 1957, in Bronxville, New York. She graduated from Menlo Business School in California.

Cindy married *<u>Jean-Claude Alten</u>* of Rochester, New York, son of Felix Alten and Jacqueline LaLiberté, on August 4, 1983. They divorced, having two sons.

On June 13, 1992, Cindy married *<u>Thomas DeLotto</u>* in Barnegat, New Jersey. He was born on March 2, 1957, the son of Peter and Alice DeLotto of Wayne, New Jersey. Tom is a regional manager with Westrec Marina Management, Inc. in Monmouth, New Jersey, the largest marina management company in the United States. The family lives in West Long Branch, New Jersey.

### Children of Cynthia Ann Gager

IX. **<u>Tyler Harrison Alten</u>**, son of Cindy Gager and Jean-Claude Alten, born in Nantucket, Massachusetts, on September 13, 1983.

IX. **<u>Logan Charles Alten</u>**, younger son of Cindy Gager and Jean-Claude Alten, born in Rhode Island on November 6, 1987. He was named after his great-uncle Logan T. Robertson.

VIII. **<u>Annchen Perin Gager</u>**, born on October 16, 1959, in Atlanta, Georgia. She received her BA from the University of New Hampshire. Annchen married *Robert Kramer Brown* in Wellesley, Massachusetts, on May 10, 1986. The son of Roberta Cook and H. Harding Brown of Westfield, New Jersey, Bob was born on February 22, 1952. He attended Union College in New Jersey, received his law degree from Suffolk University Law School, and is a partner in a leading law firm in Chatham, New Jersey, specializing in commercial real estate. They have two children and live in Watchung, New Jersey.

### Children of Annchen Perin Gager

IX. **<u>Jay Alexander Brown</u>**, born on January 2, 1988, in Summit, New Jersey.

IX. **<u>Amanda Danson Brown</u>**, born on August 31, 1993, in Summit, New Jersey.

VII. **<u>Reuben Lyman Perin Jr.</u>**, oldest son of Virginia Danson and Reuben Perin Sr., was born on March 14, 1938, in Cincinnati, Ohio. He is a 1961 graduate of the University of Colorado in Boulder, Colorado.

On July 2, 1966, Reuben married *Susan Patricia Procter* in Box-near-Bath, England. Susan was born on October 13, 1942, in Bogner Regis, Sussex, England. Her father, Paul Michael Procter, a career military officer and a Royal Air Force pilot in World War II, was killed in a training accident shortly after the war. Susan's mother is Pamela Jean Norman of Sussex, England, who now resides with her second husband in Princeton, New Jersey.

Susan attended the Eastbourne School of Domestic Economy in Sussex, England, and the Parsons School of Design in New York. She also studied at Columbia University in New York City. A former fashion model, Susan is an accomplished interior designer and painter. Susan and Reuben have two children.

Reuben spent over three decades in the steel industry with the U.S. Steel Company (now called USX Corporation), ultimately rising to the position of Executive Vice President of the company. He retired from USX in 1997 but is continuing to provide consulting services for the company. Reuben is an avid mountaineer and outdoor sportsman. In late 1998, he and his son completed an arduous thirty-day trek in Bhutan in an extremely rugged and remote part of the high Himalayas.

Since 1997, Reuben and Susan have been living in Sun Valley, Idaho. They also built a spectacular summer home, designed by their architect son, in the Sawtooth Range of the Rocky Mountains near Stanley, Idaho.

**Children of Reuben Lyman Perin Jr.**

VIII. <u>**Serena Ash Norman Perin**</u> was born on November 30, 1968, in Rye, New York. In 1990, Serena received her BA in business economics from Brown University in Providence, Rhode Island. She married *Henry Middleton Vinton* on July 25, 1998, in Stanley, Idaho. He was born on July 3, 1965, in Chappaqua, New York, son of Joan Catherine Hassett and Lewin Leonard Vinton Jr.

They live in San Francisco, California, where Serena is vice president and portfolio manager of the Franklin Templeton Group, managing over $1 billion in fund assets.

VIII. <u>**Reuben Lyman Perin III**</u> was born on April 25, 1970, in Rye, New York. He received the BA from the School of Architecture of Cornell University in 1994 and works with Walker-Warner Architects in San Francisco. Reuben also does freelance design and construction-supervision work on projects throughout the United States. He enjoys aggressive outdoor activities and has done extended solo mountain biking in Italy and elsewhere, as well as high mountain trekking in the Himalayas with his father.

VII. <u>**Edward Bridge Danson Perin**</u> (called "Dan") was born in San Francisco, California, on March 19, 1943, son of Virginia Danson and Reuben L. Perin Sr. His career has been in business and finance, first in banking on Wall Street in New York and, beginning in the early 1980s, in Arizona. He has retired from those activities and taken up landscape painting.

Dan married *Laura Evans* on July 7, 1973, in Detroit, Michigan. Born on May 2, 1946, in Nashville, Tennessee, Laura is the daughter of Jessica (called "Jo") Osmond and Tommy Evans, MD. She is a fiction writer and was one of the first female vice presidents of a major New York bank. Laura and Dan have no children and make their home in Scottsdale, Arizona.

VII. **Cynthia Robertson Perin**, daughter of Virginia Danson and Reuben Perin Sr., was born on March 1, 1948, in Cincinnati, Ohio. Possessed of a lyric soprano voice, Cindy studied opera in New York and has performed at the Aspen Arts Festival in Colorado. Cindy is also an accomplished equestrian and has participated in championship-level horse shows in various parts of the United States. She rode "The Irishman" in Madison Square Garden in medal and Maclay equitation and hunter classes.

In 1970, in Scarsdale, New York, Cindy married *Gregg Leonard Morris*, son of Arlene Teschler and Dr. Alvin Morris. Born in Michigan on January 21, 1951, Gregg was a steeplechase jockey. They divorced in 1975, having no children. Cindy moved to South Carolina, where she was engaged to a professional polo player, Les Flerx Jr. He was critically injured in a polo accident in Texas. Cynthia took care of Les for two years, staying with him in a nursing home, until he died in 1980. She then lived for a while in Paris, Kentucky, working on staff at the *Thoroughbred Record* magazine.

Cynthia Perin now resides in West Sedona, Arizona. She plays competitive amateur tennis throughout the United States and rides her Palomino quarter horse.

## 6-C.2: CYNTHIA PERIN (1907-1973)
### Daughter of Georgia Dumbreck Robertson

VI. **Cynthia Perin** was born on February 26, 1907, in Cincinnati, Hamilton County, Ohio. Called "Bumpy" by her grandfather Charles D. Robertson, she was the fourth child of Georgia Dumbreck Robertson and Lyman Perin (5-C.1 above).

On March 28, 1930, she married *James Donald Mawhinney*, known as "Don." He was born on October 28, 1898, in Litchfield, Connecticut, to Jean Anderson (born on June 17, 1878; died on October 9, 1948) and William Carlton Mawhinney (born on April 15, 1875; died on May 26, 1949). Don Mawhinney attended Clemson University in South Carolina, dropping out to enroll in the US Army's Officer Candidate School during World War I. After the war, Don attended Carnegie Institute of Technology in Pittsburgh, Pennsylvania, completing undergraduate studies and obtaining a degree in architecture. He then moved to Cincinnati, where he was in the 107th Cavalry, Ohio National Guard. Always an avid horse-man, he met Bumpy at a horse show.

Bumpy and Don Mawhinney had three children. The family moved from Cincinnati to Asheville, North Carolina, around 1937, where Don worked on developing residential property owned by Bumpy's uncle Reuben B. Robertson Sr. In 1940, the Army Reserves were called up for World War II, and as a reserve officer in the Quartermaster Corps, Don was activated. He was first stationed in Falls Church, Virginia, and later sent to Panama to work on development of Howard Air Force Base there. Bumpy and the three small children moved to Panama with Don, staying there until the Japanese bombed Pearl Harbor in 1942.

That attack led to evacuation of all American families in Panama, and Bumpy and the children moved back to Asheville for the duration of World War II. They stayed for an extended period in the home of Bumpy's cousin Logan Robertson on Fairmont Terrace in the Grove Park section of Asheville while Logan and his family were away because of his military duty. Reuben Robertson Sr., Bumpy's uncle, became almost a surrogate grandfather for the Mawhinney children, as their own grandfather Lyman Perin had died a few years before. Visits from "Uncle Reuben" were much appreciated by the children, as he usually brought pralines, sugar cane, or other treats for them.

After the war, Don remained in the Army Corps of Engineers with the rank of lieu-tenant colonel. First stationed in Japan to work on post-war reconstruction programs, Don was later transferred to a civilian position with the Army in Virginia. They moved to south-ern Arizona after Don's retirement.

On February 26, 1970, after playing eighteen holes of golf, Don suffered a severe heart attack and died in Green Valley, Arizona. He was seventy-one. Bumpy died at age sixty-six in Green Valley on May 12, 1973, also after a heart attack. Both were cremated, and their ashes are at the National Memorial Cemetery of the Pacific in the "Punchbowl" Crater in Honolulu, Hawaii.

**Children of Cynthia Perin**

VII. **Perin Mawhinney**, son of Cynthia and Donald Mawhinney and the first great-grandchild of Cynthia and Charles D. Robertson, was born on June 13, 1931, in Cincinnati, Hamilton County, Ohio. Perin graduated from the United States Military Academy at West Point, New York, in 1954. His roommate, Dick Farmer, later married Perin's cousin "Cherie" Norburn (6-C.3 below).

After his undergraduate studies, Perin served in the US Army Corps of Engineers and completed a master's degree in personnel administration at George Washington University in Washington, D.C. He later went into real estate in Chapel Hill, North Carolina, building and selling modular houses with his cousin Logan Robertson Sr. He moved to Tucson, Arizona, in 1974, still working in real estate.

Perin married *Wendy Lou Houston* on April 20, 1957, in Toronto, Canada. They divorced in November 1969, having no children.

Perin's second marriage was on November 7, 1969, at the Fort Ruger Army Post atop the Diamond Head volcano in Honolulu, Hawaii, when he married *Dolores ("Dee") Mullen*. She was born in Cincinnati, Ohio, on August 6, 1933, daughter of Rose Tebben and John Mullen. Dee attended the College of Mount St. Joseph in Cincinnati, from which she received a B.S. in mathematics in 1958. In 1960, she received a master's degree in social work (MSW) from St. Louis University in St. Louis, Missouri.

Perin has been involved in various real estate and investment ventures. Dee is a psychotherapist and, since 1993, has been in practice with the Palo Verde Behavioral Health Professional Association in Tucson, Arizona. She is a member of the Academy of Certified Social Workers and is listed in the publication *Who's Who of American Women*. They have one son and reside in Tucson.

**Child of Perin Mawhinney**

VIII. **Matthew Perin Mawhinney** was born on March 30, 1972, in Chapel

Hill, North Carolina. Matt graduated with a liberal arts degree from the University of Arizona in Tucson. He is working in Tucson.

VII. **Ann Mawhinney** was born on August 15, 1933, in Cincinnati, Hamilton County, Ohio, the oldest daughter of Cynthia Perin and James Donald Mawhinney. She attended Mary Washington College in Fredericksburg, Virginia, but dropped out to accompany her family to Japan, where her father was stationed with the Army Corps of Engineers. There she met her future husband, who was serving on General Douglas MacArthur's headquarters staff in Japan. Later, Ann attended Pomona State College in California and obtained her teachers certificate.

Ann was married on December 27, 1953, in Tokyo, Japan, to *John Ferris McGrew*. Born on August 23, 1928, in Marshalltown, Iowa, he was the son of Lucille Anna Ferrise and Vern McGrew. John McGrew attended the United States Naval Academy at Annapolis, Maryland, earning a Bachelor of Science degree, and served in the US Air Force in G-2 Intelligence. Ann and John McGrew lived in Southern California and had three children. They divorced around 1972.

Ann married *Paul Raymond Jarvela* on September 4, 1982, in Arcata, California. He was born on November 5, 1922, in Linden Grove, St. Louis County, Minnesota. His parents were Senia Saari and William Andrew Jarvela, both natives of Finland. Ann and Paul made their home in the north coastal town of Arcata, California. Paul Jarvela headed the Redwood Inspection Service of the California Redwood Association and was a recognized expert on lumber quality and grading. He died on November 25, 1997, in Arcata. Ann is now living in Sun City, California.

**Children of Ann Mawhinney**

VIII. **Martha Jean McGrew**, eldest daughter of Ann Mawhinney and John McGrew, was born on December 8, 1954, in St. Alban's, Long Island, New York. After a brief marriage to *John McGovern*, a professional bicyclist, she then married *Gerald Sarvas*. The son of Ida Frydman and Milton Edward Sarvas, Gerald was born on June 16, 1952, in Long Beach, California. Gerald and Martha Jean divorced about 1984.

Martha Jean attended Sonoma State University in Sonoma, California, where she was a Hutchins Scholar and majored in education. She obtained a Master's Degree in Education from the University of Washington in Seattle, then taught school in Alaska and in the Virgin Islands. She lives in Coral Gables, Florida, working in the Linda Ray Clinic, a local community organization funded by grants from the University of Miami. Her work involves rehabilitation therapy for infants and young children, including crack cocaine babies and other handicapped and disadvantaged children.

### Children of Martha Jean McGrew

IX. **<u>Dharia Ann McGrew</u>**, born on October 3, 1977, in Forestville, Sonoma County, California. Dharia graduated in 1999 with a degree in biology from Mount Holyoke College in South Hadley, Massachusetts.

IX. **<u>Isaac Templeton Sarvas</u>**, born on December 24, 1979, in Santa Rosa, Sonoma County, California. He is a student at the University of California at Santa Barbara. He is an avid tennis player and interested in law and politics.

VIII. **<u>James Donald McGrew</u>**, son of Ann Mawhinney and John McGrew, born on September 5, 1957, at Norton Air Force Base in San Bernardino, California. Jim McGrew obtained a B.S. in finance at Long Beach State College and later earned an M.B.A. from Pepperdine University. He is the finance program manager with ORIX Credit Alliance, Inc. in Pasadena, California, involved with equipment financing transactions, and teaches finance part-time at local colleges.

Jim married *Georgia Thompson* on January 5, 1980, in Long Beach, California. The daughter of Dot Thomas and William Thompson, Georgia was born on January 31, 1953, in Barrington, Illinois. Jim and Georgia are devout Christians. With three sons, including identical twins, they live in Riverside, California.

### Children of James Donald McGrew

IX. **<u>John Christian McGrew</u>**, one of the twins, born on July 29, 1983, in Long Beach, California.

IX. **William Thompson McGrew**, a twin, born on July 29, 1983, in Long Beach, California.

IX. **Garrett James McGrew**, born on March 18, 1995, in Riverside, California.

VIII. **Jennifer Ann McGrew**, youngest daughter of Ann Mawhinney and John McGrew, was born on February 3, 1964, in Monrovia, California. She received a B.A. in economics at Long Beach State College in 1986 and has held various jobs in the fields of finance and banking.

Jennifer married *Robert Morrill Wadley* on January 21, 1990, in Seattle, King County, Washington. He was born on July 26, 1960, in Tampa, Florida, the son of Allison Allen and William Wadley and served as a Chief Petty Officer with the US Navy. They divorced in March 1994, having no children. After living for a period in Central Florida, where she worked in computer services, Jennifer moved to Clarksville, Tennessee, the home of her aunt and uncle Cindy and Eldon Buckner.

On April 17, 1996, Jennifer McGrew married *David Harvey Haxton* in Clarksville, Tennessee, with Rev. William Buckner (Eldon's brother) officiating. The son of Shirley and Harvey Haxton, David was born on December 3, 1966, in Illinois. They had one daughter and divorced in 1999. Jennifer resides in Murfreesboro, Tennessee, and is working for SunTrust Bank in Nashville.

### Child of Jennifer Ann McGrew

IX. **Sarah Johanna Haxton**, born on October 13, 1996, in Clarksville, Tennessee.

VII. **Cynthia Mawhinney** (called "Cindy"), daughter of Cynthia Perin and James Donald Mawhinney, was born on October 21, 1936, in Cincinnati, Ohio. She attended Duke University, but her studies were interrupted to get married. Later, Cindy received a B.S. and a M.A. from Austin Peay State University in Clarksville, Tennessee.

Cindy's first marriage was to *Robert Clinton Roylance* on September 15, 1956, in Falls Church, Virginia. He was born on March 15, 1932, in Maryland, the son of Caroline Schumach and William G. Roylance. After two children, they divorced in 1972.

Cindy then married *Eldon Ezekiel Buckner Jr.* in Clarksville, Tennessee, on June 19, 1973. Eldon, the son of Ruth Bumpus and Eldon Ezekiel Buckner Sr., was born on November 25, 1927, near Cumberland Furnace in Dixon County, Tennessee. They have one daughter and live in Clarksville. Eldon, a real estate broker, owned and operated a Coldwell Banker agency in Clarksville from 1959 to 1991, when he sold the business.

**Children of Cynthia Mawhinney**

VIII.   **Thomasin Kay Roylance** (called "T.K."), daughter of Cynthia Mawhinney and Robert Roylance, was born on December 8, 1958, in Knoxville, Tennessee. T.K. is an artist and graduated with a B.A. from Austin Peay State University in Clarksville, Tennessee.

She married *Greeley McKinley Lee Jr.* (called "Mack") on June 7, 1986, in Montgomery, Alabama. He was born on November 7, 1954, in Greenville, Alabama, the son of Eva Nelle Johnson and Greeley McKinley Lee Sr. Trained as an electrical engineer, he completed undergraduate and graduate studies at Auburn University in Alabama, and he works in a family company in Greenville. T.K. and Mack Lee have two children and reside in Greenville, Alabama.

**Children of Thomasin Kay Roylance**

IX.   **Kayla McKenzie Lee**, born on January 25, 1991, in Montgomery, Alabama.

IX.   **Greeley McKinley Lee III**, born on June 2, 1995, in Montgomery, Alabama.

VIII.   **Robert Clinton Roylance II** was born on August 14, 1960, in Clarksville, Montgomery County, Tennessee, son of Cynthia Mawhinney and Robert Roylance. He is a graduate of the University of Tennessee. Bobby is a general contractor and is involved in commercial real estate as the owner of a number of properties in the Clarksville area. Bobby's partner, *Martha Elliott*, has an interior design and decorating business. They live in Clarksville.

VIII. **Cynthia Ruth Buckner**, daughter of Cynthia Mawhinney and Eldon Buckner, was born on April 23, 1974, in Clarksville, Tennessee. Unmarried, she lives Clarksville and works as the assistant to the office administrator of a large law firm in Nashville.

## 6-C.3: HOPE THOMSON ROBERTSON (1906-1973)
### Daughter of Reuben Buck Robertson

VI. **Hope Thomson Robertson** was born on March 31, 1906, in Cincinnati, Ohio, the daughter of Hope Thomson and Reuben Robertson Sr. (5-C.2 above). As an infant she moved with her parents to western North Carolina and was raised in Asheville. Hope was a graduate of Pine Manor College in Wellesley, Massachusetts, and studied art in New York at the Art Students League and other schools. She also studied writing at Columbia University. Hope pursued further artistic studies at Collegio Gazzola, near Verona, Italy, and later lived for a while in Paris, working for *Harper's Bazaar* magazine and taking sculpture classes at L'Academie de la Grande Chaumiere and L'Academie Julian.

Hope Robertson married *Bertram William Colthup* on May 23, 1931, at her parents' home in Asheville, with Rev. R.F. Campbell presiding. Bertram Colthup, a native of Royal Tunbridge Wells in Kent, England, was a director of the Paris American Art Supply Co. and served as a captain in the British Army in Ireland, India, Egypt, and Mesopotamia. He was born on September 24, 1895, son of Arthur H. Colthup. Hope and Bertram had one daughter, and divorced in 1937. During World War II, Bertram worked in the French Resistance. He was captured by the Nazis and died as a prisoner of war in a military hospital, Val-de-Grace, in Paris on August 26, 1943.

On April 10, 1939, Hope married *Russell Lee Norburn, MD* at All Souls' Episcopal Church in Biltmore Forest, Asheville, North Carolina, Rev. William C. Cravner presiding. Russell, son of Susan Lillian Strickland of Mt. Airy, North Carolina, and Charles Arwed Norburn of Rotherham, England, was born on March 7, 1893, in Danville, Virginia. As a teenager, he was awarded a Carnegie Hero Medal for keeping a friend from being swept over the one-hundred-foot-high Balsam Falls. Russell Norburn received his M.D. from Vanderbilt University Medical School in Nashville, Tennessee, and later studied at the University of Pennsylvania and Harvard. In addition to Hope's daughter by her previous marriage, she and Russell had two sons.

Dr. Norburn was a surgeon who practiced medicine for many years with his brother Dr. Charles S. Norburn. In 1928, they founded the Norburn Hospital in Asheville. The hospital grew from twenty beds at the start until, in 1946, it became a 110-bed facility located on a fifty-acre site in the heart of Asheville. It was sold to Memorial Mission Hospital in 1950, and later became one of the largest medical centers in North Carolina. Dr. Norburn also had deep interest in economics and wrote numerous articles and books on money and banking. Russell was especially critical of the Federal Reserve System. That was the focus of his book, *Mankind's Greatest Step, A New Monetary System*, as well as testimony he gave in hearings before the US House of Representatives, wherein he urged major changes in the United States monetary system. He was an outspoken advocate for fluoridation of the water supply, working with the Buncombe County Health Department to that end, despite almost hysterical community opposition.

Hope Robertson Norburn wrote poetry, articles and two books—*Above the Brink*, a collection of her poems, and *Lord Lollypop*, a poetic satire. She and her mother collaborated on two books of music—*Tunes of a Family Team* and *Melodies for Moppets*. She received numerous prizes for her paintings and sculptures. Hope's historical painting, *The Capture of General Santa Anna*, is in the Lee Davis Library of San Jacinto College in Texas. She served as president of the Asheville Civic Arts Council; as president of the American Artists Professional League, Asheville Chapter; and as president of the Asheville Branch of the National League of American Pen Women. Other interests included the Junior League of Asheville, the North Carolina Poetry Society, the Asheville Music Club, and the All Souls Episcopal Church. She also served as a member of the Girl Scout Council, the Orthopedic Hospital board, and Children's Theater board of trustees. She was featured by the *Asheville Citizen-Times* newspaper as "Woman of the Week" in October 1963.

Hope Robertson Norburn died of a heart attack on September 7, 1973, in Asheville. She was sixty-seven. Dr. Russell Norburn died in Asheville on November 27, 1989, at the age of ninety-six. Both are buried at Riverside Cemetery in Asheville.

**Children of Hope Thomson Robertson**

VII. **Laura Hope (Colthup) Norburn** (called "Cherie"), daughter of Hope Robertson and Bertram Colthup, was born on March 21, 1935, in Asheville, North Carolina. Cherie's surname was changed to Norburn after her mother's remarriage in 1939. She attended the Oldfields School in Maryland and Briarcliff College in New York.

Cherie married *Richard Albert Farmer* at All Souls Episcopal Church in Biltmore Forest, North Carolina, Rev. Issac Northrup presiding. Their wedding occurred on June 26, 1954, shortly after Dick's graduation with honors (with a rank of third in his class) from the US Military Academy, West Point, New York. Dick was born on January 8, 1932, in Carthage, Missouri, son of Joy Martin Farmer and Mildred Annabel Wheeler. Dick served with the US Army Corps of Engineers. He received master's degrees in nuclear engineering and civil engineering and, in 1969, a Ph.D. in nuclear physics from the Massachusetts Institute of Technology.

Cherie was an accomplished horseback rider and won many show ribbons and prizes. She taught horsemanship and was co-director of the Concord Pony Club in Massachusetts. She was also a talented artist, specializing in horse portraits, and her paintings received a number of awards in local art shows.

Cherie and Dick Farmer had three children. Cherie died from complications of Hodgkin's disease at the age of thirty-four on July 13, 1969, in Bedford, Massachusetts.

The following year, Dick and the children, along with five horses, moved to Colorado, where Dick worked in aerospace engineering with Martin Marietta Corporation, and they lived on a 160-acre ranch in Larkspur, Colorado. In 1971, Dick married *Susan Robinson*, who was born on September 1, 1935, in Maine. Now retired, Dick and his wife sponsor combined training events for horses and ponies on their Abbe Ranch.

**Children of Laura Hope (Colthup) Norburn**

VIII. **<u>Laura Lee Farmer</u>** (called "Lollie"), first daughter of Cherie Norburn and Dick Farmer, was born on May 27, 1956, in Stuttgart, Germany, where her father was stationed in the military. Lollie graduated from Regis University in Denver, Colorado, with a B.S. in business administration. She later received a master's degree in management from National University in San Diego, California, in 1992.

Laura married *John Joseph Gebhardt* in Denver, Colorado, on August 4, 1978. He was born on June 11, 1953, in Salina, Kansas, son of Donald Floyd Gebhardt and Dixie Louise Stephens. They divorced in 1997.

An accomplished equestrian, Laura was active in fox hunting and horse training for twenty-four years. She is an avid scuba diver with a professional rating of divemaster. Following the tradition of her mother and grandmother, Laura is an outstanding artist and sculptor. She specializes in paintings of animals and has won recognition for her work. Laura is a business manager for foreign investors and resides in Leucadia, California, a few miles north of San Diego.

**Child of Laura Lee Farmer**

IX. **<u>Trevor Ryan Gebhardt</u>**, born on July 18, 1982, in Denver, Colorado.

VIII. **<u>Cynthia Ann Farmer</u>** (called "Cindy"), born on April 29, 1960. She died at age eleven in an accident with her pony on April 17, 1971. Her ashes are buried on the ranch in Larkspur, Colorado.

VIII. **<u>Richard Robertson (Farmer)</u>** , born in Cambridge, Massachusetts, on April 28, 1961. After finishing high school in Colorado in 1979, Rick left home at the age of eighteen. At the age of nineteen, he married *Victoria Aldridge,* almost nine years older, on May 5, 1980, in Jacksonville, Florida. She was born on May 20, 1952, the daughter of John and Millie Aldridge. At her urging, Rick legally changed his surname to Robertson. They divorced in December 1988, having one son.

Rick Robertson married *Petra Anita Renz* in Jacksonville, Florida, on January 9, 1991. She was born on May 8, 1958, in Röllfeld, Lower Franconia, Bavaria,

Germany, the daughter of Karlheinz Renz and Hilde Eilbacher. They live in Jacksonville, Florida.

Rick is a shop manager for Pile Equipment, Inc. in Jacksonville. The company rents, rebuilds, and maintains construction hammers and pile-driving equipment used for deep-foundation work in construction of highways, bridges, piers, high-rise buildings, and other structures.

**Child of Richard Robertson Farmer**

IX. **Ian Gregory Robertson**, born on July 20, 1984, in Jacksonville, Florida.

VII. **Russell Lee Norburn Jr.**, born on October 25, 1941, in Asheville, North Carolina, was the son of Hope Robertson and Russell L. Norburn. He obtained a B.A. from Duke University in Durham, North Carolina. He later attained a M.A. from the Institute of Policy Sciences and Public Affairs at Duke University in 1986.

Russell married *Helen Mary Hand* on December 28, 1961, in Colchester, Essex, England. Raised in Bermuda, Helen was born on September 6, 1942, in Colchester, the daughter of Mary Fritche and John Pierce Hand Jr. of Bermuda. Russell and Helen had two sons and divorced. She remarried and is now Mrs. Preston Miller, residing in Sherrill's Ford, North Carolina.

Russell married *Gayla Dean Benignus* in September 1979. She was born about 1939 in Durham, North Carolina. That marriage also ended in divorce, with no children.

On July 16, 1983, Russell married *Jean E. Kincade* in Pittsboro, North Carolina. Jean was born on April 10, 1945, in Grenfell, Saskatchewan, Canada, the daughter of Annie Feather and Robert Henry Kincade. Jean received a Ph.D. degree in Medical Sociology, Associate Professor from Brown University in Providence, Rhode Island, and was an associate professor in the School of Public Health, University of North Carolina, working in gerontology and long-term healthcare issues. That marriage ended in divorce, with no children.

Russell Norburn Jr. set up a BMW automotive franchise, the Miller & Norburn Company, in Durham, North Carolina, and was a professional race car driver with the BMW racing team. He served as executive director of the Conservation Council of North Carolina for two years, successfully opposing the development of a proposed supercollider project in that state. He also was an avid sailor and had sailing-oriented businesses near Savannah, Georgia, and Charleston, South Carolina.

Russell Lee Norburn Jr died in Tallahassee, Florida, on June 5, 1999, as a result of a massive heart attack several weeks earlier. His ashes were interred alongside his parents at Riverside Cemetery in Asheville, North Carolina.

### Children of Russell Lee Norburn

VIII. **<u>Robert Edward Norburn</u>**, son of Helen Hand and Russell Norburn Jr., born on April 8, 1964, in Asheville, North Carolina. He graduated with a B.A. degree from the University of North Carolina at Chapel Hill. Later, he earned a B.S. degree in civil engineering from North Carolina State University.

Bob married *<u>Joni McKay</u>* in Beaufort, North Carolina, on January 9, 1988. Joni was born on April 24, 1963, in Morehead City, North Carolina, the daughter of Barbara Taylor and John Booth McKay. Joni was trained as a dental hygienist.

Bob has been a transportation planner and safety engineer with the Federal Highway Administration of the US Department of Transportation in Tallahassee, Florida, and, in 1999, was promoted to the position of environmental coordinator with that agency in Columbia, South Carolina. Joniand Bob have two daughters.

### Children of Robert Edward Norburn

IX. **<u>Cameron Nicole Norburn</u>**, born on March 26, 1991, in Raleigh, North Carolina.

IX. **<u>Taylor Christine Norburn</u>**, born on January 11, 1995. In Raleigh, North Carolina.

VIII. **<u>Christopher Scott Norburn</u>**, son of Helen Hand and Russell Norburn Jr., born on March 3, 1966, in Durham, North Carolina. He resides in Huntersville, North Carolina. Chris is with Race Parts Distribution, Inc., a company that sells auto racing parts and equipment.

VII. **Charles Robertson Clark Norburn**, son of Hope Thomson Robertson and Russell Lee Norburn, M.D., was born on June 21, 1946, in Asheville, North Carolina. Clark is a graduate of the University of North Carolina at Asheville, from which he received a B.A. degree in psychology in 1971. He also attended Schiller College near Stuttgart, Germany, and Carnegie-Mellon University in Pittsburgh, Pennsylvania, where he studied physics.

Clark has studied computer programming at the University of North Carolina at Asheville and software development at Microsoft University. He has been working on the development of an original software program for business management and financial applications. In addition, Clark is a skilled photographer.

Clark and *Celeste Lisa Carneal* were married at home in Biltmore Forest, North Carolina, on August 26, 1990. Celeste was born on September 23, 1951, in Evanston, Illinois. She is the daughter of Mercedes Ferrari of Marino, Italy, and Thomas Earl Carneal of Bluefield, West Virginia. Celeste received an Associate of Arts degree from Oakton College in Illinois in 1979 and also studied at Northwestern University, the American Conservatory of Music in Chicago, and at the Dante Alghieri School in Rome, Italy. Celeste studied the harp with the principal harpist of the Chicago Symphony Orchestra and now plays with the Blue Ridge Harp Ensemble and at the Biltmore House in Asheville, North Carolina. She is an oil painter and has also written a collection of poems and short stories. In 1992, Clark and Celeste jointly published a cassette tape of Celeste's harp music with a cover designed by Clark in his study of computer graphics at the Kodak Center for Creative Imaging in Maine.

Clark and Celeste met on a cruise ship in the US Virgin Islands, on which Celeste was working as the ship's harpist. After their wedding, both worked on a large cruise ship *Royal Viking Sky*—Celeste as the ship's harpist and Clark as computer instructor—sailing to some twenty-seven ports of call in the South Pacific, including Easter Island, Pitcairn Island, Moorea, Bora Bora, Pago Pago, New Zealand, Australia, Vanuatu, Fiji, and Christmas Island.

Clark and Celeste legally changed their names in 1991 to become Clark Robertson Norburn Carneal and Celeste Norburn Carneal. They live in Biltmore Forest, North Carolina, in the home originally built for Clark's mother in 1936, which was extensively renovated in 1978.

## 6-C.4: REUBEN BUCK ROBERTSON JR. (1908-1960)
### Son of Reuben Buck Robertson

VI. **<u>Reuben Buck Robertson Jr.</u>**, oldest son of Hope Thomson and Reuben B. Robertson Sr. (5-C.2 above), was born on June 27, 1908, in Asheville, North Carolina. He became a leading industrial manager in the paper industry and a top-level government executive before his accidental death in 1960.

Reuben attended Yale University, obtaining a B.S. degree in chemical engineering in 1930 from Yale's Sheffield Scientific School. Although he struggled at times on the academic front, Reuben was a star soccer player in college, serving as captain of the Yale team and named to the All-American team. He also played on the varsity baseball team, was a member of St. Anthony Hall, and was elected to the Aurelian Honor Society.

As a young man, Reuben's driving ambition was to follow his father's large footsteps and go into the business founded by his grandfather Peter G. Thomson, which by this time was combined into a single firm known as the Champion Paper and Fibre Company. Following college, Reuben seized an opportunity to spend four months in Germany and other parts of Europe studying forestry under the tutelage of Dr. Karl A. Schenck. In the fall of 1930, he went to work as a mill hand in the wood yard of Champion in Canton, North Carolina. With an intense determination to master the processes of pulp and paper making, he worked successively in almost all of the departments of the Canton mill. An enthusiastic, energetic, and thoroughly charming person, the handsome "Young Reuben" became a well-known and popular figure at Champion. In 1934, he was promoted to assistant to the general manager of the mill in Canton; the following year he was made vice president in the Carolina Division; and in the late 1930s, he was transferred to the Ohio Division to implement new cost-control systems and work on organizational and personnel matters.

Shortly after his move to Ohio, Reuben Jr. and *Margaret Louisa Watkins* (called "Peggy") were married on December 17, 1938, in Charleston, South Carolina. Born on November 15, 1915, in Birmingham, Jefferson County, Alabama, Peggy was the daughter of Margaret Horry Chisolm and George L. Watkins.[236] Because of her mother's early death, when Peggy was not yet four years old, she was raised by her aunt and uncle Louisa S. Chisolm and Daniel E. Huger in Charleston, South Carolina.[237] Peggy was an aspiring actress who had performed with the Barter Theater in Abingdon, Virginia, to excellent reviews and was launching a career on Broadway, but she agreed to give up the stage to start a family with Reuben.

Peggy and Reuben Robertson Jr. first set up housekeeping in a tiny frame house in the village of Glendale, a suburb of Cincinnati, Ohio. Soon he was appointed vice president and general production manager of Champion at its headquarters in Hamilton, Ohio, and he and Peggy acquired a farm near Mount Healthy, roughly halfway between Hamilton and Cincinnati, on which they started constructing a large brick home. The Second World War interrupted these plans, however, and in August of 1942, Reuben was called to Washington, D.C., to serve on the War Production Board. After a few months in that role, he transferred to active duty in the US Army. He was commissioned a captain in 1943, a major the following year, and lieutenant colonel in 1945. Reuben was discharged from the Army on October 10, 1945, (the birthdate of his third son) and returned to Ohio to resume his career with Champion.

After the war, Peggy and Reuben completed construction of their home on the estate they called "Millbrook Farm," where they raised six children and many animals.

Reuben Robertson Jr. was a dynamic and charismatic business leader. He became the Executive Vice President of Champion in 1946, and in 1950, he succeeded his father as president of the company and joined its board of directors.

Throughout his life, Reuben had a strong interest in government and public service. In 1950, President Truman appointed him as a member of the Wage Stabilization Board, on which he served until June 1951. He was appointed to the Business Advisory Council of the US Secretary of Commerce and became vice chairman of that board in 1953. At the request of President Dwight D. Eisenhower, Reuben led a team of business executives who evaluated the US Mutual Security Program in Germany, and as a result of that work, he was honored as "Man of the Year" by the National Association of Manufacturers in 1953. He was featured by *Business Week* magazine in the cover story for its August 1, 1953, issue.

In 1955, Reuben was named vice chairman of the Committee on Business Organization in the Department of Defense (a special task force of the Hoover Commission). He was asked to consider an appointment as Undersecretary of State but declined that opportunity because of his management obligations at Champion.

Later in 1955, President Eisenhower appointed Reuben Robertson Jr. as Deputy Secretary of Defense of the United States, and the family moved to Washington, D.C., for two years. In that position he was officially second in command in the Defense Department, in which are placed the US Army, Navy, and Air Force, and during the frequent absences of Charles Wilson, the Secretary of Defense, Reuben held the position of Acting Secretary. When Secretary Wilson resigned in 1957, Reuben was invited to succeed him but decided that his family and business responsibilities had to take priority. He turned down the opportunity to move into the secretary's office and instead persuaded President Eisenhower to appoint his friend and fellow Cincinnatian, Neil H. McElroy of the Procter and Gamble Co.

Resigning from the Defense Department in 1957, Reuben returned to his previous position as President of Champion Papers in Hamilton, Ohio. He held many business and civic positions in addition to his career in Champion and in government. He was a director of major industrial and financial corporations, including Procter and Gamble, the B.F. Goodrich Co., Cincinnati and Suburban Bell Telephone Co., and Wachovia Bank and Trust Co. He served as a Trustee of Miami University in Oxford, Ohio, and of Duke University in North Carolina, and as a director of the Ohio Foundation of Independent Colleges.

On March 13, 1960, at the age of fifty-one, Reuben was struck and killed by a speeding car late at night when he stopped to investigate an automobile accident on Paddock Road in Cincinnati. His death was front-page news throughout the United States. A memorial tribute delivered by the Ohio Chamber of Commerce, of which he had been a director for several years, cited Reuben Robertson Jr. as "a man of selfless integrity, vision and tireless energy" who had made great contributions "to the Nation, the State, to his community and to industry." He was buried near his father in Section 79, Lot 1, Spring Grove Cemetery, Cincinnati.

Reuben's widow, Peggy, later married Leslie A. Meek, a distinguished attorney in Cincinnati. She died on November 27, 1990, in Cincinnati at the age of seventy-five and was buried in Spring Grove Cemetery.

## Children of Reuben Buck Robertson Jr.

VII. Reuben Buck Robertson III.

One of the prerogatives of authoring a family history is that you get to write about yourself in the first person singular.

I was born on September 24, 1939, in Cincinnati, Hamilton County, Ohio. After attending the Ashville School in Ashville, North Carolina, I graduated with a B.A. degree in 1961 from Yale University, where I studied American history, literature and economics, played soccer, was a member of St. Anthony Hall, Delta Psi, and served as president of the Inter-Fraternity Council. I attended Yale Law School, from which I received my J.D. degree in 1964, and the London School of Economics in London, England.

In 1966, I settled in Washington, D.C., where I entered law practice as an associate attorney with Covington & Burling, a large law firm primarily representing corporate and industrial clients. In early 1968, I resigned that position to become a member of Senator Robert F. Kennedy's presidential campaign staff, which ended suddenly with his assassination in June 1968. I had just gotten married and heard the news from a ticker tape in a London hotel. We decided to extend the honeymoon by several weeks, since I no longer had a job waiting for me at home, and we explored various parts of Europe.

When we finally did return to Washington, I joined the US Department of Transportation to develop and prosecute, in collaboration with the Department of Justice, a series of lawsuits attacking unlawful racial discrimination in employment on interstate highway construction programs. The cases were successfully settled shortly after they were filed, and thereafter, I was asked to stay on as a special counsel in the Federal Highway Administration. In that position I helped develop and implement the federal motor vehicle safety and highway safety enforcement programs.

In 1969, with a new administration coming into power, I decided to pursue a longstanding concern about unresponsive and counterproductive government activities and became one of the early "public interest" lawyers challenging substantive and procedural practices of federal and state regulatory agencies. I helped consumer advocate Ralph Nader establish the Center for Study of Responsive Law, which sponsored teams of young lawyers and law students—nicknamed "Nader's Raiders" by the press—in studies of various agency activities and a variety of public interest litigation efforts. In 1972, I founded the Aviation Consumer Action Project to advocate consumer interests in safe and affordable air transportation, and the chairman of the U.S. Civil Aeronautics Board (CAB) appointed me to head a special committee to advise that agency on consumer interests. I also served on a special advisory committee to address needed reforms of the CAB's regulatory procedures, which published a detailed report and recommendations for simplifying the administrative rules and procedures of the agency. In 1974, I became senior attorney with the Public Citizen Litigation Group.

As a public interest lawyer during the early 1970s, I became a strong advocate for complete economic deregulation of the airline industry and enhancing the benefits of competitive market forces in air transportation. I worked for passage of the Airline Deregulation Act of 1976, which phased out the CAB after a transition period— making it the first major federal regulatory agency to be completely abolished. After its enactment, and as the deregulation act began to take effect, I was asked in 1978 by the newly-appointed chairman of the CAB, Dr. Alfred E. Kahn, to become a senior official in the agency to help plan and implement the orderly transition to deregulation and "sunset" of the CAB. Accepting that challenge, I became director of the CAB's Bureau of Consumer Protection and headed its antitrust and law enforcement programs for two years.

In 1980, I was appointed by President Carter as Chairman of the Administrative Conference of the United States and was confirmed in that position by the US Senate. I resigned the following year to resume private law practice. I have been a full-time Washington lawyer since then, specializing in commercial litigation and regulatory matters.

On June 1, 1968, I married *Victoria Hadley Emery* in New York, New York. She was born on February 9, 1947, in Cincinnati, Ohio, the daughter of Virginia Jessie Hadley and Harold Andrew Emery.[238] Victoria studied at Vassar College in Poughkeepsie, New York, from which she received her B.A. degree in political science in 1969. In 1976, she was awarded a M.A. degree in anthropology from

George Washington University in Washington, D.C. A professional archeologist, Victoria is employed by Parsons Engineering Science, working on artifacts from colonial and prehistoric American Indian sites. Victoria and I have four daughters and live in Washington, D.C.

In August 1994, the family visited Walls, Shetland, for several days. They saw Seafield in Walls, the home of my great-great-grandfather Thomas Robertson, and met some of our Robertsons who live in Shetland, including Angus and Lauretta Robertson, Eleanor Robertson Hall, and Martha ("Pat") Robertson.

### Children of Reuben Buck Robertson III

VIII. **<u>Laura Hadley Robertson</u>**, born on November 1, 1974, in Washington, D.C. She attended Reed College in Portland, Oregon, after graduating first in her class at Emerson Preparatory School in Washington. She is also a champion equestrian and is working near San Diego, California, as a horse trainer.

VIII. **<u>Victoria Hope Robertson</u>**, born on July 4, 1977, in Washington, D.C. An aspiring and talented actress, Hope is training for a stage career in New York and Washington.

VIII. **<u>Margaret Virginia Robertson</u>** (called "Maggie"), born on March 2, 1986, in Washington, D.C.

VIII. **<u>Cynthia Buck Robertson</u>**, born on October 24, 1988, in Washington, D.C.

VII. **<u>Daniel Huger Robertson</u>**, second son of Margaret L. Watkins and Reuben B. Robertson Jr., born on May 23, 1942, in Cincinnati, Ohio. He attended Denison University in Ohio and later served in the US Air Force from 1962 to 1966, attaining the rank of airman first class. Dan worked for many years as a developer and investor in real estate and restaurant projects in California and Arizona.

Daniel married *<u>Mary Elizabeth Wakefield</u>* in September 1968 in Santa Cruz, California. Mary was born on February 4, 1947, in Santa Cruz, California, the daughter of Guy and Grace Wakefield. Daniel and Mary had one daughter and divorced in 1970. Dan married again on April 23, 1979, in California. His second wife, *Judith Anne Hannover*, was born about 1945 in San Angelo, Texas, and had two children by a prior marriage, Heather and Jennifer Urrea. Daniel and Judith divorced in 1981.

Dan has developed a great interest in therapeutic hypnosis, cognitive functioning, and communications processes, including training in the field of Neuro-Linguistic Programming (NLP). He resides in Cupertino, California, and has established a private counseling and healing practice in hypnotherapy.

### Child of Daniel Huger Robertson

VIII. **Sara Hope Robertson**, born on March 24, 1970, in Santa Cruz, California. Sara works for Health Strategies Group in Palo Alto, California, a consulting firm that provides marketing advice for major pharmaceutical manufacturers. She is residing at her father's home in Cupertino.

VII. **Peter Thomson Robertson**, third son of Margaret L. Watkins and Reuben B. Robertson Jr., born on October 10, 1945, in Cincinnati, Ohio. He graduated from the University of Virginia and obtained a law degree from Boston College School of Law in Boston, Massachusetts.

Peter has worked in several high-level positions in state government, including service as general counsel of both the Massachusetts Division of Insurance and the Massachusetts Department of Securities. A recognized expert on insurance matters, Peter works as a consultant and attorney in that field in Boston. He is a director of Medical Professional Mutual Insurance Co. (ProMutual), the largest writer of medical malpractice coverage in Massachusetts, and Premier Insurance Co., a subsidiary of Travelers Insurance Co., providing auto insurance.

On June 11, 1969, Peter married *Cathryn Lee Seibert* in Grosse Pointe Farms, Michigan, a suburb of Detroit. Born on February 27, 1946, in Detroit, Cathie is the daughter of Virginia Lillian Cox [239] and Elmo Edmund Seibert. She received her B.A. degree from Michigan State University, majoring in history and political science; later, she attended Wheelock College in Boston and received a M.S. degree in human services administration. Cathie runs a childcare center.

Peter and Cathie live in Auburndale, a suburb of Boston, Massachusetts, and also have a weekend home near the Atlantic Shore in Rhode Island. They have no children.

VII. **Margaret Laurens Robertson** (called "Mardi"), first daughter of Margaret Watkins and Reuben B. Robertson Jr., was born on January 3, 1949, in Cincinnati, Ohio.

Mardi attended Western Michigan University and the University of North Carolina at Asheville, pursuing studies in geography. She and her husband, Dick, have also owned businesses making decorative artifacts and jewelry. Mardi has been a travel agent and has traveled widely throughout the world.

In June 1967, in Greensburg, Indiana, Mardi married *David Thomas White*, who was born on May 21, 1946, in Battle Creek, Michigan, and was adopted by Everette and Mary White. Mardi and David had one daughter and divorced in 1969.

On November 25, 1972, at her mother's home in Cincinnati, Mardi married *Richard Arthur LaForce Jr.* Dick was born on December 12, 1934, in Battle Creek, Michigan, son of Nettie Karr and Richard Arthur LaForce. Mardi and Dick have one daughter in addition to Mardi's daughter, Laurens, who was legally adopted by Dick. They live in Batavia, Ohio, an outlying suburb east of Cincinnati in Clermont County.

### Children of Margaret Laurens Robertson

VIII. **Lori Lyn Boren**, born on February 25, 1964, in Indianapolis, Indiana, daughter of Mardi Robertson and Robert William Foley of Boston, Massachusetts. Because her mother was then only fifteen years old and unmarried, Lori was legally adopted at birth by LaRita and Leland Boren of Upland, Indiana, where Mr. Boren has been an industrial entrepreneur and the founder of several successful businesses. The adoptive parents did not know her birth mother's identity but provided a loving, stable home.

As a young adult, Lori became determined to learn who her biological parents were and to make contact with them if possible. After years of investigation, Lori learned that her natural mother was named Margaret

Robertson, and she found a possible telephone number for her in Cincinnati. On July 3, 1991, Lori nervously called the number and for the first time made contact with Mardi, who was thrilled. Since that moment, Lori has been a welcome part of the Robertson family, as well as her adoptive parents.

Lori Boren attended college in Anderson, Indiana, where she majored in psychology. She married *Scott Lee Bowser*, who was born on June 2, 1964, son of Bonnie and Dale Bowser. Lori and Scott had two children and divorced in February 1998.

On August 18, 1998, Lori married *Bryan Keith Meyers* in Las Vegas, Nevada. Born on December 21, 1967, in Somerset, Pennsylvania, Bryan serves with the US Army at Fort Leonard Wood in Missouri, where he teaches surveying. He has a son, Kenny, from a previous marriage.

### Children of Lori Lyn Boren

IX. **Andrew Jordan Bowser**, son of Lori Boren and Scott Bowser, born on September 4, 1990, in Muncie, Indiana.

IX. **Samantha Lyn Bowser**, daughter of Lori Boren and Scott Bowser, born on April 16, 1994, in Muncie, Indiana.

VIII. **Laurens Thomson (White) LaForce**, daughter of Mardi Robertson and David White, born on December 22, 1967, in Cincinnati, Hamilton County, Ohio. Her last name was changed upon adoption by her stepfather, Richard LaForce, after her mother's remarriage in 1972. Laurens obtained a B.S. degree from the University of Findlay in Ohio and studied education at the College of Mount St. Joseph in Cincinnati. She has a teaching certificate and works as an elementary school teacher. Laurens is not married.

VIII. **Karrlyn Watkins LaForce**, daughter of Mardi Robertson and Richard LaForce, born on November 19, 1972, in Battle Creek Michigan. Karrlyn married *Troy Elliott Huff* on September 9, 1995, at the Church of Christ in Batavia, Ohio. Troy was born on October 15, 1969, in Battle Creek, Michigan, son of Bonita June Luce and Delbert Ray Huff. They have two children and reside in Batavia.

**Children of Karrlyn LaForce**

IX. <u>**Leslie June Huff**</u>, born on May 28, 1995, in Cincinnati, Ohio.

IX. <u>**Richard Elliott Huff**</u>, born on May 28, 1995, in Cincinnati, Ohio.

VII. <u>**Louisa Hope Robertson**</u> (called "Hope"), second daughter of Margaret L. Watkins and Reuben B. Robertson Jr., was born on November 21, 1952, in Cincinnati, Hamilton County, Ohio. She was seven when her father died.

Hope married *Leslie Applegate Meek Jr.* in Cincinnati on June 2, 1973. Leslie was the son of Hope's stepfather, the late Leslie A. Meek Sr., and his first wife, Elizabeth Nottingham. They divorced in 1988. Hope married *Stephen Perley* on April 22, 1995, in Cincinnati. He was born in New Jersey on December 11, 1960, son of Rona Jacobson and Howard Perley of Orange County, California. They had no children and divorced in 1996.

Hope has an abiding interest in yoga, spiritualism, and healing. She lived for almost a year in India, involved in the study of Siddha Yoga in Ganeshpuri. She is a graduate of the Barbara Brennan School of Healing in Long Island, New York, and has taught there for two years. She has also studied cabalistic healing with the Society of Souls in Princeton, New Jersey. She lives in Boulder, Colorado, and has a practice in therapeutic massage and healing.

VII. <u>**George Watkins Robertson**</u>, youngest child of Margaret L. Watkins and Reuben B. Robertson Jr., was born on May 22, 1954, in Cincinnati, Hamilton County, Ohio. He was only five when his father died in 1960.

George grew up with a strong interest in marine ecology. He graduated with a B.S. degree from the School of Natural Resources of the University of Michigan at Ann Arbor. An avid scuba diver, he is a scuba instructor with the National Association of Underwater Instructors (NAUI). George studied coral reef ecology and took a year off from his undergraduate work to travel to Thailand and Malaysia. There, he worked on coral reef research and development of a marine park off the coast of Malaysia, sponsored by the World Wildlife Fund. The coral specimens collected from the Malaysia project were donated to the Smithsonian Institution in

Washington, D.C. George received the Lyle B. Craine Award from the University of Michigan for his work on coral reef ecology and marine park development.

George Robertson married _Deborah Lynn Santavy_ on August 25, 1979, in Ann Arbor, Michigan. She was born on December 1, 1955, in Algonac, Michigan, daughter of Patricia and Anthony Santavy. They divorced in 1983, with no children.

After university, George worked for an environmental consulting firm in Washington, D.C. He then did graduate study at the Institute for Marine Studies at the University of Washington in Seattle. Before completing his thesis, however, George decided that he wanted to settle permanently in the Pacific Northwest. That would require changing his chosen career. George decided to enter the field of personal finance. After working with a mutual fund company for a year, George returned to school and qualified as a Certified Financial Planner in 1989. He has developed a growing "fee-only" (non-commission) practice and is also affiliated with a regional brokerage firm in Seattle. George is a member of the Institute of Certified Financial Planners and the International Association of Financial Planners.

George married _Mary Theresa Hecht_ on June 24, 1989, in Roche Harbor on San Juan Island, Washington. Mary was born on October 20, 1962, in Uncasville, Connecticut, daughter of Elizabeth A. Lottes and Richard J. Hecht. Mary is a certified financial planner. They have three children and live in Issaquah, Washington. The family enjoys outdoor activities, including cross-country skiing, camping, hiking, and fishing.

### Children of George Watkins Robertson

VIII. **Christopher Buck Robertson**, born on November 19, 1990, in Seattle, Washington.

VIII. **Reuben Thomson Robertson**, born on December 16, 1992, in Seattle, Washington.

VIII. **Anne Watkins Robertson**, born on July 17, 1997, in Bellevue, Washington.

## 6-C.5: LOGAN THOMSON ROBERTSON (1916-1987)
### Son of Reuben Buck Robertson

VI. **Logan Thomson Robertson** was born on April 18, 1916, in Asheville, Buncombe County, North Carolina. Named for his mother's brother Logan Gamble Thomson, he was the youngest child of Hope Thomson and Reuben B. Robertson Sr. (5-C.2 above). He graduated from Yale College in 1938.

Logan married *Evelyn Elizabeth Radeker* (called "Betty") in Biltmore Forest, near Asheville, on September 8, 1938, Rev. William C. Cravner officiating. Betty was born on April 7, 1916, in Middletown, New York, daughter of Lillian Adelaide Adams of Boston, Massachusetts, and Walter Scott Radeker of Warren, Pennsylvania. She attended Hood College in Frederick, Maryland. Logan and Betty divorced after their three children were grown. She died on May 5, 1993.

Following his marriage, Logan attended the Yale School of Medicine until World War II intervened. He was a captain in the US Army Air Corps, stationed at Carlisle Barracks in Pennsylvania, McDill Air Force Base in Tampa, and other places. Logan received his M.D. degree from the University of Cincinnati in 1942 and attended the Mayo Clinic in Rochester, Minnesota, for further study in radiology. He also studied at Duke University Medical School and was a resident intern at Christ Hospital in Cincinnati.

After the war ended in 1945, the family returned to Asheville, where Logan entered general practice and surgery. He affiliated with the Norburn Hospital and Clinic, which he helped to establish with his brother-in-law, Dr. Russell Norburn, and Dr. Charles Norburn. He was interested in industrial and preventative medicine, at one time providing surgical care for Southern Railway employees. Logan founded and was the president and medical director of Occupational Health Services, an organization that provided medical examinations at industrial plant sites. Logan served as a consultant to the Surgeon General of the United States, the New York State Civil Service Commission, the National Aeronautics and Space Administration (NASA), and the director of NASA's Kennedy Space Flight Center, and was regarded as a pioneer in the field of industrial medicine.

Logan also was involved in a variety of business ventures in the Asheville area and elsewhere. Unfortunately, these investments were too far ahead of their time or proved otherwise unviable. One company, called Rondesics, Inc., developed low-cost modular housing based on the innovative design concepts of R. Buckminster Fuller, the visionary architect/engineer. Logan was involved in development of the Southern Cross Club, the first resort property on Little Cayman Island in the British West Indies. In the 1950s, his company, Daniels Business Services, was one of the first firms in Asheville to offer computerized data-processing services on a commercial basis. He was also involved in unsuccessful resort development and automobile retailing ventures in Asheville. Logan served as president of the Asheville Rotary Club, was a member of the board of directors of the Asheville Chamber of Commerce, and was active in various organizations in the medical field.

On September 13, 1966, in Buncombe County, North Carolina, Logan married *Mary Jane Mesnard*, daughter of Lillian Kohvakka and Leo Mesnard. Mary Jane was born on March 8, 1931, in Grand Rapids, Michigan, and died of emphysema on May 10, 1975, in Asheville. She was apparently buried at Calvary Churchyard in Fletcher, North Carolina, although no grave marker has been located. Mary Jane and Logan Robertson had one daughter. In addition, Mary Jane's three children by a previous marriage—Thomas, Caroline, and Joseph B. ("J.B.")—also lived with them and took the surname Robertson.

Logan's third marriage was to *Judith Scouten*, who was born in Brunswick, Georgia. They had no children, but Logan's youngest daughter, Amorette, and three children from a prior marriage of Judith's—Jennifer, Jonathan, and Laura (who also took the name Robertson)—lived with them. Together with the children, Logan and Judith moved "back to nature" about 1978, to a log cabin home called "Big Butte" on a small, remote farmstead that Logan owned in the mountains near Cruso in Haywood County, North Carolina. There they raised all their own food, without pesticides or chemicals. Logan believed that modern farming technologies produce vegetables and fruits that are deficient in nutrients, and he considered the American populace as a whole to be overfed but undernourished.

In later years, Logan became an outspoken exponent and practitioner of holistic medicine (an approach to healing that emphasizes treatment of the whole person and the interconnectedness of the body's parts). This approach, and Logan's unorthodox procedures for healing, ultimately led him into serious conflict with the medical establishment, which was still unresolved at his death.

Logan Thomson Robertson died in his sleep on December 16, 1987, in Bruges, Belgium, on a vacation trip to Europe with his third wife, Judith. He was seventy-one.

**Children of Logan Thomson Robertson**

VII. **<u>Laura Lee Robertson</u>** (called "Lollie"), born on February 15, 1940, in Durham, North Carolina, oldest child of Elizabeth Radeker and Logan Robertson. She attended Hollins College in Roanoke, Virginia, receiving her B.A. degree in psychology in 1961.

Lollie first married *<u>Rufus Lasher Safford</u>* in Asheville, North Carolina, on June 2, 1962. Rufus was born on March 31, 1935, in Cincinnati, Ohio, son of Theodore Safford and Katherine Schell. Lollie and Rufus lived in numerous places during their marriage, including New York City, Dallas, Atlanta, Charlotte, and Cashiers, North Carolina. They had a daughter, who died as a newborn, and two sons. They divorced, and Rufus now lives in New Mexico.

Lollie married *<u>Wilford Lee Johnson</u>* in Black Mountain, Buncombe County, North Carolina, on January 7, 1984. Wilford was born on January 20, 1934, in Marion, North Carolina, son of Artie Lamb and Clyde Bovy Johnson. They have had no children and reside in Black Mountain, North Carolina.

Lollie practices as a reflexologist and is interested in herbal medicine and healing arts. She and Wilford are followers of the Baha'i Faith, a worldwide movement which holds that all religions have the same God and that all persons are part of one spiritual family. Wilford is a singer and songwriter, inspired in his work by the concepts and beliefs of Baha'i.

**Children of Laura Lee Robertson**

VIII. **<u>Laura Melind Safford</u>**, daughter of Lollie Robertson and Rufus Safford, was born on September 21, 1964, in Asheville, Buncombe County, North Carolina. She died there just two weeks later on October 7, 1964.

VIII. **<u>Rufus Bradford Safford</u>** (called "Brad"), was born on October 7, 1965, in Charlotte, North Carolina, the oldest son of Lollie Robertson and Rufus Safford. He graduated from Berklee College of Music in Boston, Massachusetts, later studied at Massachusetts Institute of Technology (MIT), and in 1994, received a Master's degree in Electrical Engineering from Boston University.

On August 26, 1991, Brad married *Heidi Ann Friedman* in St. Thomas, US Virgin Islands. Born on December 27, 1965, in Boston, Suffolk County, Massachusetts, she is the daughter of Dawn Adele Boberg and Lawrence Boryd Friedman. Brad and Heidi live in Framingham, Massachusetts.

Heidi graduated in 1988 with a B.A. degree in sociology and management from Simmons College in Boston. She has worked since 1990 for National Medical Care at its corporate headquarters in Waltham, Massachusetts, where she is the director of Human Resources—Dialysis Services. In 1996, she earned her M.Ed. in management from Cambridge College in Cambridge, Massachusetts.

While in graduate school, Brad Safford worked on a project with the U.S. Department of Energy to develop devices and systems for tracking neutrinos (subatomic particles of matter). Having worked in engineering and marketing in the computer and vision technology industries for some years, Brad is director of research and development for Cognex Inc., a firm that makes missile guidance systems.

VIII. **<u>George Scott Safford</u>**, (called "Scott") was born on August 7, 1967, in Charlotte, North Carolina, the second son of Lollie Robertson and Rufus Safford. Scott works with his various and considerable abilities as a professional chef, carpenter, DJ, and master of ceremonies. Known to fans as "Scooterman," for several years he was a top radio disc jockey on the most popular rock station in Myrtle Beach, South Carolina.

VII. **<u>Lillian Adams Robertson</u>** (called "Happy") was born on January 4, 1944, in Tampa, Florida, daughter of Elizabeth Radeker and Logan T. Robertson. She grew up in Asheville, North Carolina.

On October 12, 1963, Happy married *Joseph Norton Shinnick*. He was born on November 22, 1938, son of Jean Norton and William L. Shinnick. They divorced, having two children.

Happy and *Rason Howard Dobbs* were married in Cruso, Haywood County, North Carolina, on July 13, 1974. Rason Dobbs was born in Meridian, Mississippi, on April 17, 1934, son of Nina Spires and Olin Carl Dobbs. An architect and builder, Rason studied building construction at Southern Technical Institute in Marietta, Georgia.

Happy and Rason are active in the Baha'i faith. She became a Baha'i in 1971 and has lived in Africa, Grenada, and the Bahamas, working with Baha'is in those places on various community-building projects, including literacy and correspondence courses. Happy has written a book, *Spiritual Being: A User's Guide*, published in 1997 by George Ronald, Oxford, England (ISBN 0-85398-415-8). She and her family have spent much time on boats, including a houseboat, which Rason designed and built, where they lived for five years with the three children. They have also lived in homes that Rason constructed on dry land, both in North Carolina and in Florida. They have one daughter and now live in a new Rason-built home in St. Petersburg, Florida.

### Children of Lillian Adams Robertson

VIII. **Robertson William Shinnick**, son of Happy Robertson and Joe Shinnick, born on December 28, 1965, in West Palm Beach, Florida. He married *Angela Darlene King* on February 22, 1991, in Black Mountain, North Carolina. She was born on October 12, 1968, in Bitburg, Germany. They are divorced, with one child. Rob is pursuing a career in the resort-hospitality business in Sea Island, Georgia. He is an avid coin collector and spends many hours with his metal detector unearthing historic relics, as well as coins, wherever he goes.

### Child of Robertson William Shinnick

IX. **Justice Robertson Shinnick**, born on April 23, 1991, in Asheville, Buncombe County, North Carolina. Justice has been adopted by his new stepfather and his last name has been changed to Arotin.

VIII. **<u>Laura Elizabeth (Shinnick) Dobbs</u>**, daughter of Happy Robertson and Joe Shinnick, born on November 28, 1968, in Norwalk, Connecticut. Called Elizabeth, her surname was changed when she was legally adopted by her stepfather, Rason Dobbs. Elizabeth graduated from the University of North Carolina at Asheville with a B.A. degree in literature.

Elizabeth married *William Joseph Shamblin III* on December 28, 1990, in Flat Rock, North Carolina. Joe, son of Jane Ellen Barr and William J. Shamblin Jr., was born on January 19, 1967, in Tuscaloosa, Alabama. Elizabeth and Joe have one child and live in Raleigh, North Carolina.

Joe works in computer security at Duke University. Elizabeth is studying for a M.S. degree in technical communications from North Carolina State University, but her main professional interest is multimedia design. She conceived and created one of the first interactive programs on the internet, called The Cyranno Server, which writes humorous love letters "for the hopelessly inarticulate." Elizabeth worked at Duke University for four years in a multimedia lab, helping professors use multimedia creatively in the classroom and designing interactive programs for the internet. She also enjoys using her considerable artistic talents as a cartoonist, short-story writer and mosaic maker, and she has volunteered her time and energy to create and maintain an internet website for "Our Robertsons."

"Really," Elizabeth says, "what I want to do eventually is have an alpaca farm in the mountains, but I'm going to have to wait until someone leaves me a bunch of money before I can pursue that dream because alpacas cost about $20,000 each, and you have to have at least two of them. If you have just one, it will die of loneliness—at least that's what the alpaca salespeople say."

### Child of Laura Elizabeth (Shinnick) Dobbs

IX. **<u>Adam Theodore Shamblin</u>**, born in Durham, North Carolina, on April 1, 1999.

VIII. **<u>Jessica Nel Dobbs</u>** (called "Jes"), daughter of Happy Robertson and Rason Dobbs, born on August 7, 1975, in Asheville, Buncombe County,

North Carolina. She has completed studies in the field of interior design at the International Academy for Merchandising and Design in Tampa, Florida. Jes's main interests lie in computer-assisted design and architectural photography.

VII. **Logan Thomson Robertson Jr.**, son of Elizabeth Radeker and Logan T. Robertson, born on June 6, 1946, in Asheville, North Carolina. On June 5, 1965, Logan married *Mary Ashley Norburn*. Mary was born on January 14, 1947, in Asheville, North Carolina, daughter of Helen Johnson and Dr. Charles S. Norburn. They had two children and divorced. Logan is in the contracting business and is developing a resort project in Bocas del Toro, Panama. He resides in Asheville.

**Children of Logan Thomson Robertson Jr.**

VIII. **Logan Scott Adams Robertson**, born on September 27, 1967, in Asheville, North Carolina, son of Logan Robertson Jr. and Mary Norburn. He attended the University of New Hampshire. On July 18, 1998, Logan Scott married *Colleen Erin McElligatt* off the coast of Edisto Island, South Carolina. Colleen was born on March 15, 1969, in Detroit, Michigan. They have one child. Logan Scott is pursuing the study of Traditional Chinese Medicine (TCM) at the Atlantic University of Chinese Medicine (AUCM) in Mars Hill, North Carolina. Colleen is a massage therapist.

**Child of Logan Scott Adams Robertson**

IX. **Taylor Logan Robertson**, born on October 21, 1998, in Asheville, North Carolina.

VIII. **Ashley Nicolette Robertson**, daughter of Mary Norburn and Logan Robertson Jr., born on July 31, 1969, in Asheville, North Carolina. Ashley and *Kenneth Brian Ferguson* (born on March 16, 1969) were married in Asheville and divorced in Oklahoma. They later remarried in Oklahoma and divorced for a second time in Tennessee. They had one son. Later, Ashley married *Jeffrey William Smith* of Pennsylvania on May 17, 1996, in Charleston, South Carolina. They divorced in May 1998, with no children.

On October 10, 1998, Ashley married _Johnny Diaz_ in Charlotte, North Carolina. He is the son of Norma Bueno and Jose Antonio Diaz Sr. and was born at Andrews Air Force Base in Prince George's County, Maryland, on October 31, 1963. Johnny has adopted Ashley's son, and they are living in Matthews, North Carolina, a suburb of Charlotte. They are starting a janitorial business in Charlotte and Matthews, North Carolina.

### Child of Ashley Nicolette Robertson

IX. **Christopher Nathanial Ferguson** (called "Nathan"), born on May 21, 1987, in Asheville, North Carolina. His name was changed to Christopher Nathanial Ferguson Diaz after his mother's marriage to Johnny Diaz.

VII. **Amorette Robertson**, daughter of Mary Jane Mesnard and Logan T. Robertson, born on August 16, 1967, in Asheville, Buncombe County, North Carolina. Her mother died when Amorette was still a small child. Amorette graduated from the University of Miami in 1991 with a major in finance. She has worked as a professional model for national advertising—featured on billboards for Coors Lite Beer—and in real estate and the mortgage business in the Miami area.

Amorette married _Anthony Stephen Morales_ in Miami, Florida, on May 15, 1994. Tony was born on February 6, 1960, in Buenos Aires, Argentina, son of Elizabeth Shaeffer of Washington State and Luis Morales of Bogota, Columbia. They divorced in 1999. They have no children.

Despite her extensive background in business and finance, Amorette decided to pursue her interest in healing arts. She returned to the University of Miami in a master's program in physical therapy. Amorette is working in outpatient orthopedics near Palm Beach, Florida.

## 6-C.6: ELSIE MARIE ROBERTSON (1905-1992)
### Daughter of Charles Andrew Robertson

VI. **<u>Elsie Marie Robertson</u>**, eldest child of Charles Andrew Robertson and Ellen May Kuhn (5-C.3 above), was born on April 15, 1905, in Cincinnati, Ohio. Elsie, a slender, strikingly handsome, and vivacious woman, married *<u>James Monroe Crowder</u>* on November 21, 1926. James, who worked in construction as a steamfitter, was born in Richmond, Virginia, on November 24, 1898, the son of Nancy Wiltshire and William Crowder. They had three daughters.

Elsie was widowed when James died of tuberculosis after a long illness on January 13, 1955. At the time of his death, James was fifty-six and Elsie was not yet fifty; their youngest child had her eleventh birthday a week later. Seven and a half years later, on October 13, 1962, Elsie married *<u>Robert Bruce Robertson</u>* (no relation). Bruce died on August 22, 1972. They lived in Richmond, Virginia, and had no children. In her later years, Elsie suffered from Alzheimer's disease. She died on February 3, 1992, in Milford, Clermont County, Ohio, at the age of eighty-six.

**Children of Elsie Marie Robertson**

VII. **<u>Phyllis Marie Crowder</u>**, born in Cincinnati, Hamilton County, Ohio, on January 7, 1929, was the eldest daughter of James Crowder and Elsie Marie Robertson.

Phyllis married her high school sweetheart, *<u>Garrett Wofford Koger Jr.</u>*, on March 1, 1947, in Maysville, Kentucky. Garrett, the son of Mary Hill and Garrett W. Koger Sr., was born on March 14, 1927, in Gadsden, Alabama, but moved to the Cincinnati area at a young age. He died of kidney failure on March 14, 1974, at age forty-seven. They had two daughters. After her daughter Deborah died suddenly at the age of twenty-two, leaving two small children, Phyllis moved to Florida around 1973 to help care for the children. In 1975, she went to work with the Criminal Investigation Division of the Internal Revenue Service in Ft. Lauderdale.

While working for the IRS, Phyllis met her second husband, *<u>Hinton DeWitte White</u>*, who was at the time the chief of the IRS Facilities Management Branch. They were married in Ft. Lauderdale on November 17, 1978. Hinton was born in

Waycross, Georgia, on July 17, 1921. Phyllis and Hinton later transferred to West Palm Beach, Florida, where she was an office manager for the US Secret Service. After working in government service for twenty years, Phyllis retired in 1995. She and Hinton moved to Maineville in Butler County, Ohio, to be near her sisters and daughter Cindy.

**Children of Phyllis Marie Crowder**

VIII.  **Cynthia Marie Koger**, born on March 28, 1948, in Cincinnati, Hamilton County, Ohio, daughter of Phyllis Marie Crowder and Garrett Koger Jr. Cindy graduated from Bowling Green State University with a degree in teaching. She married a classmate at Bowling Green, *Thomas Vogt*, about 1973. Both are teaching high school in Miamisburg, Ohio, and they live in Springboro, near Dayton, Ohio. They have no children.

VIII.  **Deborah Lee Koger**, born on August 26, 1950, in Cincinnati, Hamilton County, Ohio, daughter of Phyllis Marie Crowder and Garrett Koger Jr.

She married *Anthony Claude Walker*, and they had two sons. At the age of twenty-two, Deborah was stricken with bronchial pneumonia and died suddenly on June 4, 1973. Anthony, an engineer with Motorola Corporation, later remarried and raised the boys in their home in Boynton Beach, Florida.

**Children of Deborah Lee Koger**

IX.  **Robert Garrett Walker**, born on January 25, 1970, in Pittsburgh, Pennsylvania. He is an engineering graduate of Carnegie-Mellon University and now works in the computer field with Intel Corporation in California. He is unmarried.

IX.  **Andrew Alec Walker**, born on September 17, 1971, in Ft. Lauderdale, Florida. He served in the US Air Force and is now pursuing a degree in engineering at Texas A&M University in College Station, Texas. He is unmarried.

VII. **<u>Dorothy Mae Crowder</u>**, born on February 27, 1932, in Cincinnati, Hamilton County, Ohio, second daughter of James Crowder and Elsie Marie Robertson. She married *Bernarr McFadden Glaser* on February 11, 1950. Bernarr was born on April 18, 1930. They had four children.

Bernarr died on October 11, 1974, at the age of forty-four. Widowed at a young age with a nine-year-old daughter and a fifteen-year-old son still at home, Dorothy made a career in the business world and still works as a corporate secretary at Standard Ohio Leasing Company. She lives in the village of Milford, near Cincinnati, Ohio.

### Children of Dorothy Mae Crowder

VIII. **<u>Randy Bob Glaser</u>**, born on February 15, 1951, in Cincinnati, Hamilton County, Ohio. He first married *Veronica Wentzel*; they divorced. His second marriage was to *Marilyn Wesley* on September 13, 1980. They live in Cincinnati, Ohio, where he works as financial manager with Courtesy Chevrolet Company, a new car dealership. They have no children.

VIII. **<u>Dennis Charles Glaser</u>**, born on December 7, 1952, in Cincinnati, Hamilton County, Ohio. He graduated from the University of Cincinnati, where he was trained in the field of pharmacy, and is now a researcher with Future Health Care. He married *Joy Hammons* on June 19, 1982. They are the parents of three sons and live in Terrace Park, a suburb of Cincinnati, Ohio.

### Children of Dennis Charles Glaser

IX. **<u>Tyler Thomas Glaser</u>**, born on March 18, 1987, in Cincinnati, Ohio.

IX. **<u>Jacob Corbett Glaser</u>**, born on September 1, 1989, in Cincinnati, Ohio.

IX. **<u>Luke Brandon Glaser</u>**, born on November 18, 1992, in Cincinnati, Ohio.

VIII. **<u>James Crowder Glaser</u>**, born on November 17, 1958, in Cincinnati, Hamilton County, Ohio. On November 24, 1978, he married *Melody Cusick*.

They have two children and reside in Miami Township, Clermont County, Ohio, on the outskirts of Cincinnati. James owns a homebuilding business.

### Children of James Crowder Glaser

IX. **Amy Lynn Glaser**, born on July 14, 1979, in Cincinnati, Ohio.

IX. **James Bernarr Glaser**, born on February 2, 1981, in Cincinnati, Ohio.

VIII. **Kimberly Lynn Glaser**, born on February 4, 1965, in Cincinnati, Hamilton County, Ohio. Trained as a nurse, she married *Donald Joseph Haas*. He is a route carrier with the US Postal Service. They have three sons and live near Cincinnati in Amelia, Clermont County, Ohio.

### Children of Kimberly Lynn Glaser

IX. **Kyle Joseph Haas**, born on October 6, 1990, in Cincinnati, Ohio.

IX. **Joshua Alexander Haas**, born on February 22, 1993, in Cincinnati, Ohio.

IX. **Randall Paul Haas**, born on March 24, 1995, in Cincinnati, Ohio.

VII. **Ellen Margarete Crowder**, youngest daughter of Elsie Marie Robertson and James Crowder, was born in Cincinnati, Hamilton County, Ohio, on January 20, 1944. Attending night classes for several years, she obtained a B.A. degree in education from the University of Toledo in 1979.

Ellen married *Robert F.S. Fern* on June 9, 1962. After living for a while in Massachusetts, where Robert was attending college, they divorced in 1964. They had no children.

Ellen's second marriage took place in Cincinnati, Ohio, on September 10, 1966. *William Keith Hamilton* was born on January 23, 1942, in Warren, Ohio, the son of Lydia Elizabeth Parti and Wilbur J. Hamilton. Ellen and Bill live in Toledo, Ohio, and have one daughter and one son. Ellen taught at the University of Toledo for ten years and is now involved in teaching computer skills to employees of corporate clients and continuing-education programs for Bowling Green State University. Bill is a communications executive with the Owens-Corning Fiberglass Company in Toledo.

**Children of Ellen Margarete Crowder**

VIII. **<u>Dianne Elizabeth Hamilton</u>**, born on December 14, 1970, in Toledo, Ohio. In 1994, she graduated from the University of Cincinnati with a B.A. degree in sociology and criminal justice. She is unmarried and works most of the year at Kings Island, a large recreational theme park near Cincinnati.

VIII. **<u>Philip James Hamilton</u>**, born on April 18, 1974, in Toledo, Ohio. A student at Michigan State University studying computer science, he also is an accomplished snow boarder, president of the Michigan State Ski Club, which has some 800 members, and the drummer in a rock band called Blue Highway.

## 6-C.7: CHARLES WILLIAM ROBERTSON (1908-1972)
### Son of Charles Andrew Robertson

VI. **<u>Charles William Robertson</u>**, son of Charles Andrew Robertson and Ellen May Kuhn (5-C.3 above), was born in Cincinnati, Hamilton County, Ohio, on January 29, 1908. Charles worked in the construction trades as a pipefitter.

He married *Marion Amy Lomatsch* on June 27, 1931, at St. Paul's Lutheran Church in Olean, Indiana. She was born in Olean on September 6, 1910, the daughter of Mortz Lomatsch and Wilhelmina ("Minnie") Katenbrink. They lived in Cincinnati and were the parents of three children.

Charles W. Robertson died in Cincinnati on December 20, 1972, at the age of sixty-four. His widow, Marion, died in Cincinnati on October 17, 1976, at age sixty-six. Both were buried in Olean, Indiana.

**Children of Charles William Robertson**

VII. **<u>Betty Joanne Robertson</u>** was born in Cincinnati, Hamilton County, Ohio, on February 26, 1932. On September 9, 1950, Betty married *Gene Clarence Winterhalter* in Cincinnati. Gene was born on July 1, 1928, in Cincinnati, the son of

Frieda and Clarence Winterhalter. He had worked as a retail credit manager, first in Cincinnati and, later, in Toledo, Ohio. They had four children. Gene died on April 4, 1968, in Toledo at the age of thirty-nine. Betty was then thirty-six years of age.

Some years later, Betty married *Gordon Charles Wickfeldt* on September 18, 1982, in Cincinnati. Gordon was born in Cincinnati on March 22, 1918, and worked for F&M Printing Company. He died of a heart attack on January 15, 1996, while vacationing in Florida.

Betty is active in the Lutheran Church and recently retired from the retail department store business. She lives in the Blue Ash suburb of Cincinnati, Ohio.

### Children of Betty Joanne Robertson

VIII. **Gary Gene Winterhalter**, born on December 18, 1951, in Cincinnati, Hamilton County, Ohio, the first son of Betty Joanne Robertson and Gene Winterhalter. He attended the University of Toledo.

Gary married *Joanne Farmer*, who was born on January 17, 1950, in Toledo, Ohio. He and Joanne live in Argyle, Texas, north of the Dallas-Fort Worth area, and have three children. Gary is executive vice president of a company that supplies fixtures and equipment for beauty shops and salons.

### Children of Gary Gene Winterhalter

IX. **Brianna Audris Winterhalter**, born on September 16, 1979, in Akron, Ohio.

IX. **Adrienne Serena Winterhalter**, born on January 3, 1983, in Akron, Ohio.

IX. **Stephen Gene Winterhalter**, born on January 30, 1986, in Akron, Ohio.

VIII. **Michael Wayne Winterhalter**, born in Cincinnati, Hamilton County, Ohio, on August 25, 1953, the second son of Betty Joanne Robertson and Gene Winterhalter. On July 26, 1974, in Cincinnati, Ohio, Mike married *Vicki Biehle*. She was born on September 8, 1953, in Loveland, Clermont County, Ohio, the daughter of Margaret and George Biehle. Mike and Vicki reside in Cincinnati,

Ohio, and have two daughters. He works for Precision Motors, which sells and services luxury automobiles, and Vicki is an anesthetist.

### Children of Michael Wayne Winterhalter

IX. **Jennifer Lynne Winterhalter**, born on February 9, 1981, in Cincinnati, Hamilton County, Ohio.

IX. **Rebecca Anne Winterhalter**, born on July 22, 1984, in Cincinnati, Hamilton County, Ohio.

VIII. **Bruce William Winterhalter**, born on October 27, 1957, in Toledo, Ohio, the third son of Betty Joanne Robertson and Gene Winterhalter. He is a graduate of the University of Cincinnati, where he studied accounting.

On June 28, 1986, in Cincinnati, he married a woman named *Connie* (whose maiden name is not available to us). They live in Loveland, Clermont County, Ohio, and have two children. Bruce works as an accountant with the Baldwin Piano Company in Loveland.

### Children of Bruce Winterhalter

IX. **Bradley William Winterhalter**, born on June 20, 1988, in Cincinnati, Hamilton County, Ohio.

IX. **Heather Marie Winterhalter**, born on February 5, 1991, in Cincinnati, Hamilton County, Ohio.

VIII. **Lori Ann Winterhalter**, daughter of Betty Joanne Robertson and Gene Winterhalter, was born on May 18, 1961, in Toledo, Ohio. On April 25, 1987, she married *Douglas Finamore* in Cincinnati, Ohio. Doug was born on June 30, 1960, in Hamilton, Butler County, Ohio. They live in Deer Park, near Cincinnati, Hamilton County, Ohio, and have two sons.

### Children of Lori Ann Winterhalter

IX. **Shawn Michael Finamore**, born on September 24, 1988, in Cincinnati, Hamilton County, Ohio.

IX. **<u>Joshua David Finamore</u>**, born on January 21, 1993, in Cincinnati, Hamilton County, Ohio.

VII. **<u>Delores Ann Robertson</u>** (called "Dee"), second daughter of Marion Lomatsch and Charles W. Robertson, born on November 21, 1940, in Cincinnati, Hamilton County, Ohio. She graduated with a Bachelor of Science degree from the College of Nursing and Health of the University of Cincinnati.

Dee is married to *<u>Hugh Joseph Lewin</u>* (called "Joe"). He was born on January 3, 1940, in Cincinnati, the son of Gustav Lewin and Vera Mae Burnett. Dee and Joe were married at Eastminster Presbyterian Church in Cincinnati on November 24, 1961, and are active in the Lutheran Church. They have four children.

Dee is certified as a gerontologist and worked in physical therapy at Good Samaritan Hospital in Baltimore. Joe is a graduate of the College Conservatory of Music of the University of Cincinnati and has worked in the television industry in Cincinnati as well as Richmond, Virginia, and other parts of the United States. Until 1996, he was general manager of the WMAR television station in Baltimore, Maryland. He then accepted a position in Moscow, Russia, with Story First Communications, a California company that operates eight television stations in the major Russian cities. They resided in Moscow, and Dee worked as a nurse in the US Embassy there. They have now returned to the States and have settled near Harrisburg, Pennsylvania, where Joe is managing a television broadcast station.

### Children of Delores Ann Robertson

VIII. **<u>Christopher Charles Lewin</u>** was born on March 7, 1963, in Cincinnati, Hamilton County, Ohio. He graduated in 1984 from Miami University in Oxford, Ohio, with a B.A. degree in English. Chris works in sales of industrial equipment with Allied Abrasives in Cincinnati. He also takes graduate business courses at Xavier University in Cincinnati, working toward a M.B.A. degree.

On April 20, 1991, Chris married *<u>Ann Richards</u>* in Cincinnati, Ohio. The daughter of Sally and Buzz Richards, Ann was born on May 7, 1962, in Connecticut. With two daughters, they live in Cincinnati.

### Children of Christopher Charles Lewin

IX. **Emily Ann Lewin**, born on March 8, 1994, in Cincinnati, Ohio.

IX. **Rachel Sarah Lewin**, born on June 24, 1995, in Cincinnati, Ohio.

VIII. **Andrew Burnett Lewin**, born on December 25, 1964, in Cincinnati, Hamilton County, Ohio. He studied wildlife management at Hocking Technical School in Ohio.

Andy Lewin married *Elizabeth Ann Carroll* (called "Beth") on April 8, 1989. Beth, the daughter of Betty and James Carroll, was born on February 22, 1963, in Winchester, Virginia, where her mother is president of F&M Bank. They have three children and live in Clear Brook, Winchester, Virginia.

Beth Lewin is the founder and president of Carroll Construction Company, a paving and road-construction contracting business in which her husband, Andy, is also active. They also own the Piccadilly Kitchen Store in Winchester.

### Children of Andrew Burnett Lewin

IX. **Jenna Ann Lewin**, born on October 29, 1990, in Winchester, Virginia.

IX. **Jacob Andrew Lewin**, born on September 9, 1993, in Winchester, Virginia.

IX. **Brett Alexander Lewin**, born on June 5, 1995, in Winchester, Virginia.

VIII. **Joel David Lewin**, born on October 24, 1966, in Shreveport, Louisiana. He graduated in 1989 from the College of William and Mary in Williamsburg, Virginia, earning a degree in business administration, and did postgraduate work in the field of sports administration at Ohio University in Athens, Ohio.

Joel married *Eleanor Carroll* in Long Island, New York, on May 21, 1994. Eleanor was born on May 23, 1967, in New York. Her parents, Mary and Patrick Carroll, are Irish nationals now residing in New York. Eleanor received her B.A. degree from William and Mary and, in 1996, received a Master's degree in business administration from Fordham University in New York. Joel works in television program sales for Time Warner in New York City. They live in Rockville Center, Long Island, New York, and have two children.

### Children of Joel David Lewin

IX. **<u>Deirdre Lewin</u>**, born on January 14, 1998, in Rockville Center, New York.

IX. **<u>Pierce Charles Lewin</u>**, born on March 12, 1999, in Rockville Center, New York.

VIII. **<u>Cara Ann Lewin</u>**, born on February 18, 1971, in Cincinnati, Hamilton County, Ohio. She is a 1992 graduate of Radford College in Virginia, where she majored in communications.

Cara married *Christopher Scott Rathel* at the historic Long Branch Plantation in Millwood, Virginia, on September 20, 1997. He was born in Winchester, Virginia, the son of Linda Lee Branton and Freddie Larry Rathel of Columbus, Georgia. They are living in Winchester, Virginia, where Cara is attending Shenandoah University to obtain her teaching certificate. They have one child.

### Child of Cara Ann Lewin

IX. **<u>Emma Catherine Rathel</u>**, born on July 31, 1999 in Winchester, Virginia.

VII. **Thomas William Robertson**, born in Cincinnati, Hamilton County, Ohio, on June 15, 1943. He graduated from Withrow High School in Cincinnati and worked for the Cincinnati & Suburban Bell Telephone Company. On about October 1, 1968, he married *Ellie Butler* in Cincinnati. They had one son, Scot, and divorced. Tom died in Cincinnati, Ohio, on December 12, 1981. Ellie still lives in Cincinnati.

### Child of Thomas William Robertson

VIII. **<u>Scot William Robertson</u>**, born in Cincinnati, Ohio, on March 18, 1970. He graduated from Ohio State University, majoring in telecommunications and electronic media. Scot founded a private investigation company, Vision Investigations, in Westerville, Ohio.

On December 11, 1993, Scot married *Marcia Elizabeth Lowder* in Columbus, Ohio. The daughter of Harriett and Jerry Lowder, Marcia was born on December 30, 1969, in Bloomington, Indiana. They divorced, having no children.

## 6-C.8: GRACE ELIZABETH ROBERTSON (1918-1995)
### Daughter of Charles Andrew Robertson

VI. **Grace Elizabeth Robertson**, oldest daughter of Georgia Conner and Charles Andrew Robertson (5-C.3 above), was born on May 20, 1918, in Cincinnati, Hamilton County, Ohio. She married *Alfred John Guidi*, who was born on May 27, 1917, son of Pietro Guidi of Barga in Tuscany, Italy. They lived in Cincinnati and had three sons. Al Guidi owned and operated an automotive transmission company for some thirty-seven years. He died on April 20, 1990, at the age of seventy-two. Grace died on February 21, 1995, in Cincinnati, Ohio. They are both buried in Oak Hill Cemetery.

**Children of Grace Elizabeth Robertson**

VII. **Ronald Arthur Guidi**, born on October 28, 1942, in Cincinnati, Hamilton County, Ohio, is the oldest son of Grace Robertson and Alfred Guidi. His wife was *Cathy* (maiden name unknown). They had one daughter and divorced. Ronald lives in Newtown, near Cincinnati.

**Child of Ronald Arthur Guidi**

VIII. **Samantha Noel Guidi**, born on December 24, 1986, in Cincinnati, Ohio.

VII. **John Charles Guidi**, second son of Grace Robertson and Al Guidi, was born on March 28, 1947, in Cincinnati, Ohio. John first married *Barbara Webb*. After one son, the marriage ended in divorce. In 1984, John married *Priscilla Bardes* of Cincinnati, daughter of Priscilla Garrison and Oliver Bardes. They divorced after having two children.

**Children of John Charles Guidi**

VIII. **Anthony Franchot Guidi**, born on June 6, 1966, in Cincinnati,

Hamilton County, Ohio, son of Barbara Webb and John Guidi. He received the B.Arch. degree in architecture from the University of Cincinnati in 1987.

In 1988, Tony married _Gina Lawhorn_; they later divorced. Second, he married _Amanda Tinney_, daughter of Carol Fisher and John Tinney, in Cincinnati in 1991. They have two daughters. Tony runs Link Network Systems, a computer firm in Cincinnati specializing in network applications for businesses.

### Children of Anthony Franchot Guidi

IX. **Lauren Ashley Guidi**, born on September 17, 1993, in Cincinnati, Ohio.

IX. **Grace Alexandra Guidi**, born on September 28, 1998, in Cincinnati, Ohio.

VIII. **Richy Guidi**, born on May 31, 1985, in Cincinnati, Hamilton County, Ohio, son of Priscilla Bardes and John Guidi.

VIII. **Christian Guidi**, born about 1989, in Cincinnati, Hamilton County, Ohio.

VII. **Alfred John Guidi Jr.**, born on June 2, 1955, in Cincinnati, Hamilton County, Ohio, third son of Grace Robertson and Alfred Guidi. He married _Kimberly Anne Hughes_ in Cincinnati on September 16, 1977. Kim was born in Cincinnati on December 31, 1957, daughter of William Edward Hughes and Joan Irene Poppe (who is a genealogist and expert in the early settlements of Hamilton County). Kim works for Electronic Data Systems (EDS), and Al handles sales of two-way radio communications systems for Motorola in Northern Kentucky. They live in Florence, Kentucky, and have three children.

### Children of Alfred John Guidi Jr.

VIII. **Gina Marie Guidi**, born on March 9, 1979, in Cincinnati, Hamilton County, Ohio. She works for Delta Air Lines in Cincinnati.

VIII. **Angela Michelle Guidi**, born on June 9, 1982, in Cincinnati, Hamilton County, Ohio.

VIII. **Michael Angilo Guidi**, born on November 1, 1983, in Cincinnati, Hamilton County, Ohio.

## 6-C.9: JAMES REUBEN ROBERTSON (1922-1997)
### Son of Charles Andrew Robertson

VI. **James Reuben Robertson** was born on November 13, 1922, in Cincinnati, Ohio. The youngest child of Georgia Conner and Charles Andrew Robertson (5-C.3 above), Jim's father died when he was only four months old.

He married *Dorothy Grosch* (called "Dottie") in Cincinnati, Ohio, on July 17, 1947. She was the daughter of Kate Graf and Charles Grosch and was born in Cincinnati on October 15, 1920. Dottie and Jim had three children and lived in the Cincinnati area, where he worked as a pipefitter in construction. Dottie died of a stroke on May 16, 1997, and Jim died just a month later, on June 21, 1997. He was seventy-four.

**Children of James Reuben Robertson**

VII. **Katherine Ann Robertson**, eldest daughter of Dorothy Grosch and James R. Robertson, was born on December 29, 1948, in Cincinnati, Ohio. She first married *Dallas Spear* in Cincinnati, Ohio, on September 22, 1967. He worked in archeology. They had no children and divorced in 1970. Second, Kathy married *Clifford Bradley Himmler* on December 22, 1970, in Cincinnati. Brad was born on November 10, 1943, the son of Lois Abenshaun and Clifford C. Himmler. They had one son and divorced in 1994. Kathy owns and manages a restaurant called the Hungry Bear Diner in Batavia, Ohio, a suburb of Cincinnati.

**Child of Katherine Ann Robertson**

VIII. **Brian Himmler**, son of Katherine Robertson and Brad Himmler, was born on May 18, 1973, in Cincinnati, Ohio. He married *Alicia McGown* of Detroit in Las Vegas, Nevada, and they make their home in Cincinnati.

A professional bowler, Brian plays on the Professional Bowlers Association (PBA) tour. Noted for a powerful, gutsy style of bowling, he placed second in the 1997 Tucson Open and is one of the top ten members of the PBA tour. On April

12, 1997, Brian was featured on national television as a challenger in the Bud Light Championship, shown on ABC's *Wide World of Sports*. The commentators described Brian on that show as a "really good young player" and emphasized that "we're going to hear about Brian Himmler in the future."

VII. **James Melvin Robertson** (called "Jamie"), son of Dorothy Grosch and James R. Robertson, was born on July 4, 1950, in Cincinnati, Ohio. Jamie married *Sandra Taylor*, daughter of Virginia and Robert C. Taylor, on June 12, 1970, in Cincinnati. Divorced in 1976, they had two children.

On February 19, 1994, Jamie married *Janice Strohl* in Cincinnati, Ohio. Janice was born on February 19, 1953, in Columbus, Ohio, the daughter of Jo Anne and Joseph Strohl. A business graduate of Eastern Kentucky University, Jamie is the manufacturing manager for Senco, an industrial fastener company that manufactures pneumatic nailing machines and staple guns. Janice works for the Procter & Gamble Company. They reside in Anderson Township, a suburb of Cincinnati.

### Children of James Melvin Robertson

VIII. **James Ryan Robertson** (called "Ryan"), born on April 13, 1973, in Cincinnati, Ohio. Ryan graduated with a B.S. degree in business from the University of Cincinnati. He married *Michelle Anne Weckesser* on July 18, 1998, in Cincinnati. She is a native of Cincinnati, the daughter of Linda and Gerhardt Weckesser of Germany. Ryan and Michelle live in Cincinnati.

VIII **Heather Jo Robertson**, born on May 23, 1976, in Cincinnati, Ohio. She received her B.A. degree from Ohio University in Athens, Ohio. Heather lives in Cincinnati and is an elementary school teacher.

VII. **Tami Lynn Robertson**, second daughter of Dorothy Grosch and James R. Robertson, was born on September 20, 1964, in Cincinnati, Ohio. She married *Glenn Alan Schrichten* on September 10, 1988, in Cincinnati. Glenn, the son of Rosella Fillie and Gordon Schrichten, was born on November 15, 1959, in Cincinnati and works in the maintenance department in a large retail mall. Tammy is employed as a bookkeeper in the hardware business in Cincinnati. They have no children.

## 6-C.10: Esther Kathryn Robertson (1915- )
### Daughter of William Hillman Robertson

VI. **Esther Kathryn Robertson**, second daughter of Sarah Rebekah Leisher and William Hillman Robertson (5-C.4 above), was born in Canton, Haywood County, North Carolina, on October 20, 1915. She married *Ralph Schofner Crawford* on August 11, 1941, in Buncombe County, North Carolina. He was born in Camden, Benton County, Tennessee, on July 1, 1912, the son of Vera McElyes and Albert Boyd Crawford of Tennessee. They had two children.

Ralph died in Hendersonville, North Carolina, on January 9, 1969, and is buried in Shepard Memorial Park near there. Esther is retired from General Electric Company, where she worked as an executive secretary, and resides in Hendersonville.

**Children of Esther Kathryn Robertson**

VII. **Laura Jeanne Crawford**, born on August 7, 1946, in Buncombe County, North Carolina. She graduated from King College in Bristol, Tennessee, with a B.A. degree in psychology and did graduate study at the University of Tennessee.

Laura married *Howard Edwin Overcast* in the First Presbyterian Church in Hendersonville, North Carolina, on December 21, 1968. He was born on June 20, 1947, in Knoxville, Tennessee, son of Helen Love McClellan and Dr. Woodrow Webb Overcast. Ed is an economist in the natural gas industry. They had daughters and are divorced. Laura resides in Lilburn, Georgia, a suburb of Atlanta, and works in the property and casualty department of Safeco Insurance Company.

**Children of Laura Jeanne Crawford**

VIII. **Jennifer Dawn Overcast**, born on October 7, 1972, in Burlington, Alamance County, North Carolina. She received a B.S. degree in chemistry from Furman University in 1994 and is working on a doctorate in analytical chemistry at the Georgia Institute of Technology (Georgia Tech) in Atlanta.

VIII. **Kimberly Michelle Overcast**, born on September 1, 1976, in Johnson City, Tennessee. She is a student at Georgia State University with a dual major in English and Spanish.

VIII. **Rebekah Love Overcast**, born on April 11, 1978, in Chattanooga, Tennessee. She is a student at the University of Alaska in Fairbanks, Alaska.

VIII. **Bethany Ann Overcast**, born on August 29, 1980, in Manchester, Hartford County, Connecticut.

VII. **William Boyd Crawford**, born on August 31, 1947, in Buncombe County, North Carolina. Bill pursued a military career in the U.S. Army, retiring with the rank of lieutenant colonel.

On April 25, 1970, Bill Crawford married *Julia Ann Ulmer* in the Methodist Church in Walterboro, South Carolina. She was born on December 21, 1947, at Fort Bragg, North Carolina, daughter of Eunice Murdaugh and Colonel Boswell Risher Ulmer Jr. of Walterboro. Both Bill and Julie are graduates of Baptist College in Charleston, South Carolina. They have two children and live on a farm in Ashland City, Tennessee.

During his military career, Bill served in Vietnam, in Germany, in the Pentagon in Washington, D.C., and at various other Army posts. At the time of his retirement, he was stationed at Fort Campbell, Kentucky, (his fourth tour of duty there). Since then, Bill and Julie have been involved in the antique business and have a company called Kitchen Kupboard Antiques.

### Children of William Boyd Crawford

VIII. **William Boyd Crawford Jr.**, born on February 13, 1972, at Ft. Rucker, Alabama. On August 1, 1998, he married *Clara Savage* in Franklin, Tennessee.

VIII. **Kelly Diane Crawford**, born on December 29, 1974, in Clarksville, Tennessee. She is pursuing a degree in education at Austin Peay State University. She has one son.

### Child of Kelly Diane Crawford

IX. **Riley William Crawford**, born on December 14, 1997, in Clarksville, Tennessee.

## 6-C.11: WILLIAM DAVIS ROBERTSON (1917- )
### Son of William Hillman Robertson

VI. **<u>William Davis Robertson</u>**, fourth child of Sarah Rebekah Leisher and William Hillman Robertson (5-C.4 above), was born in Canton, North Carolina, on August 29, 1917. On June 16, 1940, Bill married *Nettie Mae Robertson* in Greenville, South Carolina. Born on May 14, 1920, in Macon County, North Carolina, Nettie's parents were Margarette Pearl Sorrells and Robert Monroe Robertson. Bill and Nettie have four children. Bill retired from Champion International after forty-two years of service, and they reside in Canton, North Carolina.

**Children of William Davis Robertson**

VII. **<u>Sandra Lee Robertson</u>**, first daughter of Nettie Mae and William Davis Robertson, was born on January 16, 1942, in Waynesville, Haywood County, North Carolina. She married *Robert Edward Lee* on March 28, 1963, in Spartanburg, South Carolina. The son of Naomi Gregg and Orrin Lee, he was born on January 9, 1942. They had one daughter and divorced.

Sandra's second marriage was in Las Vegas, Nevada, on October 1, 1967. *James Franklin Hudson Jr.* was born on February 11, 1938, in Chicago, Illinois, son of Irene Altheide and James Frank Hudson. They live in Albuquerque, New Mexico. She is manager of Sandia Laboratories in Albuquerque. James is an engineer.

**Child of Sandra Lee Robertson**

VIII. **<u>Rebekah Kristine (Lee) Hudson</u>** (called "Kris"), daughter of Sandra Lee Robertson and Robert Edward Lee, was born on June 6, 1964, in Albuquerque, New Mexico. Her last name was changed to Hudson upon adoption by her mother's second husband in 1968. Kris married *James Robert Reddin* on November 27, 1987, in Mount Holly, Arkansas. The son of Alice Lawana Gandy and Robert Ward Reddin, James was born on March 8, 1968. They have two children and reside in Haywood County, North Carolina.

**Children of Rebekah Kristine (Lee) Hudson**

IX. **<u>Branden Scott Reddin</u>**, born on May 4, 1988, in El Dorado, Union County, Arkansas.

IX. **<u>Colby Ryan Reddin</u>**, born on February 15, 1991, in Asheville, Buncombe County, North Carolina.

VII. **<u>Charles William Robertson</u>**, oldest son of Nettie Mae and William Davis Robertson, born on August 17, 1947, in Asheville, North Carolina. Unmarried, Charlie works at the Little Boy Restaurant in Canton, North Carolina.

VII. **<u>James Jerome Robertson</u>**, second son of Nettie Mae and William Davis Robertson, born on March 30, 1949, in Waynesville, Haywood County, North Carolina. James married *Vicki Lynn Kuykendall* in Haywood County. They have no children. After they moved to Los Angeles, California, they divorced.

James married *Tina Turner* on May 14, 1976, in Las Vegas, Clark County, Nevada. Tina was born on July 10, 1960, in Hagerstown, Maryland, the daughter of Patricia Socks and Erwin George Turner and the adoptive daughter of Patricia Sprankle and Frederick Turner. Tina and James had two daughters, both of whom currently live with their mother in Williamsport, Maryland. James lives in Asheville, North Carolina, where he is a newspaper pressman.

**Children of James Jerome Robertson**

VIII. **<u>Shelley Dawn Robertson</u>**, born on April 11, 1977, in Arcadia, Los Angeles County, California.

VIII. **<u>Jessica Ann Robertson</u>**, born on January 31, 1980, in La Mirada, Orange County, California.

VII. **<u>Kathryn Elizabeth Robertson</u>**, second daughter of Nettie Mae and William Davis Robertson, was born on February 21, 1955, in Waynesville, Haywood County, North Carolina. On August 1, 1973, she married *Stanley Aldrege Shumolis* of Haywood County, North Carolina, son of Lucille Ann Henderson and George Wayne Shumolis. Now divorced, they had one daughter.

Kathryn married *Michael Dale Warren* (called "Duke"), the son of Rheba Metcalf and Wayne Doyle Warren, on September 2, 1989, in Haywood County, North Carolina. He was born there on September 3, 1957. They reside near Canton, North Carolina, and have a daughter.

**Children of Kathryn Elizabeth Robertson**

VIII. **Tracy Yvonne Shumolis**, born on March 2, 1974, in Haywood County, North Carolina, daughter of Kathryn Robertson and Stanley Shumolis. She is a 1996 graduate of Berea College in Berea, Kentucky, where she studied horticulture. Tracy married *Brian Thomas Russell* on September 28, 1996, at the Canton Presbyterian Church in Canton, North Carolina. He is the son of Luzean and Tommy Russell. Tracy works at the world-renowned gardens of the Biltmore Estate in Asheville.

VIII. **Josey Kathryn Warren**, born on October 14, 1992, in Haywood County, North Carolina, daughter of Kathryn Elizabeth Robertson and Michael Dale Warren.

## 6-C.12: DOROTHY HOPE ROBERTSON (1926- )
### Daughter of William Hillman Robertson

VI. **Dorothy Hope Robertson** (called "Dodie"), twin sister of George Reuben Robertson, was born in Canton, North Carolina, on December 22, 1926, the daughter of Sarah Rebekah Leisher and William Hillman Robertson (5-C.4 above).

On October 11, 1944, during World War II, Dodie married *Michael Romanchuk*, the older brother of her sister-in-law Mary Romanchuk Robertson, who had married Dodie's brother Bert (5-C.4 above). Michael was born on October 30, 1919, in Allentown, Pennsylvania, the son of Theodore Frank Romanchuk and Mary Gowan Farynick of Emmaus, Pennsylvania, a suburb of the Allentown/Bethlehem area. He was a master technical sergeant with the U.S.Marine Corps during World War II, on active duty in the South Pacific theater.

Dorothy and Michael settled in Hellertown, Pennsylvania, and had four children, including a son who died as a young man in Vietnam. Their daughters were the first set of twins born in the Norburn Hospital in Asheville, North Carolina. Dorothy and Michael were active in the Moravian Church, a Protestant denomination founded in the eighteenth century by Czech followers of the martyr Jan Hus. Dodie, with a lyric soprano voice, is a soloist for the church choir.

Michael worked for thirty-two years as a welder and in other jobs with the Champion Spark Plug Company before retiring in 1982. He died of a heart attack on October 29, 1997, one day short of his seventy-eighth birthday.

**Children of Dorothy Hope Robertson**

VII. **Michael George Romanchuk**, born in Asheville, Buncombe County, North Carolina on October 18, 1946. He was very interested in the Boy Scouts as a lad and became an Eagle Scout and patrol leader. Blond, blue-eyed, tall and muscular, he was a student leader and played quarterback on the football team while in high school. Mike enlisted in the military service following graduation. He died of injuries suffered in combat in Danang, Vietnam, on December 26, 1966. He was only twenty years old. A lance corporal in the U.S. Marine Corps, Mike was working as radio man in an amphibious armored vehicle when it was destroyed by a land mine. He lived for a few days after the explosion, but the injuries he suffered proved too severe for him to survive. Mike is buried in Hellertown, Pennsylvania.

VII. **Dorothy Amelia Romanchuk** (called "Amy"), another second-generation twin, was born in Asheville, North Carolina, on August 30, 1947. She married *Charles Joseph Schamenek III* on November 25, 1967, in Hellertown, Northampton County, Pennsylvania. He was born on April 1, 1940, in Pennsylvania, the son of Ann Gombocz and Charles Joseph Schamenek Jr. Amy and Charlie divorced about 1981. They had two children, who live with their father in Missouri City, Texas.

Amy's second marriage was to *Gary Straughan* on March 20, 1992, in Houston, Texas, with another ceremony held in Downey, California, where he was the pastor of a Moravian church. He has three grown children from a previous marriage. They reside in Hope, Indiana.

**Children of Dorothy Amelia Romanchuk**

VIII. <u>**Vanessa Colette Schamenek**</u>, born on May 2, 1971, in Galveston, Texas. She graduated from Abilene Christian University in Abilene, Texas, with a degree in psychology in December 1994.

VIII. <u>**Alexander Schamenek**</u>, born on August 24, 1972, in Galveston, Texas. Alex is taking courses in architectural design.

VII. **Rebekah Mary Romanchuk** (called "Becky") is a second-generation twin sister of Amy Romanchuk. She was born in Asheville, North Carolina, on August 30, 1947. She married *Gary Lee Ruhf* in Elkton, Maryland, on February 13, 1969. Gary was born on December 10, 1946, in Bethlehem, Northampton County, Pennsylvania. He is the son of Edward Reissmiller and Dorothy Marley—Dorothy's second husband was Carl Ruhf, hence the name—and served in the U.S. Marines in Vietnam. They live in Bethlehem, Pennsylvania and have two children.

**Children of Rebekah Mary Romanchuk**

VIII. <u>**Michael Eldon Ruhf**</u>, born on November 9, 1969, in Kaneohe, Oahu, Hawaii. He lives in Allentown, Pennsylvania, and has one child.

**Child of Michael Eldon Ruhf**

IX. <u>**Joshua Dillon Lee Ruhf**</u>, born on August 21, 1993, in Allentown, Pennsylvania.

VIII. <u>**Heather Rebekah Ruhf**</u>, born on May 15, 1975, in Allentown, Lehigh County, Pennsylvania. Heather married *Fred Anthony III* (called "Trey") on December 21, 1994, and they have two children. They live in Ashley, Pennsylvania. Fred works as an electrician.

**Child of Heather Rebekah Ruhf**

IX. <u>**Damian Eagle Anthony**</u>, born on December 7, 1993, in Allentown, Pennsylvania.

IX. **Michael Hawk Anthony**, born on November 30, 1995, in Wilkes-Barre, Pennsylvania.

VII.  **Martin Keith Romanchuk** (called "Marty"), born in Allentown, Pennsylvania, on May 17, 1955. Unmarried, he lives in the Allentown, Pennsylvania, area and works in the computer field. He has also been taking course work at Allentown Community College, which is associated with Pennsylvania State University.

## 6-C.13: ALICE RUBY ROBERTSON (1917-1982)
### Daughter of Albert Dewey Robertson

VI. **Alice Ruby Robertson**, eldest daughter of Edith Emma Signor and Albert Dewey Robertson (4-F above), was born on June 11, 1917, in Fort Monroe, Virginia. On December 2, 1933, in North Carolina, Alice married *William Degyansky*. He was born on November 22, 1910, in Altoona, Pennsylvania, son of Fanny and Albert Degyansky. Bill was a career military officer, retiring from the U.S. Army with the rank of lieutenant colonel after twenty-eight years of service.

Alice and Bill had one son. Bill died in 1965 in El Paso, Texas, and Alice died there on February 7, 1982, at the age of sixty-four.

**Child of Alice Ruby Robertson**

VII. **Albert William Degyansky**, only child of Alice and Bill Degyansky, was born on January 20, 1943, at Fort Monroe, Virginia. Al attended Texas A&M University in College Station, Texas, graduating in 1964 with a B.A. degree in business administration. He was commissioned as an infantry officer, serving in the U.S. Army in the Vietnam War and elsewhere for twenty years. In 1975, the Army sent him back to graduate school at Northwest Missouri State University, from which he received his M.B.A. in 1975.

After retiring from the Army with the rank of lieutenant colonel, Al went to work for General Motors in military vehicles production in Indiana. He later transferred to Allison Gas Turbines Company, where he works on producing generators for Navy ships.

Al married *Diana Louise Lewis* on June 13, 1965. Diana, the daughter of Eulalia ("Lila") Chavaria and William Lewis, was born in Silver City, New Mexico, on September 22, 1942. She and Al were the parents of a son and a daughter, Andy and Dena. Diana died in Carmel, Indiana, on February 14, 1991.

Al remarried on September 1, 1995, in Gatlinburg, Tennessee. His second wife is *Meribeth Miller*. She has a son from a previous marriage, Andrew Paskins. Meribeth and Al reside in Fishers, Indiana, near Indianapolis.

### Children of Albert William Degyansky

VIII. **Andrew William Degyansky** was born on August 9, 1971, in Cincinnati, Ohio. Andy completed his undergraduate college education at Regis University in Denver, Colorado, earning a Bachelor of Arts degree in the field of psychology. He is the director of a preschool program in Arvada, Colorado, and is pursuing a postgraduate degree in education at Regis. Andy's partner is *Emily Taylor*, a native of Indianapolis. Avid skiers, they live in Louisville, Colorado, between Denver and Boulder and convenient to the ski slopes of the Colorado Rocky Mountains. They have one son.

### Child of Andrew William Degyansky

IX. **Ashton William Degyansky**, born on April 21, 1996, in Louisville, Colorado.

VIII. **Dena Louise Degyansky**, born on January 4, 1974, in Cincinnati, Hamilton County, Ohio. An outstanding tennis player, she graduated from Purdue University in Lafayette, Indiana, with a Bachelor of Science degree in hotel management. Dena works in convention sales for Hyatt Hotels in Chicago, Illinois.

## 6-C.14: ALBERTA DAISY ROBERTSON (1921- )
### Daughter of Albert Dewey Robertson

VI. **Alberta Daisy Robertson** (called "Bertie"), second daughter of Edith Emma Signor and Albert Dewey Robertson (4-F above), was born on April 18, 1921, in Fort Monroe,

Virginia. She has been crippled since infancy as a result of polio contracted when she was three months old. Bertie defied medical predictions that she would not even survive childhood and has been able to enjoy a productive and adventurous life.

At the age of nineteen, Bertie married *Carl Joseph Bender* on September 7, 1940, in Fort Monroe. He was born on August 17, 1917, in McKeesport, Pennsylvania, the son of Otelia Loeprich and Joseph Bender. Carl's career was in the military service with the U.S. Army and U.S. Air Force, in which he was a warrant officer and technical sergeant. Until 1953, when they were finally able to settle in at MacDill Air Force Base in Tampa, Florida, the family had to move frequently from place to place as a result of Carl's military transfers. He retired from the service in June 1959.

Bertie and Carl raised four sons. In 1957, Bertie was honored as "Mother of the Year" at MacDill Air Force Base. Carl also was a talented musician, singer, and entertainer and frequently gave performances playing trumpet, mandolin, and other instruments at clubs and parties in the Tampa area. In addition to those talents, he handled an extensive home delivery service for the *Tampa Tribune* newspaper.

Carl died of a stroke on August 20, 1975, in Tampa, Florida, three days after celebrating his fifty-eighth birthday. Bertie lives in the family home in Tampa with two of her grown sons. Taking advantage of her ability to "beat the odds," Bertie is a dedicated Bingo player and claims to come out ahead. She also travels frequently to visit relatives in Cincinnati.

**Children of Alberta Daisy Robertson**

VII. **Carl Albert Bender**, oldest son of Alberta Robertson and Carl Bender, was born on November 5, 1941, in Fort Monroe, Virginia. He married *Barbara Oliver*. They later divorced, and she remarried. A talented musician and entertainer, Carl sings and plays guitar professionally, with a vocal style and quality similar to John Denver. He resides at his mother's home in Tampa, Florida.

**Children of Carl Bender**

VIII. **Matthew Cadell Bender**, born on September 29, 1969, in Olean, New York. He married *Leika McKinney*, who was born in New Port Richey, Florida. With two children, they divorced in October 1994. Matthew also has an infant son. In late 1997, he was residing with his mother in Okeechobee, Florida, and working in construction.

**Children of Matthew Cadell Bender**

IX. **Lacie Mali Bender**, born on January 23, 1992, in Gainesville, Florida.

IX. **Jonathan Beau Bender**, born on October 19, 1994, in Gainesville, Florida.

IX. **Robert William Bender**, born about October 1995.

VII. **Henry Allen Bender**, born on October 26, 1943, in Jessup, Georgia. Following his high school graduation in Tampa, Florida, Henry worked in banking. Later, he was employed at an insurance brokerage company in Chicago, where he met and fell in love with *Kathleen Frances Burns*. They were married in Chicago, Illinois, on October 12, 1968. Kathy was born on October 23, 1948, in Evergreen Park, Illinois, the daughter of Margaret Madigan and Edward Burns.

Henry and Kathy settled in California. Henry works in the insurance brokerage business there, and Kathy attends John F. Kennedy University in Orinda, California. They have two grown sons and reside in Hayward, California.

**Children of Henry Allen Bender**

VIII. **Michael Allen Bender**, born on February 21, 1970, in Oak Park, Illinois. He lives in Hayward, California, working as a manager in a glass company. He is unmarried.

VIII. **Kevin Christopher Bender**, born on December 19, 1971, in Oak Park, Illinois. He married *Cynthia Scadera*. on February 3, 1991, in Watertown, New York. Cynthia was born about July 30, 1970, in Watertown. Kevin joined the U.S. Army following his junior year in high school and served for several years as an enlisted man. He is now a civilian employee of the Army at Fort Drum near Watertown, New York, where the couple lives. They have no children.

VII. **William Edward Bender**, born on July 17, 1945, in McKeesport, Pennsylvania. Bill married *Mary Frances McGee.* on July 30, 1966, in Tampa, Florida. She was born on July 27, 1948, at MacDill Air Force Base in Tampa, Hillsborough County, Florida, the daughter of Mary Ellen Greenleaf and John Nathaniel McGee.

Mary and Bill have one son, Brian, and have lived since March 1977 at Islamorada in the Florida keys. Having worked for years as a licensed air conditioning contractor, Bill retired from that business and became a backcountry fishing guide and charter boat captain. Mary is a merchandising representative for American Greetings.

### Child of William Edward Bender

VIII. **Brian Stephen Bender**, born on December 1, 1974, in Tampa, Hillsborough County, Florida. He married *Tami Anne Wester*, daughter of Mr. and Mrs. Burton D. Wester, in Gainesville, Florida, on March 12, 1997.

VII. **Robert Bender**, youngest son of Alberta Robertson and Carl Bender, was born on September 28, 1948, at Tindall Air Force Base, Panama City, Florida. Bob married *Denise Claire Destremps* on June 20, 1970, in St. Petersburg, Florida. Denise was born on January 5, 1952, in Fall River, Massachusetts.

Bob and Denise had two children, Christina and Bobby. They divorced in August 1981. Bob was with the *Tampa Tribune* newspaper company for over twenty-seven years, rising to crew-operator-in-charge. In 1997, he moved to Cincinnati, Ohio, and is working there in the printing business. He is engaged to marry Barbara Martin of Cincinnati in the spring of 1998.

Bob is very interested in the spiritual side of life and, in particular, the writings and prophecies of the mystic Edgar Cayce. Bill was involved for several years in production management for the "Up With People" movement.

### Children of Robert Bender

VIII. **Christina Louise Bender** (called "Christie"), born on January 9, 1971, in Tampa, Hillsborough County, Florida. She married *Al Alexander* in St. Petersburg, Florida, on July 19, 1994. Now living in Tampa, Christie and Al have one daughter.

### Child of Christina Louise Bender

IX. <u>**Haley Ann Alexander**</u>, born on July 11, 1997, in St. Petersburg, Florida.

VIII. <u>**Robert Scott Bender**</u>, born on November 30, 1973, in Tampa, Florida. Bob married *Star Hyatt* about 1996 in St. Petersburg, Florida. They have a daughter and live in St. Petersburg.

### Child of Robert Scott Bender

IX. <u>**Alissa Bender**</u>, born on May 16, 1996, in St. Petersburg, Florida.

## 6-C.15: ESTHER LOIS ROBERTSON (1924- )
### Daughter of Levi Morton Robertson

VI. <u>**Esther Lois Robertson**</u>, the daughter of Pearl Munsey and Morton Robertson (4-F above), was born in Cincinnati, Hamilton County, Ohio, on November 7, 1924. In 1941, at the age of sixteen, Esther married *Joseph Hancel Hamilton.* Joseph, the son of Mary Curtis and William Hamilton, was born on December 13, 1919, in Cincinnati. They had two children and later divorced. Joseph is deceased.

At the age of twenty, and with two small children from her first marriage, Esther married *Richard Conrad Winkelbach* on August 31, 1945, in Cincinnati, Ohio. Born on March 27, 1919, in Cincinnati, Richard was the son of Margaret Hoffman and Fred Winkelbach. Both of Esther's children grew up using the surname Winkelbach. Esther and Richard also adopted a son. They live in Anderson Township, a suburb of Cincinnati.

### Children of Esther Lois Robertson

VII. <u>**Bonnie Lou Hamilton**</u>, daughter of Esther Robertson and Joseph Hamilton, was born on October 26, 1941, in Cincinnati, Hamilton County, Ohio. Bonnie married *Carl Taylor Jr.* on October 15, 1960, in Cincinnati. He was born about July 5, 1935, in Cincinnati. They have two sons. Carl worked as a machinist in the Ford Motor Co. plant in Batavia, near Cincinnati, until his retirement, and Bonnie worked as a secretary. The family lived for sixteen years in a historic farmhouse in Ohio before moving to Florida around 1993.

**Children of Bonnie Lou Hamilton**

VIII. **David Scott Taylor**, born in Cincinnati, Ohio. Dave married *Wanda Sue Gilreath*, and they had one child. They are now divorced.

**Child of David Scott Taylor**

IX. **David Scott Taylor II.**

VIII. **Daniel Louis Taylor**, born in Cincinnati, Ohio. Dan married *Virginia Ruth Godwin*. They had one daughter and divorced.

**Child of Daniel Louis Taylor**

IX. **Danielle Christine Taylor**.

VII. **Joseph Albert Hamilton**, born on May 15, 1943, in Cincinnati, Ohio, the son of Esther Robertson and Joseph Hamilton. Joe used Winkelbach as his last name while growing up but took back the name Hamilton upon his marriage. Joe married *Karen A. Murphy*. They had one son and divorced. Joe lives in Withamsville, Ohio, a suburb of Cincinnati.

**Child of Joseph Albert Hamilton**

VIII. **Joseph Albert Hamilton Jr.**, born about October 10, 1970, in Cincinnati, Ohio. Unmarried, he works as an apprentice pipe insulator in Cincinnati.

VII. **Richard Louis Winkelbach** (called "Rich") is the adopted son of Richard Winkelbach and Esther Lois Robertson. He married *Gail Phole* in 1983, and they have two daughters.

**Children of Richard Louis Winkelbach**

VIII. **Ashley Nicole Winkelbach**, born on May 26, 1985, in Cincinnati, Ohio.

VIII. **Brittney Elizabeth Winkelbach**, born on September 2, 1990, in Cincinnati, Ohio.

## 6-C.16: ALBERT JIRAH ROBERTSON (1927-1996)
### Son of Levi Morton Robertson

VI. **Albert Jirah Robertson** (called "Bud"), son of Pearl Munsey and Levi Morton Robertson (4-F above), was born on March 19, 1927, in Cincinnati, Hamilton County, Ohio. He attended vocational school in Cincinnati and enlisted in the U.S. Navy in World War II. Following his military service, Bud worked as a construction pipefitter. He died in November 1996.

In September 1950, Bud Robertson married *Laurel J. Corell* in Cincinnati, Ohio. The daughter of Stella Everhart and Arthur Lewis Corell, Laurel was born on August 22, 1927, in Hamilton County, Ohio. She died of cancer in May 1993 in Cincinnati. Bud and Laurel raised a son and twin daughters.

### Children of Albert Jirah Robertson

VII. **Albert Louis Robertson** (called "Bud"), son of Laurel Corell and Albert J. Robertson, born on August 13, 1952 in Cincinnati, Hamilton County, Ohio. He earned a degree in business at Indiana State University in Terre Haute, Indiana in 1974.

Bud married *Angela Mia Rhoades* on October 7, 1978, in Columbus, Indiana. Angela was born on January 1, 1952, in Columbus, Indiana, the daughter of Wilma Jean White and Jack L. Rhoades. Angela also graduated with a business degree from Indiana State, where they met. Angela is an independent company representative for a linen company in New York and a rug company in Virginia. Buddy is a partner in and chief operating officer of Rhoades Aviation, a company founded by his father-in-law and headquartered in Columbus. The company is involved in charter air transportation and other aviation-related businesses.

Angela and Bud Robertson live in Columbus and have one daughter, Brooke.

### Child of Albert Lewis Robertson

VIII. **Brooke Lauren Robertson**, born on January 26, 1988, in Columbus, Indiana.

VII. **Deborah Jean Robertson**, twin daughter of Laurel Corell and Albert J. Robertson, was born on February 5, 1955, in Cincinnati, Hamilton County, Ohio. She married *Gregory David Lewton* in Cincinnati on November 15, 1974. Gregory, born on June 5, 1955, in Greenfield, Ohio, is the son of Reba Cunningham and John Calvin Lewton and works as a police officer with the Cincinnati Police Department. Living in Cincinnati, Ohio, they are parents of a son and a daughter.

**Children of Deborah Jean Robertson**

VIII. **Gregory Brandon Lewton**, born on December 28, 1978, in Cincinnati, Ohio. He is a student.

VIII. **Jennifer Lauren Lewton**, born on June 27, 1986, in Cincinnati, Ohio.

VII. **Donna Sue Robertson**, one of the twins born to Laurel Corell and Albert J. Robertson, was born on February 5, 1955, in Cincinnati, Hamilton County, Ohio. Donna worked for many years in sales and marketing in the cosmetics business. She retired as territorial sales manager for Giorgio Perfumes to be a full-time mother.

Donna married *Gary Kaufmann* on April 8, 1979, in Cincinnati, Ohio. He was born in Piqua, Ohio, on January 12, 1953, the son of Virginia Nicodemus and Norman Kaufmann. They have one child and live in Anderson Township, a suburb of Cincinnati. Gary has been employed by the United Parcel Service for about a decade and works as a UPS Center Manager in Cincinnati.

**Child of Donna Sue Robertson**

VIII. **Kurt Edward Kaufmann**, born on February 25, 1991, in Cincinnati, Ohio.

## 6-C.17: Ivy Catherine Robertson (1924- )
### Daughter of Magnus Robertson

VI. **Ivy Catherine Robertson**, eldest daughter of Violet Dryborough and Magnus Robertson (5-C.5 above), was born on January 31, 1924, in Kelliher, Saskatchewan, Canada. On January 19, 1941, she married *Karl Ludwig Lundgren*, who was born in 1898 and died in

June 1960. They had five children and divorced. Ivy then married *Frederick Reisig*, who was born on April 18, 1915, and died in 1984. She later married *Al Hunter*, from whom she is divorced. Ivy resides in Port Alberni, British Columbia, Canada.

**Children of Ivy Catherine Robertson**

VII. **Karl Leonard Lundgren**, born on February 16, 1943. Leonard married *Jackie Judith Schilling* on July 8, 1967, in Surrey, British Columbia. She was born on September 22, 1946. They have three children.

### Children of Carl Leonard Lundgren

VIII. **Cindy Michelle Lundgren**, born on June 26, 1969. She married *Bob Prowse* on September 12, 1992, and they have two daughters. Bob was born on July 24, 1964.

### Children of Cindy Lundgren

IX. **Jenna Michelle Prowse**, born on June 9, 1993.

IX. **Nicole Debra Prowse**, born on April 30, 1996.

VIII. **Bonnie June Lundgren**, born on November 16, 1970. On September 7, 1990, she married *Kevin Barry Alcock*, who was born on February 14, 1969. They have one child and live in Houston, British Columbia, Canada.

### Child of Bonnie Lundgren

IX. **Christina Raine Alcock**, born on August 25, 1995.

VIII. **Debra Colleen Lundgren**, born on October 1, 1972. She is single and lives in Osoyoos, British Columbia.

VII. **Shirley Lundgren**, born on February 21, 1944, in Calgary, Alberta. On September 15, 1962, Shirley married *John William Belansky*, who was born on December 8, 1943, and they have two children. John and Shirley live on a farm in Aldergrove, British Columbia, where they grow mushrooms, and John also works in logging.

### Children of Shirley Ann Lundgren

VIII. **Leanne Michelle Belansky**, born on August 24, 1963. She married *Guy Walton* on May 11, 1994, in Aldergrove, British Columbia. He was born on July 7, 1959.

VIII. **Grant William Belansky**, born on June 1, 1965. On May 24, 1988, he married *Tracy Redford*, who was born on April 19, 1976. They stay at his parents' farm in Aldergrove and have three children.

### Children of Grant William Belansky

IX. **Ross William Belansky**, born on August 30, 1991.

IX. **Taylor Stephanie Belansky**, born on August 15, 1995.

IX. **Logan Grant Belansky**, born on January 31, 1998.

VII. **Sharon June Lundgren**, born on September 25, 1945. As an adventurous young woman, Sharon left Canada in 1965 and moved to Southern California. After some years there, she relocated to Scottsdale, Arizona.

On November 26, 1971, Sharon and *Charles David Rossie* were married in Scottsdale, Arizona. He was born in Fostoria, Ohio, on September 3, 1926. Charles owned a Ford automobile dealership in Arizona. When he sold that business, the family moved to Woodland Hills, California, where Charles owned a Lincoln-Mercury dealership. They have two children and now reside near the Pacific Coast in San Clemente, California. Sharon works in development for the University of California at Irvine, and Charles is semi-retired.

### Children of Sharon June Lundgren

VIII. **Christina Louise Rossie**, born on September 5, 1973, in Scottsdale, Arizona. She received a B.A. degree in political science from the University of California at Santa Barbara.

VIII. **Charles David Rossie II**, born on August 21, 1975, in Scottsdale, Arizona. He is a business student at the University of Colorado in Boulder.

VII. **John Wayne Lundgren**, born on April 19, 1947, in Melfort, Saskatchewan, Canada. On December 27, 1969, he married *Glenda James*, who was born on October 28, 1951. They divorced in November 1990, having had three children. On October 24, 1992, John married *Ann Marmont*, who was born on January 3, 1957. They reside in Surrey, British Columbia.

### Children of John Wayne Lundgren

VIII. **Carl James Lundgren**, born on August 12, 1970. He is a chiropractor in Lima, Peru.

VIII. **Shelly Ann Lundgren**, born on October 13, 1971.

VIII. **Cathleen Teresa Lundgren**, born on December 20, 1973.

VII. **Margaret Louise Lundgren**, born on July 15, 1950, in Vancouver, British Columbia. On February 14, 1969, she married *Patrick Joseph Michael McCarthy*, who was born on March 15, 1947. They live in Langley, British Columbia, and have three children.

### Children of Margaret Louise Lundgren

VIII. **Cheryl Lynn McCarthy**, born on January 16, 1971. On July 18, 1998, she married *Albert Graham Techlenborg*, born on May 3, 1967.

VIII. **Patricia Ann Margaret McCarthy**, born on July 23, 1972. On June 27, 1998, she married *Owen Anderson*, who was born on April 10, 1972. They have one child.

### Child of Patricia Ann Margaret McCarthy

IX. **Justin Todd Brewer**, born on April 4, 1993.

VIII. **Michael Justin Joseph McCarthy**, born on November 5, 1974. On September 3, 1995, he married *Amy Lynn Reich*, born on August 5, 1974.

## 6-C.18: Margaret Isabella Robertson (1927-1997)
### Daughter of Magnus Robertson

VI. **Margaret Isabella Robertson** (called "Bella"), second daughter of Violet Dryborough and Magnus Robertson (5-C.5 above), was born on May 11, 1927, in Prince Rupert, British Columbia. She married *Harold Martin Hyggen* in 1947, and they had five children. Harold was born on November 25, 1912, in Weldon, Saskatchewan. They divorced, and Harold died on January 13, 1990, in Nanaimo, British Columbia. Bella then married *Paul Collett*.

Bella died on August 11, 1997, in Port Alberni, Vancouver Island, British Columbia. She was seventy.

**Children of Margaret Isabella Robertson**

VII. **Trevor Magnus Hyggen**, born in Kinistino, Saskatchewan, Canada, on May 13, 1947. On October 14, 1967, Trevor married *Sheila Levang*, with whom he had two children. They divorced in September 1978. Trevor then married *Patsy Lee Shaw* on March 12, 1982; she was born on November 7, 1949. They live in Port Alberni, Vancouver Island, British Columbia, where Trevor works in a lumber mill operation.

**Children of Trevor Magnus Hyggen**

VIII. **Shelley Rae Hyggen**, born on January 19, 1968.

VIII. **Chad Allen Harold Hyggen**, born on September 8, 1970.

VII. **Orval Garnet Hyggen**, born on November 16, 1948, in Birch Hills, Saskatchewan, Canada. On July 4, 1974, Orval married *Linda Ruth Journeay*, who was born on February 28, 1950. Linda has a daughter, Pamela Ruth Journeay, and Linda and Orval have two sons. Orval is a long-haul truck driver, and they live in Alberta Beach near Edmonton, Alberta.

**Children of Orval Garnet Hyggen**

VIII. **Orval Garnet Hyggen**, born on July 16, 1975.

VIII. **Stanley Lorne Murphy Hyggen**, born on January 10, 1978.

VII. **Linda Marilyn Hyggen**, born on September 25, 1950, in Melfort, Saskatchewan, Canada. On January 3, 1969, she married *Kidd Roger Fiddler*, who was born on May 12, 1937. They had four children and divorced. Linda now lives in Port Alberni, British Columbia.

### Children of Linda Hyggen

VIII. **Peter Harold Fiddler**, born on May 15, 1969, on Vancouver Island, British Columbia.

VIII. **Richard Peter Fiddler**, born on May 14, 1970, on Vancouver Island, British Columbia; he is deceased.

VIII. **Margaret Ann Fiddler**, born on October 2, 1971 on Vancouver Island, British Columbia. She has one son.

### Child of Margaret Ann Fiddler

IX. **Thomas Robert Fiddler**, born on May 5, 1989.

VIII. **Elsie Lynn Fiddler**, born on February 16, 1973, on Vancouver Island, British Columbia; she has two children.

### Children of Elsie Lynn Fiddler

IX. **Adam Robert Fiddler**, born on October 30, 1993.

IX. **Lynn Linda Rose Fiddler**, born on December 26, 1996.

VII. **Curtis Martin Hyggen**, born on April 3, 1952, in Port Alberni on Vancouver Island, British Columbia. On November 15, 1974, Curtis married *Sharon Louise Mork*, who was born on October 9, 1954. They had two children and divorced. Second, Curtis married *Christiane Lambert* on September 26, 1987, in Vancouver, British Columbia. The daughter of Irene Duclos and Jean Guy Lambert, Christiane was born on January 29, 1953, in Sherbrooke, Quebec. Curtis and Christiane reside in Aylmer, Quebec, near the Canadian capital, Ottawa. A butcher by trade, Curtis heard a religious calling in the mid-1990s and became an ordained minister. Christiane works in the Canadian Department of Fisheries and Oceans in Ottawa. Together, they founded and are co-pastors of a branch of the Pentecostal church in Aylmer.

**Children of Curtis Martin Hyggen**

VIII. **Jason Harold Hyggen**, born on February 18, 1975, in Port Alberni, British Columbia.

VIII. **Jamie Lynn Hyggen**, born on March 2, 1978, in Langley, British Columbia.

VII. **Scott Bradley Hyggen**, born on March 3, 1960. He married *Lola Rose Penner*, who was born on April 8, 1961. They have two children. Scott lives in Vanderhoof, British Columbia.

**Children of Scott Bradley Hyggen**

VIII. **April Jolene Hyggen**, born on June 8, 1993.

VIII. **Amy Lee Anne Hyggen**, born on April 16, 1996.

## 6-C.19: EILEEN DELLA ROBERTSON (1931- )
### Daughter of Magnus Robertson

VI. **Eileen Della Robertson**, fourth daughter of Violet Dryborough and Magnus Robertson (5-C.5 above), was born on April 24, 1931, in Melfort, Saskatchewan. She grew up on her father's farm in Beatty until the family relocated to Vancouver Island, British Columbia.

On April 11, 1953, Eileen married *James Douglas Kelley* in Duncan on Vancouver Island, British Columbia. He was born on July 30, 1924, in Forestburg, Alberta, Canada, the son of Edith McMahon and James Bernard Kelley. Jim was a heavy-duty mechanic with the Royal Canadian Air Force, retiring with the rank of corporal in 1964. Eileen had a son by a previous relationship, and she and Jim have three children. They live in Abbotsford, British Columbia, a few miles from the Canada-US border. They spent two weeks in Shetland in August 1973, visiting cousins there, and again visited for two weeks in 1978.

**Children of Eileen Della Robertson**

VII. **Gary Miles Robertson** was born on May 24, 1950, in Prince Albert, Saskatchewan. Information of Gary withheld at his request.

**Child of Gary Miles Robertson**

VIII. <u>**James Magnus Robertson**</u>, son of Mary Crilly and Gary Robertson, was born on March 19, 1989, in Abbottsford, British Columbia.

VII. <u>**Wayne Douglas Kelley**</u> was born on November 29, 1953, in Comox on Vancouver Island, British Columbia. He married *Patricia Braun*; she had three children, who were adopted by Wayne. They reside in Surrey, British Columbia.

**Children of Wayne Douglas Kelley**

VIII. <u>**Theresa Joanne Kelley**</u>, born on May 26, 1976, twin sister of Lisa. She is unmarried.

VIII. <u>**Lisa Marie Kelley**</u>, twin sister of Theresa, born on May 26, 1976. On April 26, 1997, she married *Derrick Lupien*, who was born on April 14, 1972.

VIII. <u>**Grahame Matthew Kelley**</u>, born on July 19, 1974. He married *Tara Marie Gombec* on July 1, 1995. Tara was born on July 6, 1976. They have two children.

**Children of Grahame Matthew Kelley**

IX. <u>**Logan James Douglas Kelley**</u>, born on November 9, 1995.

IX. <u>**Austin William Matthew Kelley**</u>, born on August 18, 1998.

VII. <u>**Heather Ann Kelley**</u> was born on September 5, 1955, in Comox on Vancouver Island, British Columbia. On August 30, 1975, Heather married *Russell Bertram Stockley*, who was born on April 20, 1955. They live in Peachland, British Columbia, and Heather works for the British Columbia Telephone Company. They have no children.

VII. <u>**Edith Eileen Kelley**</u> was born on March 28, 1958, in Pembroke, Ontario. On July 26, 1979, in Barbados, British West Indies, she married *Stephen Fear* of Ontario, Canada. They had no children and divorced in December 1988. Edie lives in Toronto with her partner, *Peter Van Bodegom*, who was born on June 26, 1956, and she helps him in raising his two daughters by a previous marriage, Jenna Ann Van Bodegom and Christi Rae Van Bodegom.

## 6-C.20: JOHN THOMAS WATT (18??-1921)
### Son of Thomas Twatt

VI. **John Thomas Watt**, first son of Catherine Nicolson and Thomas Twatt (5-A.11 above), was born before 1890 in Shetland. John and two of his younger brothers immigrated to the United States and settled in Brooklyn, New York. He married *Winifred McCann* from Newfoundland, and they had two daughters. John died about 1921 at an early age. His widow later married Edwin Giles, an officer in the merchant marine, who later worked in construction. They settled in the area of Boston, Massachusetts. Edwin died in 1959.

**Children of John Thomas Watt**

VII. **Catherine Watt**, born in Brooklyn, New York on January 29, 1915. She married *Alfred Leroy Drown* about 1936. He was a construction crane operator. They have two children and reside in Stoneham, Massachusetts.

**Children of Catherine Watt**

VIII. **Allen Leroy Drown**, born on November 15, 1937, in Boston, Massachusetts. On November 17, 1958 in Nashua, New Hampshire, Al married *Jacqueline Fuller,* who was born in Lynn, Massachusetts, on March 18, 1938. They had six children and reside in Randolph, Massachusetts. Al worked as a construction crane operator for thirty-five years before retirement.

**Children of Allen Drown**

IX. **Scott Allan Drown**, born on September 7, 1959, in Quincy, Massachusetts. He died in infancy, just a week after his birth.

IX. **Dana James Drown**, born on September 30, 1960, in Quincy, Massachusetts. He first married *Cindy* (maiden name unavailable); they had one son and divorced. He later married *Marie* (maiden name unavailable), who was born in England. They have four children.

**Children of Dana James Drown**

X. **Dustin Drown**, son of Cindy and Dana Drown, born on April 28, 1981.

X. **Lacie Drown**, daughter of Marie and Dana Drown, born on October 4, 1984, in Arkansas.

X. **Ross Drown**, son of Marie and Dana Drown, born on October 16, 1985, in Arkansas.

X. **Hollie Drown**, one of twin daughters of Marie and Dana Drown, born on October 28, 1987, in Missouri.

X. **Ashley Drown**, twin daughter of Marie and Dana Drown, born on October 28, 1987, in Missouri.

IX. **Teresa Lee Drown**, born on November 11, 1961, in Quincy, Massachusetts. She married *Robert Banden*, an engineer in the merchant marine, on May 27, 1999, in Cape Cod, Massachusetts.

IX. **Peter Gregory Drown**, born on May 22, 1963, in Quincy, Massachusetts.

IX. **Tracy Jean Drown**, born on July 7, 1967, in Quincy, Massachusetts.

IX. **Nancy Ann Drown**, born on January 29, 1970. She is a physical therapist, working at Massachusetts General Hospital.

VIII. **Marilyn Drown**. She married *George Gustin,* and they had two daughters and divorced. Marilyn lives in Woburn, Massachusetts.

**Children of Marilyn Drown**

IX. **Lynn Gustin**

IX. **Lauren Gustin**

VII. **Winifred Watt**, born on August 20, 1917 in Brooklyn, New York. On October 22, 1938, she married *Peter John Feeley* of Medford, Massachusetts. Peter was born on November 5, 1907, the youngest of eight children. As a young man,

Peter played baseball for a while in the minor leagues. He later worked for the US Postal Service, first as a letter carrier and then as a superintendent. They had four children and lived in a home they built in 1949 in Stoneham, Massachusetts. Peter died in 1966 in Stoneham at the age of fifty-eight.

After Peter's death, Winnie married *Francis Xavier Connors* about 1972; they had no children. Winnie died in 1997 at the age of eighty and is survived by her second husband at the family home in Stoneham.

### Children of Winifred Watt

VIII. **Peter John Feeley Jr.**, son of Winifred Watt and Peter John Feeley, born on February 13, 1941. Peter served in the U.S. Marine Corps in Vietnam and later returned home after his father died in 1966. He married *Teresa Raboin*; they had no children. Peter worked as a roofer and died of a brain tumor about 1986.

VIII. **Edwin Michael Feeley**, son of Winifred Watt and Peter John Feeley, born on April 1, 1943, in Medford, Massachusetts. He married *Mary Gail Dutney*, daughter of Kathleen and Dexter Dutney, on May 24, 1969. They have five children and reside in North Reading, Massachusetts. Ed is a sales representative with Massachusetts Envelope Company.

### Children of Edwin Michael Feeley

IX. **Kathleen Edith Feeley**, born on December 5, 1967, in Woburn, Massachusetts. On May 12, 1991, in Stoneham, Massachusetts, she married *Steven Joseph D'Amico*. The son of Rebecca Cole and Carmello D'Amico, Steven was born on March 9, 1970, in Lynn, Massachusetts. They have three children.

### Children of Kathleen Edith Feeley

X. **Stephen Carmello D'Amico**, born on December 21, 1990, in Winchester, Massachusetts.

X. **Michael Ryan D'Amico**, born on June 1, 1993, in Salem, Massachusetts.

X. **Katielyn Edith D'Amico**, born on June 21, 1994, in Salem, Massachusetts.

IX. **Peter John Feeley III,** born on November 4, 1969. He is unmarried. He was a professional baseball player in the minor leagues with the Detroit Tigers organization for several years. No longer an active player, he is working with the Mo Vaughn Motivational Sports training camps.

IX. **Edwin Michael Feeley Jr.**, born on December 2, 1970. Eddie and his partner, *Laurie Tatrow*, and they have one child.

**Child of Edwin Michael Feeley Jr.**

X. **Christopher Michael Feeley**, born on April 21, 1995.

IX. **Colleen Ann Feeley**, born on December 24, 1977.

VIII. **Margaret Ann Feeley** (called "Peggy") was born on August 16, 1944, in Medford, Massachusetts, the daughter of Winifred Watt and Peter John Feeley. She married *Peter Jay Daniels* on May 21, 1966, in Stoneham, Massachusetts. Peggy was a financial analyst and project specialist in corporate finance for Compaq Computer Corporation after its acquisition of Digital Equipment Corp., where she previously worked. Peter, an electrical engineer, is lab chief at Lincoln Laboratories of the Massachusetts Institute of Technology. They have one son and reside in Stoneham.

**Child of Margaret Ann Feeley**

IX. **Kevin Michael Daniels**, born on October 17, 1969. He married *Laura Paciorek* in September 1998. They are both qualified mechanical engineers; they have no children.

VIII. **Kathleen Mary Feeley**, daughter of Winifred Watt and Peter John Feeley, was born on October 12, 1950, in Medford, Massachusetts. On May 1, 1971, she married *Robert John Paul Leger* in Stoneham, Massachusetts. He was born on November 29, 1949, in Monckton, New Brunswick, Canada. They divorced in 1983. Kathy has an adopted daughter and lives in Malden, Massachusetts.

**Child of Kathleen Mary Feeley**

IX. **Julie Anne Leger**, born on November 10, 1980, in Newburyport, Massachusetts.

# ENDNOTES

*IGI in these notes refers to the International Genealogical Index*

1  Tide-lumps = sea piling up suddenly in a tideway.

2  Norah C. Kendall of Melbourne, Australia, a descendant of Shetland emigrants in the nineteenth century, has written of these practices and their effects in her 1998 book titled *With Naught But Kin Behind Them*. Her book can be ordered from the Shetland Times Bookstore in Lerwick.

3  Membership in the SFHS is open to anyone interested in family history. The modest annual dues entitle members to receive the excellent quarterly journal of the Society, *Cootin Kin*. The Society's address is 6 Hillhead, Lerwick, Shetland ZE1 OED, Scotland, UK.

4  Although recording the sources from which family information is obtained is essential in serious genealogical research, we have not attempted to list all source materials for the information in this book. However, we have included IGI references, including batch and serial numbers, where available, for birth, christening, and marriage events involving our ancestors in order to aid further research and review; these references are found in numbered notes at the end of the text.

5  The Clan Donnachaidh Society, PO Box 742, Edinburgh EH4 3UP, Scotland, is a membership organization with active branches throughout the United States, Canada, Australia, and New Zealand. It sponsors various events and publishes an annual magazine that includes historical and genealogical articles about the Robertsons. The Society also maintains the Clan Donnachaidh Museum, located in the heart of the Highlands at Bruar, a few miles from Blair Atholl and Pitlochry in Perthshire.

6  The story of the battle and its aftermath is well told in John Prebble's detailed history, *Culloden* (Penguin Books, 1961). An excellent article titled "Clan Donnachaidh in the '45" by James Irvine Robertson, focusing on the involvement of Robertsons in particular, was published in the 1995 *Clan Donnachaidh Annual*.

7  IGI M110092-0282

8  IGI C110092-0211

9  IGI C110092-0991

10  IGI C110092-1087

11   IGI M110092-0508

12   IGI C110092-2207

13   IGI M110094-0153

14   IGI M110094-0180, M110094-0233

15   Malcolm Robertson was born in 1772 or 1775 to Bess Magnusdaughter and Jerom Robertson, who were married on October 4, 1750, at Aithness, Sandsting & Aithsting Parish. (IGI M110092-0106). Jerom thus would have been considerably older than our forefathers Thomas and John Robertson. Malcolm's daughter Mary Robertson married John Nicolson on November 12, 1830, and their daughter Anderina married Robert Johnson and had numerous children. The Johnson family immigrated to New Zealand, joining a pioneering settlement at the remote outpost of Karamea on the Western shore of the South Island.

16   IGI C110092-2334

17   IGI C110092-2603

18   IGI C110092-1315

19   IGI C110092-0402

20   IGI C110092-0435

21   According to Alan Beattie, editor of the Shetland Family History Society, Umphray was the surname of a prominent local landlord of the time. The Kirk Session Minutes for Walls Parish record that Laurence Umphray in 1741 held the position of "Ruling Elder" in Elvister; he died in 1758.

22   IGI C110092-0315

23   Stuart Robertson, a Shetland native now residing in Inverness, Scotland, has traced ancestors on his grandmother's side back to Robertsons living in Walls Parish. Although they were in the same small villages at the same times, and even had similar or identical first names, he believes our families probably were not related.

24   IGI 7621005-53, M110092-0502

25   IGI C110092-2101

26   IGI M110094-0273

27   IGI C110094-0837

28   IGI C110094-0932

29   IGI C110094-1031

30   IGI C110094-1259

31   IGI C110094-1367

32  IGI C110094-1457

33  IGI C110094-1551

34  IGI C110092-2232

35  IGI C110092-2330

36  IGI C110092-2487

37  IGI M110094-0233

38  IGI M110094-0153

39  IGI M110094-0444

40  IGI C110091-0118

41  IGI C110092-1083

42  IGI 7628762-95; also M110092-0421 (S & A)

43  The IGI also lists a record of their marriage dated January 26, 1796, in Sandsting & Aithsting Parish. This was possibly a later registration in Jerom's home parish of the marriage that had occurred earlier in Walls.

44  In 1740, Thomas Gifford of Busta reportedly owned three quarters of Delting Parish and two thirds of Northmaven. He had massively increased his holdings by taking over the estates of other landlords who became bankrupt because of declining market conditions some years earlier. Norah Kendall, in *With Naught But Kin Behind Them*, (pp. 130 – 131), notes: "Much of the Gifford money and estates had been accrued throughout the many generations who acted as chamberlain or factor."

45  The livestock was to be kept in "steelbow," a term meaning that the number of sheep had to be rigidly maintained and returned by the farmer to the landlord at the end of his tenancy.

46  N. Kendall, *supra* at pp. 131 – 132, quoting a 1798 report by Sir John Sinclair titled "General View of the Agriculture of the Northern Counties and Islands of Scotland."

47  Documentation on the case is preserved in the Shetland Archives at Lerwick [SC12/6/1797/21/1].

48  Old Walls Parish Records [GS F 14505 pt. 7] show Thomas Robertson's birth date as September 6, 1796; however, this could simply be a record of a later baptism in Walls Parish, if the child had been born at Vementry in Aithsting.

49  IGI 7628762-59

50  IGI 7628762-60

51  IGI 7628762-62

52  IGI 7628762-65

53   IGI 7628762-19

54   Based on an entry in the Walls Parish Register of Deaths showing that a Robert Robertson died on August 27, 1827, and was then "about 68" years of age, that would indicate that a birth date around 1759 – 1760. However, assuming this was the same individual and that his father was born in 1745, that would mean his father would have been fifteen or sixteen at the time of Robert's birth, which seems unlikely. Stuart Robertson suggests that John Robertson may have been born before 1745.

55   IGI 7628762-90

56   IGI C110092-0946

57   IGI 7628762-52

58   IGI 7628762-52

59   IGI 7628762-26

60   IGI 7127820-74, 7127820-49

61   IGI C110124-0026

62   The 1841 Census of Delting Parish records Peter Jamieson as being sixty years of age, meaning he was born in about 1781. Peter's wife, Janet, was listed as being fifty-five, putting her birth about 1786. Thomas, then age twenty, was still living at home, as were an older brother, Arthur (twenty-five), and a younger sister, Elizabeth Jamieson (fifteen), according to the census report.

63   IGI 7628762-58

64   IGI 7628762-28

65   IGI 7628762-18

66   IGI M110054-0286

67   IGI M110094-0217

68   IGI C110052-3982

69   IGI C110094-0856

70   IGI C110094-0957

71   IGI C110094-0379

72   IGI C110094-1161

73   IGI C110094-1245

74   IGI 7628762-19

75   IGI M110122-0046

76   IGI M110122-0046 (re: "Agness Robertsdaughter")

77   IGI M110122-0097 (re: "Agnes Johnsdaughter")

78 This information was posted on the internet by John Watt on January 14, 1999.

79 IGI C110122-0131

80 IGI C110122-0550

81 IGI C110104-2661

82 IGI M110124-0156

83 IGI M110104-6740

84 IGI 6932108-42

85 IGI C110124-0568

86 IGI C110104-2664; also C110124-0622 (Tingwall)

87 IGI C110124-0684

88 IGI C110104-2665

89 IGI C110104-2666

90 IGI C110104-2667

91 IGI C110104-2668

92 IGI 2627451-52

93 IGI C110122-0659

94 IGI C110124-0050

95 IGI M110124-0007

96 IGI C110124-0041

97 IGI C110122-0253

98 The family tree of James Jeromson neatly illustrates the traditional use of patronymic surnames in Shetland. About 1714, John Jeromson had a son, John, who was called John Johnson. He in turn had a son, Magnus Johnson, born in 1736, whose children were given the surname Manson (a shortened form of Magnusson). One of these children, born in 1769, was Jerom Manson, whose children in turn used the surname Jeromson. At that point, use of patronymics stopped, and the family name thereafter was Jeromson. This information was supplied by Robert A. Coutts of Wellington, New Zealand, who has compiled a Jeromson family tree consisting of more than 1,600 individuals (including spouses).

99 Dr. Eddie Robertson has described the development of this kind of farming: "At the end of the 18th century came the first real attempt at land reclamation, when small farms known as outsets came into being. The method was to build a turf and stone dyke around a few acres of moorland, then turn the heather over by spade. Several thousand acres of arable land were cleared in this way, causing complaints from the crofters, who lost grazing land without compensation from the landlord in the form of reduced rent."

100 The children's names and dates of birth were recorded in John Robertson's Bible, which was passed down to his great grandson George Robertson of Waterloo, Walls.

101 IGI M110104-0489

102 IGI 7621005-52

103 IGI 7621005-52

104 IGI 7621005-52

105 IGI 7621005-53

106 IGI 7621005-50

107 IGI 7628762-59

108 IGI 6932108-62

109 Margaret Mouat's parents were married October 20, 1811, on Unst. Three of Margaret's sisters also came to Walls from Unst and married there: Ann Mouat, who married a sea captain named John Smith; Elizabeth Mouat, who married James Georgeson and immigrated to New Zealand in 1876; and Charlotte Mouat, who married George Georgeson. In March 1904, Margaret's son James Robertson wrote a letter to a family friend, attempting to set out the ancestry and offspring of Captain John Mouat. James said this question "can scarcely be satisfactorily answered. All that is known is Peter Mouat, Northhamersland, had three sons, of whom John was one. Whether the ancestors of Peter Mouat were Lairds (i.e., landowners) or tenants is not known." However he was able to identify Captain John's four wives and many children.

110 IGI M110124-0202

111 The property had been acquired by Gideon Henderson, a merchant, from Sir Arthur Nicolson, Baronet, in 1827. Mr. Henderson apparently ran into financial problems, for "Seafield" was conveyed to lawyers James Greig and Archibald Greig of Lerwick, as trustees for Henderson's creditors, in 1841. In 1843, the trustees sold the house and land, "together also with peat-moss in the hill or common of Forratwatt sufficient for fuel to the said house and grazing in said hill or pasture for two cattle," to Thomas Robertson, who was described in the deed as a merchant in Stove. Those apparently were the same lawyers Thomas wrote to in 1839.

112 ** "Seafield" may have been built as early as 1760, and a shop and storerooms were added around 1840, according to Angus Robertson. The house may have been built for a minister of the Church of Scotland and originally called "Brattanoust."

113 This shopman was probably the same James Georgeson who later married Margaret's sister Elizabeth Mouat and immigrated with her and two of Thomas and Margaret's daughters to New Zealand around 1878.

114 At that time in Shetland, several people might be buried in a single grave, with markers to be put up later. According to his grandson Reuben, Thomas Robertson and two of his wives,

Christina and Margaret, were all buried together in the Walls churchyard. Apparently, no markers were placed on their graves.

115 IGI C110124-0609

116 IGI C110124-0768

117 This reference work, covering the years 1837 – 1916, was compiled by L.E. Hughes (1991) and is maintained in the research library of the Cincinnati Historical Society.

118 This was related by Tina Cheyne Rankine, Ann Margaret's niece, to Blanche Robertson.

119 IGI C110124-0839

120 IGI C110124-0894

121 IGI C110124-0986

122 IGI C110124-1083

123 IGI C110124-1181

124 Like this branch of our Robertsons in Walls, the Grutquoy Robertson family had also joined the Methodist church there. Scott Robertson of Grutquoy was a leading lay member of the Methodists in Walls from the 1830s until his death in 1884, and his son Andrew Umphray Robertson was baptized by the Wesleyan minister in Walls Parish.

125 The date is listed in her father Thomas's daybook in which he recorded the children's birthdays. The IGI records Eliza's date of birth as December 8, 1856. [C110121-0130].

126 IGI C110121-0456

127 IGI C110133-0368

128 IGI 7628762-19

129 IGI M110104-0666

130 However, the IGI records all the children as having been born in Tingwall Parish.

131 IGI C110104-3623

132 IGI M110101-0258

133 GI C110104-2398

134 IGI C110104-2400

135 IGI C110104-1080

136 IGI M110101-0184

137 IGI C110104-0582

138 IGI C110104-2401

139 IGI C110104-1285

140 IGI C110104-1342, C110104-2402

141 IGI C110104-2027

142 IGI C110122-0253

143 IGI M110122-0662

144 His family illustrates the traditional use of patronymic surnames in Shetland. About 1714, John Jeromson had a son John, who was called John Johnson. He in turn had a son Magnus Johnson, born in 1736, whose children were given the surname Manson (a shortened form of Magnusson). One of these children, born in 1769, was Jerom Manson, whose children in turn used the surname Jeromson. At that point, use of patronymics stopped, and the family name thereafter was Jeromson. This information was supplied by Robert A. Coutts of Wellington, New Zealand, who has compiled a Jeromson family tree consisting of more than 1600 individuals (including spouses).

145 All information on this family is derived from SFHS research.

146 IGI C110122-0281

147 IGI M110124-0019

148 IGI C110124-1128

149 All information on her husband, children, and descendants is from SFHS data.

150 IGI C110121-0011

151 IGI C110121-0308

152 IGI C110121-0469

153 IGI C110121-0694

154 IGI M110124-0279

155 IGI M110124-0282

156 IGI C110124-1141

157 IGI C110121-0490

158 IGI C110121-0729

159 IGI C110123-0023

160 IGI C110123-0232

161 IGI M110084-0234

162 IGI M110124-0141

163 IGI C110124-0525

164 IGI M110121-0089

165 IGI C110124-0564

166 Our information on Catherine's children and grandchildren comes from SFHS research.

167 IGI C110124-0621

168 IGI C110124-0675

169 IGI C110124-0728

170 IGI C110124-0788

171 IGI M110121-0177

172 IGI C110124-0838

173 IGI C110124-0924

174 IGI C110124-1002

175 IGI C110124-1062

176 IGI C110124-1169

177 IGI C110121-0021

178 IGI C110093-0053

179 IGI C110093-0227

180 IGI C110093-0411

181 IGI C110094-1828

182  Laurence's parents, Christina Ridland (1818 – 1884) and Peter Robertson (1810 – 1889), are buried at Westerskeld Cemetery.

183  Charles D. Robertson's mother, Christina Dumbreck, was not a Shetland native but was born and raised in Edinburgh. Charles was told that his father had made her acquaintance while Christina was visiting the rectory of an Episcopal minister in Shetland, but Charles knew virtually nothing about his mother or her ancestors. Research efforts aided by Stuart Robertson in Scotland have established that Christina's parents were Mary Cromar and Charles Dumbreck and have provided further information about her family roots in Scotland.

184  In April 1867, a shipping agent reported to the Registrar of Shipping at Lerwick that Charles D. Robertson, then residing in the United States, was still registered as owner of the *Charles*, although the sloop was broken up as unfit for sea around 1863.

185 Alan Beattie, the knowledgeable editor of the Shetland Family History Society journal *Coontin Kin*, suggests that Thomas Robertson's friend was a prominent Shetlander named Arthur Anderson. About four years older than Thomas, Mr. Anderson had started his working career in fish curing. He served in the Royal Navy during the Napoleonic Wars and then went to London, becoming a clerk in a shipping company. A man of great aptitude and energy, Mr. Anderson rose steadily in the business and eventually founded the Peninsular & Oriental Steam Navigation Co. (known as P&O) to operate scheduled services to Spain, Portugal, and later, Egypt. Soon the P&O line was operating around the Cape of Good Hope to India and the Far East. In 1837,

Mr. Anderson founded the Shetland Fishery Company on Vaila, the island opposite Walls in Vaila Sound, and over the years must have had dealings with Thomas Robertson in connection with his fish curing-and-export business. Elected as a member of parliament to represent the Orkney and Shetland Islands, Arthur Anderson also founded the Anderson Educational Institute in Lerwick, which became Anderson High School, Shetland's principal educational institution.

186  Reuben Buck, born in 1791 in the town of Clarendon, Rutland County, in Western Vermont, was the first child of Moses Buck and Cynthia Crary, who were married in Clarendon on February 12, 1790. We do not know where Moses Buck came from or who his parents were. Reuben's mother Cynthia's parents were Dorothy ("Dolly") Randall, a descendant of the John Gallup family – among the first pilgrims to arrive in the American colonies in the early 17th Century – and Ezra Crary of Voluntown, Connecticut, whose ancestor Peter Crary first came to America in the 1660s. Ezra Crary was a patriot who served in the Connecticut assembly during the American Revolution.

Reuben Buck's first wife died of tuberculosis in 1833. A widower with several children, Reuben then remarried on July 20, 1834, in Nunda, Livingston County, New York. His second wife was Fanny Morton Dewey, the widow of Eliphalet Dewey. Fanny was born on April 24, 1795 in Paris, Oneida County, New York, the daughter of Elishaby Mack and Levi Morton (1770-1840) of Madison County, New York. Levi Morton was descended from some of the first pioneer settlers of Athol, Massachusetts, which was named after Atholl, Scotland and to have descended from the Duke of Atholl. Fanny Morton Buck's grandfather Samuel Morton – an ancestor of most if not all of Our Robertsons in the United States – was a Revolutionary soldier mustered as a private in April, 1775, to fight against the British forces in the Battle of Lexington, one of the first and most famous of the armed conflicts of the war.

After their marriage, Reuben and Fanny Morton Buck moved to Fredonia in Chautauqua County, New York, where their two children, Cynthia Ann and Jirah Dewey Buck, were born. They all moved again to Belvedere, Illinois in the 1840s and, a decade later, to Janesville in Rock County, Wisconsin. Reuben died there at the age of 61 on April 27, 1853, another victim of tuberculosis, and was buried at Oak Hill Cemetery. Fanny Buck survived for another 22 years; she died on January 18, 1875, at the age of 79, at Johnstown, Barry County, in southern Michigan.

Source: Charles Morton, Morton Family Record, 1668-1881 (privately printed, 1881)

187  At that time Cynthia's daughter Esther was nine years old. She grew up to marry Charles's half-brother Andrew Umphray Robertson, fifteen years his junior, who immigrated to Cincinnati around 1880 with the aid and encouragement Charles. Andrew and Esther were married on Christmas Day 1881.

188 Charles Robertson's close friend and brother-in-law, Dr. Jirah D. Buck, who had also moved to Cincinnati about 1870, was also of a serious intellectual and philosophical bent. He helped organize and became the dean and a professor of medicine of Pulte Medical College, later made part of Ohio State University, and he served as president of the American Institute of Homeopathy. Active in the Masonic fraternity, he authored numerous books and articles on philosophy and psychology. Dr. Buck was elected to the Cincinnati Literary Club in 1872, the same year as Charles. Upon his death, the *Cincinnati Times-Star* newspaper described him as "the world's leading authority on Masonry" and stated, "His studies and writings on Masonry, spiritualism, vegetarianism, theology, theosophy, psychology, New Thought, Christian Science and historical and scientific researches won him international fame. Dr. Buck was of imposing appearance and was one of Cincinnati's most beloved characters."

189 Reuben B. Robertson Sr. graduated in 1900 from Yale, the first of his family to earn a university degree, and, in 1903, earned a bachelor of laws (LL.B.) from the University of Cincinnati. After a few years working under his father's guidance in the law firm of Robertson and Buchwalter, he moved to North Carolina in 1906 to pursue a career in business. He became a leader in the pulp and paper industry, widely respected for his enlightened approached to labor-management relations and sound forestry practices.

190 Charles Robertson was one of the official commissioners elected to oversee the annexation of the city of Avondale into Cincinnati.

191 A family Bible, which has been passed down to Annchen Perin Gager, records the year of her birth as 1872 instead of 1870.

192 IGI M110121-0227

193 The marriage date is based on a letter from Charlotte's daughter Agnes O'Brian to her cousin William Hillman Robertson in 1920. Records found by Kate Mitchell in her family research put the date three years later—July 1, 1878—but this information appears to have been recorded much later and appears to be incorrect. Kate also found a death certificate for Frank O'Brian giving his birth year as 1849, which she also believes is inaccurate. Before the 1900s, original records were written by local officials and clerks whose handwriting was often unclear, and other secondary records were hand copied from the originals. Years later, the information may have been transcribed again. Problems in deciphering words and numbers in this process easily lead to errors in the "official" records.

194 Molesworth lasted for sixty-seven years as a merino sheep station. The flock had to be driven to Buttergill for shearing, a long and often difficult journey. Stragglers were shorn at Molesworth, and that wool was taken by packhorse to Buttergill, where it was pressed and made ready to go with the main clip to the London Sales.

195 From Kate Mitchell's interview notes with her grandmother Agnes Lyver, March 14, 1991.

196 Greta Robertson and Charles were witnesses to the will of Jirah D. Buck, Charles's brother-in-law, which was executed on September 1, 1914; after Dr. Buck died, Greta appeared in the Hamilton County probate court proceedings on January 19, 1917, and authenticated the will.

197 A copy of Greta's letter is in the Reuben B. Robertson collection at the University of North Carolina at Asheville.

198 Morton may have been named after an ancestor of his grandmother Cynthia Buck. Cynthia's grandfather was Levi Morton (1770 – 1840) of Madison County, New York, a descendant of the first settlers of Athol, Massachusetts. That town was named after Athol in Scotland because the Morton family claimed to have originated there and to have descended from the Duke of Athol. See Charles Morton, *Morton Family Record, 1668 – 1881* (privately printed, Missouri, 1881). Another Levi Morton, born in Vermont and probably unrelated, was a prominent Wall Street banker and political leader who served as vice president of the United States under President Harrison from 1889 to 1892 and was elected governor of New York in 1895. According to his daughter Esther, Morton Robertson changed his first name from Levi to Louis when he enrolled in the U.S. Navy.

199 IGI C110124-0026

200 IGI M110124-0279

201 IGI C110124-0090

202 IGI C110124-1110

203 IGI C110121-0216

204 IGI C110121-0451

205 IGI C110121-0640

206 IGI C110121-0918

207 IGI M110124-0282

208 IGI C110124-0219

209 IGI C110124-1025

210 IGI C110124-1151

211 IGI C110121-0140

212 IGI C110121-0410

213 Information from the SFHS indicates that Jemima Twatt married a man named Francis William Gray, born in 1883, and had four children: Barbara, Francis James, Evelyn, and John William Gray; that the first daughter, Barbara, married John Georgeson; the son, Francis, married Margaret Jane Isbister; and Jemima's daughter Evelyn married Thomas Andrew Cheyne and had three daughters, Barbara, Alice, and Josephine Cheyne. As several of our Robertsons

in Shetland dispute this information, and we have not been able to verify it, it has not been included in the text.

214 IGI C110121-0616

215 IGI C110121-0824

216 IGI C110123-0305

217 IGI C110123-0411

218 IGI C110093 0053

219 IGI C110093-0411

220 The Mrs. Cheyne mentioned in Margaret's letters was Christina Robertson, widow of Robert Cheyne, who died in September 1934 at the age of eighty-seven; Mrs. Georgeson was Ann Elizabeth Robertson, who had married George Georgeson and died in March 1935 at the age of eighty-five; Mrs. Thomson was Agnes Robertson, who was married to James Thomson and was seventy-five years of age in 1935; Mrs. O'Brian was Charlotte Robertson, then eighty-three, widow of Francis O'Brian. All four sisters, daughters of Margaret Mouat and Thomas Robertson (3-B), immigrated to New Zealand in the 1870s. Charlotte's daughter Elizabeth Lyver had also died suddenly, in September 1934, at the age of forty-three.

221 IGI 7621005-50

222 IGI C110121-0140

223 "Ness's Story, A Personal Tribute," by Sonja Mitchell, Nelson College for Girls Sixth Form English Project (1994). We are very grateful to Sonja for sharing this report and letting us quote from it. More from Sonja's report about her grandmother appears in Part 6-B.10 below.

224 "Ness's Story, A Personal Tribute," by Sonja Mitchell, Nelson College for Girls Sixth Form English Project (1994). We are very grateful to Sonja for sharing this report and letting us quote from it. More from Sonja's report about her grandmother appears in Part 6-B.10 below.

225 According to Delphine Slattery, her name was recorded as Lynch on their daughter's birth certificate and as Jenkins on her husband Peter Jamieson's death certificate.

226 Notes in a family Bible in the possession of Annchen Perin Gager show Georgia's birth in October 1872, not 1870; however, this would conflict with the recorded birth of her younger brother Charles D. Robertson Jr. on September 19, 1872, and appears to be in error.

227 At birth he was given the name Reuben Robertson Perin but decided as a young man to change it in order to include Lyman as the middle name in honor of his father.

228 May 22, 1962, letter from Reuben Robertson Sr. to Reuben Robertson III.

229 Laura Gamble was born October 6, 1853, in Louisville, Kentucky; she married Peter G. Thomson in 1875 and died January 20, 1913, in Cincinnati, Ohio. Her ancestors included

General Benjamin Logan, one of the first pioneer settlers of Kentucky, and a great military leader in fights against Indians aligned with the British during the Revolutionary War; Colonel Richard Clough Anderson, an officer in George Washington's Continental Army, who served as an aide to Lafayette and was involved in many of the important battles of the Revolution; and Ann Clark, whose famous brothers included General George Rogers Clark, the Revolutionary War hero who led American troops against the British forces in the capture of Vincennes, and General William Clark, who, with Merriwether Lewis, conducted the first exploratory expedition across the American continent to the Pacific Coast.

230  Peter Gibson Thomson, son of Alexander Thomson and Mary Ann Edwards, was born on December 16, 1851, in Cincinnati, Ohio. He was the grandson of Peter Thomson, who emigrated from Scotland to America in 1824. Peter G. Thomson's father and grandfather had both died by the time he was fourteen, leaving Peter the great responsibility of looking after his family at an early age. Young Peter got his start in business as a shipping clerk for a bookstore operated by Robert Clark Co. in 1871; he opened his own bookstore six years later. By 1884, he was engaged in making children's books, toys, and games, and he founded the Champion Coated Paper Company in Hamilton, Ohio, which started production of fine printing paper in 1894. To ensure a source of wood pulp needed for papermaking, he founded the Champion Fibre Company at Canton, North Carolina, and the new company acquired thousands of acres of timberland in the mountains of Western North Carolina. Peter G. Thomson became one of the leaders of the American pulp and paper industry, and his enterprise grew into one of the largest forest-products companies in the world. He died on July 10, 1931, in Cincinnati.

231  In 1935, the Champion Fibre Company merged with the Champion Coated Paper Company of Hamilton, Ohio, under the combined name of Champion Paper and Fibre Company.

232  Years ago, following the deaths of Reuben Robertson Sr. and Reuben Robertson Jr., control of Sit-N-Whittle and the other cabins and facilities at Lake Logan returned to Champion International Corporation. However, the company allowed some members of the family to have a Robertson family reunion there in 1992.

233  There is a family legend that his bunk on the overnight ferry from Aberdeen to Lerwick was so narrow that Reuben, a very large man, couldn't pry himself out in the morning, so the ship's crew members were called in to extricate him. Very possibly, the story was invented by Logan Robertson, a notorious teaser and practical joker. Reuben told a different story about the ferry trip: venturing below to check out the sleeping quarters, he had found a cabin with only two bunks. He asked where his son was to sleep, and the steward replied that a cradle would be brought in right away. Reuben roared with laughter, because Logan was over six feet tall.

234  John Laurenson is also from a Shetland family. His great-grandparents were Helen Robertson and Laurence Laurenson, both born in 1831, who were married in Walls Parish and immigrated to New Zealand. Ship passenger lists preserved in the National Archives in Wellington show

the Laurenson family arriving at Nelson on November 8, 1874, on the *Ocean Mail*. Helen and Laurence Laurenson, together with their four young children, were among the immigrant families selected by the provincial authorities for a new settlement in the remote, inaccessible area of Karamea on the west coast of the South Island. The first two years in this settlement turned out to be a disaster for the settlers, according to historian Susan Butterworth, as the land reserved for them was swampy and largely worthless for cultivation. Helen Laurenson's parents were Mary Irvine and Scott Robertson of Walls Parish. Research to date has not revealed any connection between them and our Robertson ancestors who lived in Walls Parish at the same time.

235 Margaret's father, Kenneth Nelson Kingsford Huffam, was born May 27, 1895, at Oriental Bay, Wellington, New Zealand. The son of Richard and Sofia Huffam, he was married on March 19, 1924, to Margaret's mother, Euphemia Agnes Catherine Gower. "Phemia" was born on October 19, 1897, and died on August 1, 1986, at age eighty-eight. Her parents were Benjamin Gower and Martha Euphemia Bowen. Kenneth and Phemia had homes at Roseneath and Khandallah near Wellington.

Ancestors of both Kenneth and Phemia were among the earliest settlers of New Zealand. His Huffam forebears arrived in New Zealand from the Isle of Wight in 1869, and her Gower and Bowen ancestors arrived in New Zealand around the 1840s. (Bowen Street in downtown Wellington was named after an ancestor.) New Zealand was populated only by Maori tribes until the early 1800s. Except for a few pioneer settlements and trading posts, significant immigration to New Zealand did not begin until around 1840.

236 Margaret Horry Chisolm, daughter of Robert Chisolm Jr. and Margaret Horry Laurens, was born on July 27, 1891, in Birmingham, Jefferson County, Alabama; she died on November 12, 1919, of childbirth complications, leaving two small children. Her husband, George LeGrand Watkins, born on June 8, 1886, in Faunsdale, Marengo County, Alabama, was the son of John Franklin Watkins and Caroline C. Abernathy. He graduated from the University of the South at Sewanee, Tennessee, a noted football player and team captain in his senior year, 1906. George earned a law degree at the University of Alabama, practiced law for a time in Birmingham, Alabama, and was a pilot with the US Navy Air Corps. After Margaret's death, George moved to Tulsa, Oklahoma, where he became a newspaperman and well-known columnist. Later, he was a water commissioner and was instrumental in developing the Spavinaw dam and reservoir to assure Tulsa's future water supply. George Watkins became the mayor of Tulsa in 1932, and later was appointed by President Franklin D. Roosevelt as the postmaster of Tulsa, a job he held for many years. He died on March 16, 1962, in Tulsa.

237 On both sides of her ancestry, Peggy Watkins descended from Scotch Highlanders and French Huguenots, who were among some of the earliest settlers in the American South. Several of her ancestors were leaders and heroes in the American Revolution. They include Henry Laurens of

South Carolina, who was president of the Continental Congress during the Revolution, was captured at sea by the British and imprisoned for over a year in the Tower of London, later was exchanged for Lord Cornwallis after the British military leader surrendered at Yorktown, and then negotiated the treaty of peace that ended the Revolutionary War. Another ancestor was John Rutledge, who was governor of South Carolina during the Revolution, one of the principal authors of the US Constitution, and served as chief justice of the US Supreme Court. Peggy's Chisolm forebears originated from the area north of Loch Ness in Inverness-shire, Scotland; that family can be traced back over 900 years to the time of William the Conqueror.

238 Victoria's mother was born in Ohio on October 22, 1928, the daughter of Leola Bennett White and Edmund James Hadley. She died in Cincinnati on January 31, 1988. Her father was a housing developer in the Cincinnati area. He was born September 25, 1922, in King's Mountain, Kentucky. The son of Andrew Paxton Emery and Florence Smith, Harold died in Cincinnati on August 16, 1960.

239 Cathie's mother is the grandniece of the late James M. Cox, who once served as governor of the State of Ohio and was once the official nominee of the Democratic Party for president of the United States.

# Index

# B

## C

## D

## H

## I

Inkster, Evangentine G.
  (SP) David Georgeson (V)  68

Irvina, Margaret (VIII)  129

Irvine, Elizabeth
  (SP) Jerom Robertson (III)  21, 22

Irvine, Elizabeth Catherine (VIII)  129

Irvine, Lillias
  (SP) Peter Henry Williamson (VI)  132

Irvine, Margaret
  (SP) Frederick Moffat (VI)  64

Irvine, Norman James
  (SP) Freda Brown (VII)  128

Irvine, Norma (VIII)  128

Isbister, Brian
  (SP) Avril Young (VIII)  126

Isbister, Magnus (IX)  126

Isbister, Robert (IX)  126

## J

Jakeman, Henrietta Lavinia (Teddy)
  (SP) Lawrence James Alexander (Laurie)
    Cheyne (VI)  220

James, Glenda
  (SP) John Wayne Lundgren (VII)  327

James, Patricia
  (SP) Magnus Fraser Lawrie (VII)  135

Jamieson, Alfred Peter (VI)  164

Jamieson, Alison (Alice) Guthrie
  (SP) Thomas Robertson (IV)  37

Jamieson, Arthur Henry (V)  105

Jamieson, Beatrice (Bessie)
  (SP) Thomas Robertson (II)  14

Jamieson, Derek
  (SP) Denise Mary Watt (IX)  149

Jamieson, Edward Norman (VI)  164

Jamieson, Elizabeth Jessie Margaret (V)  104

Jamieson, Eliza Margaret (Lill) (V)  105

Jamieson, Elspeth
  (SP) John Thomson Jeromson (IV)  62

Jamieson, Francis Herbert (VI)  164

Jamieson, Helen Robina (VI)  105

Jamieson, James (V)  105

Jamieson, Jessie Margaret (V)  104

Jamieson, Kathleen (VI)  105

Jamieson, Laura Helen
  (SP) Martin Edward Williamson (VI)  131

Jamieson, Lesley Avril (X)  149

Jamieson, Louisa Bridget (VII)  164

Jamieson, Loyal Lubeck (VI)  164

Jamieson, Lynn
  (SP) George Peter Johnson (VIII)  197

Jamieson, Mary Elizabeth Irvine (V)  104, 161

Jamieson, Mary Margaret (VII)  164

Jamieson, Noel Hanley (VII)  164

Jamieson, Norman Edward Thomas (VII)  164

Jamieson, Peter John (VII)  164

Jamieson, Peter (V)  104, 163

Jamieson, Robert Andrew (V) [1]  104

Jamieson, Robert Andrew (V) [2]  104

Jamieson, Robina Charlotte (V)  105

Jamieson, Robina Mariea (VI)  104

Jamieson, Ruth Laura
  (SP) Peter Tait (VI)  107

Jamieson, Thomas Andrew
  (SP) Laureen Williamson (VII)  131

Jamieson, Thomas Gifford
  (SP) Robina Robertson (IV)  28, 102, 103,
    104

## **M**

# R

## Y